the demographics of empire

the
demographics
of empire

The Colonial Order
and the
Creation of Knowledge

*Edited by Karl Ittmann,
Dennis D. Cordell,
and Gregory H. Maddox*

Ohio University Press • Athens

Ohio University Press, Athens, Ohio 45701
www.ohioswallow.com
© 2010 by Ohio University Press
All rights reserved

Printed in the United States of America

Ohio University Press books are printed on acid-free paper ⊗ ™

17 16 15 14 13 12 11 10   5 4 3 2 1

Library of Congress Cataloging-in-Publication Data
The demographics of empire : the colonial order and the creation of knowledge / edited by
Karl Ittmann, Dennis D. Cordell, and Gregory H. Maddox.
    p. cm.
  Includes bibliographical references and index.
  ISBN 978-0-8214-1932-8 (hc : alk. paper) — ISBN 978-0-8214-1933-5 (pb : alk. paper) —
ISBN 978-0-8214-4348-4 (electronic)
  1. Africa—Population—History—Research. 2. Demography—Africa—History. I.
Ittmann, Karl. II. Cordell, Dennis D., 1947– III. Maddox, Gregory. IV. Title.

HB3661.A3D439 2010
304.6096—dc22

2010033820

For Michael Fuller,

Leonore Ittmann, and

Gerald and Joyce Maddox

contents

acknowledgments

This book grew out of a workshop held at Texas Southern University (TSU) in Houston on 8–9 November 2002, which was supported by a grant from the U.S. Department of Education's Title VI Undergraduate International Studies and Foreign Languages Program. The editors would like to thank the other colleagues who participated in the workshop, Nupur Chaudhuri and Karen Kossie-Chernyshev of TSU and Kerry Ward of Rice University. The editors also gratefully acknowledge the support of TSU, Southern Methodist University, and the University of Houston. Texas Southern also provided assistance for the publication of this volume.

Counting Subjects

Demography and Empire

DENNIS D. CORDELL, KARL ITTMANN, AND GREGORY H.MADDOX

In 1977, Ian Pool, writing about the challenges of historical demography in Africa, noted,

> African historical demography may depart significantly from classical
> historical demography. . . . The African historical demographer will
> probably be forced to build upon the existing methodology and
> perhaps may have to create his own new tools. In this we would be
> merely following what is becoming almost a tradition in African
> studies and is certainly typical of the two parent disciplines of history
> and demography.[1]

This statement still holds true more than a quarter century later. The challenge facing scholars interested in the historical demography of Africa remains the need to balance defensible demographic analysis with the effort to reflect the complexities of African history. The broader reproduction of any society is a combination of births, deaths, and migrations related to strategies that individuals and social groups adopt to reproduce themselves in different eras and contexts. Reproduction is thus both biological and profoundly social. Moreover, it changes through time. Such social reproduction requires reproducing labor for the work of society on a day-to-day basis, as well as reproducing people from one generation to the next. These strategies are all intertwined with and grow out of specific patterns of economic activity and social organization. They are also influenced by political systems, values, and other cultural constructs. These strictly demographic factors and broader societal factors combine to shape a "demographic regime."[2]

Beginning in the 1960s, European historical demographers contended that Western Europe possessed a unique traditional regime, characterized by late age of marriage, low rates of birth outside marriage, and relatively slow growth— factors that, taken together, distinguished it from other regions of the world. In recent years, scholars have rejected this generalization because subsequent research has brought to light a diversity of population patterns even among the Western European societies whose study gave rise to the theory.[3] African historical demographers have also begun to highlight the diversity of African demographic regimes in recent years, as they have debated issues such as the impact of the transatlantic slave trade; the size of African populations in the modern era; and the degree to which Africa possessed, now or in the past, a unitary demographic regime characterized by low population densities, high birthrates, and high levels of mortality from endemic diseases such as malaria.[4]

Orthodox demographic thought predicted that in the later twentieth century, African societies would experience declining fertility, a change predicted by the theory of the demographic transition. Indeed, in a few places across the continent, fertility did decline slightly in the 1990s—but not everywhere, not uniformly, and not for the same reasons.[5] Based on the experience of a small number of European societies in the modern era, initial formulations of the paradigm of the demographic transition posited that high levels of mortality characterized all societies in the past, accompanied by correspondingly high levels of fertility to assure survival. The resulting population increase was slow. Early in the modern era, transition theory contends, the provision of better housing, less-contaminated water, and broader public health measures promoted declines in mortality. However, fertility levels, maintained by social custom and belief, remained high, resulting in dramatic increases in population. Only later did fertility drop to levels closer to replacement, thus producing the "modern" demographic regime of low mortality and low fertility. The contributions to this volume dispute the facile assumption that "traditional" societies, whether in Africa, Europe, or anywhere else, exhibited a single demographic regime characterized by high fertility and high mortality.[6]

Using existing historical sources, the essays in this book reconstruct the demographic regimes of African societies within the contexts of the colonial states that circumscribed them. The sources for colonial population data, like all historical sources, are incomplete and imperfect in various ways. These essays acknowledge these limitations but nonetheless aim at producing well-founded analyses to help us understand the roles that demographic theory, practice, and policy played in the governance of colonial states in Africa. They demonstrate that African societies existed in a diversity of demographic contexts and displayed varied demographic regimes, hence underscoring the need to turn to new kinds of evidence and fresh perspectives to reconstruct those circumstances at the local and regional levels.

The essays in this collection are implicitly and explicitly comparative. Each author writes about a different part of the continent but is aware of the connections between regions and of the need to consider both European and African patterns to arrive at new syntheses about the demographic history of colonial empires in Africa. This implicitly comparative approach extends beyond the numbers to consider how colonial regimes apprehended the demographic regimes of societies that they administered and how they produced the demographic data on which they based policy and action. Colonial representations of population constituted part of the larger discourse of power and control central to the exercise of authority. Colonial practices of counting and then mobilizing people were also integral to the assertion of hegemony. At the same time, by taking the colonizers' understandings of their own metropolitan populations into consideration, many of the authors also demonstrate how Europeans projected their own conceptions of population and population dynamics and their own fears of dramatic demographic change onto the people of their empires—the non-European "Others." Before turning to the essays themselves, we will locate our essays within larger historical and theoretical contexts.

In his seminal work on nationalism, Benedict Anderson noted the critical importance of the colonial census in enumerating and targeting colonial subjects. The generation of the types of knowledge embodied in a census was not uncontested, though. The new discipline of demography initially provided a means of bringing uniformity to masses of inconsistently collected and contradictory data in Europe. Later, demographic methods served to document, trace, forecast, and, one could say, routinize the reproduction of colonial populations abroad. In the colonial context, demography served as one of the tools that defined the colonial subject as an Other subjugated to European control and European agendas for "improvement."[7] Anderson focused on quantification in Southeast Asia, but his insights may be applied to other parts of the colonial world. The essays here on Africa and the British and French empires by historians and social scientists examine the multifaceted nature of the demography of empire in the nineteenth and twentieth centuries. They raise three related questions. First, how have historians and demographers understood the concept of population in the colonial world? Second, what were African demographic realities, and how did they channel the development of colonial systems of power on the continent? And third, how did metropolitan and colonial demographies interact in this period, both ideologically and physically?

To reconstruct what Anderson referred to as the "grammar" that guided the deployment of the classificatory and quantitative schemes of the various colonial states in different periods, we will first examine the history of the relationship between demography and state power since the rise of the population sciences in Europe in the eighteenth century. This history brings together ideas about population, the development of quantitative techniques, and the use of demographic data by the state. In the seventeenth and eighteenth centuries, most observers argued that a large and growing population was proof of a prosperous and well-ordered society.[8] According to these "*populationniste*" theorists, the duty of the ruler and the state lay in encouraging population growth by securing peace and prosperity.[9] Yet, as the work of Frederick Whelen and others on eighteenth-century population thought in Europe reveals, these same observers believed that contemporary peoples were less numerous than in the past, and they feared imminent demographic decline.[10] Building on the ideas of writers such as Montesquieu, eighteenth-century population discourse focused on the reasons for this dire state of affairs, arguing for social, political, and economic changes to forestall demographic collapse.[11] Such arguments offered implicit, and occasionally explicit, political judgments of the merits of governments and the potential for human progress over the long term. At the same time, through the development of statistics and what the British referred to as "political arithmetic," statisticians, officials, and governments devised more sophisticated quantitative techniques to improve their knowledge of population sizes and trends.[12] Such efforts laid the foundation for the modern census and also documented the new reality of population growth that became an important concern for nineteenth-century demography.

The publication of Thomas Malthus's *Essay on Population* in 1799 signaled a sea change in demographic thought. His model of population dynamics, which proposed that populations tend to grow toward the limit of subsistence, brought new perspectives and approaches to the analysis of poverty and economic progress in the early nineteenth century. For Malthus, population growth was a major force in a larger providential universe in which a need to counter increasing pressure on the supply of subsistence items afforded people the incentive for moral and physical improvement, thus promoting progress. For these "natural laws" to function, the state needed to remain on the sidelines. Malthusian thought was folded into political economy—a human representation of the law of diminishing returns.[13] The quantitative evidence of population growth recorded by the "modern," periodic censuses introduced in Europe and North America at the beginning of the nineteenth century reinforced and lent credibility to the commonsense conclusions of observers who witnessed the dramatic growth of urban populations at the time. The causal links proposed between population expansion, the growth of poverty, and potential social disorder transformed demography into drama—more than an abstract science of numbers.[14] As part of its duties, the state assumed the responsibility to measure and quantify the "social body"—part of a larger reimagining and reshaping of government in the new era of liberal and democratic politics.[15]

By the end of the nineteenth century, however, classical Malthusianism was on the wane. In Europe, the end of widespread subsistence crises and dramatic advances in industrial productivity laid to rest the specter of a Malthusian problem of "overpopulation."[16] Instead, new demographic anxieties emerged. Many observers now feared the impact of falling birthrates, which in France helped trigger the rise of a natalist movement that would receive official sanction.[17] In other countries, falling fertility rates—particularly among the upper classes—fueled concerns about shifts in the racial and class composition of society. In England, the eugenics movement argued that the higher fertility of the poor would inevitably lead to the decline of the nation, as the "less fit" made up an ever larger proportion of the population.[18] These new demographic worries helped justify the expansion of state welfare provisions and intervention to address the problem.[19]

New demographic tools in the form of probability theory and mechanical aids to tabulation and calculation produced more accurate data and laid the groundwork for modern demographic analysis.[20] Later, this connection between the growth of state power and the elaboration of demographic analysis found sinister expression in the emergence of the totalitarian states of the twentieth century. The histories of Italy, Germany, and the Soviet Union in the twentieth century underscore how ideological constructions may shape the design of quantitative measures and also bend demographic analysis to serve the state.[21] The ultimate expression of this trend may be found in the complicity of some demographers whose quantitative analyses assisted the perpetration of the Holocaust.[22]

However, more recent thought and research on these topics has grown out of inquiry into the growth of the welfare state, on the one hand, and, on the other, new initiatives to conceptualize the relationship between state and society—embodied most notably in the work of Michel Foucault.[23] Foucault proposed an all-encompassing biopolitics. In his analytical framework, demography functioned as a technology of power, measuring, classifying, and ordering the population to foster state control at the meso level of the family and the micro level of the individual. Foucault's oeuvre opened an avenue for other scholars to reconsider and re-present the relationship between state exercises in quantitative measurement exemplified by the census—usually presented to the public as objective, empirical knowledge—and the visible and invisible political and institutional forces and agenda behind their use. Some scholars believe that Foucault exaggerated his representation of the state as a monolith possessed of an insatiable appetite for power and knowledge—an overemphasis that perhaps grew out of the influence of the French state's ideology of hypercentralization on Foucault himself.[24] Notwithstanding these reservations, it is clear that European states with widely differing structures and systems expanded the quantitative investigation of their populations during this period, imposing more uniform schemes of classification. And yet, though all of these states were, broadly speaking, liberal capitalist regimes, they exhibited considerable differences in how and why they collected information. In each country, social groups pushing for the elaboration of demographic analyses competed to promote their agendas, lobbying the state to incorporate them in its programs. In looking at this range of state policy and action, it is important to distinguish between left-of-center welfare reformers and ardent racists and eugenicists. The history of such initiatives in Great Britain offers an instructive example.[25]

When we turn toward the colonial world, other difficulties emerge. Foucault's work focused primarily upon Europe and did not acknowledge colonial empires and race as central features of modernity.[26] Indeed, his model of state power is not appropriate for the complicated stories of Europe's colonial possessions. The fragmented and contradictory nature of what may be termed "the modern demographic project" becomes clearer through examination of the use of quantitative measures by the colonial state. For the colonial powers, the alien and radically heterogeneous nature of their possessions made them opaque and more in need of study. Beyond enumeration, a desire for mapping led to a preoccupation with the thorny issues of race and ethnicity, which assumed far greater significance in the colonial state than in the metropole.[27] However, the conceptual and empirical bases for quantitative grids incorporating race and ethnicity remained elusive, leading to the deliberate restriction, compression, and simplification of differences and ambiguities. As Anderson pointed out, Europeans constructed categories from their own frames of reference and experiences for colonial societies, categories that often did not take into consideration those used by the colonized themselves.[28]

This reification of race and ethnicity represented only one distortion in the quantitative explorations of the colonial state. The lack of financial and human resources was another equally debilitating handicap. Faced with a far more complex and difficult technical and cultural enterprise, colonial states had to make do with much smaller budgets than their metropolitan counterparts. Last but not least, the emphasis on welfare prevalent in discussions of European demography played only a minor role in the calculations of colonial states—at least before World War II. For most of their histories, the colonial states pursued demographic policies and practices aimed at military control, tax collection, extraction of resources, and labor recruitment.[29] In the colonies, the collection of quantitative data for these ends revealed the interests of the colonial states more nakedly. Ironically, then, given Foucault's neglect of the colonies, the implications of the inquisitorial state that he and his fellow travelers mapped out are most apparent in the colonial context.[30]

Early research on the quantitative dimensions of the colonial state focused on British India, where the British state both subsumed existing systems of data collection from the Mughal Empire and devised its own techniques for studying the population.[31] Bernard Cohen's work on the census in British India underscored the fact that data collection, far from being a neutral act, helped construct understandings of caste by both colonizer and colonized.[32] Later scholars have documented the ways in which quantitative assessments of the colonial state created new "facts" on the ground. Many of these studies built on Edward Said's theorization of Orientalism and associated work in Indology, arguing that the colonial practice of imagining and counting categories provoked an indigenous response that led Indians themselves to privilege religious identity within Indian modernity.[33]

However, several recent studies challenge the idea that specifically European forms of enumeration created these identities in their totality, insisting instead that methods of counting communities used by the British in India were adopted from practices in earlier, precolonial states. This research maintains that such approaches to enumeration reflected existing, albeit fluid, identities and relationships and were not simply the products of the imposition of Western constructions.[34]

More attention is now being directed to how indigenous groups understood their identities outside the realm of state power and how they attempted to transform colonial understandings into forms of resistance. Despite these caveats, however, most scholars still agree that the colonial project in India underwent an important shift in the later nineteenth century, becoming more comprehensive and intrusive. This change reflected the creation of a "new" colonial state in the wake of the Rebellion of 1857 and the further thrust of the state into new arenas, such as public health and education.[35]

In Africa, too, demography was a colonial creation, even though African populations had prior histories. In the long term, climate change, disease, the development of food production systems, and the expansion of long-distance trade all shaped African population. Migration, within and out of sub-Saharan Africa, altered the demographic profiles of African societies. Beginning in the 1500s of the current era, forced migration in the form of the slave trade from western Africa took millions of Africans into the Atlantic world. The trade left a lasting mark on populations in the New World while impacting populations in Africa in diverse ways as well.[36] Finally, the intensification of commerce during the early modern era brought a greater mobility of people, goods, and diseases in the Indian Ocean as well as the Atlantic; the nineteenth century witnessed an increase in the number of people from Africa enslaved in the Indian Ocean world.[37]

Despite little concrete knowledge of African demographic regimes, Europeans arrived with presuppositions about Africa's population drawn from a variety of sources. The work of eighteenth-century students of political arithmetic, the writings of early explorers, and Malthus's publications portrayed Africa as underpopulated as a result of warfare, insecurity of property, slavery, polygamy, and prolonged breast-feeding.[38] Arguments emphasizing insecurity and slavery served to justify European conquest. In the early years of European colonization, the violence and upheaval of conquest as well as the lack of administrators and resources overshadowed the collection and analysis of demographic data about newly vanquished populations. For the most part, European colonial regimes made do with rudimentary estimates compiled by local colonial administrators, indigenous agents of the colonial regimes, and outside observers. Limited attention was given to technical assessments of the accuracy or consistency of information or how it was gathered. Only in the 1920s and 1930s did European colonial authorities attempt to refine the enumeration of their subjects and apply demographic methods by then common in the metropole to the analysis of colonial populations.[39]

Nowhere were the limitations of colonial demography more apparent than in Africa. Catholic parish registers recording births, deaths, and marriages appeared shortly after the earliest Portuguese contacts with the kingdom of Kongo in the late fifteenth and sixteenth centuries. Portuguese censuses of Luanda and other settlements in Angola followed.[40] Other initiatives specifically intended to enumerate colonial populations were common in the later modern period.[41] However, the first modern censuses and sample surveys in Africa south of the Sahara date only from the 1940s for the Portuguese colonies and from the 1950s for the others.[42] In part, this late arrival of the modern demographic state derived from widespread violence and flight associated with initial colonial conquests after 1885, as well as the subsequent imposition of the Pax Europa. The creation of the colonial state and the infrastructures required to sustain it also requisitioned African wealth and labor, which made people exceedingly reticent about coming into contact with authorities or accurately reporting the size of their families and communities.

Different regions of Africa, of course, had different demographic histories. In the first few decades of the nineteenth century, for example, West African societies continued to suffer the ravages of the Atlantic slave trade, which was then about to enter a clandestine and violent final phase that did not trail off until the 1880s. Only after 1850 did West African populations begin to recover from two centuries of very slow growth and population loss. Central and East Africa, by contrast, experienced more pronounced losses from the continued export of people into the Indian Ocean trading network right up to 1900.[43] In southern Africa, the spread of white settlers into the interior in the first couple of decades of the nineteenth century provoked a chain reaction of violence and migration, upending societies from today's eastern South Africa all the way north to what is now Tanzania. In Central, East, and southern Africa, these bouts of violence, social dislocation, and migration fueled dramatic rises in the incidence and prevalence of disease among people and their livestock.[44]

European campaigns of conquest magnified these demographic disruptions, provoked massive movements of population across the continent, and brought high levels of mortality.[45] Many Africans resisted initial conquest. In some cases, superior European arms overwhelmed them rather quickly, although costs in lives remained high. In other cases, notably among decentralized societies, conquest translated into drawn-out military expeditions that imposed European authority village by village, accompanied by very high levels of mortality and even higher levels of flight. A final indignity came with the spread of rinderpest in the central, eastern, and southern parts of the continent after 1888. The disease came with cattle that the Italian army brought to Eritrea during their hapless attempt to conquer Ethiopia. It destroyed herds across the continent, caused severe food shortages, and promoted the spread of the tsetse fly and the sleeping sickness that it carried.[46] As a result, the continent and its societies entered the colonial era in tumult.

The need for labor in a variety of forms shaped the demographic agendas of colonial regimes. European schemes to count and classify African populations and analyze results were far from perfect, and many were policies and practices devised for colonies elsewhere. But beyond simple enumeration, the perpetual search for labor, including a growing need for migrant labor, led colonial states to try to alter the demographic regimes of African populations—in particular, fertility levels, patterns of illness and disease, and social organization.[47] In the French colonies, the labor project in general and forced recruitment in particular led the colonial state to undertake measures to ensure the flow of workers and to deal with the consequences of such policies domestically and internationally.[48] However, British and French authorities in the interwar years also initiated natalist policies that reflected a common European belief that the fundamental causes of the labor shortage were inadequate fertility, poor maternal care, and flight.[49]

These measures underscore the critical differences in the ways that the state functioned in the metropole and the colonies. Despite the claims of Foucault and others about the all-encompassing power of the state in Europe, only in the colonial setting, especially in Africa, could the state deploy its powers with little restraint. The forced recruitment and removal of people, intervention in agricultural and pastoral practices, and imposition of health and sanitary regimes encountered few of the legal barriers imposed by civil society in Europe.[50] Property rights, legal norms, and civil liberties in Europe, although hardly impregnable defenses, provided metropolitan citizens far more protection than colonial subjects had. In Africa and elsewhere in the colonial world and despite resistance, "natives" were more acted upon and more often subjected to demands for change and "development." Between the world wars and into the 1950s, proponents claimed that "modernized" colonialism brought the benefits of development. Yet the development imperative led the colonial state to mobilize increasingly against its subjects in order achieve its objectives—which, in turn, destabilized colonial societies.[51]

Still, the colonial state was not a Leviathan free to do whatever it wished.[52] By the interwar period, the African colonial state, although more stable and in greater control, indeed faced limits. One limit was material—the sheer scale of the task and the extremely limited resources allocated to accomplish it. This constraint became more formidable in the Depression of the 1930s, characterized by drastic drops in the prices for raw materials. As revenues dried up, ambitious development schemes remained on the drawing board or were reduced to pilot projects with limited impact. European powers also reduced the numbers of colonial administrators and the size of their administrations. These reduced colonial bureaucracies did little more than hold the line while waiting for the return of better times.[53] Even World War II, which brought a sudden ramping up of state activity and intervention, failed to change these circumstances dramatically.

Political barriers were equally daunting. The growing criticism of colonial practice by reformist officials, academics, missionaries, and political activists in Europe reduced the African colonial state's range of action. Exposés of poor living conditions, extreme exploitation, failed experiments, and the formulation of more African-centered alternatives undercut the rationale for authoritarian systems.[54] African responses to new state demands also undermined them. Whether through direct resistance or evasion, Africans seized agency, responding in their own ways to the demands they faced. Some accommodated themselves and sought to maximize their interests; others fled beyond the reach of the state. Some migrated to the new colonial cities, where control proved more elusive.[55] Still others organized social and political movements that challenged the legitimacy of the state's demand for information and power.[56] In these circumstances, the quantitative project, whether defined in terms of data collection or the use of that information to exert control, remained fragmented and incomplete.

Many of the forms and projects of the colonial state survived into the postcolonial era. In the historical and social science literature, debates over the failures of postcolonial states in Africa often focus on the relationship between these "new" states and their late colonial antecedents.[57] The prolongation into the independence era of development projects and policies designed to confiscate wealth do indeed suggest that the independent African state is primarily developmentalist, concerned more than anything else with control over fragmented local populations, amassing wealth, and acceleration of economic change.[58] Like their counterparts in the colonial era, contemporary rulers have been most attentive to the demands of the developed world and international institutions—focusing attention on demographic trends deemed important by their international patrons. In addition, these regimes have usually concentrated on urban populations to the exclusion of citizens living in rural areas.[59] In the demographic arena, this externalized focus initially led to greater efforts at improved data collection and the expansion of family planning programs but only later, if ever, to social programs aimed at rural areas or the broader health of the people.[60]

In Africa, the independence era has, according to one school of thought, brought crisis after crisis. The "Afro-pessimists" of the 1980s and 1990s argued that conflicts within and between states, as well as manipulation from beyond the continent, have given rise to a large number of "failed" or "hollow" states.[61] Countries such as Ethiopia, Sudan, Somalia, and the Sahel region of West Africa have suffered repeated food shortages and famine brought on by climatic variation, rapacious regimes, and political instability. Beginning in the 1980s and 1990s, the HIV/AIDS epidemic resulted in much higher mortality in eastern and southern Africa—wiping out the gains made in life expectancy since independence.[62] Other observers have called for nuance, pointing out that such problems do not plague all parts of Africa. Even in regions racked by conflict, communities have found ways to reproduce themselves and create space for renewal. The need to understand such local dynamics further complicates efforts to develop general demographic models for Africa.

The ten essays in this book reexamine how these understandings evolved and suggest new ways in which historians and others might reconstruct the demographic history of Africa in the modern era. Taken together, the chapters ahead cover the period from the late eighteenth century through the postcolonial era. For the most part, they assess the experience of regions under British and French control in the colonial era. New theoretical approaches, new evidence, and the slow accumulation of detailed historical studies of different regions have enhanced our knowledge of Africa's population history. *The Demographics of Empire* opens with three overviews that probe the intellectual history and the production of knowledge about African demography and argue for new theories and methods.

Dennis Cordell's chapter engages the literature on the historical demography of colonial Africa and South Asia in an effort to understand why research and publication plummeted in the 1990s. He suggests that the decline in research may well be attributed to postmodern and postcolonial approaches to the social sciences in general and fields such as historical demography that privilege quantitative data in particular. Preoccupied with analysis of how knowledge is produced and used to project power, Cordell contends, postmodern and postcolonial scholarship called into question the objectivity of historical sources. To be sure, these issues were by no means new to historians or demographers, whose analyses routinely contend with imperfect data. However, many postmodern and postcolonial studies became mired in their often legitimate criticism, failing to suggest any way forward—any way "to know" anything at all. Without explicitly voicing such a conclusion, they left the impression that the past was not knowable. Cordell suggests that these new perspectives in African studies in the 1980s and 1990s probably discouraged research in African historical demography and social science history in general. Later in the chapter, however, he reviews recent research that incorporates postmodern and postcolonial perspectives but moves beyond the simple rejection of historical sources to reassess their value and usefulness with greater nuance. The chapter also considers new work in historical population studies in Africa that does not adopt the perspectives of either postmodernism or postcolonialism.

Karl Ittmann's essay takes as its theme the question of how theory and history shaped British views of African population in the modern era and how these views affected colonial policies. Ittmann reviews the literature of African population and places it within the larger context of an evolving discourse of imperial population. This discourse linked British ideas of domestic population with those of the larger world and the empire in particular. For the British, Africa represented a place where "nature has continued to dominate man," leaving African populations unable to control their reproduction.[63] In the initial stage of British rule, this fundamental belief led to a focus on underpopulation and policies designed to bolster health and reproduction as well as improve the supply of labor. From the 1940s on, however, officials and demographers began to raise concerns about accelerating population growth and its possible impact upon plans for economic and social development. Ironically, as British rule ended, it was fear of overpopulation that dominated demographic discourse and served as the rationale for the creation of international family planning programs built upon existing British institutions and expertise.

Raymond Gervais and Issiaka Mandé's essay examines the construction of demographic knowledge and systems of data collection in French West Africa in the years prior to 1946. The authors demonstrate that despite ministerial directives in 1904, 1909, and 1921 imposing the collection of uniform categories of demographic data, a lack of training, paltry resources, and extraordinarily unrealistic expectations about the technical capacities of colonial administrations at all levels made it impossible to meet metropolitan demands. For local administrators, the annual census tours of their districts were much more important as symbols of their authority than as realistic exercises in collecting demographic information.

The limitations of expertise and resources were often masked by a language of power emanating from the center that made it impossible for administrators to question unreasonable expectations without putting their careers in jeopardy. Rather, they felt compelled to respond with obfuscation and numbers that they knew were incomplete and inaccurate. By the 1930s, these initiatives become more realistic, but World War II then delayed their implementation.

Thomas McClendon examines the invention and transmission of conventional wisdom about the history of population in South Africa. In his essay, he also explores the debate over the size and composition of the African population of the new British colony of Natal in southern Africa in the early nineteenth century, as well as efforts by officials and settlers to measure and track that population. Some observers believed that many Africans in Natal were immigrants who had entered the territory in large numbers to take advantage of the security that British rule provided in the wake of Shake Zulu's *mfecane*. This belief led officials to classify and attempt to remove many Africans in order to limit their claims to land and resources in a territory now open to British settlement. As a corollary, the colony's secretary of native affairs, Theophilus Shepstone, set up a network of "native reserves" to confine African settlement. McClendon demonstrates that contemporary officials and later generations of historians accepted this view of Natal's population despite the lack of accurate estimates of the precolonial population or postsettlement censuses. Precolonial population also figured in the debate over whether the mfecane was, in fact, a historical myth used to rationalize the expansion of European power. McClendon concludes by discussing how the debate over depopulation and indigenity in the nineteenth century prefigured debates over similar issues in apartheid and postapartheid South Africa.

In "Counting and Recounting," John Cinnamon juxtaposes two sets of perspectives that two groups of people—the French and the locals—adopted in efforts to comprehend migration and depopulation in what is today called Gabon. Focusing first on the Minkébé forest in the north in the early decades of the twentieth century, Cinnamon presents oral accounts collected since 1990 that remember these demographic events in qualitative ways as stories of personal and group conflict, flight, and eventual return. He contrasts these local understandings of events and environment with the early French colonial gaze, which was quantitative, producing numerical estimates and analyses preoccupied with labor, mortality, and production. Yet the essay goes beyond these conventional dichotomies of African/European and qualitative/quantitative to explore variant narratives within each community. Broadening his view to encompass all of Gabon and neighboring French colonies, Cinnamon then explores the different French assessments of the region's demographic fortunes. Man-on-the-spot assessments now preserved in the colonial archives differ in important ways from those of colonial social scientists written over the same period. Cinnamon demonstrates in a convincing and empirical way the importance of pursuing variant African and French visions in order to arrive at multiple, global understandings of demographic changes in the equatorial forest and what they meant—to all who lived them.

The demographic conceptions of officials and their impact upon policy also constitute the central theme of Meshack Owino's examination of the Kenya labor corps, known as the Pioneer Corps, during World War II. Owino shows how officials persisted in their belief that the western provinces of Kenya possessed virtually unlimited "reserves" of labor that could be mobilized for the war effort. These beliefs, which dated back to the early days of the protectorate, had played a crucial role in the founding of the Carrier Corps in East Africa during World War I, with disastrous results for local people. This debacle, however, failed to dissuade officials from mounting an analogous effort before World War II. Men such as S. H. Fazan confidently proceeded with the creation of the new unit, the Pioneer Corps, despite difficulties in recruiting that stemmed from Kenyans' painful memories of the earlier experience.

Sheryl McCurdy discusses European views of health and maternity in the trading center of Ujiji on the shores of Lake Tanganyika. She combines colonial and mission archival records with oral history to reconstruct the experiences of African women before and after the colonial conquest. She argues that the population of Ujiji had long been transitory in many respects, with coastal traders, slaves, and local rural dwellers mingling in the town. The disruptions of the early colonial era further caused instability for individuals in the town. European observers, both missionaries and German and British colonial officials, blamed low fertility and high infant mortality on lax morals. McCurdy shows that town dwellers had created fluid sets of relationships in the face of the constant disruption of town life in the later nineteenth and early twentieth centuries. She notes: "Together, the culture of divorce, remarriage, and alternate relationships, as well as the effects of sexually transmitted infection, smallpox, malaria, tuberculosis, cholera, influenza, typhoid fever, and anemia, created an environment where couples were less likely to conceive. And even among those who did conceive, the rates of miscarriage, stillbirth, and infant and child mortality were extremely high." McCurdy concludes by pointing out that concerns of Europeans about the perceived demographic crisis of Ujiji/Kigoma find their echoes in contemporary debates about the causes and effects of the HIV/AIDS epidemic.

Gregory Maddox addresses another central theme in the demographic history of Africa—the assumed relationships between environment, health, and population growth that observers argue determine the structure and size of the continent's populations. Drawing on evidence from East Africa about interactions between people and their physical and biological environments, Maddox argues that they must be read in a more flexible and nuanced fashion. In particular, he investigates how new work on the history of disease, especially malaria, challenges the widely held view that Africans lacked the ability to control their exposure to disease. In place of neo-Malthusian models, Maddox asserts the need to see how environmental homeostasis and equilibrium situations arose in part from African patterns of land use and settlement. These practices were severely disrupted by intensified commerce—especially the Indian Ocean slave trade in the eighteenth and nineteenth centuries—and the Western colonial intervention that followed. The fallout included increased violence, mobility, and overwhelming epidemics among people and animals. Finally, Maddox turns to mortality and population in the postwar and postcolonial eras. Although acknowledging the importance of health initiatives since 1945, he identifies fertility-driven population growth and the uncertain impact of the HIV/AIDS epidemic as new factors that lie outside the traditional paradigm. Maddox concludes by calling for greater collaboration between historians and scientists in studying the history of African environments and health.

The following chapter by Meredeth Turshen explores how colonial government policies on reproduction and sexuality affected women in British, Belgian, and French colonies in Africa primarily in the decades between the two world wars. Turshen adopts a gender perspective, which focuses attention on how relations between women and men, both European and African, affected women's lives. Her analysis seeks to avoid arguments of economic determinism while at the same time acknowledging the real material interests that influenced the colonial policies that had the greatest impact on women. After all, research to date underscores the fact that questions related to labor and its reproduction—from day to day and generation to generation—were the primary demographic policy concerns of all colonial regimes most of the time. However, Turshen shows that this primary concern about the reproduction of labor affected women in ways that were indirect as well as direct and unintended as well as intended. The impact could also be quite nuanced on occasion. To illustrate these points, the chapter explores three major themes: the imposition of statutory law, the creation of customary law, and how both shaped family law and policies; direct interventions to shape population growth by providing or withholding maternity and birth control services; and the impacts on women of disease dispersion and environmental disruption. The chapter concludes with discussions of several specific areas of colonial policy that had major demographic consequences.

Patrick Manning's essay sets out to formulate new estimates for African population over the period 1750 to 1950. Dissatisfied with the existing scenarios, many of which are based on thin evidence, Manning begins his reconstruction with the first reasonably accurate estimates of African population in 1950 and 1960 and works backward. As part of this method, he turns to existing colonial records, filling gaps in vital rates with estimates for nineteenth-century India. The analysis takes into account the different regions of Africa, assessing variations in their demographic regimes and their experiences of slavery and colonialism. Manning proposes continental population totals for 1930 (180 million) and 1850 (150 million) that are substantially higher than previous estimates. He suggests that we need to revise our overall understanding of African demographic history because these numbers imply a much larger population in 1700, given the impact of the slave trade on the continent and lower growth rates for the period 1850 to 1950. His conclusions suggest that the modern era represents a break with older patterns of slower growth. Manning also proposes a corrective to the conventional portrayal of Africa as a continent that remained "underpopulated" well into the nineteenth century.

Taken together, these essays comprise the latest installment in efforts to understand the histories of population in Africa that stretch back to the late 1970s. *The Demographics of Empire* follows published proceedings from seminal conferences on African historical demography convened at the Centre of African Studies at the University of Edinburgh in 1977 and 1981, as well as issues of *Cahiers d'Études Africaines* and *Annales de Démographie Historique* devoted to the same theme in 1987. This volume is perhaps even more a direct descendant of the more focused essay collections edited by Dennis Cordell and Joel Gregory in 1987 and Bruce Fetter in 1990.[64] We hope this latest collective intellectual effort will stimulate other scholars to follow in what has become a persistent, if low-profile, mission to understand more fully African populations in what the revered English historical demographer Peter Laslett called "past time."[65]

Notes

1. D. Ian Pool, "A Framework for the Analysis of West African Demography," in *African Historical Demography: Proceedings of a Seminar Held in the Centre of African Studies, University of Edinburgh, 29th and 30th April 1977*, ed. Christopher Fyfe and David McMaster (Edinburgh: African Studies Centre, University of Edinburgh, 1977), 57.

2. For a more thorough discussion of the demographic regime, see Dennis D. Cordell, Joel W. Gregory, and Victor Piché, "African Historical Demography: The Search for a Theoretical Framework," in *African Population and Capitalism: Historical Perspectives*, ed. Dennis D. Cordell and Joel W. Gregory, 2nd ed. (Madison: University of Wisconsin Press, 1994), 14–32.

3. Jean-Claude Chesnais, *La transition démographique: Étapes, formes, implications économiques—Étude de séries temporelles, 1720–1984, relatives à 67 pays* (Paris: Presses Universitaires de France, 1986); John Knodel, *Demographic Behavior in the Past* (Cambridge: Cambridge University Press, 1988).

4. See C. C. Wrigley, "Population in African History," *Journal of African History* 20, no. 1 (1979): 127–31; John Iliffe, "The Origins of African Population Growth," *Journal of African History* 30, no. 1 (1989): 165–69; Thomas Spear, "Africa's Population History," *Journal of African History* 37, no. 3 (1996): 479–85.

5. Thérèse Locoh and Véronique Hertrich, eds., *The Onset of Fertility Transition in Sub-Saharan Africa* (Liège, Belgium: International Union for the Scientific Study of Population, 1994). See also Population Council, *The Unfinished Transition* (New York: Population Council, 1996).

6. For a nuanced statement of this theme, see John Iliffe, *The African Poor* (Cambridge: Cambridge University Press, 1987).

7. Benedict Anderson, *Imagined Communities: Reflections on the Origin and Spread of Nationalism* (New York: Verso, 1991), 163–70.

8. For seventeenth-century England, see Mildred Campbell, "'Of People Either Too Few or Too Many': The Conflict of Opinion on Population and Its Relation to

Emigration," in *Conflict in Stuart England,* ed. Basil D. Henning (New York: New York University Press, 1960), 169–201. For a general overview, see J. Overbeek, *History of Population Theories* (Rotterdam, the Netherlands: University of Rotterdam Press, 1974).

9. See Annie Vidal, *La pensée démographique: Doctrines, théories et politiques de population* (Grenoble, France: Presses Universitaires de Grenoble, 1994), 26–32.

10. Frederick Whelan, "Population and Ideology in the Enlightenment," *History of Political Thought* 12, no. 1 (1991): 35–72; Jacqueline Hecht, "From 'Be Fruitful and Multiply' to Family Planning: The Enlightenment Transition," *Eighteenth Century Studies* 32, no. 4 (1999): 536–51; Sylvana Tomaselli, "Moral Philosophy and Population Questions in Eighteenth Century Europe," *Population and Development Review* 14, issue supplement "Population and Resources in Western Intellectual Tradition" (1988): 7–29; Carol Blum, *Strength in Numbers: Population, Reproduction and Power in Eighteenth Century France* (Baltimore, MD: Johns Hopkins University Press, 2002).

11. Blum, *Strength in Numbers,* 11–20; Vidal, *La pensée démographique,* 33–40.

12. Julian Hoppit, "Political Arithmetic in Eighteenth-Century England," *Economic History Review,* n.s., 49, no. 3 (1996): 516–40; Theodore M. Porter, *The Rise of Statistical Thinking, 1820–1900* (Princeton, NJ: Princeton University Press, 1986), 4–5, 17–39. It is telling to note that statisticians were first known as "statists," so named for the close association between enumerating and recording and the rise of the modern state.

13. Donald Winch, *Malthus* (Oxford: Oxford University Press, 1987); John Toye, *Keynes on Population* (Oxford: Oxford University Press, 2000), 13–36.

14. Porter, *Rise of Statistical Thinking,* 17.

15. In England, attention focused on the functioning of the Poor Laws. An extensive and contentious literature exists on the subject. For an overview, see Peter Mandler, "The Making of the New Poor Redivivus," *Past and Present* 117 (1987): 131–57. For a general treatment of population issues in England, see Warren Robinson, "Population Policy in Early Victorian England," *European Journal of Population* 18, no. 2 (2002): 153–73. For a study of French ideas, see Jacques Donzelet, *The Policing of Families* (New York: Pantheon, 1979), and Vidal, *La pensée démographique,* 43–63.

16. The reasons for this declining influence have received little attention from scholars of Malthus and Malthusianism, who tend to concentrate on the reception of his ideas during his life and times. See William Petersen, *The Politics of Population* (Garden City, NY: Doubleday, 1964), 46–48.

17. There is an extensive literature on this topic. See William Schneider, *Quality and Quantity: The Quest for Biological Regeneration in Twentieth Century France* (Cambridge, MA: Harvard University Press, 1990); Andres Reggiani, "Procreating France: The Politics of Demography, 1919–1945," *French Historical Studies* 19, no. 3 (1996): 725–54; Joshua Cole, *The Power of Large Numbers: Population, Politics, and Gender in Nineteenth-Century France* (Ithaca, NY: Cornell University Press, 2000); Ella Camiscioli, "Producing Citizens and Reproducing the 'French Race': Immigration, Demography, and Pronatalism in Early Twentieth Century France," *Gender and History* 13, no. 3 (2001): 593–621.

18. The classic account is Richard Soloway, *Demography and Degeneration* (Chapel Hill: University of North Carolina Press, 1990). Also see Porter, *Rise of Statistical Thinking,* 40–92.

19. For Britain, see Anna Davin, "Imperialism and Motherhood," *History Workshop Journal* 5 (1978): 9–65.

20. Edward Higgs, "The Statistical Big Bang of 1911: Ideology, Technological Innovation and the Production of Medical Statistics," *Social History of Medicine* 9, no. 3 (1996): 409–26.

21. Carl Ipsen, *Dictating Demography: The Problem of Population in Fascist Italy* (Cambridge: Cambridge University Press, 1996); Paul Weindling, *Health, Race, and German Politics between National Unification and Nazism, 1870–1945* (Cambridge: Cambridge University Press, 1989); David Horn, *Social Bodies: Science, Reproduction, and Italian Modernity* (Princeton, NJ: Princeton University Press, 1994); Mark Adams, "Eugenics in Russia, 1900–1940," in *The Wellborn Science,* ed. Mark Adams (Oxford: Oxford University Press, 1990), 153–216; David Hoffman, "Mothers in the Motherland: Stalinist Pronatalism in Its Pan-European Context," *Journal of Social History* 34, no. 1 (2000): 35–54.

22. William Seltzer, "Population Statistics, the Holocaust, and the Nuremberg Trials," *Population and Development Review* 24, no. 3 (1998): 511–52.

23. In addition to his *Discipline and Punish* and *The History of Sexuality,* most scholars also cite his essay "Governmentality." See Michel Foucault, Graham Burchell, Colin Gordon, and Peter Millere, *The Foucault Effect: Studies in Governmentality* (Chicago: University of Chicago Press, 1991), 87–104.

24. Martin Hewitt, "Bio-politics and Social Policy: Foucault's Account of Welfare," *Theory, Culture and Society* 2, no. 1 (1983): 67–84.

25. Simon Szreter, *Fertility, Class and Gender in Britain, 1860–1940* (Cambridge: Cambridge University Press, 1996).

26. Ann Stoler, *Race and the Education of Desire: Foucault's History of Sexuality and the Colonial Order of Things* (Durham, NC: Duke University Press, 1995).

27. Richard Baxstrom, "Governmentality, Bio-power and the Emergence of the Malayan-Tamil Subject on the Plantations of Colonial Malaya," *Crossroads: An Interdisciplinary Journal of Southeast Asian Studies* 14, no. 2 (2000): 49–78.

28. Anderson, *Imagined Communities,* 164–70.

29. For a detailed case study, see Dennis D. Cordell and Joel W. Gregory, "Labour Reservoirs and Population: French Colonial Strategies in Koudougou, Upper Volta, 1914 to 1939," in *African Historical Demography,* vol. 2, ed. Christopher Fyfe and David McMaster (Edinburgh: African Studies Centre, University of Edinburgh, 1981), 51–104. A condensed version, lacking most tables, appeared with the same title in the *Journal of African History* 23, no. 2 (1982): 205–24. Other examples may be found among the essays in Cordell and Gregory, eds., *African Population and Capitalism: Historical Perspectives,* 2nd ed. (Madison: University of Wisconsin Press, 1994).

30. Gyan Prakash, *Another Reason: Science and the Imagination of Modern India* (Princeton, NJ: Princeton University Press, 1999), esp. 123–26.

31. C. A. Bayly, *Empire and Information: Intelligence Gathering and Social Communication in India, 1780–1870* (Cambridge: Cambridge University Press, 1996).

32. Bernard Cohen, "The Census, Social Structure and Objectification in South Asia," in Cohen, *An Anthropologist among the Historians and Other Essays* (Oxford: Oxford University Press, 1987), 224–54.

33. Edward Said, *Orientalism* (New York: Pantheon, 1978); Robert Inden, *Imagining India* (Bloomington: Indiana University Press, 2000). See the essays in Carol Breckenridge and Peter van der Veer, *Orientalism and the Postcolonial Predicament: Perspectives on South Asia* (Philadelphia: University of Pennsylvania Press, 1993), as well as Jyotsna G. Singh, *Colonial Narratives/Cultural Dialogues: "Discoveries" of India in the Language of Colonialism* (New York: Routledge, 1996), 52–78.

34. Tim Alborn, "Age and Empire in the Indian Census, 1871–1931," *Journal of Interdisciplinary History* 30, no. 1 (1999): 61–89; Norbert Peabody, "Cents, Sense, Census: Human Inventories in Late Precolonial and Early Colonial India," *Comparative Studies*

in Society and History 43, no. 4 (2001): 819–50; Sumit Guha, "The Politics of Identity and Enumeration in India c. 1600–1990," *Comparative Studies in Society and History* 45, no. 1 (2003): 148–67.

35. Prakash, *Another Reason,* 127–43; David Arnold, *Colonizing the Body: State Medicine and Epidemic Disease in Nineteenth-Century India* (Berkeley: University of California Press, 1993).

36. On this debate, see Philip Curtin, *The Atlantic Slave Trade: A Census* (Madison: University of Wisconsin Press, 1968); Paul E. Lovejoy, *Transformations in Slavery: A History of Slavery in Africa,* 2nd ed. (Cambridge: Cambridge University Press, 2000); Joseph E. Inikori, "Measuring the Atlantic Slave Trade: An Assessment of Curtin and Anstey," *Journal of African History* 17, no. 2 (1976): 197–223; Walter Rodney, *How Europe Underdeveloped Africa* (Washington, DC: Howard University Press, 1974); Patrick Manning, *Slavery and African Life: Occidental, Oriental and African Slave Trades* (Cambridge: Cambridge University Press, 1990).

37. Dirk Hoerder, *Cultures in Contact: World Migrations in the Second Millennium* (Durham, NC: Duke University Press, 2002), 366–404.

38. Thomas Malthus, *An Essay on Population,* vol. 1 (London: J. M. Dent and Sons, 1914), 89–98. For the problems with early European accounts, see Norman Etherington, "A False Emptiness: How Historians May Have Been Misled by Early Nineteenth Century Maps of South-Eastern Africa," *Imago Mundi* 56, no. 1 (2004): 67–86, and John Caldwell and Thomas Schindlmayr, "Historical Population Estimates: Unraveling the Consensus," *Population and Development Review* 28, no. 2 (2002): 183–204. Citing new sources that include records of archaeological excavations in West Africa and reinterpreting older sources, Louise Marie Diop-Maes sharply contests the conventional wisdom that Africa was "underpopulated." See Diop-Maes, *Afrique noire: Démographie, sol et histoire* (Paris: Présence Africaine and Khepera, 1996).

39. See Robert Kuczynski, *Demographic Survey of the British Colonial Empire,* vol. 1, *East Africa,* and vol. 2, *West Africa* (London: Oxford University Press, 1948).

40. See, for example, John Thornton, "An Eighteenth Century Baptismal Register and the Demographic History of Manguenzo," in *African Historical Demography,* ed. Christopher Fyfe and David McMaster (Edinburgh: African Studies Centre, University of Edinburgh, 1977), 405–15; José Curto, "Sources for the Pre-1900 Population History of Sub-Saharan Africa: The Case of Angola, 1773–1845," *Annales de Démographie Historique,* 1994, 319–38; Curto and Raymond R. Gervais, "The Population History of Luanda during the Late Atlantic Slave Trade, 1781–1844," *African Economic History* 29 (2001): 1–59; Curto and Gervais, "The Population History of Luanda during the Late Atlantic Slave Trade, 1781–1844: Addenda," *African Economic History* 30 (2002): 155–62; Curto, "The Anatomy of a Demographic Explosion: Luanda, 1844–1850," *International Journal of African Historical Studies* 32, nos. 2–3 (1999): 381–405.

41. For discussions of the kinds of demographic data available for Africa before the contemporary period and methodologies that promote their exploitation for population history, see Dennis D. Cordell and Joel W. Gregory, "Historical Demography and Demographic History in Africa: Theoretical and Methodological Considerations," *Canadian Journal of African Studies* [*Revue Canadienne des Études Africaines*] 14, no. 3 (1980): 389–416; Cordell and Gregory, "Earlier African Historical Demographies," *Canadian Journal of African Studies* [*Revue Canadienne des Études Africaines*] 23, no. 1 (1989): 5–27; Gregory, Cordell, and Raymond Gervais, *African Historical Demography: A Multidisciplinary Bibliography* (Los Angeles: Crossroads, 1984), v–xiv.

42. Frank Lorimer, *Demographic Information in Tropical Africa* (Boston: Boston University Press, 1961); William Brass, Ansley Coale, Paul Demeny, Don Heisel, Frank Lorimer, Anatole Romaniuk, and Etienne Van De Walle, *The Demography of Tropical Africa* (Princeton, NJ: Princeton University Press, 1968); Bruce Fetter, ed., *Demography from Scanty Evidence* (Boulder, CO: Lynne Rienner, 1990); Francis Gendreau, "Les opérations statistiques de collecte des données démographiques dans l'Afrique noire coloniale," *Annales de Démographie Historique,* 1987, 33–50; Eliane Doemschke and Doreen S. Goyer, *The Handbook of National Population Censuses: Africa and Asia* (New York: Greenwood, 1986).

43. On the impact of the slave trades, see Manning, *Slavery and African Life,* and Lovejoy, *Transformations in Slavery.*

44. Mike Davis, *Late Victorian Holocausts: El Niño Famines and the Making of the Third World* (New York: Verso, 2001); Marc H. Dawson, "Smallpox in Kenya, 1880–1920," *Social Science and Medicine* 13B (1979): 245–50; Meredeth Turshen, *The Political Economy of Disease in Tanzania* (New Brunswick, NJ: Rutgers University Press, 1984), 21–39; Carolyn Hamilton, ed., *The Mfecane Aftermath: Reconstructive Debates in Southern African History* (Johannesburg, South Africa: Witwatersrand University Press, 1995).

45. John Caldwell, "The Social Repercussions of Colonial Rule: Demographic Aspects," in *UNESCO General History of Africa,* vol. 7, *Africa under Colonial Domination, 1880–1935,* ed. A. Adu Boahe (London: Heinemann Educational Books, 1985), 458–86; Catherine Coquery-Vidrovitch, "Les populations africaines du passé," in *Population et socétéss en Afrique au sud du Sahara,* ed. Dominique Tabutin (Paris: L'Harmattan, 1988), 51–72.

46. See John Ford, *The Role of the Trypanosomiases in African Ecology: A Study of the Tsetse Fly Problem* (Oxford: Clarendon, 1971); James Giblin, "Trypanosomiasis Control in African History: An Evaded Issue?" *Journal of African History* 31, no. 1 (1990): 59–80; Helge Kjekshus, *Ecology Control and Economic Development in East African History: The Case of Tanganyika, 1850–1950* (Heinemann: London, 1977); Gregory H. Maddox, James L. Giblin, and Isaria N. Kimambo, eds., *Custodians of the Land: Ecology and Culture in the History of Tanzania* (Athens: Ohio University Press, 1996), 43–66.

47. In addition to the essays in Cordell and Gregory, *African Population and Capitalism,* see David Anderson, "Depression, Dust Bowl, Demography and Drought: The Colonial State and Soil Conservation in East Africa during the 1930s," *African Affairs* 83, no. 331 (1984): 321–41; Raymond Dummett, "Disease and Mortality among Gold Miners of Ghana: Colonial Government and Mining Company Attitudes and Policies, 1900–1938," *Social Science and Medicine* 37, no. 3 (1993): 213–32; Thaddeus Sunseri, *Vilimani: Labour Migration and Rural Change in Early Colonial Tanzania* (Portsmouth, NH: Heinemann, 2002).

48. Frederick Cooper, *Decolonization and African Society: The Labor Question in French and British Africa* (Cambridge: Cambridge University Press, 1996); Alice Conklin, *A Mission to Civilize: The Republican Idea of Empire in France and West Africa, 1895–1930* (Stanford, CA: Stanford University Press, 1997); Dennis D. Cordell, Joel W. Gregory, and Victor Piché, "The Demographic Reproduction of Health and Disease: Colonial Central African Republic and Contemporary Burkina Faso," in *The Social Basis of Health and Healing in Africa,* ed. Steven Feierman and John M. Janzen (Berkeley: University of California Press, 1992), 39–61; Hilaire Babassana, *Travail forcé, expropriation et formation du salariat en Afrique noire* (Grenoble, France: Presses Universitaires de Grenoble, 1978); Babacar Fall, *Le travail forcé en Afrique occidentale française (1900–1945)* (Paris: Karthala, 1993); Abebe Zegeye and Shubi Ishemo, eds., *Forced Labour and Migration: Patterns of Movement within Africa* (London: Hans Zell, 1989).

49. Carol Summers, "Intimate Colonialism: The Imperial Production of Reproduction in Uganda, 1907–1925," *Signs* 16, no. 41 (1991): 787–807; Jean Allman, "Making Mothers:

Missionaries, Medical Officers and Women's Work in Colonial Assante, 1924–1945," *History Workshop Journal* 38, no. 1 (1994): 23–47; Nancy Rose Hunt, "'Le Bébé en brousse': European Women, African Birth Spacing and Colonial Intervention in Breast-Feeding in the Belgian Congo," *International Journal of Historical Studies* 21, no. 3 (1988): 401–32; Dennis D. Cordell, "Où sont tous les enfants: La faible fécondité en Centrafrique," in *Population, reproduction, sociétés: Perspectives et enjeux de démographie sociale,* ed. Dennis D. Cordell, Danielle Gaureau, Raymond R. Gervais, and Céline Le Bourdais (Montreal: Les presses de l'Université de Montréal, 1993), 257–82.

50. Kirk Arden Hoppe, *Lords of the Fly: Sleeping Sickness Control in British East Africa, 1900–1960* (Westport, CT: Greenwood, 2003); Maryinez Lyons, *The Colonial Disease: A Social History of Sleeping Sickness in Northern Zaire, 1900–1940* (Cambridge: Cambridge University Press, 1992); Rita Headrick, *Colonialism, Health and Illness in French Equatorial Africa, 1885–1935,* ed. Daniel R. Headrick (Atlanta, GA: African Studies Association, 1994).

51. For an example, see Jean Filopovich, "Destined to Fail: Forced Settlement at the *Office du Niger, 1926–1045*," *Journal of African History* 42, no. 2 (2001): 239–60.

52. For a discussion of the weaknesses and limits of the late colonial state, see Bruce Berman, "The Perils of Bula Matari: Constraint and Power in the Colonial State," *Canadian Journal of African Studies* 31, no. 3 (1997): 556–70, and John Darwin, "What Was the Late Colonial State?" *Itinerario* 23, nos. 3–4 (1999): 73–82.

53. Stephen Constantine, *The Making of Colonial Development Policy, 1920–1940* (London: F. Cass, 1984), 195–226.

54. Helen Tilley, "The African Research Survey, Ecological Paradigms and British Colonial Development, 1920–1940," in *Social History and African Environments,* ed. William Beinart and JoAnn McGregor (Oxford: Oxford University Press, 2003), 109–30.

55. See Bill Freund, *The African City: A History* (Cambridge: Cambridge University Press, 2007); David M. Anderson and Richard Rathbone, eds., *Africa's Urban Past* (Portsmouth, NH: Heinemann, 2005); Steven J. Salm and Toyin Falola, eds., *African Urban Spaces in Historical Perspective* (Rochester, NY: University of Rochester Press, 2005).

56. Monica Van Beusekom, *Negotiating Development: African Farmers and Colonial Experts at the Office du Niger, 1920–1960* (Portsmouth, NH: Heinemann, 2002).

57. Berman, "Perils of Bula Matari," 568–70. See also M. Crawford Young, *The African Colonial State in Comparative Perspective* (New Haven, CT: Yale University Press, 1994).

58. Christophe Bonneuil, "Development as Experiment: Science and State Building in Late Colonial and Post-colonial Africa, 1930–1970," *Osiris* 15, no. 1 (2001): 258–81.

59. Mahmood Mamdani, *Citizen and Subject: Contemporary Africa and the Legacy of Late Colonialism* (Princeton, NJ: Princeton University Press, 1996).

60. Aderanti Adepoju, "Military Rule and Population Issues in Nigeria," *African Affairs* 80, no. 318 (1981): 29–47.

61. Jeffrey I. Herbst, *States and Power in Africa: Comparative Lessons in Authority and Control* (Princeton, NJ: Princeton University Press, 2000).

62. See Susan Hunter, *Black Death: AIDS in Africa* (New York: Palgrave Macmillan, 2003); Philip W. Setel, *A Plague of Paradoxes: AIDS, Culture, and Demography in Northern Tanzania* (Chicago: University of Chicago Press, 1999); John Iliffe, *The African AIDS Epidemic: A History* (Athens: Ohio University Press, 2006).

63. William Macmillan, *Africa Emergent* (London: Faber and Faber, 1938), 40. For more on Macmillan's career, see John Flint, "Macmillan as Critic of Empire: The Impact of an Historian on Colonial Policy," in *Africa and Empire: W. H. Macmillan, Historian and Social*

Critic, ed. Hugh Macmillan and Shula Marks (Aldershot, UK: Published for the Institute of Commonwealth Studies by Temple Smith, 1989).

64. Fyfe and McMaster, *African Historical Demography,* vols. 1 and 2; *Cahiers d'Études Africaines* (Démographie historique) 28, 1–2, No 105/106 (1987); *Annales de Démographie Historique,* 1987; Cordell and Gregory, *African Population and Capitalism;* Fetter, *Demography from Scanty Evidence.*

65. Peter Laslett, *The World We Have Lost: England before the Industrial Age* (New York: Scribner's, 1965).

1

African Historical Demography in the Postmodern and Postcolonial Eras

DENNIS D. CORDELL

At the Third African Population Congress held in Durban, South Africa, in 1999, I presented a "census" of publications on African historical demography that had appeared since two landmark Edinburgh seminars on the topic in 1977 and 1981.[1] My aim was to show demographers working on Africa—most of whose research is astonishingly ahistorical—that in recent decades, the labors of historians, anthropologists, and indeed even a few of their own number had laid the foundations for the serious historical study of African population. I assumed that such research was expanding. I hoped that presenting a paper at an international meeting of more than a thousand specialists on African demography would convince some that African historical demography is possible despite the scarcity of the sacrosanct forms of demographic data cherished by demographers.[2] I also hoped that an overview of research might encourage more demographers to introduce historical dimensions into their own work. To my surprise, the presentation drew an audience of several hundred. Questions and comments were numerous, and debate flourished.

However, the true significance of my paper lay elsewhere. My census suggested that all was not right with the world. The enumeration showed that publications in English about the history of African population had grown slowly but steadily through the late 1970s and the 1980s. However, contrary to my expectations, the number of books, as well as articles published separately or in essay collections, peaked at more than thirty in 1990, plummeted to five in 1991, and remained minimal for the remainder of the decade, except for 1994 when it climbed to ten.

I asked myself what lay behind this apparent reversal in research on African population history. I concluded that perhaps the rise of postmodern and postcolonial studies in the 1980s had led scholars of African history and Africanist social science and their students—the scholars of the 1990s—to turn their energies and enthusiasm away from social and economic history to cultural studies. Both postmodernism and postcolonialism raise questions about what is undoubtedly perceived as the apparent hyperempiricism, overgeneralization, quantitative bias, and hegemonic interest characteristic of demographic research. Demography, perhaps more than any other discipline in the social sciences, has been the handmaiden of the state. Censuses, surveys, and other demographic exercises are more often than not the work of state agencies; and the state deploys demographic data to administer or control its inhabitants. International organizations and agencies, which also have sponsored considerable demographic research, are extensions of the global state system. Postmodern theorists such as Michel Foucault and his successors, then, would undoubtedly dispute the objectivity and hence the validity of quantitative data collected by the state and its agents. For their part, postcolonial scholars have also roundly criticized the collection of demographic data in the colonies of the European empires.

A couple of other factors also undoubtedly contributed to the decline in research in African population history. First, demography has been marginalized in the contemporary academy. Population studies are most often housed in departments of sociology, anthropology, or economics. Nonetheless, the field has remained segregated from the other social sciences, including history. Students of these disciplines seldom learn much demography. At best, they see demography as comprising discrete sets of methods learned piecemeal to answer questions raised by their research agendas in other fields. Second, demographic research has been closely linked to contemporary public policy issues and the local, national, and international institutions that foster them.[3] Such research has focused mainly on the contemporary period. Neither focus nor funding has favored historical studies.

However, these two features have characterized demography as a discipline since World War II. They do not date from the early 1990s, when I pinpoint the decline in new research. So they do not explain it. Postmodernism and postcolonialism, by contrast, were new to Africanist history and the social sciences in the 1980s and 1990s—some years after both had begun to influence other fields of study. Thus, it seems appropriate to explore the impact of postmodernism and postcolonialism on the production of knowledge in the field.

The objective of this chapter is not to savage postmodernism and postcolonialism, though I do indeed look first at why postmodernism and postcolonialism may well have turned attention away from African historical demography for a time. This analysis is by no means as exhaustive as my census published in 2000, but it concludes on a more positive note. In recent years, a few scholars of population history in Africa have incorporated postmodern and postcolonialist perspectives, while still respecting earlier critical traditions characteristic of history and demography. Others have not been dissuaded from producing solid studies, which adhere to the best critical traditions of history and demography, with little reference to postmodern and postcolonial research. In the sections that follow, I will offer definitions of postmodernism and postcolonialism, and then I will look at how each has impacted historical studies. Finally, I will review recent research on African historical demography in light of both.

Postmodernism: Defining the Undefinable

Postmodernism is marked by two characteristics, both inimical to definition. First, postmodernism defines itself in terms of its nemesis—modernism. The standard-bearers of postmodernism have written extensively about characteristics of modernism: belief in the forward march of progress and reason; focus on the emergence of the modern individual graced with an anchored, centered identity; and confidence that modern individuals, aided by science and sangfroid, will deduce objective truths about the world. Second, the founding figures of postmodernism have not only shied away from developing a definition, they have also insisted that such an effort contradicts their enterprise, which is, in part, to deny the existence of universal truths or metanarratives. Indeed, George Ritzer suggests that intellectuals most commonly associated with postmodernism—Jean Baudrillard, Michel Foucault, Jacques Derrida, Jean-François Lyotard, and Jacques Lacan—would even deny that they were or are postmodernists.[4] Ironically, then, it is perhaps "modernists," who, in their "modern" efforts to articulate postmodern critiques, have done the most to delineate postmodernism.[5]

Postmodernism is associated with several core concepts. First, it contests the conviction that modernity has brought progress and that science promises an ever more rational and enlightened future. Postmodernists cite as support for their skepticism the horrors of the last century—two world wars, the genocide of the Armenians that opened the century, the Holocaust and the dropping of atom bombs that marked the 1930s and 1940s, and the genocides in the Balkans and Rwanda that brought it to a close. To this list, we might also add the colonial era—the "new" imperialism of the late nineteenth century and the first half of the twentieth century. After 1850, Western societies often used their great gains in military technology to inflict horrendous death and destruction on the peoples of Africa, Asia, and the Americas.[6] Ironically, the colonizing powers justified their actions by claiming that the suffering and sacrifice were theirs—a "white man's burden" and "civilizing mission" to promote progress.

Second, postmodern texts submit that the prime movers of human action are not reason and logic but less predictable and less "knowable" influences. Pauline-Marie Rosenau writes that postmodern thinkers "tend to accord great importance to more pre-modern phenomena such as 'emotions, feelings, intuition, reflection, speculation, personal experience, custom, violence, metaphysics, tradition, cosmology, magic, myth, religious sentiment, and mystical experience.'"[7] Most often through Michel Foucault and Jacques Derrida, postmodernism looks back to Friedrich Nietzsche, the nineteenth-century philosopher who characterized knowledge itself—the great achievement of the modern scientific age—as "an invention that masks a will to power."[8]

Third, postmodernist authors reject "metanarratives," analytical frameworks that offer total explanations. Ryan Bishop defines metanarratives as "grand theories for the generation of knowledge. Each theory . . . claims to be universal in regard to truth and application."[9] Baudrillard has written that "the great drives or impulses, with their positive, elective, and attractive powers are gone."[10] Lyotard has echoed him with his declaration that postmodernism is "an incredulity toward metanarratives."[11] Historians Joyce Appleby, Lynn Hunt, and Margaret Jacob identify the dominant metanarratives of the post–World War II era as modernization theory, Marxism, and the *Annales* school. They observe, too, that these theoretical frameworks were exclusionary: "All three major schools of history had left women and minorities out of their accounts or had treated them in stereotypical ways."[12]

Fourth, distrust of metanarratives and the identification of such grand theories with strategies for power and control has led postmodernists rather to direct attention to texts and language. They have analyzed or "unpacked" texts to reveal discourses of power, position, and identity rather than universal truth or knowledge. The objective of analysis is to situate "knowledge" by demonstrating how it is produced, by whom, and for what end. This exercise leads to "historicizing" texts—locating them in their own particular historical contexts.

Finally, language is obviously integral to the analysis of texts. Bishop writes that "the problems posed by language, rhetoric, and representation with regard to knowledge production and legitimation form an essential element of postmodernism."[13] This concern about language led to a "linguistic turn" in the late 1970s and 1980s.[14] Postmodernist presumptions of a chasm between language and speech and between signifier and signified led to questions about gaps between the meanings of words—as used by different people of the same society and era, by people of the same society in different eras, and by people of different societies in the same or different eras. Roland Barthes and Claude Lévi-Strauss applied Ferdinand de Saussure's analysis of language/speech to the interpretation of signs in general, giving rise to semiotics.[15]

Attention to systems of signs, in turn, promoted attention to the broader role of culture in analyzing societies. The linguistic turn, then, gave way to the "cultural turn." The notion of text also stretched to embrace tangible and even nontangible cultural artifacts. These developments and the rise of cultural studies, taken together, aroused concern among historians. Appleby writes that "[historians] rely on the stability of word meanings at two points: when they write their interpretations of the past and when they read the texts that serve as evidence of the past. Thus, for [some] historians, the linguistic turn has precipitated an epistemological crisis."[16]

Postmodernism and History

Postmodern scholarship draws from a common well of thinking about history greatly influenced by Foucault. Foucault regarded history as a succession of discourses, each of which arose in "concrete historical conditions" to explain the world in terms of prevailing structures of power.[17] For Foucault, the historian's task was to historicize these discourses to reveal power relationships, rather than to try to understand the origins of people and events—much less the causal relationships among them. There were two dimensions to historicizing discourse. Foucault referred to the first as the "archaeology of knowledge," how a particular discourse or discursive environment constructed knowledge across fields of knowledge or disciplines in the same era. For the modern period, for example, an archaeology of knowledge would privilege inquiry into how modernist discourse was reflected in discursive practices characteristic of history, literature, politics, economics, and science. The second task was uncovering a "genealogy of knowledge" or showing how "discursive formations" succeeded each other through time. Once such discursive environments were brought to light, Foucault and his successors focused attention on contradictions within discourses to illuminate sites of contestation or struggle. Bringing to light each contradiction unveiled still deeper levels of contradiction and contestation. The objective, then, was to uncover or peel back each layer of discourse to reveal layers beneath it, a process that was never expected to arrive at the "truth." Derrida baptized this kind of analysis "deconstruction."[18]

Discursive events take the form of texts. Hence, the analysis of texts and their location in the larger "discursive formation" was crucial. For Foucault and Derrida, the web of language was determinant in fashioning "understanding" and fostering action, rather than any external reality. For historian Appleby and her colleagues, this postulate undercut historical analysis: "Women and men are stripped of the meaningful choices whose reality had once served to distinguish human beings from animals. Change comes about through . . . slips in the fault lines of broad discursive configurations . . . not through self-determined human action."[19] As postmodernism expanded its sphere from language and discourse to culture, it implicitly called into question the "usability" of the evidence employed by historians to understand the past. Postmodernist criticism undermined regard for historical texts as authored sources, as well as the physical evidence remaining from other eras.

Postmodernism's denunciation of a positivist and universalizing modernism followed earlier schools of thought that called into question accepted tenets of historiography. By the late 1960s, for example, the rise of social history had underscored the ways that "traditional interpretations . . . had excluded marginal or nonconforming historical groups."[20] Searching for a new universal narrative, some scholars explored the ways that the outsiders resisted domination and yet struggled to become part of the nation. Social historians offered "a more complex picture of the past. . . . Ironically, [however, their work also] fostered the argument that history could never be objective." Such doubts opened the doors to the broader issues raised by postmodernist criticism. In Western Europe, the student protests of the late 1960s asked similar questions about the ways nationalist elites and the educational establishments excluded many social groups—writing them out of the historical experience of the nation.

Finally, the end of colonial empires and the emergence of new nationalist intellectual elites and educational systems in Asia and Africa also attacked the hegemonic, modernist narratives of the West. Still, these narratives persevered and even thrived under new names: colonies became "developing" states, which together made up the "developing" world, whose teleology remained decidedly modernist. A generation later, however, intellectuals from Asia, Africa, and other parts of the non-West, along with some Western scholars, raised new questions.

Postcolonialism: Epistemology and Empire

If postmodernism defies categorization and denies the existence of a master narrative, postcolonialism is marked by a multiplicity of definitions.[21] Kamala Visweswaran writes that when used as a noun, *postcolonial* suggests a "movement, condition, or character . . . that is far more cohesive than the term warrants." However, when employed as an adjective, *postcolonial* describes myriad conditions, "everything from certain critics, intellectuals, bodies of theory or literature, and entire peoples or societies; to a mode of consciousness, a state formation, an historical period, and, finally, the condition of the (post)modern world itself." Indeed, Visweswaran concludes, "there is little consensus about what the term means or even whether it should be used at all."[22]

Nonetheless, as a descriptor for the second half of the twentieth century, *postcolonial* has meaning. *Postwar,* the usual term for the decades after 1945, has been common currency mainly in the North—in North America, Europe, and the former Soviet Union. *Postcolonial* is perhaps more meaningful for the rest of the planet. Between 1945 and the 1990s, more than seventy-five former colonies attained political independence.[23] If China is acknowledged to have been an "informal" colony of European powers in the nineteenth century, then about 80 percent of the earth's people live in these new states today. However defined, *postcolonial* is a major chronological marker.

The term is of double provenance. The work of Edward Said is the best-known and most recent inspiration for postcolonialist analysis. In 1978, Said published *Orientalism,* an intellectual history analyzing how European scholars and visitors in the early modern period described "the Orient." Their descriptions, Said submitted, produced a much broader discourse that reduced peoples and societies in southwest Asia and North Africa to a homogenized and unchanging population of "Orientals," whose characteristics were binary opposites of those of Europeans.[24] He called this package of description, interpretation, and policy "Orientalism," borrowing a term coined earlier to refer to similarities in subject and style among artists and authors from Europe whose works portrayed this part of the world. Through case studies, Said traced how this essentializing European discourse translated into policy and action in the era of European colonialism. He suggested, too, that Orientalism continues to shape Western views of the rest of the world. Said's work pushed scholars to reread the writings of imperialism through these new glasses; that exercise constitutes postcolonial analysis.

Said attributed three dimensions to Orientalism. The first was academic: "Anyone who teaches, writes about, or researches the Orient . . . either in its specific or its general aspects is an Orientalist, and what he or she does is Orientalism."[25] The second dimension was broader: a "style of thought, based upon an ontological and epistemological distinction made between 'the Orient' and (most of the time) 'the Occident.'" This style of thought characterized numerous writers across many fields, who "have accepted the basic distinction between East and West." The third dimension was more explicitly about power and hegemony: "Taking the late eighteenth century as a very roughly defined starting point, Orientalism can be discussed and analyzed as the corporate institution for dealing with the Orient—dealing with it by making statements about it, authorizing views of it, describing it, by teaching it, settling it, ruling over it."

Said acknowledged his debt to postmodernism through Foucault, who provoked him into thinking about Orientalism as a discourse that "was able to manage—and even produce—the Orient." In addition, Said acknowledged in *Culture and Imperialism* that "what partly animated my study of Orientalism was my critique of the way in which the alleged universalism of fields such as the classics (not to mention historiography, anthropology, and sociology) was Eurocentric in the extreme."[26] Like all discourse, Orientalism grew out of power. It reinforced the belief among Europeans that they and their institutions were entitled to rule the Orient. It became second nature.

Although postmodernism and postcolonialism both call assumed truths into question, their objectives are not the same. As Vijay Mishra and Bob Hodge point out, "If for postmodernism the object of analysis is the subject as defined by humanism, with its essentialism and mistaken historical verities, its unities and transcendental presence, then for postcolonialism the object is the imperialist subject, the colonized as formed by the processes of imperialism."[27]

Citing a specific example of this difference, Mishra and Hodge note that Salman Rushdie raises questions about "historical certainties" in his novel *Midnight's Children* in a way that recalls postmodernism. However, Rushdie also incorporates magical narratives from the classic texts of the *Mahabharata* and the *Kathasaritasagara*, which may be seen as calling on non-Western metanarratives to offer alternatives to those of colonialism and the West.[28]

The second provenance of postcolonialism is an explicitly political body of thought and texts on the impact of European domination. Visweswaran reminds us that "the racial basis of colonial society and the extent to which it served as an instrument of colonial power was discussed anthropologically" as early as 1951.[29] As an example, he cites the French sociologist Georges Balandier, who noted that intellectuals such as the Italian psychologist O. Mannoni and two Martiniquans—the physician Frantz Fanon and the poet-politician Aimé Césaire—had also explored how European colonialism reduced colonial people to a lesser, homogenized Other.[30] Published first in *Revue Volonté* in 1939 and reprinted many times, Césaire's powerful poem "Cahiers d'un retour au pays natal" explores the psychological onslaught that accompanied European hegemony and then sounds a clarion call for colonial peoples to claim European stereotypes and use them as weapons against colonial rule.[31] The poem became the anthem for the Négritude movement, which called into question the moral integrity of what the French termed *"la mission civilisatrice"* (the civilizing mission) and the British termed "the white man's burden." Négritude proclaimed that African heritage and black skin were positive and beautiful.[32]

As an aside, it should be added that in the early 1900s, African American writers such as Charles W. Chestnutt and Zora Neale Hurston, among others, probed the psychological impact of hegemonic white racism on people of African heritage.[33] African Americans in the United States may not have been colonial subjects, but they lived in a colonial situation. They, too, were the Other. Another intellectual of the French Empire, the Tunisian philosopher Albert Memmi, acknowledged as much in the mid-1960s by dedicating the English translation of his seminal volume *The Colonizer and the Colonized* to "the American Negro, also colonized."[34]

Said's naming and exploration of Orientalist discourse in the 1970s and earlier Négritude critiques resonated powerfully among scholars of the former colonies and, in particular, scholars *from* these parts of the world. A group from South Asia founded what they called a "subaltern school." They reinterpreted colonialism and later nationalist movements, making three powerful points: colonialism and nationalism were discourses that grew out of Western hegemony, both homogenized the non-West and its people, and both excluded the mass of South Asians as agents in their own history. Drawing on Antonio Gramsci's writings on agency and dominated classes, Gayatri Chakravorty Spivak's essay "Can the Subaltern Speak?" joined *Orientalism* as a seminal text.[35]

As with postmodernism, the postcolonial definition of texts broadened to include other artifacts of culture and morphed into cultural studies. Postcolonial scholars have scrutinized works of fiction, European travel literature, and historical documents and material evidences of empire produced by European observers and European authorities. Despite an ironic tendency to overgeneralize and homogenize non-Western cultures and societies, postcolonial studies have revealed both the very obvious and the more subtle ways that colonialism cast its gaze, categorized the Other, and transmitted it globally. Postcolonialism has recast how scholars now read the history of the colonial and postcolonial eras.

Postcolonialism, Postmodernism, and History

Postmodernism implies a gaze across time, between the era of the modern and whatever has succeeded it. However, when and even if the era of modernism ended remains ambiguous. Postcolonialism, by contrast, has an explicitly historical project. Patrick Williams and Laura Chrisman insist on the emphatically historical and engaged character of postcolonial analysis:

> If texts exist in what . . . one would call a dialectical relationship with
> their social and historical context, . . . then an analysis of the texts
> of imperialism has a particular urgency, given their implication in
> far-reaching, and continuing, systems of domination and economic
> exploitation. This involves an understanding of present circumstances as
> well as the ways in which these are informed by, perpetuate, and differ
> from situations which preceded them, and the complex interrelation of
> history and the present moment provides the terrain on which colonial
> discourse analysis and post-colonial theory operate.[36]

Historians have not, by and large, enthusiastically embraced postcolonialism. This comment by Williams and Chrisman gives an inkling as to why this might be so. First, the focus of postcolonial analysis is said to be on "the texts of imperialism," with little reference to the many other kinds of evidence that historians examine. Most historians look beyond texts to the broader social, economic, political, and cultural contexts that conditioned their production. Given that the pioneers of postcolonial analysis were most often scholars of literature and not historians, a preoccupation with texts is perhaps not surprising. Said, himself a scholar of comparative literature, wrote, "My method is to focus as much as possible on individual works, to read them first as great products of the creative or interpretative imagination, and then to show them as part of the relationship between culture and empire."[37]

Postcolonial scholars have analyzed texts other than novels. Ivo Kamps and Jyotsna Singh, for example, have edited a collection of essays on travel literature about the Middle East, Africa, and India.[38] Elsewhere, Singh has explored the "discovery" literature on India, in order "to join contemporary moves to de-naturalize history: to show that it is not objectively or providentially created and that it is yoked to specific, sometimes discrete agendas."[39] Singh's comment and similar remarks by other postcolonial scholars suggest that, for them, it is a revelation to learn that historical evidence may be biased, inaccurate, or incomplete. In *Colonial Narratives,* Singh concludes that although the "discovery" trope of travel literature offers a basis for critical reflection, it also calls into question the use of travel narratives as sources for history.[40]

The idea that historical texts are biased and conditioned by their production is not news to historians. All historical sources are biased, all are incomplete, and none are completely accurate—indeed, this may be said for virtually all kinds of data in all fields. For historians of the non-West, dismissing the entire corpus of travel literature is not the way to deal with the epistemological concerns raised by postcolonial scholarship. The solution is to reread travel accounts carefully, analyze the multiplicity of discourses they represent, pay close attention to the circumstances of their production and use as well as their content, and then compare them with the myriad other kinds of historical sources to arrive at plausible scenarios about past events.

Historians and social scientists who study Africa embarked on critical reconsiderations of travel accounts and other sources beginning in the 1960s. A sample of these different kinds of critical projects may be found in *History in Africa: A Journal of Method (HA)*, beginning with its first issue in 1974.[41] The *HA* "bibliography" includes essays, such as that by Gérard Chouin, that reread travel narratives in light of discourse theory or that carefully examine, as in articles by John Cinnamon and Dmitri Van den Bersselaar, the ways that bodies of knowledge from the colonial era influenced the development of modernist Africanist social science and the colonial state.[42] Scholars have also sounded travel literature and oral sources for silences—clues about people and topics not addressed. Richard Roberts and Donald Moore have theorized research on fieldwork with explicit reference to the literature on hegemony by postmodern icons such as Foucault.[43] Many others, such as Kathryn Barrett-Gaines, offer careful close readings of narrative texts and the biographies of their authors.[44]

John Hanson provides an example of still another kind of critical perspective published by *HA* in his analysis of the ways that African oral testimonies have been embedded in travel narratives.[45] Others, such as Paola Ivanov, study particular regions or ethnic groups to evaluate how the European narratives have presented them to the larger world.[46] Articles such as that by Selena Axelrod Winsnes have explored how the processes of editing and translation have reshaped historical sources.[47] Last but not least, African historians have engaged since 1980 in the collection, annotation, and production of the *Fontes historiae africanae,* critical editions of major travel narratives originally written in West European languages and Arabic.[48] Although problematic, historical sources for Africa are limited. Hence, it is very important not to dismiss and discard them but to learn how to use them critically.

In quite another vein, Walter E. A. van Beek has reassessed the work of a founding anthropologist-ethnologist in African studies—in this instance, Marcel Griaule, whose writings on the Dogon in the 1940s and 1950s, in the former colony now known as Mali, came to be regarded as classics. J. E. G. Sutton has followed up with a reevaluation of the impact of two major archaeologists on history writing in East Africa.[49] Articles in *HA* have also proposed the critical examination of nondocumentary, cultural "texts." Christraud M. Geary, for example, wrote the introduction to a series of articles on "Sources and Resources for the Study of African Material Culture" published in the 1994 issue; two years later, Colleen Kriger followed with an essay about using museum collections as historical sources, illustrated by a detailed case study.[50]

To return to the earlier comment by Williams and Chrisman, many historians would also disagree with the priority they assign to interpreting historical texts in terms of how they interact with "present circumstances." Historians are dedicated first to trying to understand past circumstances and moments that led to the creation of texts, while acknowledging that contemporary concerns influence their choice of topics. Appleby, Hunt, and Jacob write that history is different from fiction because it arises from "curiosity about what actually happened in the past. Beyond the self—outside the realm of the imagination—lies a landscape cluttered with the detritus of past living, a mélange of clues and codes informative of a moment as real as this present one."[51] Acknowledging postmodern and postcolonial critiques, they make the case for "qualified objectivity," writing that "we have redefined historical objectivity as an interactive relationship between an inquiring subject and an external object." However, material objects from the past do exist, and historians build their arguments by documenting and interpreting them.

To be more specific, it is instructive to look at how a historian of South Asia has reacted to postcolonial scholarship. At the high tide of postcolonial dominion in the academy, Robert Frykenberg published *History and Belief,* whose last chapter, "History as Rhetoric: A Disputed Discourse," levels serious charges against "Post-Orientalism."[52] First, Frykenberg takes aim at Said, condemning him *not* for raising questions about how colonialism itself shaped our knowledge of the non-West but rather for rhetoric "blinded by its own rage." Second, Frykenberg charges that postcolonial discourse is itself homogenizing and generalizing, overlooking great differences among many societies subjected to several European colonial regimes. This criticism holds a mirror up to the postcolonial charge that colonialism created a nondifferentiated non-West. He makes the very important point that the historiography of South Asia is more complicated than postcolonialism admits: "For every one European scholar who worked to uncover the cultural riches of India's past, there were scores (perhaps hundreds) of Indian scholars committed to the same task."

Third, Frykenberg excoriates postcolonial scholars,[53] who, he writes, ignore examples of "colonialism" antecedent to the European variety, such as the rise of modern Hinduism (which itself is a blend of "syncretistic canons") or "the equally 'colonizing' roles of Sanskrit, Persian, and other 'classical' canons in India." The chapter includes three other examples to show that India's modern history and the impact of British colonialism are more ambiguous, complex, and contradictory than the "clear, neat, and simple perspectives" proposed by postcolonialism. To wit, he observes: "Thirty thousand [Indian] notables put their signatures on a petition begging the government for English-medium colleges"; Hindu scholars led the rise of the "'Indish' (Anglo-Indian English) literary canon and its assimilation of other indigenous canons"; and finally, it was European missionaries who advocated in favor of indigenous languages and resisted the imposition of English because they believed that such a policy would support continued domination by the Hindu ruling classes.

However, underlying all of these specific charges is anger about a deeper, more fundamental matter. For Frykenberg, Said and the "post-Orientalism" that he engendered display a "disregard, if not contempt, for mere facts or for critical rules of evidence [that] springs from his postmodernist scorn for any concrete objective reality." Postmodernism posits that it is impossible to know, which allows postcolonialism the freedom to engage in rhetoric about the colonial experience unencumbered by a deep knowledge of the relevant historical sources, languages, and local cultures and traditions.

What impact has postmodernism and postcolonialism had on scholarship? At the outset of this chapter, I hypothesized that the rise of postmodernism and postcolonialism may have contributed to the decline in research in African historical demography, at least initially in the 1990s. Such seems to have been the case in other fields. In a content analysis of major journals on French history in English and French published between 1976 and 1990 aimed at assessing the impact of postmodernism, Thomas Schaepter documented an important shift away from political, economic, social, and diplomatic history to cultural and intellectual history. Articles in English on French political and diplomatic history declined by half, and publications on economic and social history dropped by a quarter. Essays in French on political and diplomatic history fell by one-fourth, and those on economic and social history were down 50 percent. In contrast, publications on intellectual and cultural history in both languages doubled over the same period.[54] Even in cultural history, Appleby and her colleagues write that "the central task" shifted to "decoding meaning, rather than inferring causal laws of explanation."[55]

In Indian history, according to Richard Eaton, postmodernism (and postcolonialism) played out differently but with analogous effects.[56] First, Eaton concludes that these analytical perspectives led scholars away from studying the precolonial history of South Asia. Despite the imperial conquests of earlier non-European powers in the subcontinent, which produced their own empires, colonial history translated simply into the history of British conquest and rule. Everything before became a homogeneous "non-British, noncolonial" India, which postcolonial studies did not supply the analytical tools to address. Of 118 proposals submitted to the American Institute of Indian Studies for research in Indian history in 1996, for example, the vast majority were "crowded into the nineteenth or twentieth century."[57] Second, Eaton notes, the emphasis on British colonial history translated into research proposals in the 1980s and 1990s largely limited to studying texts in colonial archives: "Most ended up in London, and a few in national or state archives in India, studying colonial records that were then subjected to discourse analysis."[58] Concern was not with the collection and analysis of empirical data. Hence, young scholars ceased doing fieldwork, with unfortunate and ironic results:

> What the turn to discourse analysis did was to enable scholars to cast new interpretive spins on data that not only were already published (and which were, conveniently, in English), but also were relatively accessible. For Americans, this then made it feasible not to go to India or to undertake original field research, while providing unlimited opportunities for armchair theorizing. . . . It is worth recalling, after all,

that a telling feature of classical Orientalist scholarship on India had been precisely its detached, armchair quality.[59]

A similar climate has inhibited research and open discussion about the types of sources used to do social history elsewhere. Ben Johnson, a historian of the American Southwest, presented a paper on ethnic Mexican racial formations in Texas in the 1930s and 1940s at a meeting in Mexico of scholars from the Americas. He explored how postrevolutionary Mexican politics impacted Mexican American racial self-conceptions and relations with non-Hispanics. Compiling records of marriage in San Antonio in the 1930s between people with and without Hispanic surnames, Johnson found that 30 percent of Hispanics married outside their ethnic community. He compared these findings with Jewish outmarriage rates in the mid-twentieth century and used his findings to evaluate current thinking about the role of "amalgamation" in U.S. history. Many colleagues at the conference dismissed the marriage records:

> The response, pretty vehement, from some was to ask "what do you actually think you're measuring," and to argue that such data were meaningless because they reified the racial categories being used, and assumed that there were such fixed groups of people as "Anglos" and "Mexican Americans," "Blacks," etc. I argued that such data were surely sloppy and were in fact essentialist, but surely they told us something, capturing change over time, . . . the difference between anti-black and anti-Mexican racism, and the like.[60]

Johnson's colleagues simply rejected the possibility of using ethnic categories of the 1930s to understand marriage patterns—rather than looking closely at the sources to see what reasonable conclusions might be drawn from admittedly imperfect data. Such an adamant rejection of marriage registers as useful historical records precludes, of course, one of the major sources for research in historical demography.[61] It seems likely that such negative reactions from colleagues would discourage research in historical demography or social history in general—particularly by young scholars at the beginning of their careers.

However, if postmodernism asserts that objective knowledge of any external reality is impossible, it may be argued that postcolonialism is less nihilistic. Like postmodernists, postcolonialist scholars raise serious questions about the veracity of texts. But their objections are more specific. They charge that colonial texts are distorted in fundamental ways by Europeans and European states that set themselves above and apart from those they ruled. Presumably, then, postcolonialist scholarship should eventually show the way to correcting distortions of the Orientalist gaze, making it feasible to produce more balanced knowledge about the colonial history of the vast parts of the world once under European rule.

Postcolonialism, Postmodernism, and Population History in South Asia and Africa

Before concluding that postmodernism and postcolonialism deny the possibility of history, it is useful to look specifically at how both have influenced research in a particular field—in this case, the historical demography of empires. As the anecdote about the conference in Mexico illustrates, it is fair to say that postmodernist and postcolonial critics have been particularly dismissive of quantitative data, judged to be among the most egregious products of modernist and colonialist empiricism. The next few pages review research on Southeast and South Asia and Africa appropriate for this volume. I will first consider censuses. The initial postmodern/postcolonial studies of censuses appeared in the 1980s and 1990s, focusing on Asia. By and large, they explored how these counts contributed to distorted visions of colonial populations. Since 2000, at least a couple of scholars have analyzed West African censuses in light of the postmodern/postcolonial criticism of enumerations in Asia. However, their studies move on to evaluate how the empirical data collected in the counts may be useful for population history.

Among demographers and administrators, discussion and debate about censuses have long been common conversation, and the technical literature on how to improve the accuracy of such enumerations is vast. Courses on demographic techniques always cover the very concrete "what" and "how" of the census. Postcolonial criticism has directed greater attention to how authorities conceptualized such enumerations, to how they elaborated the categories used to describe colonial populations, and later to how people responded to such classification schemes. In *Imagined Communities,* Benedict Anderson analyzed how the British in Malaya, the Dutch in today's Indonesia, and the Spanish in the Philippines classified the populations of their colonial possessions in arbitrary ways that were influenced more by their stereotypes of local peoples and the social categories used at home than by local realities.[62] They routinely conflated ethnic, religious, and social categories. Anderson examined British censuses in Malaya in greater detail, and, paraphrasing Charles Hirschman, he concluded that "as the colonial period wore on, the census categories became more visibly and exclusively racial. Religious identity, on the other hand, gradually disappeared as a primary census classification."[63] For Malaya, "on the whole the large racial categories were retained and even concentrated after independence, but now re-designated, and re-ranked as 'Malaysian,' 'Chinese,' 'Indian,' and 'Other.'"[64] Colonial categories lived on into the postcolonial era.

Postcolonial writing on the census in South Asia or colonial India (today's India, Pakistan, and Bangladesh) appeared first in the 1980s. Bernard Cohn's seminal essay, "The Census, Social Structure and Objectification,"[65] published in 1987, argues that British census questions about Indian societies and populations led Indians to objectify their culture: "They in some sense have made it into a 'thing'; they can stand back and look at it themselves, their ideas, their symbols and culture and see it as an entity."[66] For anthropologist Cohn, censuses in South Asia are useful exercises in data collection that illustrate this more global theme. Not only did the British "other" South Asians and their societies, if you will, but colonialism and the census led South Asians to "other" themselves.

Cohn traces the history of the census. Enumerations between 1780 and 1870 were fragmentary, focused more on assembling "systematic information" on land tenure, potential tax revenue, and agricultural production than population.[67] Administrators of the British commercial company that governed parts of South Asia at that time required local officers to "summarize pre-existing records which might yield quantitative information of a social and economic sort." These subordinates often included population estimates in their reports, as well as descriptions and their own impressions of the character of people belonging to castes and tribes in their jurisdictions. Estimates of total population appeared as early as 1820.[68]

In ensuing decades, these estimates led to requests for more precise population data. District officers developed methodologies to assess the size of settlements. For example, a common procedure was to report house counts by castes—the endogamous social and occupational groups into which many societies in India were organized—and then to multiply these totals by the "average" number of people thought to live in a household typical of each caste. Castes were also associated with different livelihoods, so that household sizes attributed to specific castes were later transformed into household sizes according to occupation. Such assumptions and associations led to "conceptual problems built into the economic categories of the census." Vague definitions of family and household and of the age-groups "adult" and "children" introduced further ambiguities.

Cohn's discussions of some conceptual issues clearly derive from postmodern/ postcolonial scholarship. However, others echo concerns long raised by scholars and technicians who formulate censuses and demographic surveys. For example, Cohn reviews four decennial enumerations beginning with the first modern census of 1871–72, drawing attention to problems identified at the time: people avoided census enumerators because they associated the count with tax collection, accurate lists of villages and towns were difficult to assemble, and distinctions between villages and towns were ambiguous.[69]

Cohn elaborates on caste and the census, embarking on a recognizably postcolonial analysis. He cites G. S. Ghurye, who commented already in 1932 that "the conclusion is unavoidable that the intellectual curiosity of some of the early officials is mostly responsible for the treatment of caste given in the census, which has been progressively elaborate in each successive census since 1872."[70] Echoing Said's charge that colonial views of colony promoted uniformity, Cohn concludes that "from the beginning of the census operations it was widely assumed that an all-India system of classification of castes could be developed."[71] He asks two other "postcolonial" questions, although, again, both had already been raised in the colonial era by M. N. Srinivas and Ghurye: First, why did the British record the caste of individuals—was it curiosity or was it part of a strategy to divide and rule? Second, how did this British preoccupation promote caste consciousness and lead to "the use of the census for validation of claims to new status within the caste system"?

Cohn adds other postcolonial queries. How did these census operations influence the "views which both administrators and social scientists developed about the Indian social system"?[72] Why did the British become fixated on recording caste? How did the number, names, and ethnic and religious definitions of caste vary from one part of India to another? How did caste boundaries shift over time? How did new castes appear while older ones sometimes disappeared? And how did the British colonial government attempt to impose uniform caste labels and definitions? The article ultimately concludes that the census indeed raised levels of caste consciousness, ultimately contributing to more intense communal politics in both colonial and independent India. This is an important conclusion. It seems remarkable, however, that Cohn never attempts to use quantitative data collected in the course of what then were arguably some of the largest demographic operations ever undertaken in the non-West to assess the impact of evolving caste definitions. He writes not a word about how these "imperfect" data may be interpreted in light of the issues he raises.[73] His loud silence leaves the impression that nothing can be done with these data.

Citing intervening publications on the colonial census, anthropologist Arjun Appadurai writes that "the precise and distinctive links between enumeration and classification in colonial India have not been specified, and that is what I propose to do."[74] Appadurai notes that cadastral exercises aimed at asserting conceptual as well as physical control over land laid the groundwork for later operations concerning "human communities and their enumeration."[75] He theorizes that counting and producing numbers created an impression of control. The *métropole* required numbers to assess requests for resources. Moreover, translating different kinds of data into numbers also made it possible to compare things that were otherwise different.[76] Analogous to Cohn's analysis of caste, Appadurai argues first that "colonial body counts" created homogeneity out of heterogeneity and then that such exercises contributed to "a polity centered around self-consciously enumerated communities."[77] Pointing to publications such as the *Journal of the Statistical Society of London,* which published its first issue in 1838, demographer D. Ian Pool suggests that this desire for quantitative data on India was part of a larger Victorian "passion for moral statistics."[78]

Again, having raised the important and insightful questions about the production of demographic knowledge by the Indian colonial state, Appadurai does not assess how the process of producing data may have shaped the profile of the collected data or their analysis. He reviews, for example, the contents of massive quantitative documents of the emerging bureaucracy, such as *The Joint Report of 1847:*

> This is prose composed partly of rules, partly of orders, partly of appendices, and partly of letters and petitions which must be read together. In this prose, the internal debates of the revenue bureaucracy, the pragmatics of

rule formation, and the rhetoric of utility always accompanied the final recommendations by authorities at various levels of new technical practices. These are documents whose manifest rhetoric is technical (that is, positivist, transparent, and neutral), but whose subtext is contestatory (in regard to superiors) and disciplinary (in regard to inferiors).[79]

The essay does not assess how these documents may be used to learn more about the history of colonial India. Perhaps this reticence stems from the anthropologist's reluctance to engage historical and demographic documents. Given that better data do not exist, however, the challenge is to identify weaknesses and omissions and then figure out how to interpret them. As with Cohn, Appadurai's silence leaves the impression that these sources are not "usable."

Ironically, an Indian demographer has begun to reconsider Indian censuses in the light of postcolonial scholarship. Ram Bhagat analyzes how caste categories in Indian enumerations evolved through time. He begins an article in *Genus* by observing that "the discipline of demography is not accustomed to view census as having an interface with society and power."[80] He acknowledges that "census categories are not neutral, but are politically constructed," and then, in a move truly rare among demographers anywhere, he reviews the analyses of postcolonial scholars such as Cohn and Appadurai.

Bhagat offers an empirical analysis of Indian colonial censuses, focusing on problems of definition, caste, and religion. He looks concretely at the evolution of caste and related categories such as "tribe" and "race" from the enumeration of 1871–72 through the last colonial census in 1941.[81] He offers examples of how caste definitions evolved in particular parts of the country, thereby laying an empirical foundation for possible reanalysis of the data. Implicitly, Bhagat also shows that postcolonial critiques of the colonial census are not revelations. Roughly a century ago, the British were aware that caste was not an immutable label. Bhagat cites E. A. Gait, census commissioner for the 1911 count:

> Apparently caste looked [like a] fixed and immutable category, but this is by no means the case. In fact, new castes come up as necessity arises and old disappears. The process of change is slow and imperceptible ..., but it is nevertheless always going on. When one section of a caste develops peculiarities of any kind—a different occupation, habitat or social practice, or more rarely, a different religious cult—the tendency is for it to regard itself and to be regarded by the rest of the caste, as something different. The feeling grows stronger with time, until at last it, or the main body of the caste, withdraws from the marriage league. The result is a new sub-caste, and often, in the end, a new caste.[82]

Bhagat also explores how Indians perceived and reacted to the classifying practices of the colonial census: "Many people thought that the object of the census was to fix the relative social positions of the different social classes and deal with questions of social superiority."[83] Again, this observation is not new. In 1924, Ghurye noted that people of lower castes claimed membership in higher castes in an effort to elevate their social status.[84] Like Cohn, Bhagat concludes that the colonial census created greater caste consciousness.[85]

The remainder of Bhagat's article looks at how colonial counts influenced the postindependence censuses beginning in 1951. The Indian government sought to encourage national unity by suppressing caste in the census. However, to offer recompense to groups that historically had suffered discrimination, the constitution provided for new official categories and special benefits for underprivileged people, identified and classed in "Scheduled Castes" (SC) and "Scheduled Tribes" (ST). Groups not included in the SC and ST designations soon claimed membership in these categories, and the government had to figure out how to evaluate the legitimacy of their demands. The "disappearance" of caste in the census led to an increased emphasis on collecting data related to religion, which was also necessary to determine membership in the Scheduled Castes.[86]

Thus, Bhagat underscores an important contradiction in the contemporary census. Caste had been omitted to promote national unity at the same time that determining who qualifies for special benefits required information about caste. This contradiction intensified in the 1990s when a government commission looked into the plight of marginal social groups, or "Other Backward Classes" (OBCs), and recommended reserving jobs for them. Because a primary barrier to people in the OBCs is membership in lower castes, data on caste was again required for job reservation. The government, nonetheless, refused to include questions about caste on the next census in 2001. In the absence of recent caste data, the commission resorted to a caste list from the 1931 colonial census! Near the end of his essay, Bhagat explores what he terms the "enumeration dilemma," emphasizing that "in India, from the point of view of access to state power, caste and religion have been two competing identities in the political sphere."[87]

However, rather than suggesting, explicitly or implicitly, that the colonial gaze of the census is an insurmountable barrier to knowledge of history, Bhagat concludes that the ways in which the census has looked at India's population are now themselves part of Indian history and may be usefully analyzed within existing traditions of data criticism in history and demography. He cites a scholar of caste: "If caste returns as a critical enumerative category for the Indian state in the new millennium, it both carries the enormous contradictions of this legacy and points to new possibilities for social transformation and political citizenship. Caste, in these terms, is neither tragedy nor farce, but history itself."[88] Bhagat does not move on in his short article to reconsider numerical data from the Indian censuses, but he does analyze specific uses of caste categories in successive enumerations. His critique invites more focused reanalyses of quantitative data from individual districts collected in specific counts.[89]

Shifting to Africa, essays in 2002 and 2003 by historians Brian Peterson and Dmitri Van den Bersselaar show how it is possible to incorporate postcolonial criticism directed at censuses, arrive at concrete conclusions about the quality of data, and then move on to use them as historical sources. At the beginning of his essay about enumerating Muslims in the French colony of Soudan (today's Mali) after World War II, Peterson repeats the postcolonial refrain about "the census as an exercise of colonial bureaucratic power," noting, too, that it "was a complex social and political process that must be 'deconstructed.'"[90] He sets out to try to determine what proportion of people in the southern part of the colony were Muslims. He concurs with contemporary observers that the reported percentages were exaggerated but wonders by how much and how to arrive at more acceptable estimates.

The essay sets the context in a postcolonial perspective by exploring French stereotypes about Muslims and followers of African religions. Peterson observes that since their earliest expeditions, the French feared Muslim fundamentalists and followers of the Wahhabiyya movement in particular. At the same time, they considered Muslims to be of higher culture than non-Muslims, and in places such as southern Mali, they used Muslims as guides and interpreters. Hence, when French officials on census tours asked local people about religion, they often replied that they were Muslims, despite obvious clues that they continued to adhere to local religions. The French acknowledged such syncretism, constructing a category they referred to as "Islam noir," or "black Islam," which allowed them to classify West Africans on the Islamic frontier as Muslims, even if they observed earlier religious traditions at the same time.[91]

In addition to the European colonial gaze, however, Peterson explores an earlier, external Muslim colonial gaze. The people of southern Mali had long suffered raids by outsiders, mainly Muslims. Because raiders were more likely to take "pagans" captive than Muslims, people quite practically presented themselves as Muslims. Before the French ever appeared, then, many people in southern Mali declared themselves Muslim when in fact they were not.[92] Muslim identity in southern Mali in the colonial period was a product of this twice-refracted vision. Peterson thus shows how conceptualizations associated in the postcolonial literature exclusively with European colonialism had longer and more complicated histories.

However, the major epistemological significance of Peterson's essay lies elsewhere. After analyzing the conceptualization, definitions, and methodologies of French colonial censuses, Peterson confirms that they exaggerated the numbers of Muslims. But he goes beyond Cohn and Appadurai to ask, "How did the power-laden context of the census tour affect the 'purity' of the data collected?"[93] He acknowledges that colonial officials themselves eventually "began to place more faith in qualitative records" as a way of assessing the accuracy of the quantitative data. Rather than rejecting the census as a historical source, Peterson concludes that the data on Muslims in southern Mali are useful but must be assembled and interpreted with care. He is suspicious of data aggregated at the level of the *circonscription,* or district, a process that probably compounded errors. But he believes that quantitative information aggregated at the level of the smaller *canton,* or county, when assessed along with qualitative sources such as "the observations of colonial officials, and the testimonies of elders," makes it "possible to identify key correlations." Peterson identifies an important way forward, which still incorporates postcolonial criticism: "There is plenty of middle ground between the two extremes of reading statistics uncritically on the one hand, and discarding them as 'colonial constructions' on the other. The next step is to track the ways in which the state used such statistics, and how, in turn, the 'objects' (and agents) of their collection were affected."

As part of another research project, Van den Bersselaar analyzes the 1921 census of southern Nigeria.[94] He wonders why historians have not written much on colonial statistical data, speculating that they "should be able to say something more definite about the reliability of these data."[95] At the outset, he, like Peterson, demonstrates awareness of postcolonial criticism, which he combines seamlessly with the time-honored questions that historians ask: "If we know more about the process by which these statistics were collected, for which aims, and with what preconceived ideas in mind, we should be able to establish, if not a margin of error, then at least some idea of which aspects of colonial statistics are more reliable than others. Furthermore, the process of colonial data-collecting was linked to establishing ethnic and other categories, which have since become generally accepted."[96]

The 1921 census in Nigeria, unlike counts in 1901 and 1911, aimed at complete coverage. Among scholars, it is regarded as better than that of 1931, which came on the heels of popular uprisings in the southeast in 1929 and 1930.[97] World War II precluded a count in 1941. As a result, the 1921 census is somewhat of a benchmark for the first half of the twentieth century.[98]

Van den Bersselaar combines the historian's classic approach to evaluating sources with postcolonial insights. He, too, has read Anderson and Cohn.[99] In addition, he asks questions that historians have long asked about a source: who created it, and what were the circumstances of its production? Although Van den Bersselaar could not locate the raw data collected in the 1921 count, the census is still an exceptional source because one identifiable individual compiled, evaluated, and "adjusted" the data. Moreover, that person left a reasonably detailed record of what he did and why. P. A. Talbot, the census officer for southern Nigeria, was "an experienced Colonial Officer with a longstanding interest in anthropology." Van den Bersselaar pointedly notes that "he was not, however, a statistician." Five years after the census, Talbot published a four-volume abstract of more than thirteen hundred pages, with volumes on local and regional history and ethnography as well as on population. The census data constituted less than a fourth of the compendium.[100]

The initial analysis is conceptual. For example, the author notes two overarching constraints in formulating census questions. First, the 1921 count was part of a larger census of the British Empire; as such, authorities wanted to collect data that could be compared across the colonies. Second, census categories derived from, and resembled, those used in British counts. Both produced a questionnaire and plan for analysis that was somewhat inappropriate for the context of southern Nigeria. Van den Bersselaar then moves on to discuss a specific problem. Following British enumerations, the 1921 census form asked that people be identified as adults or children, males or females, and it defined fifteen years of age as the divide between girls and adult women. In 1921, few people in southern Nigerian could document their chronological age. In northern Nigeria, age fifteen was associated with life transitions commemorated by social rites, so reasonable estimates of age might be inferred by asking young women about such events. This was not, however, the case in southern Nigeria. Talbot wrote that the "natives have but the vaguest ideas on this subject," which led him to conclude that the numbers of people recorded as girls and boys in the 1921 count were probably too low.[101]

Van den Bersselaar repeats the familiar observation that colonial regimes devised schemes of data collection and classification ostensibly to describe their colonial possessions but also to assert their control.[102] Cohn calls these schemes of data collection "investigative modalities," submitting that they differed according to time and place. In India, for example, the colonial regime "assumed the requisite facts could be discovered through history." Van den Bersselaar, citing Jan Vansina, suggests that early on "in Africa the same function was provided by ethnography."[103] Standardized ethnographic questionnaires identified what information should be collected and included uniform formats for recording it. Given this predilection, Talbot's abstract of the 1921 census included much more ethnographic data than demographic data. This tendency was intensified in Nigeria, where, under Governor Frederick Lugard, local administrators were ordered to "make their own notes about African culture, and indeed every District Office contained an Intelligence Book in which relevant observations were recorded."[104] However, a decisive shift took place in the British colonies in Africa in the 1920s, from an ethnographic to an enumerative modality that privileged quantitative data. As a result, later censuses did not collect nearly as much ethnographic data, so the 1921 count came to be regarded as the definitive catalog of the ethnic groups in southern Nigeria. Even so, the ethnic categories devised for the 1921 census were problematic.[105]

Like Peterson, Van den Bersselaar goes beyond observations about shortcomings of the 1921 count to assess how the way it was formulated and carried out influenced data quality. The operation was divided into a township census and a provincial census. The township enumeration was nominative: "The aim . . . was the direct enumeration of every individual," and "an enumerator visited each house" on the same day.[106] The provincial count extended over two months, although a single form was used to record the population of each village or neighborhood. Not surprisingly, Van den Bersselaar concludes that the township census was the more accurate in terms of the actual population count, occupation, and ethnic identity. Then Talbot evaluated the census totals. Initial tabulations were submitted to district officers, who usually judged that the counts were too low. Talbot then adjusted them, increasing counts between 5 and 100 percent! Van den Bersselaar points out that "these corrections were not based on any statistical evidence, but merely reflected the intuition of the District Officers."[107] The latter part of the essay offers conceptual critiques and concrete evaluations of other categories of data.[108]

Van den Bersselaar, therefore, does not dismiss the census but assesses how conceptual problems raised by the colonial gaze and how specific operational obstacles may have affected its quality. He offers specific assessments. First, he states that, "as a result of these 'corrections' the usefulness to historians of the published population census data for the provinces must be regarded as extremely limited."[109] However, he continues, "the population data included from the township census, and figures relating to foreign residents, appear to be more directly useful. Of course, considering the fluidity of the urban population at the time, there can be no doubt that these figures are also underestimates, but at least they are underestimates arrived at through a consistent methodology."[110] Finally, he observes: "The detailed discussions of the way in which the 1921 census data were produced and corrected, and of the form that the published report took, help historians to understand the type of source the colonial census constitutes, and which aspects are likely to be more or less reliable than others. It does not give us any clear pointers to correct the data, but it does give an idea of where the problems are likely to be."[111]

The analyses by Peterson and Van den Bersselaar suggest that more than a quarter century after Said's *Orientalism,* some scholars of population are integrating postmodern and postcolonial insights about historical sources in a productive way. They have moved beyond the blanket rejection of demographic sources implicit in earlier postmodern and postcolonial analyses. They have also declined to reread colonial history exclusively through the lens of postcolonial theory. Research such as theirs requires descending from theory to the nitty-gritty application of theoretical insights to the evaluation of detailed bodies of data.

Two other historians of Africa have drawn on postmodern and postcolonial theory in a different way to analyze how institutional demands and constraints of the French Empire in West Africa shaped the production of demographic data in the first half of the twentieth century. Raymond R. Gervais and Issiaka Mandé document a contradiction.[112] During this period, the upper levels of the colonial administration in West Africa and in France issued circulars requesting more data about the societies that they ruled. At the same time, Gervais and Mandé show, colonial administrators at the local level received neither the training nor the trained staff needed to respond to these requests with accurate data. Administrators completed forms and sent reports filled with quantitative and qualitative information on the populations of their districts. Unfortunately, the data were of very uneven quality.

If earlier assessments of colonial censuses by Cohn and Appadurai implicitly disregard their value as historical sources by failing to suggest how to evaluate empirical data in light of their criticism, Gervais and Mandé implicitly admit the eventual possibility of using colonial data collected in French West Africa. Much of their criticism of demographic data collection is based on contemporary sources from within the French colonial bureaucracy itself—notably, reports by colonial inspectors who made regular tours to assess the workings of the colonial bureaucracy or who were dispatched to investigate particular crises. Given this institutionalized mechanism for identifying and presumably correcting administrative shortcomings, it is possible to argue that the colonial administration itself possessed the capacity to identify how increasing demands of the bureaucracy for information and limited local resources distorted the "demographic realities" reported from the colonies. In their chapter, Gervais and Mandé do not go on to examine how unrealistic demands for data and shortcomings in the responses to them skewed empirical data. However, this next step is implied in their earlier research.[113]

These scholars of African population history have labored to incorporate postmodern and postcolonial criticism into their research, but others have continued to produce insightful research on the historical demography of Africa without reference to these perspectives. This body of research, too, seems to have grown in recent years. For example, a group of Finnish scholars has analyzed African parish registers in the tradition of European historical demography. Harri Siiskonen, Anssi Taskinen, and Veijo Notkola have collected and analyzed data from parish registers kept by churches founded by the Finnish Missionary Society in Ovamboland in Namibia beginning in 1870.[114] The registers, recording marriages, births, and deaths among members of the congregations, permit detailed analyses of identifiable populations over time. The three scholars mined the most complete registers to reconstruct families from several parishes.[115] Their research also integrates techniques for analysis and adjustment derived from contemporary demography.

The authors suggest that their analyses of parish registers pave the way to move beyond long-standing debates between "the natalistic and anti-natalistic school over changes in fertility and mortality in Sub-Saharan African societies during the precolonial and early colonial period."[116] The natalist perspective holds that most demographic change in Africa before the modern era had to do with the rise and decline of mortality, given that the need to survive in harsh environments induced uniformly high levels of fertility in African societies. The antinatalists maintain that the history of population change was more complex—societies did not at all times and in all circumstances maximize births; mortality levels varied in time and place; and rates and patterns of marriage were various, producing different patterns of reproduction and population change.[117] Studies of the histories of African populations must not be limited to tracking changes in fertility and mortality rates—an approach privileged by the natalists—but must also include the analyses of the evolution of social structures. Age structures, for example, were not systems in equilibrium. This point is powerfully illustrated in the chapter by Gregory Maddox in this volume and in the sophisticated work of Anne-Marie Péatrik on the demographic history of the Meru of Kenya.[118]

Siiskonen, Taskinen, and Notkola offer robust demographic and historical critiques of the different categories of data.[119] In a historiographical and methodological essay in *History in Africa,* they open with a history of European counts of

African populations. They do not refer to the postcolonial critiques of colonial censuses by Anderson, Cohn, and Appadurai or the essays by Peterson and Van den Bersselaar on counts in West Africa. They do, though, underscore the problems with African censuses in the colonial and postcolonial eras: incomplete coverage, lack of simultaneity, and the ways that fiscal and recruitment objectives usually undermined these counts. They discuss contemporary censuses and surveys, noting that the data they have collected are problematic for doing history because they are retrospective and people do not always recall information accurately. These are all classic issues among demographers.

In contrast to these sources, which record data at one moment in time, Siiskonen, Taskinen, and Notkola point out that parish registers recorded demographic events over time, usually close to the dates they occurred, and hence are more accurate for historical studies. The authors survey the literature on parish registers in Africa. Such records are more common than might be supposed but still rare enough to preclude studies at the level of the continent or large regions. The authors also knowledge their variable quality: "Despite commonly accepted principles of keeping parish registers, the practices of writing down vital events have differed noticeably between parishes. Some priests, both European and African, were more interested in preaching to their parishioners than doing office work."[120] Applying the logic and standard techniques of demographic analysis, the authors conclude that mortality among infants and children was perhaps underreported. Church custom dictated that their names be recorded only after baptism, and some obviously died before receiving that rite.[121] Siiskonen, Taskinen, and Notkola close with an urgent call to find and preserve these sources. After all, they write, "parish registers are the first written sources in sub-Saharan Africa to describe the life of African people."[122]

Two other recent monographs take another approach to research on population history in Africa. Rather than focusing on censuses or parish registers, classical sources for historical demography, Jan Kuhanen and Shane Doyle combine the wide variety of information on population available in colonial records, missionary documents, and oral accounts to explore reasons for the decline of population in Uganda.[123] Neither author accepts demographic data at face value but rather confronts data from different sources. Kuhanen does not integrate a lot of quantitative data collected at the level of the colony into his analysis, except in his estimate of the numbers of people who migrated into Buganda and in a table on cotton production between 1914 and 1938.[124]

At the beginning of *Poverty, Health and Reproduction in Early Colonial Uganda,* Kuhanen reviews the shortcomings and the possibilities offered by his various bodies of data. Throughout, he brings other types of information to bear on his topic. First, he sets the study in a broad theoretical context, drawing on recent work on poverty, hunger, and health. Throughout, he confronts empirical data, both quantitative and more often qualitative, with theory and with studies of disease and health in other parts of the world. Second, he explores the ways that colonial officials and missionaries "constructed" the African world. Particularly enlightening is his history of the colonial and missionary understandings of sexually transmitted infections and how they conditioned the way that government and civil authorities dealt with their spread. This approach draws on the research of scholars such as Steven Feierman, which, if not explicitly postcolonial, certainly shares with postcolonial scholarship a concern about categories of knowledge, how they are conceived, and how they condition perception.[125] Finally, Kuhanen offers a close reading of data from Mengo Hospital and evaluates them based on what he has found in other sources: "Despite these shortcomings, the Mengo Hospital case files are a rich source of evidence providing much-desired grassroot-level information. Individual case histories offer a window for understanding the reproductive problems faced by women in early colonial Buganda, for example, thus providing means of explaining the demographic developments observed at that time."[126]

Kuhanen determines that focused local research by scholars intimately familiar with the societies and situations they study offers a valuable avenue for better understanding the evolution of African populations. As for the history of reproduction in Uganda, a specific concern, Kuhanen rejects the generalization that African peoples everywhere and at all times maximized fertility, so that demographic history is uniquely driven by changes in mortality. Agreeing with Juhani Koponen, Kuhanen offers a more nuanced view: "Fertility in African societies appeared high in the eyes of the European colonists, but ... it was actually quite low in parts of East and Central Africa and had already been low or moderate in the pre-colonial era."[127]

Shane Doyle's volume focuses on the evolution of the population of Bunyoro, a precolonial kingdom that the British eventually incorporated into colonial Uganda. He sets this colonial history in the larger context of precolonial social and political development. He also explores the relationships between armed conflict and famine and disease. Like Kuhanen, Doyle suggests that understanding the demographic history of colonial Bunyoro "requires an analysis of a wide range of factors." Such a judgment implies, of course, recourse to many kinds of data, which ensures that he will not fall captive to a single "text." Based on scattered demographic data, most of them qualitative, the book reaches bold conclusions about colonial conquest: "Bunyoro suffered unprecedented demographic decline in the 1890s," "the scale and intensity of colonial conquest in Bunyoro was unmatched in east Africa," and the "disruption of the 1890s appears to have profoundly altered Bunyoro's disease environments."[128] However, deficiencies in quantitative data lead him understandably to avoid being more specific: "An estimate of the mortality caused by the war of conquest in Bunyoro is impossible."[129]

Doyle is less cautious in accepting demographic data from the colonial era. At the beginning of the first of two chapters where he presents much of his information on population, he offers a careful critique of colonial statistics on population, which bespeaks familiarity with contemporary demographic approaches to data criticism. Without fully explaining why, however, Doyle goes on to include data from the 1911 and 1921 Bunyoro censuses with little reservation, noting only that "the early censuses may have been inadequate, but they appear to have been done better in Bunyoro than in much of Africa, as everyone in the district was apparently counted."[130] He simply compares the demographic data on Bunyoro with statistics collected in Buganda, Busoga, Ankole, and Tooro, justifying this approach because "problems associated with the collection of vital statistics by chiefs would probably have been more or less the same."[131] It is probably true that, taken together, the many types of qualitative data that Doyle pulls together do confirm his conclusions in a general way. However, presenting quantitative data with so little analysis of the categories devised for their collection or their accuracy suggests a level of precision and confidence that is misleading. Indeed, it reinforces postcolonial criticism of the way that scholars have used colonial texts.

However, in *Crisis & Decline in Bunyoro,* Doyle is more critical on how the perceptions of colonial authorities and missionaries shaped colonial medicine and understandings of and approaches to health problems such as sexually transmitted diseases in particular. Doyle refers to historians such as Megan Vaughan, whose work has been informed by postcolonial scholarship.[132] Near the end, he offers a short analysis of colonial surveys of four Bunyoro villages or parishes done between 1936 and 1961. Although Doyle again offers very little in the way of data criticism, the information he presents suggests that these surveys are quite rich. Like Kuhanen and like Siiskonen, Taskinen, and Notkola, Doyle concludes, based on these surveys, that "a better understanding of the complexity of Africa's recent population history will only come about from detailed local studies."[133]

By Way of Conclusion

The present essay is the culmination of a long search for explanation. I have recounted how my earlier "census" of publications on African historical demography had quite unexpectedly revealed a decline in the appearance of new monographs, essay collections, and articles beginning in the early 1990s. In late 2002, I presented a keynote address at a population history conference that raised the possibility that the shift away from historical studies in African population was attributable to the influence of postmodernism and postcolonialism, with their suspicion of texts, quantitative and qualitative empirical data, and colonial sources on colonial history. I explored these ideas further in a paper presented in 2003 at the annual meeting of the African Studies Association. Other panelists and fellow scholars in the audience responded energetically to my ideas and contributed their own.

The findings presented here on the impact of postmodernism and postcolonialism on research on African population history support my initial hunch. As the intellectual history reveals, these perspectives were common currency in literary studies in Europe in the 1970s, in Indian history in the 1980s and 1990s, and in North America a few years later. In part, the postcolonialism of Said represented a reformulation of some key ideas of postmodernism and their application to colonial texts. He acknowledged his debt to this body of writing. Hence, post-colonialism joined postmodernism in analyses of the literatures, cultures, and then the histories of the former European colonies—beginning with South Asia and Southwest Asia (the West's Middle East). These critical and very thought-provoking avenues of analysis soon made their appearance in African studies. Their rising prominence in the scholarship of the late 1980s and early 1990s on Africa coincided fairly closely with the drop in research on African historical demography.

The message—distrust of texts in general, colonial texts in particular, and, beyond that, quantitative data—discouraged research on precisely the kinds of sources used to study African population history. My own "census" of the production of knowledge was confined to research on African historical demography in English and limited to the years between 1977 and 2000. I have not carried that census forward to the present. However, the examples of the impact of postmodernism and postcolonialism on French history and South Asian history reported in this essay, along with the bias against social history and its sources expressed by scholars of the Americas at a conference in Mexico, confirm my assessment.

Nonetheless, this long journey has also taken unexpected turns. First, postcolonial scholars have directed serious attention to fundamental issues related to historical demography. Unlike scholars at the conference with Johnson in Mexico, who dismissed his findings out of hand, Cohn and Appadurai have engaged demographic sources such as the census. They have asked critical questions about how colonial authorities formulated categories, the impact of such categories on how people identified themselves, and the ways that the search for quantitative data both led to overgeneralizations about colonial peoples and societies and created new "realities." In so doing, they have added new critical questions to those raised by classical demographic analysis, for example, about the formulation and comprehensibility of census questions or about how to discern and correct inaccurate reporting of information such as age, date and place of birth, and date and length of residence in a region whose population is being counted.

But these early postcolonial studies failed to go beyond criticizing the conceptualization and application of categories to evaluate their impact on the quality of the empirical data; they also failed to hazard a suggestion about if or how the data might be used for historical research. The void left in the wake of this failure to take the next step left the impression that such data are not usable, just as similar analyses of travel literature implied that these sources are of limited value for writing history. However, I would argue that because postcolonial critiques in this vein have become more commonplace since the 1990s, younger scholars of African population history such as Peterson and Van den Bersselaar have now gone beyond analyzing conceptualization of censuses to assess the viability of the empirical data that they collected.

It is important, too, to recall the new research on African population history discussed earlier that does not incorporate postmodern or postcolonial critiques. This work is excellent. Beyond that, scholars more focused on postmodern and postcolonial criticism may now review the findings of Siiskonen, Taskinen, and Notkola and of Kuhanen and Doyle in light of these perspectives. Although they do not use the same terminology, the authors of these more classic studies also express suspicion of metanarratives and overgeneralization. They all believe that our knowledge of African population history will best be served by careful local studies and close readings of sources by scholars familiar with the contexts in which they are situated. Such studies will provide the solid foundation for writing the population histories of Africa's regions and, ultimately, the continent itself.

Developments since 2000 suggest that the insights of postmodernism and postcolonialism, which provoked such controversy shortly before, are making their way into the eclectic collection of analytical tools that historians and other social scientists use to understand the past and the contemporary world. The dramatic appearance of new theoretical perspectives is by no means exceptional in recent history, although the rhythm with which they appear seems to be accelerating. Each new perspective has claimed to recast totally the past and present in its image, each has provoked outrage, and each has left behind another valuable lens for viewing the world. For instance, the rise of social history in the middle of the last century "relativized" the more elitist historiography that preceded it. The materialist social history that followed has now made it impossible for historians to ignore social class. And the dependency school of thought has altered our way of thinking about relationships between the peripheries and centers of world systems, however defined.

Postmodernism and postcolonialism have changed how we look at the production of knowledge, the role of power in its production, and the ways that they both shape identities and categories of perception. Both also privilege "close readings" and lexical analysis, which have made scholars and students in all fields more aware of how the use of language produces meaning. Jyotsna Singh's volume will not lead scholars to disregard travel accounts in writing Indian history. It will undoubtedly foster more critical readings of that literature.

The field of demography itself, often characterized as a continuing bastion of modernization theory and unexamined positivism (which is to say modernism), has also opened its doors to postmodern analysis. In a paper presented in 1993 at a congress of the International Union for the Scientific Study of Population, Louis Sabourin described postmodernism as a "widespread state of mind across an increasing number of disciplines," rather than a school of thought.[134] The lessons for demography, he wrote, are several. First, demographers' efforts to arrive at a universal theory of population change were unrealistic. Second, the multiplicity of methods that demographers deploy to track and explain demographic phenomena already constituted an implicit admission that comprehensive and uniform explanations do not exist for population change. Third, the rise of the so-called Third World in the second half of the twentieth century, which defined itself explicitly as different from the capitalist West and socialist societies, made it impossible to ignore the heterogeneity of demographic phenomena. Sabourin also cautioned that systematic approaches to understanding social phenomena had serious limits:

"Theories may describe and explain numerous social phenomena but they do not always end up—contrary to what often happens in pure science—explaining and making predictions about phenomena that are themselves changing."[135] Sabourin suggested that the search for understanding and knowledge, even about global issues such as population growth, must be local and specific.

A decade later, in *Demography in the Age of the Postmodern,* Nancy Riley and James McCarthy also pleaded for an approach to demographic research and analysis that is more self-conscious in its methodology, less preoccupied by "a search for a universal, unifying theory," and open to a multiplicity of approaches. They argued for an "affirmative postmodernism," which is to say an approach that adopts postmodern perspectives with the aim of producing usable analyses of the real world. Such an approach, they suggested, would offer "indeterminancy" rather than "determinism," "difference rather than synthesis," and "complexity" rather than "simplification."[136] They included case studies to illustrate how such a perspective sheds light on challenging topics. In 2007, the influential journal *Population,* for a long time the holy grail of positivist demography, published a series of articles on the state of the discipline, calling for greater openness to other disciplines and greater attention to explaining phenomena rather than measuring them.[137] Focusing on population studies in Africa, the demographer Victor Piché also counseled similar openness to postmodernism:

> The point here is not quantitative versus qualitative, or anthropology versus demography, but the possibility and the challenge to carry out sophisticated in-depth surveys which lean on postmodern lessons, namely insisting on different levels of discourse (narratives), abandoning excessive reductionism and the idea of a universal theory, and aiming at the complexities of peoples lives. It could be argued that in certain respects African demography is already moving along these lines. In this sense, African demography remains a continent of demographic innovation and imagination.[138]

Although inhibited in the 1990s by the influence of postmodernism and postcolonialism, historical studies in African population now seem likewise to be responding to and profiting from the challenges presented by these theoretical perspectives. Such a creative response is not new. It seems appropriate to allow Ian Pool, a demographer of Africa, to have the last word, taken from the paper he presented at the first Edinburgh conference on African historical demography in 1977: "The African historical demographer will probably be forced to build upon the existing methodology and perhaps may have to create his own new tools. In this, we would be merely following what is becoming almost a tradition in African studies, and is certainly typical of the two parent disciplines of history and demography."[139]

Notes

1. Dennis D. Cordell, "African Historical Demography in the Years since Edinburgh," *History in Africa* 27 (2000): 61–89 (hereafter, this journal will be cited as *HA*).

2. Dennis D. Cordell and Joel W. Gregory, "Historical Demography and Demographic History in Africa: Theoretical and Methodological Considerations," *Revue Canadienne des Études Africaines/Canadian Journal of African Studies* 14, no. 3 (1980): 389–416; Cordell and Gregory, "Earlier African Historical Demographies," *Revue Canadienne des Études Africaines/Canadian Journal of African Studies* 23, no. 1 (1989): 5–27.

3. I would like to thank Stacey Colwell for this observation.

4. George Ritzer, *Postmodern Social Theory* (New York: McGraw-Hill, 1997), 2.

5. To be sure, defining oneself in oppositional terms is nothing new. Marx, whose writings are the bedrock of socialist and communist thought, devoted most of *Das Kapital,* his magnum opus, to a detailed and insightful analysis and critique of the rise of capitalism in Great Britain. The communist society that he envisioned was almost an afterthought, a vague and veiled vision of utopia described in far fewer pages at the end.

6. Daniel R. Headrick, *The Tools of Empire: Technology and European Imperialism in the Nineteenth Century* (New York: Oxford University Press, 1981). For broader surveys, see Scott B. Cook, *Colonial Encounters in the Age of High Imperialism* (New York: HarperCollins, 1996); Sven Lindqvist, *"Exterminate All the Brutes": One Man's Odyssey into the Heart of Darkness and the Origins of European Genocide,* trans. Joan Tate (New York: New Press, 1996).

7. Pauline Marie Rosenau, *Post-modernism and the Social Sciences: Insights, Inroads, and Intrusions* (Princeton, NJ: Princeton University Press, 1992), 6. Rosenau is cited in Ritzer, *Postmodern Social Theory,* 9.

8. Joyce Appleby, Lynn Hunt, and Margaret Jacob, *Telling the Truth about History* (New York: W. W. Norton, 1994), 208.

9. Ryan Bishop, "Postmodernism," *The Encyclopedia of Cultural Anthropology* (New York: Henry Holt, 1996), 994. Although Nietzsche is most often cited as the forerunner of postmodern thought, he was by no means alone in his doubts about modernity, progress, and reason. Intellectuals such as Sigmund Freud, Henrik Ibsen, Oswald Spengler, Martin Heidegger, Aldous Huxley, and Fyodor Dostoyevsky, among others, expressed similar reservations.

10. Jean Baudrillard, *The Transparency of Evil: Essays on Extreme Phenomena,* trans. James Benedict (London: Verso, 1993), 72.

11. Jean-François Lyotard, *The Postmodern Condition: A Report on Knowledge,* trans. Geoff Bennington and Brian Massumi (Minneapolis: University of Minnesota Press, 1984). Lyotard is cited in Bishop, "Postmodernism," 994.

12. Appleby, Hunt, and Jacob, *Telling the Truth about History,* 217.

13. Bishop, "Postmodernism," 996. Here, the postmodernists drew from the work of Ferdinand de Saussure. Writing in the early twentieth century, de Saussure differentiated between language, or formal grammatical structure, and speech, or the spoken word, which adheres much less closely to the structure of language. In speech, the spoken word (or signifier) refers to what Ritzer calls "the meaning of the word that is called forth in the mind of the recipient" (or signified). Together, signifier and signified constitute a "sign." For de Saussure, the system of signs that constitutes a particular language/speech system and the signs' meanings are often more determined by the relationship between the signs than their relationship with an existential reality. For example, "cold" derives its

meaning more from "hot" than from an objective quality of the world outside. Language, then, exists apart from reality. See Ritzer, *Postmodern Social Theory,* 29.

14. See, for example, George E. Marcus and Michael M. J. Fischer, *Anthropology as Cultural Critique: An Experimental Moment in the Human Sciences* (Chicago: University of Chicago Press, 1986).

15. Ritzer, *Postmodern Social Theory,* 29–30, 36.

16. Joyce Appleby, "One Good Turn Deserves Another: Moving beyond the Linguistic; —A Response to David Harlan," *American Historical Review* 94, no. 5 (1989): 1326.

17. Luc Ferry and Alain Renaut, *French Philosophy of the Sixties: An Essay on Anti-humanism* (Amherst: University of Massachusetts Press, 1990), 11. See Michel Foucault, *The Order of Things: An Archaeology of the Human Sciences* (New York: Vintage Books, 1973). This volume originally appeared as *Les mots et les choses* (Paris: Gallimard, 1966).

18. Ritzer, *Postmodern Social Theory,* 38–41; Appleby, Hunt, and Jacob, *Telling the Truth about History,* 215.

19. Appleby, Hunt, and Jacob, *Telling the Truth about History,* 224.

20. The two quotations in this paragraph are from ibid., 217 and 200, respectively. For examples of more inclusive histories, see Edward Countryman, *Americans: A Collision of Histories* (New York: Hill and Wang, 1996), and Ronald Takaki, *A Different Mirror: A History of Multicultural America* (New York: Little, Brown, 1993). This effort provoked a backlash by "traditionalists." See, for example, Robin Wilson, "Taking on 'Half-Baked' History: At Penn State, an Education Professor Wants to Inspire His Students to Teach America's Past the Old-Fashioned Way," *Chronicle of Higher Education* 53, no. 28 (16 March 2007): A10, A12–A13.

21. Vijay Mishra and Bob Hodge, "What Is Post(-)colonialism?" in *Colonial Discourse and Post-colonial Theory: A Reader,* ed. Patrick Williams and Laura Chrisman (New York: Columbia University Press, 1994), 284.

22. Kamala Visweswaran, "Postcolonialism," in *The Encyclopedia of Cultural Anthropology,* ed. David Levinson and Melvin Ember (New York: Henry Holt, 1996), 988. See also Zine Magubane, "Postcolonialism," in *New Encyclopedia of Africa,* ed. John Middleton and Joseph C. Miller (New York: Scribner's, 2008), 4:206–7.

23. Visweswaran, "Postcolonialism," 989.

24. Edward W. Said, *Orientalism* (New York: Random House, 1978).

25. Quotations in this paragraph are from ibid., 2–3.

26. Edward W. Said, *Culture and Imperialism* (New York: Alfred A. Knopf, 1993), 44.

27. Mishra and Hodge, "What Is Post(-)colonialism?" 281.

28. Ibid., 282.

29. Visweswaran, "Postcolonialism," 989.

30. Georges Balandier, "The Colonial Situation: A Theoretical Approach," in *Social Change: The Colonial Situation,* ed. Immanuel Wallerstein (New York: John Wiley and Sons, 1966). Among these texts, see O. Mannoni, *Psychologie de la colonisation* (Paris: Éditions du Seuil, 1950); Frantz Fanon, *Peau noire, masques blancs* (Paris: Éditions du Seuil, 1952); Aimé Césaire, *Discours sur le colonialisme* (Paris: Présence Africaine, 1955).

31. The definitive edition is also the most accessible: Aimé Césaire, *Cahiers d'un retour au pays natal* (Paris: Présence Africaine, 1956).

32. This tradition of resisting hegemonic representations among people of African heritage continues. Examples include the "black is beautiful" movement, which arose in the United States in the 1960s; South Africa's "black consciousness" campaigns of the 1980s; and Afrocentrism, a more contemporary school of thought that focuses attention

on the contributions of African heritage peoples to world civilization. The movement also led European intellectuals to raise questions about the legitimacy of colonialism. See Jean Genet's play *Les nègres* (Paris: Marc Barbezat-L'Arbalète, 1958), which was published just before the independence of most French colonies in Africa.

33. See, for example, Charles W. Chestnutt, *Paul Marchand F.M.C.* (Princeton, NJ: Princeton University Press, 1999). Written in the late 1910s but not published until this edition, Chestnutt's novel is an incisive treatment of race, color, and social status in Louisiana shortly after the American purchase of the territory from France. See Hurston selections published in the 1940s and reprinted in *I Love Myself when I am Laughing, and again when I'm Mean and Impressive: A Zora Neale Hurston Reader*, ed. Alice Walker (New York: Feminist Press, 1979): "The Pet Negro System" (156–62), "My Most Humiliating Jim Crow Experience" (163–64), "Crazy for This Democracy" (165–68), and "What White Publishers Won't Print" (169–73).

34. Albert Memmi, *The Colonizer and the Colonized*, trans. Howard Greenfeld (Boston: Orion Press, 1965), v. Memmi revisits this topic in *Portrait du décolonisé* (Paris: Gallimard, 2004), which concludes that even if the former colonies are now "post-colonies," their people are not decolonized and remain in thrall to forces of the *métropole*.

35. Gayatri Chakravorty Spivak, "Can the Subaltern Speak?" in *Marxism and the Interpretation of Culture*, ed. C. Nelson and L. Grossberg (Basingstoke, UK: Macmillan Education, 1988), 271–313. See also Gyan Prakash, "Subaltern Studies as Postcolonial Criticism," *American Historical Review* 99, no. 5 (1994): 1475–90.

36. Patrick Williams and Laura Chrisman, "Colonial Discourse and Post-colonial Theory: An Introduction," in *Colonial Discourse and Post-colonial Theory: A Reader*, ed. Patrick Williams and Laura Chrisman (New York: Columbia University Press, 1994), 4.

37. Said, *Culture and Imperialism*, xxii.

38. Ivo Kamps and Jyotsna G. Singh, eds., *Travel Knowledge: European "Discoveries" in the Early Modern Period* (New York: Palgrave, 2001).

39. Jyotsna G. Singh, *Colonial Narratives, Cultural Dialogues: "Discoveries" of India in the Language of Colonialism* (New York: Routledge, 1996), 8.

40. Ibid., 1–14.

41. See, for example, Paul Edward Hedley Hair, "Barbot, Dapper, Davity: A Critique of Sources on Sierra Leone and Cape Mount," *HA* 1 (1974): 25–54; Albert van Dantzig, "Willem Bosman's *New and Accurate Description of the Coast of Guinea:* How Accurate Is It?" *HA* 1 (1974): 101–9.

42. Gérard Chouin, "Seen, Said, or Deduced? Travel Accounts, Historical Criticism, and Discourse Theory: Towards an 'Archaeology' of Dialogue in Seventeenth-Century Guinea," *HA* 28 (2001): 53–70; John M. Cinnamon, "Missionary Expertise, Social Science, and the Uses of Ethnographic Knowledge in Colonial Gabon," *HA* 33 (2006): 413–32. Dmitri Van den Bersselaar, "Missionary Knowledge and the State in Colonial Nigeria: On How G. T. Basden Became an Expert," *HA* 33 (2006): 433–50. See also Cinnamon's chapter in this volume.

43. Richard Roberts and Donald Moore, "Listening for Silences," *HA* 17 (1990): 319–25. This essay introduces four other articles on "Silences in Fieldwork."

44. Kathryn Barrett-Gaines, "Travel Writing, Experiences, and Silences: What Is Left Out of European Travelers' Accounts—The Case of Richard D. Mohun," *HA* 24 (1997): 53–70.

45. John H. Hanson, "African Testimony Reported in European Travel Literature: What Did Paul Soleillet and Camille Piétri Hear and Why Does No One Recount It Now?" *HA* 18 (1991): 143–58.

46. See Paola Ivanov, "Cannibals, Warriors, Conquerors, and Colonizers: Western Perceptions and Azande Historiography," *HA* 29 (2002): 89–217. After noting that "as a result of the research of E. E. Evans-Pritchard, the Azande are among the best-known African peoples," Ivanov writes that "it is all the more surprising that the relevant sources for their history have never been subjected to serious critical examination" (89–90).

47. Selena Axelrod Winsnes, "Voices from the Past: Remarks on the Translation and Editing of Published Danish Sources for West African History during the Eighteenth and Nineteenth Centuries," *HA* 14 (1978): 275–85.

48. *Fontes historiae africanae* has sponsored three series: the Series Varia of six accounts, which appeared between 1980 and 1990; the Series Arabica, which has published eleven volumes to date; and the New Series, launched in 1997, which now includes seven items.

49. Walter E. A. van Beek, "Haunting Griaule: Experiences from the Restudy of the Dogon," *HA* 31 (2004): 43–68; John Edward Sutton, "Denying History in Colonial Kenya: The Anthropology and Archaeology of George Wynn Brereton Huntingford and Louis Seymour Bazett Leakey," *HA* 33 (2006): 287–320; Sutton, "Archaeology and Reconstructing History in the Kenya Highlands: The Intellectual Legacies of G. W. Huntingford and Seymour B. Leakey," *HA* 34 (2007): 297–320.

50. Christraud Geary, "Introduction," *HA* 21 (1994): 321–23; Colleen Kriger, "Museum Collections as Sources for African History," *HA* 23 (1996): 129–54.

51. Appleby, Hunt, and Jacob, *Telling the Truth about History,* 259. All quotations in this paragraph are taken from that page.

52. Robert Eric Frykenberg, *History and Belief: The Foundations of Historical Understanding* (Grand Rapids, MI: William B. Eerdmans, 1996), 287–93. References and quotations in the next several paragraphs are from those pages.

53. As an example, Frykenberg cites Gauri Viswanathan, who published *Masks of Conquest: Literary Study and British Rule in India* (New York: Columbia University Press, 1989).

54. Thomas J. Schaeper, "French History as Written on Both Sides of the Atlantic: A Comparative Analysis," *French Historical Studies* 17 (1991), tables 1 and 2, on 242–43. Schaeper is cited in Appleby, Hunt, and Jacob, *Telling the Truth about History,* 219n34.

55. Appleby, Hunt, and Jacob, *Telling the Truth about History,* 219–20.

56. Richard Eaton, "(Re)imag(in)ing Otherness: A Postmortem for the Postmodern in India," *Journal of World History* 2, no. 1 (2000): 57–78.

57. Ibid., 73n53.

58. Ibid., 73.

59. Ibid., 73 and 73n54. See also Bryan O. Palmer, *The Reification of Language and the Writing of Social History* (Philadelphia: Temple University Press, 1990).

60. Benjamin Johnson to Dennis Cordell, e-mail message, 27 March 2007.

61. On the development of methods for family reconstitution based on parish records, which, of course, include data on marriage, see Michel Fleury and Louis Henry, *Nouveau manuel de dépouillement et d'exploitation de l'état civil ancien* (Paris: INED, 1965); Louis Henry, *Techniques d'analyse en démographie historique* (Paris: INED, 1980); Jacques Dupâquier, *Pour la démographie historique* (Paris: Presses Universitaires de France, 1984), 24–42; Dennis Willigan and Katherine A. Lynch, *Sources and Methods of Historical Demography* (New York: Academic Press, 1982), 57–78, 161–92, 203–22.

62. Benedict Anderson, *Imagined Communities: Reflections on the Origin and Spread of Nationalism,* 2nd ed. (New York: Verso, 1991), 164–70.

63. Ibid., 164–65; Charles Hirschman, "The Meaning and Measurement of Ethnicity in Malaysia: An Analysis of Census Classifications," *Journal of Asian Studies* 46, no. 3

(1987): 552–82; Charles Hirschman, "The Making of Race in Colonial Malaya: Political Economy and Racial Ideology," *Sociological Forum* 1, no. 2 (1986): 330–62.

64. Anderson, *Imagined Communities,* 165.

65. Bernard S. Cohn, "The Census, Social Structure and Objectification in South Asia," in Cohn, *An Anthropologist among the Historians and Other Essays* (Delhi: Oxford University Press, 1987), 224–54.

66. Cohn, "Census," 229.

67. Ibid., 233–38. See those pages for the quotations in this paragraph and the following.

68. Walter Hamilton, *A Geographical, Statistical, and Historical Description of Hindostan and the Adjacent Countries,* 2 vols. (London, 1820; repr., Delhi: Oriental Publishers, 1971). Hamilton is cited in Cohn, "Census," 232.

69. Cohn, "Census," 238–41.

70. Ibid., 241, citing G. S. Ghurye, *Caste and Race in India* (London: K. Paul, Trench, Trubner, 1932), 158.

71. Cohn, "Census," 243.

72. Ibid., 241.

73. This silence is particularly notable given that in his notes, Cohn identifies Indian scholars who have grappled with how to use these data. See, for example, "Census," 252–53n25: "Durgaprasad Bhattacharya and Bibhavati Bhattacharya have collected and published all printed estimates for the population of India in the period 1820–30, as well as some district and town censuses. They have also tried to summarize the methods used in obtaining these estimates. . . . The Bhattacharyas have projected eight volumes on the population estimates of India between the eighteenth century and 1872."

74. Arjun Appadurai, "Number in the Colonial Imagination," in *Modernity at Large: Cultural Dimensions of Globalization,* ed. Arjun Appadurai (Minneapolis: University of Minnesota Press, 1996), 114–35. Appadurai first published this article in 1993.

75. Ibid., 125.

76. Ibid., 117, 119, 120.

77. Ibid., 133.

78. Pool made this observation in his evaluation of this manuscript for Ohio University Press in 2009.

79. Appadurai, "Number," 121. Appadurai cites the report: Government of Maharashtra, *The Joint Report of 1847: Measurement and Classification Rules of the Deccan, Gujurat, Konkan and Kanara Survey* (Bombay: Government of Maharashtra, 1975). Presumably, the government of Maharashtra reprinted this report because it deemed the document was valuable for understanding the history of the state.

80. Ram B. Bhagat, "Census and Caste Enumeration: British Legacy and Contemporary Practice in India," *Genus* 62, no. 2 (2006): 119–34. The quotation comes from p. 119.

81. Ibid., 121–26.

82. Edward Albert Gait, *Census of India, 1911,* vol.1, *India, Part I—Report* (Calcutta: Government Printing, India, 1913), 371.

83. Bhagat, "Census and Caste Enumeration," 124.

84. Govind Sadashiv Ghurye, *The Caste and Class in India* (Bombay, India: Popular Book Depot, 1924), 169, cited in Bhagat, "Census and Caste Enumeration," 124.

85. Bhagat, "Census and Caste Enumeration," 126.

86. Ibid., 126–28.

87. Ibid., 131.

88. Nicholas B. Dirks, *Castes of Mind: Colonialism and the Making of Modern India* (Princeton, NJ: Princeton University Press, 2001), 302.

89. The year after Bhagat's essay on census and caste in colonial India, Magali Barbieri published a summary and evaluation of demographic sources available for the colonial history of French Indochina (today's Vietnam, Laos, and Cambodia). Her essay is a superb example of the careful and systematic way that demographers evaluate statistical sources, even though she does not indicate that she had read the work of Anderson, Cohn, or Appadurai on South Asia. Citing an article by statistician G. Bournier, published in 1943, Barbieri does acknowledge early concerns about how data were produced: "A number does not exist objectively. One can not interpret it, and therefore use it correctly, if one overlooks 'the conditions of its creation and then its nature, quality, and possibilities.'" See Barbieri, "De l'utilité des statistiques démographiques de l'Indochine française (1862–1954)," *Annales de Démographie Historique: Populations Coloniales,* no. 1 (2007): 85–126. The quotation is from G. Bournier, "La question de la statistique coloniale," *Comptes rendus trimestriels des séances de l'Académie des sciences d'Outre-Mer* 3, 5–19 March 1943, 154–78.

90. Brian Peterson, "Quantifying Conversion: A Note on the Colonial Census and Religious Change in Postwar Southern Mali," *HA* 29 (2002): 381.

91. Ibid., 383–85, 388.

92. Ibid., 390–91.

93. For quotations in this paragraph, see Peterson, "Quantifying Conversion," 388, 389, 392, respectively.

94. Dmitri Van den Bersselaar, "Establishing the Facts: P. A. Talbot and the 1921 Census of Nigeria," *HA* 31 (2004): 69–102.

95. Ibid., 69.

96. Ibid.

97. Ibid., 72.

98. Scholars of later censuses in Nigeria are well aware of these issues. Van den Bersselaar cites two of them: Babatunde A. Ahonsi, "Deliberate Falsification and Census Data in Nigeria," *African Affairs* 87, no. 349 (1988): 553–62, and S. A. Aluko, "How Many Nigerians? An Analysis of Nigeria's Census Problems, 1901–63," *Journal of Modern African Studies* 3, no. 3 (1965): 371–92.

99. Van den Bersselaar, "Establishing the Facts," 74–75.

100. Percy Amaury Talbot, *The Peoples of Southern Nigeria. A Sketch of Their History, Ethnology and Languages, with an Account of the 1921 Census* (London: Oxford University Press, 1926). Also see Talbot, *Peoples of Southern Nigeria,* 1:v. Talbot is cited in Van den Bersselaar, "Establishing the Facts," 71. Talbot noted in the introduction, however, that he had supplied the government with five times as much statistical data as appeared in the final edition.

101. Van den Bersselaar, "Establishing the Facts," 72–73.

102. Bernard Cohn, *Colonialism and Its Forms of Knowledge: The British in India* (Princeton, NJ: Princeton University Press, 1996), 3, 5, cited in Van den Bersselaar, "Establishing the Facts," 74–75.

103. Jan Vansina, "The Ethnographic Account as a Genre in Central Africa," *Paideuma* 33 (1987): 435, 438–39. Vansina is cited in Van den Bersselaar, "Establishing the Facts," 75.

104. Van den Bersselaar, "Establishing the Facts," 76–79.

105. Ibid., 83–85, 89–92.

106. Ibid., 81.

107. Ibid., 88.

108. Ibid., 92–101.

109. Ibid., 89.

110. Ibid.

111. Ibid., 102.

112. Raymond R. Gervais, *Contribution à l'étude de l'évolution de la population de l'Afrique occidentale française, 1904–1960* (Paris: Centre Français sur la Population et le Développement, 1993); Raymond R. Gervais and Issiaka Mandé, "Comment compter les sujets de l'Empire? Les étapes d'une démographie impériale en AOF avant 1946," *Vingtième siècle* 2007/3, no. 95, 63–74. A revised version of the second article translated into English is included in this volume.

113. See, for example, Raymond R. Gervais, "Population et politiques agricoles dans le Mosi, Haute-Volta, 1919–1940" (thèse de doctorat, Université de Paris VII–Denis Diderot, 1990); Issiaka Mandé, "Les migrations du travail en Haute-Volta (actuel Burkina Faso), mise en perspective historique" (PhD diss., Université de Paris VII–Denis Diderot, 1997).

114. Harri Siiskonen, Anssi Taskinen, and Veijo Notkola, "Parish Registers: A Challenge for African Historical Demography," *HA* 32 (2005): 385–402.

115. Ibid., 395–96.

116. Ibid., 385.

117. Gwyn Campbell offers another perspective on the debate between the natalists and antinatalists. First, he points out that both interpretations make a major distinction between population change in the precolonial and colonial eras. The precolonial era is thought to be characterized by very slow growth and the colonial era by a dramatic drop in population during colonial conquest, followed by rapid increase. Second, Campbell submits that this dichotomy is too sharply drawn, citing his own research in Madagascar where the Imerina conquests of the interior in the nineteenth century (which occurred before European conquest) brought population growth and then decline. Finally, he suggests that in some cases, population changes were the result of state policy mediated by management of the environment—in the Imerina case, through the imposition of agricultural policies that initially increased yields and made for a healthier population. In short, he counsels both natalists and antinatalists to nuance their analyses and pay more attention to what he calls "natural" factors. See Campbell, "The State and Pre-colonial Demographic History: The Case of Nineteenth-Century Madagascar," *Journal of African History* 32, no. 3 (1991): 415–45.

118. Anne-Marie Péatrik, *La vie à pas contés: Génération, âge et société dans les hautes terres du Kénya (Meru Tigania-Igembe)* (Paris: Société d'Ethnologie, 1999).

119. For substantive findings, see Veijo Notkola and Harri Siiskonen, *Fertility, Mortality and Migration in Subsaharan Africa* (New York: St. Martin's, 2000).

120. Siiskonen, Taskinen, and Notkola, "Parish Registers," 391.

121. On this point, see Emmanuel Kreike's review of Siiskonen and Notkola's monograph, entitled "Family Reconstitution in African Demographic History," *Journal of African History* 42, no. 3 (2001): 533–35.

122. Siiskonen, Taskinen, and Notkola, "Parish Registers," 402.

123. Jan Kuhanen, *Poverty, Health and Reproduction in Early Colonial Uganda* (Joensuu, Finland: University of Joensuu, 2005); Shane Doyle, *Crisis & Decline in Bunyoro: Population and Environment in Western Uganda, 1860–1955* (Athens: Ohio University Press, 2006).

124. Kuhanen, *Poverty, Health and Reproduction,* 181, 220.

125. See, for example, the introduction and essays in Steven Feierman and John M. Janzen, eds., *The Social Basis of Health and Healing in Africa* (Berkeley: University of California Press, 1992).

126. Kuhanen, *Poverty, Health and Reproduction,* 27.

127. Ibid., 106. See also Juhani Koponen, "Population Growth in Historical Perspective: The Key Role of Changing Fertility," in *Tanzania: Crisis and Struggle for Survival,* ed. Jannik Boesen, Kjell Havnevik, Juhani Koponen, and Rie Odgaard (Uppsala, Sweden: Scandinavian Institute of African Studies), 42–43.

128. Doyle, *Crisis & Decline in Bunyoro,* 85, 92, 93.

129. Ibid., 85.

130. Ibid., 135.

131. Ibid., 234. Doyle offers a few critical comments on the 1931, 1948, and 1959 censuses. However, after reporting that the 1959 count probably had a "large error margin of 21 percent," he inexplicably concludes that "the 1931 and 1959 censuses will be taken as a broadly reliable guide to the changes in Bunyoro's population during his period."

132. Ibid., 150–62, 210–32. See Megan Vaughan, *Curing Their Ills: Colonial Power and African Illness* (Cambridge: Cambridge University Press, 1991).

133. Doyle, *Crisis & Decline in Bunyoro,* 246.

134. Louis Sabourin, "Postmodernisme et démographie," paper presented at the Twenty-Second World Congress of the International Union for the Scientific Study of Population, Montreal, Canada, 31 August 1993, 5. The essay later appeared with the title "Postmodernisme et démographie: Réflexions sur l'évolution de la population mondiale," *Les Cahiers du GERFI,* no. 3 (1964). GERFI is an acronym for the Groupe d'Étude, de Recherches et de Formation Internationale, at the École Nationale d'Administration Publique in Montreal, Quebec.

135. Sabourin, "Postmodernisme et démographie," 21.

136. Nancy E. Riley and James McCarthy, *Demography in the Age of the Postmodern* (Cambridge: Cambridge University Press, 2003), 17–18, 156, 162.

137. Dominique Tabutin, "Vers quelle(s) démographie(s)? Atouts, faiblesses et évolutions de la discipline depuis 50 ans," *Population* 62, no. 1 (2007): 15–32; Graziella Caselli and Viviana Egidi, "Nécessité d'une approche multidisciplinaire," *Population* 62, no. 1 (2007): 33–38; Daniel Courgeau and Robert Franck, "La démographie: Science constituée ou en voie de constitution? Esquisse d'un programme," *Population* 62, no. 1 (2007): 39–46; John Hobcraft, "Pour améliorer notre compréhension des comportements démographiques," *Population* 62, no. 1 (2007): 47–52; Jan M. Hoem, "La démographie, aujourd'hui et demain," *Population* 62, no. 1 (2007): 53–56.

138. Victor Piché, "From African Demography to African Population Studies: Beyond the Postmodern?" paper presented at the joint annual meetings of the Canadian Association of African Studies (Association Canadienne des Études Africaines) and the African Studies Association, New Orleans, LA, 11–14 November 2004, p. 7.

139. David Ian Pool, "A Framework for the Analysis of West African Historical Demography," in *African Historical Demography,* ed. Christopher Fyfe and David McMaster (Edinburgh: Centre of African Studies, University of Edinburgh, 1977), 57. A New Zealander, Pool is also the author of a population history of the Maori: *Ti Iwi Maori: A New Zealand Population—Past, Present & Projected* (Auckland, New Zealand: Auckland University Press, 1991). As an outside reviewer, he offered valuable comments on the manuscript that we submitted to the Ohio University Press and helped us turn it into a much better book.

2

"Where Nature Dominates Man"

Demographic Ideas and Policy in British Colonial Africa, 1890–1970

KARL ITTMANN

In 1925, Leo Amery, the British colonial secretary, declared at the Imperial Social Hygiene Conference,

> The problem of development in Africa is in the main, a human
> problem: it has got to be carried through by the people of the country
> themselves. At the present moment the people of Africa are neither
> in numbers nor in physique or intelligence capable of coping with
> the great task that lies before them in the development of Africa.
> The duty of statesmanship lies in the physical, moral and intellectual
> development of those people, and the physical side is the foundation
> of it. We have got to cope—and we are realizing increasingly that the
> very foundation of successful administration in Africa lies in that—
> with the health problems of that great continent.[1]

Amery expressed the prevailing view of African population among British officials during the interwar era, which focused on the problem of underpopulation. Yet within thirty years, officials began to warn about the dangers of overpopulation in Africa. This rapid shift occurred despite the fact that officials lacked accurate demographic information about the continent.[2] Rather, it reflected changed perceptions, as members of the British government discarded earlier ideas about African population. This essay explores this transition and places British ideas about African population within a larger demographic discourse of empire. It also links this discourse to the actions of officials and private individuals in Africa and the metropolis from the end of the nineteenth century to the demise of British colonial rule in the 1960s.[3] Despite changing British ideas about African population, three characteristics of this discourse remained stable. First, the British linked African demographic trends to a set of racial and cultural traits. Second, they saw African societies as unable to control nature, whether in the form of reproduction or production. And third, they argued that since Africans could not control nature, they needed British and European intervention in order to become "modern." This essay does not directly evaluate claims about African population growth in the colonial era. Literature on modern African population examines a number of critical issues, among them: variations in African demographic regimes, rates of growth before and after the colonial encounter, levels of fertility and mortality, and the causes of growth since the 1920s.[4] This research bears directly on many of the assertions made by British commentators, but determining the truth of those assertions is not my main concern. Instead, this essay focuses on the ways in which popular and academic understandings created their own reality and influenced colonial policy.

I begin with a discussion of British population discourse from the late nineteenth century until World War I, which portrayed Africans as backward and demographically stagnant. I then turn to the interwar years and the interaction between demographic ideas and British policy in Africa, particularly in the areas of labor and health, during the era of the dual mandate, as the British sought to foster the growth of African populations. The next phase began in the late 1930s, as the British government, under the twin pressures of political unrest and war, became more active in social and economic affairs and created a more interventionist colonial state in order to preserve the empire. In the postwar era, British officials and demographers expressed concern about population growth in Africa and its potential impact upon this new colonial agenda, which led to efforts to improve population data through the expansion of census and statistical departments. They also addressed the perceived impact of population growth through resettlement, agricultural programs, and the encouragement of private family planning services in parts of British Africa. Finally, I examine how British ideas and institutions influenced the postcolonial era, particularly the development of aid and population programs that sprang up in the 1960s and 1970s.

British Population Thought in the Age of Empire

British views of African population constituted part of a larger British discourse of imperial population in the nineteenth and twentieth centuries. Two men, Charles Darwin and Thomas Malthus, shaped this discourse. Although Malthusian ideas have been dominant since the 1950s, this dominance is a relatively recent phenomenon. Before the emergence of Malthusian orthodoxy in the first half of the nineteenth century, British students of population, like their counterparts elsewhere in Europe, argued that a large and growing population signified a prosperous and well-ordered society.[5] Most European observers in the eighteenth century believed that modern populations were smaller than those of antiquity and were either stagnant or declining. These assumptions provided the backdrop for debates about the merits of monarchal government and the possibilities for human progress. Malthus's insistence on the rapid growth of contemporary populations represented a decisive break. His model of population dynamics, in which populations tended toward the limit of subsistence, presented population growth, particularly among the poor, as a threat to social stability and continued progress.[6] This Malthusian view of British population waned in the middle of the nineteenth century, reflecting the absence of a Malthusian crisis in England—although not in Ireland—and the widespread belief that economic progress associated with industrialization would remove the limits on human subsistence.

Though domestic Malthusianism diminished, observers in Britain still insisted upon its applicability abroad, especially in places such as India. Indeed, Malthus was used to justify the transformation of colonial economies to Western-oriented market systems as a way of avoiding demographic disaster.[7] Malthus devoted only limited attention to African populations. In the absence of reliable statistical information, he depended upon the writings of Mungo Park and other explorers. He portrayed Africa as underpopulated due to warfare, insecurity of property, slavery, polygamy, and prolonged breast-feeding.[8] Despite their thin evidentiary base, these ideas would shape British and European views of African population into the twentieth century.

In the last quarter of the nineteenth century, Darwinian ideas began to supplant those of Malthus. Darwin found inspiration in Malthus for his early work, but his insistence on the importance of heredity and evolutionary progress laid the groundwork for a radically different analysis of demographic trends. Although Darwin's early work focused on broader issues of evolution, his later work, *Descent of Man,* explicitly dealt with human societies and race. He argued that the human demography reflected evolutionary forces at work. As groups competed for land and resources, peoples who were better adapted expanded at the expense of the less well adapted.[9] Darwin and his contemporaries pointed to the growth and overseas expansion of Britain as evidence of this process at work. They contrasted the vitality of Greater Britain with stagnant Asian societies and declining indigenous peoples in the Americas and the southwestern Pacific.[10] Darwinian population discourse classified Africans among the primitive races, isolated from the mainstream of human evolution. Limited innate endowments and harsh environments led African societies to stagnate at a low level of population. Although adapted to the tropical climate and diseases, they also suffered from their debilitating effects, lacking vigor and industry.[11] This view of African populations informed the generation of Europeans who conquered and administered Africa prior to 1914. Despite their increasing presence in Africa, Europeans knew very little about the size and composition of African populations well into the twentieth century.[12]

Lacking reliable data, they tended to view sub-Saharan Africa as underpopulated.[13] They feared that population losses from warfare and epidemics during the period of colonial conquest would exacerbate this problem and complicate the task of transforming these societies along Western lines.[14]

Darwinian population discourse emerged in an era in which a variety of biological interpretations of social phenomena, often lumped together under the term Social Darwinism, flourished.[15] The popularity of Social Darwinism spanned the ideological spectrum from socialism to authoritarian nationalism, but it rested on a common belief in the centrality of biology in human affairs.[16] Many Europeans saw the nation in racial terms and viewed warfare and political conflict as biological struggles for superiority in which the size and "quality" of the nation would play a critical role. Although Darwinian demographic discourse asserted the superiority of Europeans over other races, Darwin's belief that races could decay provoked an anxious search for signs of degeneration within Europe.[17] In France, demographic concerns focused on the slow rate of population growth, but in Britain, concerns about population "quality" displaced fears of overpopulation.[18] As fertility declined in the late nineteenth century, many in Britain believed that the higher fertility of the poor would undermine the biological fitness of their society, as the "unfit" made up an increasing portion of the population. This threat provoked various responses. The public health movement advocated increased investment in social welfare measures such as health clinics and slum clearance to improve the overall environment. Eugenicists and other hereditarians focused on the need to increase the fertility of the fit, while finding ways to limit the "breeding" of the unfit.[19] Hereditarian and environmental activists often made a connection between the poor and colonial peoples as racially different and alien. Like Africa, "Darkest London" remained unknown and vaguely threatening, only comprehensible to the missionaries and social workers who penetrated its depths. In the interwar years, this analogy would help rationalize health and labor initiatives in Africa modeled on those first advanced to address questions of poverty and social disorder at home.

The Interwar Years

World War I heightened fears about the future of Britain's population while also undermining the Darwinian analysis of population dynamics. Though Social Darwinists disagreed about the role of war in social evolution, most observers agreed that the war losses were a disaster for Britain.[20] In spite of new measures to improve maternal and infant health and the overall improvement in health conditions during the war, the mood among demographers and other students of population grew more pessimistic in the postwar years.[21] This pessimism increased in the interwar years as two trends converged. On one hand, the continuing decline of the birthrate in Europe produced a fear of depopulation.[22] On the other hand, new studies of non-European populations suggested they were growing rapidly rather than declining or reaching some Malthusian limit. Most attention focused on China, Japan, and India, but demographers also noted population growth in the Caribbean, the Middle East, and Southeast Asia.[23] These trends, by challenging the belief in European growth and non-European decay, undermined the Darwinian population model and helped revive Malthusian population ideas. Observers raised the specter of new struggles over territory and resources as non-European peoples expanded and Europeans contracted.[24]

This new demographic pattern generated concern among British intellectuals and activists. A loose coalition of eugenicists, demographers, and birth control advocates emerged in the interwar years. Members of this population movement founded organizations, most notably the Family Planning Association, that sponsored research, established clinics, and conducted informational campaigns in Britain and abroad.[25] These groups also established links to like-minded groups in the United States and Europe, formalized by a network of conferences and organizations. Their concerns centered on domestic issues such as voluntary sterilization, but they also paid attention to imperial population issues. The Eugenics Society provided much of the financial and organizational resources for the movement.[26] Socially prominent members, such as Julian Huxley, the biologist, Alexander Carr-Saunders, director of the London School of Economics (LSE), and C. E. Blacker, a physician and the society's secretary, lobbied the government about potential demographic threats to the stability of the empire and served as advisers to the Colonial Office from the 1930s through the 1950s. The population movement continued its work in the postwar era, helping to establish demography as an academic discipline and working through private agencies to provide family planning services in the empire and later in former colonies.

Despite shifts in British demographic discourse, most observers of African population in the interwar years continued to focus on underpopulation.[27] In British Africa, the losses incurred by African military and auxiliary forces in World War I, especially in East Africa, combined with the devastating impact of the influenza epidemic of 1918–19, gave greater urgency to the issue.[28] Carr-Saunders, a leading figure in interwar demography, argued that Africans suffered from a low level of development in part due to their inability to reproduce, even asserting that Africans possessed a diminished sex drive and smaller sex organs. In the face of white expansion, they suffered depopulation as a result of disease and warfare.[29] The British scientist Huxley, in *An African Journey* (1931), saw Africa's population as either stationary or in decline as a result of disease, native customs and taboos, and "the strange distaste for living or conferring life which seized upon various primitive peoples ... on being brought under the influence of an alien and incomprehensible culture."[30] William Macmillan's 1938 book, *Africa Emergent,* echoed Huxley's notion of an unstable African population propelled into modernity by Europeans. Macmillan, a well-known commentator on imperial issues, called Africa a place where "nature has continued to dominate man."[31] Citing the familiar litany of hostile environment, native customs, and disease, he identified a lack of population as the primary roadblock to African development. This argument became a staple of British commentaries about Africa in the interwar years.[32]

Although British writers focused on the innate or environmental causes of Africa's perceived demographic problems, some individuals acknowledged the role played by European imperialism. The missionary and activist J. H. Oldham raised this issue in the 1920s. Oldham believed that disease, malnutrition, and poor child care practices were partially responsible for underpopulation in British Africa.[33] However, he also noted the impact of European colonization, which encouraged the spread of disease through improved communications and labor migration. European influence disrupted African family life, as men left their villages to pursue work and returned riddled with disease and unable to readjust to tribal life. These changes resulted in a fall in the birthrate and a steady decline in population in both rural and urban areas. Oldham believed that the solution to this problem lay in the expansion of medical care and research, better nutrition through the improvement of African agriculture, child and maternal welfare services, universal education, and limits on labor demanded by European interests.[34] Africans should not, he asserted, be "left to stagnate in their reserves but under the guidance of sympathetic administrators helped forward on the path of industrial and social progress."[35] British observers such as Huxley and Macmillan agreed with Oldham's call for a more constructive imperialism and argued that future African progress depended upon the continued presence of European administrators and settlers.[36]

Colonial administrators accepted this analysis of Africa's demographic situation and its implications. In 1926, W. Ormsby-Gore, parliamentary under-secretary for the colonies and a future secretary of state for the colonies, offered his assessment in an address to the Geography Section of the British Association. He argued that most of tropical Africa suffered from a severe shortage of labor, which he linked to slow-growing or even declining populations. These problems, he suggested, reflected the poor condition of the natives and their low standards of health and hygiene. The solution lay in expanded production, improved transportation, and enhanced public health.[37] Ormsby-Gore's thinking reflected prevailing notions of trusteeship, in which colonial regimes were to offer Africans the possibility for progress within the contexts of their own "traditional societies." In this era, the heyday of the dual mandate, British colonial administrators rationalized intervention to ensure the reproduction of African labor.[38]

The discourse of African labor in British and other European colonies focused on ways to mobilize labor and guarantee a supply of healthy workers. This desire for a larger and more efficient labor supply dated from the late 1800s. As British rule in sub-Saharan Africa expanded, colonial regimes and private firms complained about a shortage of labor, caused in part by the reluctance of Africans to take on wage labor and in part by populations that were small and unhealthy. The need for workers, especially for infrastructure projects, led to forced labor.[39] Forced labor, in turn, proved disastrous for many African populations. Mortality on European work sites, the disruption of African agricultural life, and the alteration of disease environments through migration led to sharply rising death rates and perhaps even to declining birthrates.[40] The demographic consequences of forced labor, then, exacerbated the problem of obtaining sufficient African labor, undermining European claims that "free labor" would bring benefits to Africans.[41]

The desire to improve the quality and quantity of African labor linked the labor discourse with the prevailing biomedical analysis of African population. For British and other European doctors and scientists, Africa represented a unique disease environment, hostile to outsiders and debilitating for its indigenous inhabitants. This assessment led to claims that Africans were immune to some diseases, such as malaria. However, Europeans also believed that diseases such as yellow fever and sleeping sickness produced an enervated population, barely capable of reproducing itself and limited in its ability to perform physically demanding work. According to this biomedical discourse, Africa's disease environment needed to be changed through public health measures and the expansion of European medicine. The research of Megan Vaughan, David Arnold, and Sheldon Watts underscores the contradictory nature of this discourse, with its tendency to view Africa as an unchanging environment and its reliance on racially constructed ideas of disease.[42]

The problems that beset indigenous populations fueled criticism of Britain and other colonial powers by missionaries and political activists. Campaigns to reform the labor practices of Western colonial powers led ultimately to the Forced Labor Convention of the International Labor Organization in 1930.[43] In addition, the British and French hoped to improve the efficiency of African labor through health and welfare programs, a facet of what the French had come to call "*mise en valeur*" (development).[44] Colonial governments hoped that greater state regulation of labor, combined with improved sanitation and medical treatment, would blunt attacks on colonial regimes while ensuring an adequate labor supply. Although humanitarian and political motives did play a part in these innovations, British officials, like those of other colonial powers, argued that the initiatives would also bring population growth.[45]

The link between population, health, and development led the British government and private agencies to expand their public health work in the 1920s.[46] Medical experts called for measures to lower maternal and infant mortality rates.[47] Using models originally devised for working-class families in late nineteenth-century Europe, health workers formulated programs to encourage African mothers to adopt European methods of child rearing, including early weaning.[48] Such "health" measures overlapped with attacks on other practices that reduced fertility, including taboos against intercourse and abortion.[49] However, these scattered initiatives could not overcome the limited provision of public health services in the British Empire. Even though officials began to focus on the problems of indigenous health in the interwar years, they lacked the resources to transform a system centered principally on the needs of the colonial administration and the European populations of the colonies and on epidemic diseases such as smallpox. The passing of what David Arnold terms the "heroic age" of Western imperial medicine left only a bare infrastructure for health care, a flaw that became evident in the weak response of colonial governments to the flu pandemic of 1918–19.[50]

Given the limited nature of public services in Africa, the Colonial Office and local colonial governments cooperated with private agencies, such as the missionary societies and metropolitan pressure groups including the British Social Hygiene Council, to combat venereal disease, malaria, sleeping sickness, and other endemic afflictions.[51] Such arrangements allowed the colonial government to expand its reach. In Sierra Leone in the late 1920s, for example, the colonial government employed only five doctors and four African medical officers to service a population estimated at 1.5 million. To improve infant welfare efforts, the British government agreed to subsidize the work of four missionary hospitals. As the governor noted, "The experience gained by officers in charge of the Infant Welfare Clinics in Freetown has demonstrated that highly satisfactory results may be obtained, even with totally illiterate Africans, by careful, systematic and continuous welfare work."[52] Despite these efforts, the Colonial Office came under pressure from British and international groups, especially women's groups, to do more.[53]

Demography and the New Colonial State

The Colonial Office and colonial governments pursued new initiatives to bolster African populations during the interwar years, yet they remained limited in scope. Insufficient resources and the belief that African development should occur within existing institutions prevented a more active approach. Beginning in the late 1930s and continuing until the era of decolonization in the late 1950s, the British government took a far more interventionist approach to colonial rule. This shift, motivated by political unrest within the empire as well as domestic and international criticism of British imperialism, forced the Colonial Office to increase efforts to foster economic development and social welfare in the empire.[54] The turning point in this process in British Africa came in 1938 with the publication of Lord Hailey's *African Survey*. This comprehensive review of African conditions sparked a wide-ranging debate about the need for reform.[55] Even as this debate proceeded, the outbreak of World War II led to a dramatic increase in state intervention as colonial authorities made more and more demands for resources and labor to aid Britain's war effort.[56]

Significant changes in the size and structure of the colonial service accompanied this shift in imperial governance. From the early 1930s onward, the Colonial Office attempted to exert more control from London and to prod colonial regimes into a greater activism. Officials reformed the central establishment in London, creating new subject departments to supplement the traditional geographic departments that dominated the Colonial Office. Officials hoped that these departments, such as administration (1932), medicine (1934), and agriculture (1935), would increase the application of specialized knowledge in colonial affairs, which would be supplemented by the use of outside experts.[57] The Depression

and the war led to staffing shortages, but in the postwar era, the British government rapidly expanded the size of the colonial service.[58]

After 1945, the Labour government, facing economic difficulties at home and a
challenging international environment, hoped to use the empire to assist Britain's
recovery and to bolster its claims to great power status.[59] This desire produced a
more powerful imperial state that served multiple, often conflicting purposes. The
British government committed itself to economic development of the colonies
with the Colonial Development and Welfare Act of 1940, which was enlarged in
1945. Ostensibly, development would improve the standard of living of colonial
peoples and form part of a broader modernization of the social and political life of
colonial societies that would move them closer to self-rule.[60] However, given the
reluctance of the British government to set timetables for self-rule, development
plans also served to counter criticism of the empire and resist demands for greater
autonomy or independence for dependent territories.[61] The financial benefits to
London of increased colonial exports and the sequestering of colonial foreign
exchange far exceeded the amount allocated for development and welfare in the
empire.[62] These policies prevented colonial peoples from benefiting from the augmented output of their economies.[63]

Colonial officials spoke of the shared values that tied the empire to Britain,
yet the stark differences between colonial and British development revealed the
contradictions in this stance. Although the postwar British welfare state relied on
increased intervention and planning, the idea of basic rights possessed by citizens
imposed limits on state power. In the empire, however, state power operated with
fewer controls. Postwar colonial regimes often used compulsion to pursue their
goals, relying on an influx of new officials that African historians call the "second
colonial occupation."[64] The confused and coercive efforts of officials, particularly
in Africa, often failed to achieve their objectives.[65] Like other developmentalist
colonial regimes, the British often faced resistance or evasion from the erstwhile
subjects of development that revealed the limits of their power.[66]

The elevation of development to a central aim of imperial policy increased the
importance of planning by colonial regimes, which required improved demographic
information. Already in the 1930s, the Colonial Office recognized that it lacked
adequate population data. In order to improve demographic information in the
early 1940s, the Colonial Office brought in an outside expert, Robert Kuczynski, a
well-known demographer who wrote the chapter on population for Hailey's *African
Survey*. Kuczynski, the Reader in Demography at LSE, spent much of his career
concentrating on technical demography and Western population trends, but in the
late 1930s, he began to study colonial populations.[67] In 1937, he published a short
book on colonial population, followed in 1939 by a study of the population statistics
of the Cameroons and Togoland under German rule.[68] In 1939, with the support
of the Eugenics Society and its well-connected members, he received a grant from
the Carnegie Corporation to expand his study of colonial population, which culminated in his multivolume work on the subject, entitled *Demographic Survey of the*

British Colonial Empire.[69] After retiring from LSE in 1941, Kuczynski joined the Colonial Office and served as demographic adviser from 1944 until his death in 1947.

Kuczynski's work demonstrated the inadequacy of colonial population statistics. He showed that birth and mortality figures, as well as estimates of population made by untrained colonial officials, represented nothing more than educated guesses. Indeed, the quality of censuses had actually declined in the early twentieth century when the Colonial Office allowed colonial governments to conduct their own counts. Censuses varied dramatically in coverage and were not comparable. And nowhere was the problem more acute than in Africa. In the case of Nigeria, Kuczynski could not determine from existing data whether the population was growing or declining.[70] Administrators in the Colonial Office discussed ways to improve population data and attempted to implement Kuczynski's recommendations for better census taking and training of personnel.[71]

To assist Kuczynski, the Colonial Office created the Demography Advisory Group in 1943. Chaired by J. H. Hutton, professor of anthropology at Cambridge and commissioner of the 1931 Indian census, the group's members included Huxley and Carr-Saunders.[72] The body became a clearinghouse for demographic information and worked with other advisory units to address population issues relevant to their areas of concern. The Colonial Office, under its chief statistician, W. F. Searle, worked to improve the quality of colonial statistics after 1945, but demographic information about the colonies remained inadequate throughout the colonial era.[73]

Although officials and politicians recognized the importance of demographic trends for imperial policy, they failed to create a coherent response. Despite calls for a central body to address population issues and formulate an imperial population policy, British efforts remained fragmented and ad hoc during the colonial era. The Colonial Office and local colonial governments continued to exert control over imperial populations by restricting movement within colonies and the empire, even as they subsidized immigration by British subjects to the empire and the Commonwealth.[74] As during the interwar years, the Colonial Office encouraged private groups to create family planning clinics in the empire with the approval of local officials.[75] This permissive policy led local colonial regimes to pursue population control policies on their own, while allowing the British government to deny direct involvement.

Increased attention to population concerns in the empire came as yet another significant shift occurred in demographic discourse. In Britain, fears of depopulation faded with the postwar baby boom.[76] The creation of a comprehensive welfare state after 1945 committed the British government to "reconstructing" the population through expanded opportunity and the creation of a minimum standard of life for all families.[77] The greater homogeneity of British domestic population trends heightened the perceived differences with so-called underdeveloped peoples outside the metropole. American demographers such as Frank Notestein and Kingsley Davis elaborated a new model of population dynamics—the demographic transition theory that portrayed population trends as part of a universal process of modernization. The theory posited that population growth occurred during an intermediate step as traditional societies industrialized and enjoyed better health, leading to falling death rates while high birthrates persisted. As societies reached socioeconomic modernity, however, new values and social systems encouraged the use of birth control on a wide scale and fostered the emergence of small families, leading to lower birthrates and slower growth. Demographers argued that Asian and African societies were in the early stages of this transition, as exposure to Western medicine and technology reduced mortality but continued high fertility led to rapid population growth. Western governments began to consider how to control population growth in colonial and postcolonial societies as part of a larger effort to maintain international stability.[78]

New Views of African Population

This new demographic discourse emerged as British views about African populations underwent a dramatic change. Previously, the British had believed that underpopulation hampered development, but beginning in the early 1940s, experts worried about the impact of population growth in different parts of Africa upon colonial development. The increasing importance of Africa's resources and people to postwar British plans magnified the significance of these concerns.[79] As early as the 1930s, some experts highlighted local or regional population growth, usually in relationship to patterns of land use and agricultural techniques, particularly in East Africa.[80] They argued that although the overall density of population in Africa remained low, many areas, especially those with good soil, exhibited far higher densities—a point illustrated by population mapping.[81] Yet as fears of overpopulation at a regional level emerged, many in the British government continued to worry about labor scarcity as late as the 1940s. The need for strategic materials, food and other goods for the war effort, and the recruitment of Africans for military service greatly expanded the demand for labor, which led to the use of forced recruitment—and some observers feared that would reduce population growth.[82] Margery Perham proposed a study of the relationship between labor migration and demography in Africa, arguing that "war may lead to even more wasteful use of the docile African humanity."[83] This project never got off the ground, but some officials continued to view African populations from a perspective shaped by prewar notions of shortage and surplus. Thus, colonies such as Nyasaland (today's Malawi) and Kenya continued to be thought of as labor reserves for the war effort in the face of growing evidence of labor shortages as recruitment and conscription increased.[84]

African demographic trends remained unclear in the immediate postwar years. In 1947, Kuczynski felt unable to determine the direction or strength of population trends.[85] Reliable demographic data remained scarce, despite the pioneering work of scholars such as A. T. Culwick and G. M. Culwick in Tanganyika.[86] A number of observers argued that improvements in medical care and food production would ultimately lead to higher rates of growth. In 1943, Julian Huxley wrote Oliver Stanley, secretary of state for the colonies, to warn him of the potential problem of African population growth. Echoing points first advanced in *African Journey* in 1931, Huxley argued that the enhanced health services and greater prosperity would bring population growth. To forestall this possibility, he suggested that birth control programs be provided at health centers and maternity and infant welfare clinics.[87] In 1945, Andrew Cohen, one of the architects of postwar African policy, warned of predictions that the introduction of DDT would dramatically lower death rates from malaria, leading to higher rates of population growth.[88] Several postwar assessments of African population echoed these concerns.[89] In 1948, T. H. Davey, a medical adviser to the Colonial Office, argued that parts of Nigeria and Kenya were already experiencing high rates of growth and that other regions of the continent would follow if existing trends continued.[90] Postwar censuses by African colonial governments, like those undertaken in East Africa in 1948 and in northern Nigeria in 1952, seemed to confirm these more impressionistic reports.[91] International agencies, colonial governments, and independent demographic researchers reached similar conclusions.[92]

Experts and officials did not argue that British Africa as a whole suffered from overpopulation. Instead, they focused on regional problems of population, often using the term *population pressure* to describe local circumstances. This understanding of population located it within existing debates about the environment, land use, and agricultural techniques that predated World War II. Colonial regimes constructed narratives about population, the environment, and agriculture that made African behavior the root cause of poverty and social disruption, while portraying colonial interventions in African lives as a source of progress.[93] British efforts to reshape African life sought to address the perceived impact of African population growth at a regional and local level. Rather than relying on family planning programs, which only appeared at the end of the colonial era, officials hoped that resettlement programs and greater agricultural output would reduce population pressure. They rejected any suggestion that colonial policies, especially land alienation, played a role in the problem and instead focused on transforming African behavior, by coercive means if necessary. This approach generated increasing resistance from rural populations and growing support for nationalist movements.[94]

Officials saw evidence of population pressure in the Gold Coast, Nyasaland, Southern Rhodesia, and northern Nigeria, but they directed much of their attention to East Africa, especially Kenya.[95] In the interwar years, settlers and their representatives argued that African population growth threatened the viability of native reserves and produced erosion and environmental damage. These claims continued in the postwar era and found a sympathetic audience in the Colonial Office and East African governments.[96] Sir Phillip Mitchell, the governor of Kenya, called African population growth a critical issue for the future of East Africa and asked for a royal commission to study the problems of the region.[97] However, the Royal Commission on East Africa, created in 1953, rejected overpopulation as a problem, speaking instead of overcrowding and primitive agricultural methods.[98] This understanding of the issue accorded with that held by many officials.

Colonial officials saw resettlement of the land as central to their plans. Already in the 1930s, the British used forced resettlement as part of their tsetse fly control efforts.[99] In the 1940s and 1950s, resettlement programs moved people from overcrowded regions to areas officials saw as underutilized, in order to relieve overpopulation and encourage new agricultural production.[100] Resettlement schemes operated in Nyasaland (1942), Uganda (1944), Swaziland (1945–46), Nigeria (1946), and Tanganyika.[101] The scale of these projects varied, but some were quite substantial. The Nyasaland project affected 28,000 people, and a Ugandan plan to resettle former soldiers in the Kigezi district involved 15,000 people.[102] Southern Rhodesian officials forced the removal of as many as 465,000 "squatters" from white farms.[103] These efforts continued despite their cost. The Kigezi scheme cost £18,000, and one in Nigeria from 1946–51 ran to £240 per settler.[104]

The high cost of these programs reflected the difficulties of beginning new settlements in often remote areas that lacked roads or reliable water supplies. Yet officials hoped to make them model settlements and included strict rules about the nature of land use and agricultural techniques in these areas.[105] Colonial governments proved willing to use compulsion to achieve their goals. Forced removals and tight controls led to resistance from displaced groups.[106] Some settlers attempted to return to their homes; other groups moved into areas emptied by resettlement to exploit newly available land. In an attempt to maintain a forest reserve created in the Jos region of Nigeria, officials prosecuted and fined interlopers. The refusal of a local authority court to enforce the ban on settlement led to its dismissal by colonial officials.[107] Such conflicts reflected the differing perceptions of Africans and the British about land use. The desire of officials to bring new land under cultivation often contradicted established local patterns of land use designed to preserve marginal lands from overuse. Some experts recognized the value of indigenous knowledge, but in general, the British discounted the value of African ideas.[108]

British officials linked resettlement to their efforts to transform African agriculture in order to raise output and accommodate larger populations. Detailed critiques of African agriculture dated back to the interwar years and the work of E. B. Worthington and Sir Daniel Hall.[109] In the eyes of British observers, Africans relied on inefficient and destructive techniques.[110] Overuse of the land and soil erosion threatened to reduce food production even as populations increased.[111] Officials believed that only a sustained campaign to improve African farming could prevent a future crisis. Postwar agricultural policy thus took aim at African practices and used incentives and compulsory powers to force changes in behavior. Yet such programs were riddled with problems.[112] Officials refused to endorse African peasant cultivation for the market as the way forward, despite their encouragement of increased output of maize and other cash crops during the Depression and World War II.[113] Instead, they believed that large-scale production by well-capitalized European farmers would create the basis for economic modernization. However, this decision also reflected the debate about tradition and modernity in postwar Africa. British officials and politicians disagreed on the wisdom of encouraging new values and behaviors. Many of them argued a "traditional" African society, in which chiefs and communal institutions predominated, would ensure stability. They distrusted peasant cultivators producing for the market and the new urban working class.[114] Other experts and officials, however, saw the rise of the market as the best way to encourage innovation and enhance productivity. This debate took on a particular relevance in discussions of agriculture. Some thought that population growth would eliminate shifting cultivation and pastoral practices and lead to the adoption of more "modern" techniques modeled on those of British agriculture, leading to increased output.[115] Yet other experts believed that cash cropping and individual tenure accelerated the processes of soil erosion and exhaustion. Both sides agreed that only British guidance could ensure a safe transition to modernity and thus that agricultural experts needed to retain control over rural populations to ensure success.

Many in the colonial establishment remained uncertain about the wisdom of encouraging modernization, but those concerned with demographic issues believed that new values and attitudes were essential if Africans hoped to avoid a future population crisis. Whereas previously experts had argued that Africa's slow population growth demonstrated the continent's backwardness, they now said that Africa's inability to limit its growth demonstrated its failure to modernize. From the perspective of demographic theories elaborated after 1945, African families remained enmeshed in collective networks that inhibited the exercise of individual autonomy and choice. Even as mortality fell, Africans continued to bear large numbers of children, leading to rapid population growth. Officials blamed this problem on African backwardness. As J. K. Greer, a Colonial Office agricultural specialist, argued in 1948: "The utterances of Governors make it appear that most East Africans are incurably lazy and industrialization and plantations will be possible up to the point at which the few exceptional members of the community who are willing to do regular work have all been absorbed. The rest will continue to live a shiftless existence, surrounded by swarms of children."[116]

For these officials and experts, the expansion of the market offered the best solution to the agrarian and demographic problems of Africa. The growth of the market would encourage increased output and individualism in African society, which in turn would lead Africans to adopt the values necessary for fertility control.[117] As one official put it, "A voluntary limitation of families will only come when the people have been educated to more sophisticated wants—bicycles instead of babies, furniture instead of families."[118] The problem, in the eyes of officials, lay in the slow pace of social and economic change. Plans for the modernization of Africa rested on the ability of colonial regimes to foster the economic changes necessary to sustain improved standards of living while at the same time encouraging the growth of modern values among the wage earners and peasant farmers of the continent. This vision of modernity represented the latest iteration of British efforts to reshape Africans and other supposedly backward peoples.

The problems inherent in British efforts to control African populations appeared most clearly in Kenya. The creation of a white settler elite in the early twentieth century relied upon the displacement of the African population from its land and its resettlement into native reserves. As evidence mounted about overcrowding in these reserves, the British resisted land reform and instead used resettlement and agricultural schemes that targeted indigenous farmers. Colonial administrators framed the problem as one of overpopulation on the reserves and rejected land alienation as a factor. One report noted, "In Kenya, where the pressure of population is 'beyond the present, and in some cases the possible future carrying capacity of the land'; a more adequate redistribution of the African population through resettlement has been adopted as one of the main objectives of economic development."[119] Both resettlement plans and the eviction of African "squatters" from white lands in the Highlands relied on the use of force. The failure to resolve land tenure issues or allocate more land to African farmers generated increasing tensions in the postwar era and formed the background to the outbreak of the Mau Mau Insurgency.[120] British authorities responded to the revolt by employing population control as a counterinsurgency tactic. The British used forced resettlement of rural populations into controlled villages to isolate rebel forces. The Swynnerton Plan, launched at the height of the insurgency in 1953, sought to use the war to reorganize rural life by fostering a landowning peasant class producing cash crops on consolidated landholdings with new agricultural methods. The concentration of the Kikuyu in fortified villages reduced the floating population of the reserves, while providing forced communal labor for land "improvement."[121] The British also used detainee labor for agricultural projects, including several long-planned irrigation schemes, despite the fact that this practice violated international law.[122] Land became a weapon to divide the Kikuyu from one another and against other Kenyan ethnic groups. Loyalists received preferential treatment in the new settlement schemes as well as access to cheap labor.

Despite the defeat of the Mau Mau Insurgency, British plans for Africa were increasingly unrealistic given the rapidly changing political environment.[123] The drive toward the "Africanization" of local colonial services lessened the ability of Colonial Office officials to control events.[124] The decline in development funding after 1955 and the increasing pace of decolonization made officials reluctant to begin new, expensive projects. Instead, the Colonial Office began the transition toward independence, winding down development projects and making arrangements for the transfer or redundancy of colonial officials.[125] As the dismantling of the colonial state proceeded, attention turned to the transition to a postcolonial development regime that included population programs.

African Population in the Postcolonial Era

Decolonization ended direct British control over African populations, but the British continued to exert influence in the postcolonial era. British officials, scholars, and nongovernmental organizations (NGOs) helped construct the new aid programs aimed at Africa. In 1961, the British government created the Department of Technical Cooperation to coordinate aid programs in the remaining colonies and newly independent states. This agency and its successor, the Ministry of Overseas Development (ODM), created in 1964, drew much of their personnel from the ranks of the colonial service, including their director, Andrew Cohen.[126] A number of British officials, including Julian Huxley, the first head of the United Nations Educational, Scientific, and Cultural Organization (UNESCO), were central to the creation of international development programs under UN auspices that played a large role in Africa.

In the 1960s, as African states achieved independence, new demographic estimates for sub-Saharan African appeared.[127] These estimates built upon the work of demographers previously associated with the Colonial Office.[128] One of these scholars, William Brass, served in the East African Statistical Department from 1948 to 1955. Brass became an important figure in African demography and helped create the Centre for Overseas Population Studies at the London School of Hygiene and Tropical Medicine.[129] In 1961, Frank Lorimer launched a comprehensive research project on African demography at Princeton University's Office of Population Research, whose members included Brass. Their publications argued that Africa stood on the brink of rapid population growth as a result of falling mortality.[130] The United Nations Economic Commission for Africa (UNECA) echoed the Princeton group, though it produced even higher estimates of growth.[131] By the early 1970s, then, a new consensus emerged among demographers about African population growth. They warned of an escalating threat and its potential consequences for the newly independent states of the continent.[132] Much of this new research invoked demographic transition theory. Development projects began to incorporate population control measures as part of their plans, despite the reluctance of many African countries to accept them.[133]

The population programs that emerged in Africa in the 1960s and 1970s relied heavily on NGOs that operated in former British colonies. Their activities, like those of other NGOs such as Oxfam and Save the Children, reflected the shift of NGOs toward Africa as decolonization proceeded.[134] They joined an array of British missionary organizations that survived the end of imperial rule and continued to operate in former colonial states.[135] Though family planning activity in Africa dated back to the 1930s and Marie Stopes's work with South African activists, it took off in the postwar era, as concern about African population growth increased.[136] Not surprisingly, one of the earliest calls for birth control for Africans came from the settler community in Kenya.[137] In Kenya and elsewhere in British colonial Africa, private groups, with unofficial Colonial Office support, established birth control clinics. In the mid-1950s, the International Planned Parenthood Federation (IPPF) contacted physicians and other persons interested in birth control in several African countries, including Uganda, Tanzania, Kenya, Sierra Leone, and Nigeria.[138] In 1956, Edith Gates, the East African and Far East field representative of the Committee on Maternal Health, set up an IPPF field organization in Africa. Her visit to Kampala, Uganda, in 1957 led to the creation of a family planning committee in the city staffed principally by South Asian volunteers, as would be the case in much of eastern Africa. In 1959, the IPPF appointed the wife of a Colonial Medical Service officer as its regional field organizer for East Africa to work with affiliates in Nairobi, Mombasa, Dar es Salaam, Kampala, and Zanzibar. Work also began in Nigeria, Ghana, and Sierra Leone.[139] Such initiatives resembled those undertaken elsewhere in the empire by the IPPF and its predecessor, the Family Planning Association, with the cooperation of the Colonial Office. Urban hospitals and maternal and child welfare centers housed these clinics. Officials despaired of reaching the larger population in rural areas, where medical services and clinics were sparse.[140]

By the late 1950s, the IPPF enjoyed a close working relationship with the Colonial Office. Once the British government decided in 1961 to fund overseas population programs, this relationship became closer. Lacking its own personnel and clinics, the ODM funneled much of its aid through the IPPF, a process made easier by the appointment of the former governor of Mauritius, Sir Colville Deverell, as president of the IPPF.[141] Despite the early work of the organization, however, not all Africa governments welcomed family planning programs. As one official in 1967 noted, "The general impression in Africa is that the continent is under-populated, but few of the African countries have adequate demographic and other statistics to show whether their rates of growth are outrunning their capacity for economic growth."[142] Although such resistance continued, the potential benefits of cooperation and the insistence of aid donors led to the rapid expansion of family planning programs. The British both offered bilateral aid for family planning and contributed to UN efforts.[143] By the early 1980s, virtually every state in sub-Saharan Africa had created a family planning program in conjunction with international and bilateral assistance agencies, supplemented by the work of nongovernmental organizations.[144] The white minority governments of Rhodesia and South Africa linked their family planning programs to counterinsurgency efforts.[145]

Population Discourse and African History

International population programs aimed at Africans built upon a narrative of African population deeply rooted in British colonial rule. The international population establishment inherited and reproduced the British narrative of African population history. In this narrative, Africa was an underpopulated continent prior to the colonial era, characterized by high birth and death rates as a result of general poverty, slave raiding, and endemic disease. After European conquest, African

populations reeled from the shock of forced modernization and underwent a period of decline. However, growth soon succeeded decline as Western colonialism
brought internal peace, ended the slave trade, and reduced mortality rates through
public health services and modern medicine. This mortality decline, coupled with
continued high birthrates, led to a population explosion. In the final stage, Western development assistance would reduce African fertility by inculcating modern
values of individualism and equality and introducing birth control. This discourse
about African population demonstrated remarkable stability over the years. Both
the older version that emphasized underpopulation and the newer one focused on
overpopulation removed control from Africans. Both versions portrayed Africa as
a continent unable to shape and control natural forces, leaving for Western nations
the task of propelling it into the modern world using the tools of medicine and
biology or the insights of social science. Contemporary Western commentators on
Africa continue to invoke this discourse of African population to explain why the
continent remains troubled by warfare, famine, and poverty.[146]

The triumph of this Malthusian view of African population can be seen in
the evolution of ideas about development and population. In the postwar years,
proponents depicted population control as a potential remedy for poverty. At the
same time, many experts argued that development would lead to sustained fertility decline through its impact upon standards of living and social attitudes. By
the 1970s, this view had been supplanted by a more pessimistic one that argued
changes in attitudes would take too long and population growth would over-
whelm efforts at development. Therefore, population control had to come first
in order to provide time for development to occur.[147] This shift led to the abandonment of equity as a goal and an emphasis on technique and contraception as
keys to success. As was the case with the Green Revolution, Western donors and
host countries preferred the narrative of modernization and hoped for a technical
solution in the form of miracle seeds or new contraceptives.[148] The promise that
population programs would reduce poverty and jump-start development appears
to have been oversold. The dramatic fall in fertility in the last decades occurred
even as measures of global inequality stood static or worsened, particularly in sub-
Saharan Africa.[149]

The history of British discourse on African population and its influence on
contemporary Western views of Africa demonstrates how understandings of population represent more than simply a neutral scientific analysis. Ideas about population were intimately involved in the exercise of power and reflected the interests
of both experts and officials. In this sense, demography functioned as a colonial
science, like anthropology or medicine. Demographers assisted in the creation of
an African Other, one that could be understood and transformed in the name of a
universal modernity. The transition from a colonial to a postcolonial discourse retained this perspective in a new ideological and political environment. By focusing
on population growth and the behavior of Africans, contemporary Western population discourse sidesteps questions about the causes of poverty and the legacies

of European colonial rule. Its use of universal categories and neutral language also conceals the persistence of racial categories in demography. Although the decline of scientific racism discredited biological explanations of racial difference, the social sciences created new categories of inferiority, linked to underdevelopment and incomplete modernization.[150] By squeezing Africans into a single model based on Western experience, population discourse obscured the dramatic differences in demographic behavior on the continent and placed all African societies within the realm of the primitive or traditional. A critical narrative of this history allows us to challenge contemporary myths about Africa and to continue the process of rewriting African demographic history.[151]

Notes

The University of Houston provided support for this project through its Small Research Grant program. In addition, I received a grant from the Center for Immigration Research at the University of Houston. I would also like to acknowledge the assistance of Ian Pool, Meredeth Turshen, Dennis Cordell, and Greg Maddox.

1. *Proceedings of the Imperial Social Hygiene Congress, 1925* (London: British Social Hygiene Council, 1925), 1–2.

2. The classic account of this problem remains Robert Kuczynski, *Demographic Survey of the British Colonial Empire,* vol. 1, *East Africa,* and vol. 2, *West Africa* (London: Oxford University Press, 1948).

3. A similar set of ideas existed among French and Belgian colonial authorities. See Nancy Rose Hunt, "'Le Bebe en Brousse': European Women, African Birth Spacing and Colonial Intervention in Breast-Feeding in the Belgian Congo," *International Journal of African Historical Studies* 21, no. 3 (1988): 401–32, and Myron Echenberg, "'Faire du nègre': Military Aspects of Population Planning in French West Africa, 1920–1940," in *African Population and Capitalism: Historical Perspectives,* ed. Dennis Cordell and Joel W. Gregory, 2nd ed. (Madison: University of Wisconsin Press, 1994), 95–108.

4. For an introduction to this literature, see C. C. Wrigley, "Population in African History," *Journal of African History* 20, no. 1 (1979): 127–31; John Iliffe, "The Origins of African Population Growth," *Journal of African History* 30, no. 1 (1989): 165–69; Thomas Spears, "Africa's Population History," *Journal of African History* 37, no. 3 (1996): 479–85.

5. For seventeenth-century England, see Mildred Campbell, "'Of People Either Too Few or Too Many': The Conflict of Opinion on Population and Its Relation to Emigration," in *Conflict in Stuart England,* ed. Basil D. Henning (New York: New York University Press, 1960), 169–201. For a general overview, see J. Overbeek, *History of Population Theories* (Rotterdam, the Netherlands: University of Rotterdam Press, 1974).

6. Frederick Whelan, "Population and Ideology in the Enlightenment," *History of Political Thought* 12, no. 1 (1991): 35–72.

7. See Mike Davis, *Late Victorian Holocausts: El Niño Famines and the Making of the Third World* (London: Verso, 2001).

8. Thomas Malthus, *An Essay on Population,* vol. 1 (London: J. M. Dent and Sons, 1914), 89–98. For the problems with early European accounts, see Norman Etherington, "A False Emptiness: How Historians May Have Been Misled by Early Nineteenth Century Maps of South-Eastern Africa," *Imago Mundi* 56, no. 1 (2004): 67–86.

9. Charles Darwin, *The Descent of Man* (1879; repr., London: Penguin, 2004), 194–230.

10. Stephen Roberts, *Population Problems of the Pacific* (1927; repr., New York: AMS, 1969).

11. The classic Darwinian account is Alexander Carr-Saunders, *Population Problems: A Study in Human Evolution* (Oxford: Clarendon, 1922).

12. See John Caldwell and Thomas Schindlmayr, "Historical Population Estimates: Unraveling the Consensus," *Population and Development Review* 28, no. 2 (2002): 183–204.

13. For example, see G. F. Darker, "Niger Delta Natives: With Special Reference to Maintaining and Increasing the Population of Southern Nigeria," *Journal of the Royal African Society* 4, no. 14 (1905): 206–25.

14. For the complexity of the situation in East Africa, see Shane Doyle, "Population Decline and Delayed Recovery in Bunyoro, 1860–1960," *Journal of African History* 41, no. 3 (2000): 429–58.

15. Scholars increasingly see Social Darwinism not simply as a misinterpretation of Darwin but also as part of the larger intellectual context in which Darwin himself formulated ideas about evolution, progress, and the place of human societies in relation to one another. See Gregory Claeys, "The 'Survival of the Fittest' and the Origins of Social Darwinism," *Journal of the History of Ideas* 61, no. 2 (2000): 223–40; John Waller, "Ideas of Heredity, Reproduction and Eugenics in Britain, 1800–1875," *Studies in History and Philosophy of Biological and Biomedical Sciences* 32, no. 3 (2001): 457–89.

16. Mike Hawkins, *Social Darwinism in European and American Thought, 1860–1945* (Cambridge: Cambridge University Press, 1997).

17. Darwin, *Descent of Man*, 211–22.

18. For the French, see William Schneider, *Quality and Quantity: The Quest for Biological Regeneration in Twentieth Century France* (Cambridge, MA: Harvard University Press, 1990); Andres Reggiani, "Procreating France: The Politics of Demography, 1919–1945," *French Historical Studies* 19, no. 3 (1996): 725–54; Joshua Cole, *The Power of Large Numbers: Population, Politics, and Gender in Nineteenth-Century France* (Ithaca, NY: Cornell University Press, 2000); Ella Camiscioli, "Producing Citizens and Reproducing the 'French Race': Immigration, Demography, and Pronatalism in Early Twentieth Century France," *Gender and History* 13, no. 3 (2001): 593–621.

19. Daniel Kevles, *In the Name of Eugenics* (New York: Alfred A. Knopf, 1985); Richard Soloway, *Demography and Degeneration* (Chapel Hill: University of North Carolina Press, 1990); Simon Szreter, *Fertility, Class and Gender in Britain, 1860–1940* (Cambridge: Cambridge University Press, 1996), 67–282.

20. Paul Crook, *Darwinism, War and History* (Cambridge: Cambridge University Press, 1994); Richard Soloway, "Eugenics and Pronatalism in Wartime Britain," in *The Upheaval of War: Family, Work and Welfare in Europe, 1914–1918*, ed. Richard Wall and Jay Winter (Cambridge: Cambridge University Press, 1988), 369–88.

21. Jay Winter, *The Great War and the British People* (Cambridge, MA: Harvard University Press, 1986); Soloway, *Demography*, 164–72.

22. The classic statement is Enid Charles, *The Twilight of Parenthood* (London: Watts, 1934). See also Michael Teitelbaum and Jay Winter, *The Fear of Population Decline* (Orlando, FL: Academic, 1985); Soloway, *Demography*, 226–58; Pat Thane, "The Debate on the Declining Birth Rate in Britain: The 'Menace' of an Ageing Population, 1920s–1950s," *Continuity and Change* 5, no. 2 (1990): 283–305.

23. Warren Thompson, *Danger Spots in World Population* (New York: Alfred A. Knopf, 1929); Sir John Megaw, "Pressure of Population in India," *Journal of the Royal Society of Arts* 87, no. 4491 (1938–39): 134–57; Edward East, *Mankind at the Crossroads* (New York:

Scribner's, 1923); George Knibbs, *The Shadow of the World's Future* (1928; repr., New York: Arno, 1976); E. F. Penrose, *Population Theories and Their Application with Special Reference to Japan* (1934; repr., Westport, CT: Greenwood, 1973).

24. Writing alarmist tracts about non-European population became a virtual cottage industry in the 1920s and 1930s. See J. W. Gregory, *The Menace of Colour* (London: Seeley, Service, 1925); Basil Matthews, *The Clash of Colour* (1925; repr., Port Washington, NY: Kennikat, 1973); L. C. Money, *The Peril of the White* (London: W. Collins Sons, 1925); J. Swinburne, *Population and the Social Problem* (New York: Macmillan, 1925).

25. June Rose, *Marie Stopes and the Sexual Revolution* (London: Faber and Faber, 1992); Audrey Leathard, *The Fight for Family Planning: The Development of Family Planning Services in Britain, 1921–74* (London: Macmillan, 1980), 1–50. See also Richard Soloway, *Birth Control and the Population Question in England, 1877–1930* (Chapel Hill: University of North Carolina Press, 1982), 159–318.

26. Karl Ittmann, "Demography as Policy Science in the British Empire, 1918–1969," *Journal of Policy History* 15, no. 4 (2003): 425–30.

27. Edward Ross, *Standing Room Only* (New York: Century, 1927), 342; Warren Thompson, *Population Problems,* 2nd ed. (New York: McGraw-Hill, 1935), 253–54; East, *Mankind at the Crossroads,* 98–102; Lothop Stoddard, *The Rising Tide of Color* (New York: Scribner's, 1920), 87–91.

28. K. David Patterson, "The Influenza Epidemic of 1918–1919 in the Gold Coast," *Journal of African History* 24, no. 4 (1983): 485–502; David Killingray, "Labour Exploitation for Military Campaigns in British Colonial Africa, 1870–1945," *Journal of Contemporary History* 24, no. 3 (1989): 483–501; Gregory H. Maddox, "*Mtunya:* Famine in Central Tanzania, 1917–1920," *Journal of African History* 31, no. 2 (1990): 181–98.

29. Carr-Saunders, *Population,* 97–100. He repeated these arguments in his book *World Population* (1936; repr., New York: Barnes and Noble, 1965), 300–306.

30. Julian Huxley, *African View* (London: Chatto and Windus, 1931), 418.

31. William Macmillan, *Africa Emergent* (London: Faber and Faber, 1938), 40. For more on his career, see John Flint, "Macmillan as Critic of Empire: The Impact of an Historian on Colonial Policy," in *Africa and Empire: W .H. Macmillan, Historian and Social Critic,* ed. Hugh Macmillan and Shula Marks (Aldershot, UK: Published for the Institute of Commonwealth Studies by Temple Smith, 1989), 212–31.

32. Royal Institute of International Affairs, *The Colonial Problem: A Report* (New York: Oxford, 1937), 127–39; Raymond Buell, *The Native Problem in Africa* (1927; repr., Hamden, CT: Archon, 1965); I. C. Greaves, *Modern Production among Backward Peoples* (1935; repr., New York: A. M. Kelley, 1968).

33. Oldham's critique of British policy in East Africa stirred controversy in the 1920s. He became an adviser to Malcolm Macdonald. For his work, see John Cell, "Lord Hailey and the Making of the African Survey," *African Affairs* 88, no. 353 (1989): 483–85.

34. John Oldham, "Population and Health in Africa," *International Review of Missions* 15 (1926): 402–17. For a somewhat different version, see Oldham, "The Population Question in Africa," 1926, typescript in School of Oriental and African Studies, Box 206, African—General, Council of British Missionary Societies Archive.

35. Oldham, "Population Question in Africa," 34.

36. Macmillan, *Africa Emergent,* 9–49; Huxley, *African Journey,* 421–23.

37. W. Ormsby-Gore, "The Economic Development of Tropical Africa and Its Effect on the Native Population," *Geographical Journal* 68, no. 3 (1926): 240–53.

38. Penelope Hetherington, *British Paternalism and Africa, 1920–1940* (London: F. Cass, 1978).

39. Despite the widespread acknowledgment of the importance of forced labor, there is no modern comprehensive study of forced labor in this era. A number of regional and local studies exist, but the most complete study remains A. T. Nzula, I. I. Potekhin, and A. Z. Zusmanovich, *Forced Labour in Colonial Africa* (1933; repr., London: Zed, 1979).

40. Raymond Dumett, "Disease and Mortality among Gold Miners of Ghana: Colonial Government and Mining Company Attitudes and Polices, 1900–1938," *Social Science and Medicine* 37, no. 3 (1993): 213–32. For an overview, see John Caldwell, "The Social Repercussions of Colonial Rule: Demographic Aspects," in *Africa under Colonial Domination, 1880–1935,* General History of Africa 7, ed. A. Adu Boahen (London: Heinemann Educational Books, 1985), 458–86.

41. Frederick Cooper, "Conditions Analogous to Slavery: Imperialism and Free Labor Ideology in Africa," in *Beyond Slavery: Explorations of Race, Labor, and Citizenship in Postemancipation Societies,* ed. Frederick Cooper, Thomas Holt, and Rebecca Scott (Chapel Hill: University of North Carolina Press, 2000), 107–49.

42. Megan Vaughan, *Curing Their Ills* (Stanford, CA: Stanford University Press, 1991); Sheldon Watts, *Epidemics and History: Disease, Power and Imperialism* (New Haven, CT: Yale University Press, 1997), 213–68; David Arnold, ed., *Imperial Medicine and Indigenous Societies* (Manchester, UK: Manchester University Press, 1988).

43. Kevin Grant, *A Civilized Savagery: Britain and the New Slaveries in Africa, 1884–1926* (New York: Routledge, 2005), 135–66.

44. Frederick Cooper, *Decolonization and African Society: The Labor Question in French and British Africa* (Cambridge: Cambridge University Press, 1996), 1–170; Alice Conklin, *A Mission to Civilize: The Republican Idea of Empire in France and West Africa, 1895–1930* (Stanford, CA: Stanford University Press, 1997), 38–72, 212–45.

45. Hunt, "'Le Bebe en Brousse,'" 401–32; Echenberg, "'Faire du nègre,'" 95–108; Nicholas Thomas, "Sanitation and Seeing: The Creation of State Power in Early Colonial Fiji," *Comparative Studies in Society and History* 32, no. 1 (1990): 149–70; Lenore Manderson, "Health Services and the Legitimation of the Colonial State: British Malaya, 1786–1941," *International Journal of the Health Services* 17, no. 1 (1987): 91–112.

46. Joseph Hodge, *Triumph of the Expert: Agrarian Doctrines of Development and the Legacies of British Colonialism* (Athens: Ohio University Press, 2007), 119–25.

47. Medical Welfare Work amongst Native Women and Children, 1935, Colonial Office (hereafter cited as CO) 323/1331/11, National Archives, UK (hereafter cited as NA).

48. Carol Summers, "Intimate Colonialism: The Imperial Production of Reproduction in Uganda, 1907–1925," *Signs* 16, no. 41 (1991): 387–407; Jean Allman, "Making Mothers: Missionaries, Medical Officers and Women's Work in Colonial Assante, 1924–1945," *History Workshop* 38, no. 1 (1994): 23–47.

49. Native Women and Children, 1930, CO 323/1067/3, NA; Native Populations, Health and Progress of, 1932, CO 323/1177/21, NA.

50. David Arnold, "Introduction: Disease, Medicine and Empire," in *Imperial Medicine and Indigenous Societies,* ed. David Arnold (Manchester, UK: Manchester University Press, 1988), 1–26. For a discussion of the influenza pandemic, see David Killingray, "A New 'Imperial Disease': The Influenza Pandemic of 1918–19 and Its Impact on the British Empire," *Caribbean Quarterly* 49, no. 4 (2003): 30–49, and Terrence Ranger, "The Influenza Pandemic in Southern Rhodesia: A Crisis of Comprehension," in Arnold, *Imperial Medicine and Indigenous Societies,* 172–88.

51. British Social Hygiene Council, *Empire and Health* 1, no. 1 (1926). For a discussion of colonial medicine and venereal disease in Africa, see Vaughan, *Curing Their Ills,* 39–76, 129–54.

52. Sierra Leone Infant Welfare Work, 1928, Dispatch, 4 December 1928, CO 267/625/10, NA. The grant totaled £2,400 per year.

53. Medical Welfare Work amongst Native Women and Children, NA. For the context of feminist work on Africa, see Barbara Bush, "'Britain's Conscience on Africa': White Women, Race and Imperial Politics in Inter-war Britain," in *Gender and Imperialism,* ed. Clare Midgley (Manchester, UK: Manchester University Press, 1998), 200–223.

54. Howard Johnson, "The West Indies and the Conversion of the British Official Classes to the Development Idea," *Journal of Commonwealth and Comparative Politics* 15, no. 1 (1977): 55–83; Stephen Constantine, *The Making of British Colonial Development Policy, 1914–1940* (London: F. Cass, 1984), 195–266.

55. For the prewar period, in addition to Constantine, *Making of British Colonial Development Policy,* see R. D. Pearce, *The Turning Point in Africa British Colonial Policy, 1938–1948* (London: F. Cass, 1982); D. J. Morgan, *The Official History of Colonial Development,* vol. 1, *The Origins of British Aid Policy, 1924–1945* (Atlantic Highlands, NJ: Humanities Press, 1980); Michael Havinden and David Meredith, *Colonialism and Development: Britain and Its Tropical Colonies, 1850–1960* (London: Routledge, 1993), 187–234.

56. On the war, see J. M. Lee and Martin Petter, *The Colonial Office, War and Development Policy* (London: M. T. Smith for the Institute for Commonwealth Studies, 1982). For the postwar era, see D. J. Morgan, *The Official History of Colonial Development,* vol. 2, *Developing Colonial Resources, 1945–1951* (Atlantic Highlands, NJ: Humanities Press, 1980); Havinden and Meredith, *Colonialism,* 225–318. For an overview of the impact on Africa, see David Killingray and Richard Rathbone, eds., *Africa and the Second World War* (New York: St. Martin's, 1986).

57. Charles Jeffries, *Whitehall and the Colonial Service: An Administrative Memoir, 1939–1956* (London: University of London, published for the Institute of Commonwealth Studies by Athlone, 1972), 9–17; Charles Jeffries, *The Colonial Office* (London: Allen and Unwin, 1956), 24–115; Anthony Kirk-Greene, *On Crown Service: A History of HM Colonial and Overseas Services, 1837–1997* (London: I. B. Tauris, 1999); Lee and Petter, *Colonial Office,* 13–46; Barbara Ingram, "Shaping Opinion on Development Policy: Economists at the Colonial Office during World War II," *History of Political Economy* 24, no. 3 (1992): 689–710; Hodge, *Triumph of the Expert,* 196–206. The Social Services Department, created in 1938 to deal with issues of social welfare in the empire, became the department most directly involved in population issues.

58. The Colonial Service began the campaign in June 1945 and made 4,000 appointments from 1946 to 1948. The Colonial Service reached 11,000 in 1947 and peaked at 18,000 in 1954. Kirk-Greene, *On Crown Service,* 49–53.

59. For a general account of this period, see Kenneth Morgan, *Labour in Power, 1945–1951* (Oxford: Clarendon, 1984), 94–187, and Peter Hennesey, *Never Again: Britain, 1945–1951* (New York: Pantheon, 1993), 119–215. For a discussion of the role of the empire in the postwar era, see John Darwin, *Britain and Decolonization* (New York: St. Martin's, 1988); John Kent, *British Imperial Strategy and the Origins of the Cold War, 1944–49* (Leicester, UK: Leicester University Press, 1993); Partha Sarathi Gupta, *Imperialism and the British Labour Movement, 1914–1964* (New York: Holmes and Meier, 1975), 303–48; P. J. Cain and A. G. Hopkins, *British Imperialism: Crisis and Deconstruction, 1914–1990* (London: Longman, 1993), 263–81.

60. Ronald Hyam, "Africa and the Labour Government, 1945–1951," *Journal of Imperial and Commonwealth History* 16, no. 3 (1988): 148–72; Pearce, *Turning Point,* 90–161; Gupta, *Imperialism and the British Labour Movement,* 309–35; Cooper, *Decolonization and African Society,* 111–24.

61. Frederick Cooper, "Modernizing Bureaucrats, Backward Africans, and the Development Concept," in *International Development and the Social Sciences,* ed. Frederick

Cooper and Randall Packard (Berkeley: University of California Press, 1997), 64–92; A. J. Stockwell, "British Imperial Policy and Decolonization in Malaya, 1942–52," *Journal of Commonwealth and Imperial History* 13, no. 1 (1984): 68–87; Michael Cowen and Robert Shenton, "The Origin and Course of Fabian Colonialism in Africa," *Journal of Historical Sociology* 4, no. 2 (1991): 143–74.

62. Allister Hinds, *Britain's Sterling Colonial Policy and Decolonization, 1939–1958* (Westport, CT: Greenwood, 2001), and Gerald Krozewski, *Money and the End of Empire: British International Economic Policy and the Colonies, 1947–58* (New York: Palgrave, 2001).

63. R. J. Butler, "The Ambiguities of British Colonial Development Policy, 1938–1948," in *Contemporary British History, 1939–1961: Politics and the Limits of Policy,* ed. Anthony Gorst, Lewis Johnson, and W. Scott Lucas (London: Pinter, 1991), 119–40, and Butler, "Reconstruction, Development and the Entrepreneurial State: The British Colonial Model, 1939–1951," *Contemporary British History* 13, no. 4 (1999): 29–55.

64. D. A. Low and A. Smith, "The New Order," in *History of East Africa,* vol. 3, ed. D. A. Low and A. Smith (Oxford: Clarendon, 1976), 12.

65. In addition to Cooper, *Decolonization and African Society,* see Jane Lewis, *Empire State Building: War and Welfare in Kenya, 1925–1952* (Oxford: Oxford University Press, 2000); Roderick Neumann, "The Postwar Conservation Boom in British Colonial Africa," *Environmental History* 7, no. 1 (2002): 22–47; Dorothy Hodgson, "Taking Stock: Ethic Identity and Pastoralist Development in Tanganyika, 1948–1958," *Journal of African History* 41, no. 1 (2000): 55–78; Andres Eckert, "Regulating the Social: Social Security, Social Welfare and the State in Late Colonial Tanzania," *Journal of African History* 45, no. 3 (2004): 467–89; Eric Worby, "Discipline without Oppression: Sequence, Timing and Marginality in Southern Rhodesia's Post-war Development Regime," *Journal of African History* 41, no. 1 (2000): 101–25.

66. Christopher Bonneuil talks about the creation of the developmentalist state in colonial Africa in "Development as Experiment: Science and State Building in Late Colonial and Postcolonial Africa, 1930–1970," *Osiris* 15, no. 1 (2000): 258–81. Also see James Scott, *Seeing Like a State* (New Haven, CT: Yale University Press, 1998), 223–63. For the limits of colonial state building, see Bruce Berman, "The Perils of Bula Matari: Constraint and Power in the Colonial State," *Canadian Journal of African Studies* 31, no. 3 (1997): 556–70, and John Darwin, "What Was the Late Colonial State?" *Itinerario* 23, nos. 3–4 (1999): 73–82. For French programs, see Monica van Beusekom, *Negotiating Development: African Farmers and Colonial Experts at the Office du Niger, 1920–1960* (Portsmouth, NH: Heinemann, 2002).

67. Ralf Dahrendorf, *LSE: A History of the London School of Economics and Political Science, 1895–1995* (Oxford: Oxford University Press, 1995), 249–66; Jose Harris, *William Beveridge: A Biography* (Oxford: Clarendon, 1997), 277–83; Eugene Grebenik, "Demographic Research in Britain," *Population Studies* 45, supplement, "Population Research in Britain" (1991): 7–10; "Memoir: R. R. Kuczynski," *Population Studies* 1, no. 4 (1948): 471–72; David Glass, "Robert Rene Kuczynski," *Journal of the Royal Statistical Society* 110, no. 4 (1947): 383–84.

68. Robert Kuczynski, *Colonial Population* (London: Oxford University Press, 1937); Kuczynski, *The Cameroons and Togoland* (London: Oxford University Press, 1939).

69. Population Problems in the Colonies, 1937, CO 323/1523/1, NA.

70. Memo from Robert Kuczynski, Personnel for Reorganization of Colonial Population and Vital Statistics, 7 December 1944, Demography 1943–44, CO 927/10/1, NA; Proposal for Population Count in Nigeria, 1944–45, CO 859/126/3, NA.

71. Social Service-Census, 1944, CO 859/125/8, NA.

72. In addition, G. M. Culwick, the ethnographer and colonial official who coauthored a series of groundbreaking studies of African population, became a member. The group also enrolled staff from the Colonial Office whose work focused on the West Indies and Africa. Demography, 1943–44, CO 927/10/1, NA.

73. Minute by W. F. Searle, 19 January 1950, Staff Training of Colonial Government Statisticians, 1950, CO 852/1076/1, NA; Appointment of Statisticians General, 1948–50, CO 877/39/2, NA; Conference of Colonial Government Statisticians, 1951–53, CO 1042/146, NA.

74. Kathleen Paul, *Whitewashing Britain: Race and Citizenship in the Post-war Era* (Ithaca, NY: Cornell University Press, 1997).

75. Karl Ittmann, "The Colonial Office and the Population Question in the British Empire, 1918–1962," *Journal of Imperial and Commonwealth History* 27, no. 3 (1999): 68–74.

76. Glen O'Hara, "'We Are Faced Everywhere with a Growing Population': Demographic Change and the British State, 1955–64," *Twentieth Century British History* 15, no. 3 (2004): 243–66.

77. Soloway, *Demography,* 312–62; Jay Winter, "Population, Economists and the State: The Royal Commission on Population, 1944–49," in *The State and Economic Knowledge: The American and British Experiences,* ed. Mary Furner and Barry Supple (Cambridge: Cambridge University Press, 1990), 436–60; Pat Thane, "Population Politics in the Post-war British Culture," in *Moments of Modernity: Reconstructing Britain, 1945–1964,* ed. Becky Conekin, Frank Mort, and Chris Waters (London: River Oram, 1999), 114–33.

78. Dennis Hodgson, "Demography as Social Science and Policy Science," *Population and Development Review* 9, no. 1 (1983): 1–33; John Sharpless, "World Population Growth, Family Planning, and American Foreign Policy," *Journal of Policy History* 7, no. 1 (1995): 72–102; Dennis Hodgson, "Orthodoxy and Revisionism in American Demography," *Population and Development Review* 14, no. 4 (1988): 541–67; Susan Greenhalgh, "The Social Construction of Population Science," *Comparative Studies in Society and History* 38, no. 1 (1996): 26–65; Simon Szreter, "The Idea of the Demographic Transition and the Study of Fertility Change: A Critical Intellectual History," *Population and Development Review* 19, no. 4 (1993): 659–701.

79. John Kent, "Bevin's Imperialism and the Idea of Euro-Africa," in *British Foreign Policy, 1945–56,* ed. M. Dockrill and John Young (New York: St. Martin's, 1989), 47–76.

80. A. Walter, a government statistician, estimated African population growth at 1 to 1.5 percent per year in his testimony to the Kenyan Land Commission in 1933. Other reports in the mid-1940s estimated rates as high as 2 percent a year. A. R. Robertson, "The Human Situation in East Africa," *East African Medical Journal* 34, no. 2 (1947): 81–97; S. J. K. Baker, "The Distribution of Native Population over East Africa," *Africa: Journal of the International African Institute* 10, no. 1 (1937): 37–54; Lord Hailey, *An African Survey* (London: Macmillan, 1938), 811–13.

81. F. Dixey, "The Distribution of Population in Nyasaland, *Geographical Review* 18, no. 2 (1928): 274–90; C. R. Niven, "Some Nigerian Population Problems," *Geographical Journal* 85, no. 1 (1936): 54–58.

82. David Killingray estimates that 500,000 Africans served in imperial military units from 1939 to 1945, the vast majority as laborers and construction workers. Killingray, "Labour Mobilization in British Colonial Africa for the War Effort, 1939–46," in Killingray and Rathbone, *Africa and the Second World War,* 68–96. Kenneth Vickery, "The Second World War Revival of Forced Labor in the Rhodesias," *International Journal of African Studies* 22, no. 3 (1989): 423–37.

83. M. Perham to Warden of Nuffield College, 10 October 1939, Nuffield College Proposed Labour Investigation—Africa—1939, CO 847/17/12, NA.

84. See Meshack Owino's chapter in this volume.

85. Proposal for Population Count in Nigeria, 1944–45, CO 859/126/3, NA.

86. A. T. Culwick, "The Population Trend," *Tanganyika Notes and Records* 11 (1941): 13–17; A. T. Culwick and G. M. Culwick, "A Study of Population in Ulanga, Tanganyika Territory," *Sociological Review* 30, no. 4 (1938): 365–79, and *Sociological Review* 31, no. 1 (1939): 25–43. Colonial officials paid attention to such reports. One official argued that "this population report seems to me to be of greatest importance and interest." Papers Tanganyika, 1938 Publications, CO 691/167/10, NA.

87. Extract of letter from J. Huxley to Oliver Stanley, 17 July 1943, Birth Control West Africa, 1943, CO/859/62/17, NA.

88. Andrew Cohen to J. B. Williams, 16 February 1945, Demography—Social Service Research, 1945, CO 927/10, NA.

89. Standards of Living in Relation to Population Problems in Middle East and Central Africa, 1948, CO/927/73/1, NA; E. D. Pridie, The Effect of Raising the Standard of Living on Population, Working Party on Food Supplies and Communism, 1949, CO 537/4472, NA.

90. T. H. Davey, The Growth of Tropical Populations, Meetings and Papers of Colonial Advisory Medical Committee, 1948, CO 859/152/4, NA.

91. C. J. Martin, "The East African Population Census, 1948: Planning and Enumeration," *Population Studies* 3, no. 3 (1949): 303–20; R. Mansell Prothero, "The Population Census of Northern Nigeria, 1952: Problems and Results," *Population Studies* 10, no. 2 (1952): 166–83.

92. L. T. Badenhurst, "Population Distribution and Growth in African," *Population Studies* 5, no. 1 (1951): 23–34; A. T. Grove, "Soil Erosion and Population Problems in South-East Nigeria," *Geographical Journal* 117, no. 3 (1951): 291–304; J. F. M. Middleton and D. J. Greenland, "Land and Population in West Nile District, Uganda," *Geographical Journal* 120, no. 4 (1954): 446–55; Glenn Trewartha and Wilber Zelinsky, "Population Patterns in Tropical Africa," *Annals of the Association of American Geographers* 44, no. 2 (1954): 135–62; W. B. Morgan, "Farming Practices, Settlement Patterns and Population Density in South-Eastern Nigeria," *Geographical Journal* 121, no. 3 (1955): 320–33; Trewartha, "New Population Maps of Uganda, Kenya, Nyasaland and Gold Coast," *Annals of the Association of American Geographers* 47, no. 1 (1957): 1–58. Government statisticians in the early 1950s estimated Nigeria's population growth at 1.3 percent to 1.7 percent per year, the Gold Coast at 2.0 percent, and the Central African Federation at 2.8 percent. R. A. Cooper to the Secretary of the East Africa Royal Commission, 7 July 1953, 2nd Conference of Colonial Government Statisticians, 1953–54, CO 1034/16, NA. The governor of Southern Rhodesia claimed that his territory had one of the highest growth rates in world, which led to pressure on the land. Governor of Southern Rhodesia to Secretary of State, 9 November 1950, Affairs in Southern Rhodesia, 1950, CO 936/62/3, NA. A UN study in 1951 noted population pressure in the Gold Coast (Ghana), Nyasaland (Malawi), and Kenya. Note on Land Distribution in the African Territories, Special Committee on Information Submitted by NSGT Land Distribution, 1951, CO 936/46/1, NA.

93. Fiona Mackenzie, "Contested Ground: Colonial Narratives and the Kenyan Environment, 1920–1945," *Journal of African Studies* 26, no. 4 (2000): 698–718.

94. David Throup, *Economic and Social Origins of Mau-Mau* (Athens: Ohio University Press, 1988); John McCracken, "Conservation and Resistance in Colonial Malawi: The 'Dead North' Revisited," in *Social History and African Environments,* ed. William Beinart and Joann McGregor (Athens: Ohio University Press, 2003), 155–74; L. Cliffe, "Nationalism and the Reaction to Enforced Agricultural Change in Tanganyika during the

Colonial Period," in *Socialism in Tanganyika: An Interdisciplinary Reader,* ed. L. Cliffe and J. Saul (Nairobi: East African Publishing House, 1972), 17–24.

95. Note on Land Distribution in the African Territories, NA.

96. European representatives from East Africa raised the issue at the East African Medical Conference in 1945. In August 1946, another representative met with Robert Kuczynski and Andrew Cohen, then under-secretary of state for the colonies, to press for a census in East Africa. In August 1947, the Fabian Colonial Bureau wrote to Creech Jones to raise the question of overpopulation in the region. Memo on Colonial Medical Policy, 1945–48, CO 859/155/1, NA; Notes of a Meeting, 14 August 1946, Papers of E. B. Worthington, MSS Africa since 1425, Box 5, File 3, Rhodes House, Oxford; Letter from the Fabian Colonial Bureau to A. Creech Jones, 24 April 1947, Greenridge Papers, MSS British Empire since 1877, 285 Box 14, File 2, Rhodes House, Oxford.

97. *Land and Population in East Africa: An Exchange between the Secretary of State and the Governor of Kenya on the Appointment of a Royal Commission* (London: HMSO, 1952).

98. East Africa Royal Commission, *Report* (London: HMSO, 1955), 30–40.

99. Kirk Arden Hoppe, *Lords of the Fly: Sleeping Sickness Control in British East Africa, 1900–1960* (Westport, CT: Greenwood, 2003), 105–42. In one case in Nigeria, officials hoped to create a forest reserve in the evacuated area. Report by Dr. T. A. M. Nash, Anchua Rural Development and Resettlement Scheme, 1946–47, CO 583/296/3, NA.

100. East Africa Agricultural Policy, 1951, CO 691/215, NA. For a discussion of such schemes, see Scott, *Seeing Like a State,* 225–29, and Bonneuil, "Development as Experiment," 261–69.

101. Resettlement of Africans from Overpopulated Areas, 1951, CO 583/311/4, NA; Congested Areas in Cholo District Nyasaland, 1944–45, CO 525/196/2, NA; Resettlement of Africans from Overpopulated Area, 1947–48, CO 583/296/4, NA; Uganda Protectorate Agricultural Development and Resettlement Schemes, 1953, CO 892/15/8, NA.

102. For more on the Kigezi plan, see Grace Carswell, *Cultivating Success in Uganda: Kigezi Farmers and Colonial Policies* (Athens: Ohio University Press, 2007), 59–62.

103. Chris Youe, "Rebellion and Quiescence: Kenyan and Rhodesian Responses to Forced Removals in the 1950s," in *Agency and Action in Colonial Africa: Essays for John Flint,* ed. Chris Youe and Tim Stapleton (Houndmills, UK: Palgrave, 2001), 172–94.

104. Note on Land Distribution in the African Territories, NA.

105. Throup, *Economic and Social Origins,* 120–38.

106. Grace Carswell, "Multiple Historical Geographies: Responses and Resistance to Colonial Conservation Schemes in East Africa," *Journal of Historical Geography* 32, no. 2 (2006): 398–421.

107. A. T. Lennox-Boyd to Reverend R. W. Sorenson, 22 November 1951, The Resettlement of Africans from Birom in the Jos Division of Nigeria, 1951, CO 554/370, NA.

108. Helen Tilley, "African Environments and Environmental Sciences: The African Research Survey, Ecological Paradigms and British Colonial Development, 1920–1940," in Beinart and McGregor, *Social History and African Environments,* 109–30.

109. E. B. Worthington, *Science in Africa* (1938; repr., New York: Negro Universities Press, 1969), and Sir A. Daniel Hall, *The Improvement of Native Agriculture in Relation to Population and Public Health* (London: Oxford University Press, 1936). For a discussion of this discourse, see Melissa Leach and Robin Mearns, eds., *The Lie of the Land: Challenging Received Wisdom on the African Environment* (Oxford: International African Institute in association with James Currey, 1996), and David Anderson, "Depression, Dust Bowl, Demography and Drought: The Colonial State and Soil Conservation in East Africa during the 1930s," *African Affairs* 83, no. 332 (1984): 321–41.

110. Hodge, *Triumph of the Expert*, 146–66, 180–96, 231–51; Hodgson, "Taking Stock," 56–57; Worby, "Discipline," 104–5; McCracken, "Conservation and Resistance," 163–73. The British extended this critique to African's relationship to forests and wild game. See Neumann, "Postwar Conservation," 31–35; James Fairhead and Melissa Leach, "Rethinking the Forest Savanna Mosaic: Colonial Science and Its Relics in West Africa," in Leach and Mearns, *The Lie of the Land*, 105–23.

111. The geographer Robert Steel, whose work was supported by Colonial Welfare and Development funds, warned of erosion and soil exhaustion as a consequence of population pressure in Gold Coast and Sierra Leone. R. W. Steel, "Some Geographical Problems of Land Use in West Africa," *Transactions and Papers of the Institute of British Geographers* 14 (1948): 27–42, and Steel, "The Population of Ashanti: A Geographical Analysis," *Geographical Journal* 112, nos. 1–3 (1948): 64–77.

112. Hodge, *Triumph of the Expert*, 206–51.

113. Throup, *Economic and Social Origins*, 6–8, 77; Anderson, "Depression, Dust Bowl," 325–26.

114. Cooper, *Decolonization and African Society*, 43–56, 208–16; Throup, *Economic and Social Origins*, 72–77.

115. Memo by Colonial Office, Native Land Tenure, CSSRC Minutes and Papers, 1944, CSSRC (44) 33, CO 901/1, NA.

116. Memo by J. K. Greer, 11 March 1948, Growth of Tropical Populations, 1949, CO 859/154/6, NA.

117. Worby, "Discipline," 109–11.

118. Minute by Francis, 18 March 1948, Growth of Tropical Population, 1949, CO 859/154/6, NA.

119. By one estimate, officials devoted £3 million to resettlement and agricultural schemes in Kenya from 1945 to 1950. UN Report on Non-Self-Governing Territories Settlement Policies, 1951, A/AC.35.L.61, 17 October 1951, Special Committee on Information Submitted by NSGT, Land Distribution, 1951, CO 936/46/1, NA.

120. David Anderson, *Histories of the Hanged: The Dirty War in Kenya and the End of Empire* (New York: W. W. Norton, 2005), 119–51, Throup, *Economic and Social Origins*, 91–119.

121. Anderson, *Histories of the Hanged*, 122–25, 235–38, 293–97; David Percox, *Britain, Kenya, and the Cold War: Imperial Defense, Colonial Security, and Decolonization* (London: I. B. Tauris, 2004), 60–63, Caroline Elkins, *Imperial Reckoning: The Untold Story of Britain's Gulag in Kenya* (New York: Henry Holt, 2005), 103–6, 116–17, 125–30, 265–68.

122. William Adams and David Anderson, "Irrigation before Development: Indigenous and Induced Change in Agricultural Water Management in East Africa" *African Affairs* 87, no. 349 (1988): 520. The Hola camp, the site of a massacre of detainees, provided labor to one of these projects. See Elkins, *Imperial Reckoning*, 345–46.

123. Cooper, "Modernizing Bureaucrats," 78–81; Lewis, *Empire State Building*, 363–73.

124. Richard Symonds, *The British and Their Successors* (Evanston, IL: Northwestern University Press, 1966), 119–208.

125. Kirk-Greene, *On Crown Service*, 64–91; Hodge, *Triumph of the Expert*, 251–53.

126. For the background to the creation of the DTC and ODM, see D. J. Morgan, *The Official History of Colonial Development*, vol. 3, *A Reassessment of British Aid Policy*, and vol. 4, *Changes in British Aid Policy* (Atlantic Highlands, NJ: Humanities Press, 1980), 236–70 and 13–32.

127. Richard Stephens, *Population Pressures in Africa South of the Sahara* (Washington, DC: Population Research Project, George Washington University, 1958); K. M. Barbour

and R. M. Prothero, eds., *Essays on African Population* (New York: Praeger 1962); Frank Lorimer, *Demographic Information on Tropical Africa* (Boston: Boston University Press, 1961).

128. For example, see T. E. Smith, ed., *The Politics of Family Planning in the Third World* (London: Allen and Unwin, 1973).

129. Grebenik, "Demographic Research," 22.

130. William Brass, Ansley Coale, Paul Demeny, Don Heisel, Frank Lorimer, Anatole Romaniuk, Etienne Van De Walle, *The Demography of Tropical Africa* (Princeton, NJ: Princeton University Press, 1968).

131. See John Caldwell, "Introduction," in *The Population of Tropical Africa,* ed. John Caldwell and Chukuka Okonjo (New York: Columbia University Press, 1968), 3–27.

132. Robert Steel, "Problems of Population Pressure in Tropical Africa," *Transactions of the Institute of British Geographers* 49 (1970): 1–14; Thomas Dow, "Fertility and Family Planning in Africa," *Journal of Modern African Studies* 8, no. 3 (1970): 445–57; D. Ian Pool, "The Development of Population Policies," *Journal of Modern African Studies* 9, no. 1 (1971): 91–105.

133. Donald Warwick, *Bitter Pills: Population Policies and Their Implementation in Eight Developing Countries* (Cambridge: Cambridge University Press, 1982). On Africa, see John Caldwell, "Family Planning in Continental Sub-Saharan Africa," in Smith, *Politics of Family Planning,* 50–66; Lisa Richey, "Family Planning and the Politics of Population in Tanzania: International to Local Discourse," *Journal of Modern African Studies* 37, no. 3 (1999): 457–87; Amy Kaler, "A Threat to the Nation and a Threat to the Men: The Banning of Depo-Provera in Zimbabwe, 1981," *Journal of Southern African Studies* 24, no. 2 (1998): 347–76.

134. Firoze Manju and Carl O'Coil, "The Missionary Position: NGO's and Development in Africa," *International Affairs* 78, no. 3 (2003): 567–83.

135. John Hailey, "Ladybirds, Missionaries and NGO's: Voluntary Organizations and Co-operatives in 50 Years of Development—A Historical Perspective on Future Challenges," *Public Administration and Development* 19, no. 5 (1999): 467–86; John Stuart, "Overseas Mission, Voluntary Service and Aid to Africa: Max Warren, the Church Missionary Society and Kenya, 1945–1963," *Journal of Imperial and Commonwealth History* 36, no. 3 (2008): 527–43.

136. Susanne Klausen, "The Imperial Mother of Birth Control: Marie Stopes and the South African Birth Control Movement, 1930–1950," in *Colonialism and the Modern World,* ed. Gregory Blue, Martin Bunton, and Ralph Crozier (Armonk, NY: M. E. Sharpe, 2002), 182–99.

137. The English writer Elspeth Huxley and the former director of the Kenyan Medical Service, A. R. Patterson, both raised the issue of the high birthrate of Africans in the colony and suggested improved education and health services as means of transforming African attitudes and encouraging the limitation of family size. Huxley cited in Lewis, *Empire State Building,* 183; A. R. Patterson, "The Human Situation in East Africa: Part I—On the Increase of the People," *East African Medical Journal* 24, no. 2 (1947): 81–97.

138. Tanzania was formed by the union of Tanganyika and Zanzibar in 1964.

139. SP/FPA A21/1, General Correspondence, Africa, 1952–1960, Family Planning Association Papers, Contemporary Medical Archives Center, UK. Also see Beryl Suitters, *Be Brave and Angry: Chronicles of the International Planned Parenthood Federation* (London: International Planned Parenthood Federation, 1973), 136–41.

140. Margaret Hadley, an IPPF member who worked with the Colonial Office, noted: "In East Africa . . . facilities for proper medical control are limited but demand is growing;

in small upcountry stations there are no European chemist shops, only the local 'duka.'" Population—General Information and Enquiries, 1957–9, CO/859/1026, NA.

141. In 1965, the ODM gave the IPPF a Colonial Development and Welfare grant of £7,625, which grew to £12,980 in 1966–67, including £6,000 for an IPPF regional office for East Africa at Nairobi. This grant increased to £50,000 for 1967–68 and for 1968–69, with a further increase to £100,000 per year for the next two years. Draft Memo on Population Policy and UK Aid by R. H. Cassen, Population Control General Policy Part A, 1967–69, Overseas Development Ministry (hereafter cited as OD) 25/222, NA; Population Control Cooperation with IPPF Part A, 1967–69, OD 25/233, NA; Cooperation with IPPF 1973–75, OD 62/59, NA.

142. Brief for Economic Commission for Africa, 8th Session, Lagos, February 1967, Population Control General Policy Part A, 1967–69, OD 25/222, NA.

143. In addition to Kenya, the countries of Malawi, Gambia, and Ghana received aid. Family Planning, The Gambia, 1970–72, OD 30/312, NA.

144. Fred Sai, "Changing Perspectives of Population in Africa and International Responses," *African Affairs* 87, no. 347 (1988): 267–76.

145. Barbara Brown, "Facing the 'Black Peril': The Politics of Population Control in South Africa," *Journal of Southern African Studies* 13, no. 2 (1987): 256–73; Michael White, "Nationalism, Race and Gender: The Politics of Family Planning in Zimbabwe, 1957–1990," *Social History of Medicine* 7, no. 3 (1994): 447–71; Amy Kaler, *Running after Pills: Politics, Gender, and Contraception in Colonial Zimbabwe* (Portsmouth, NH: Heinemann, 2003), 43–56.

146. John Iliffe, *The African Poor: A History* (Cambridge: Cambridge University Press, 1987). For a more extreme version, see Jared Diamond, *Collapse: How Societies Choose to Fail or Succeed* (New York: Viking, 2005), 311–28.

147. Szreter, "Idea of the Demographic Transition," 659–701.

148. Eric Ross, *The Malthus Factor: Poverty, Politics and Population in Capitalist Development* (London: Zed Books, 1998); John Perkins, *Geopolitics and the Green Revolution: Wheat, Genes and the Cold War* (New York: Oxford University Press, 1997); Nick Cullather, "Miracles of Modernization: The Green Revolution and the Apotheosis of Technology," *Diplomatic History* 28, no. 2, (2004): 227–54.

149. Frank Furedi, *Population and Development: A Critical Introduction* (New York: St. Martin's, 1997).

150. Cooper, *Decolonization and African Society,* 323–86. For this process within Britain, see Chris Waters, "'Dark Strangers' in Our Midst: Discourses of Race and Nation in Britain, 1947–1963," *Journal of British Studies* 36, no. 2 (1997): 207–38.

151. In addition to Cordell and Gregory's work, see *African Historical Demography,* vols. 1 and 2, ed. Christopher Fyfe and David McMaster (Edinburgh: African Studies Centre, University of Edinburgh, 1977 and 1981). See also Helge Kjekshus, *Ecology Control and Economic Development in East African History: The Case of Tanganyika, 1850–1950* (London: Heinemann, 1977); Gavin Kitching, "Proto-industrialization and Demographic Change: A Thesis and Some Possible African Implications," *Journal of African History* 24, no. 2 (1983): 221–40; Juhani Koponen, *People and Production in Late Precolonial Tanzania: History and Structures* (Helsinki: Finnish Historical Society, 1988); Gwyn Campbell, "The State and Pre-colonial Demographic History: The Case of Nineteenth-Century Madagascar," *Journal of African History* 32, no. 3 (1991): 415–45.

3

How to Count the Subjects of Empire?

Steps toward an Imperial Demography in French West Africa before 1946

RAYMOND R. GERVAIS AND ISSIAKA MANDÉ

The gathering of population data contributed to the birth of official statistics in European states,[1] and as such, it assured the preeminence of modern state structures in the management of human resources. In contrast, colonial expansion constituted a privileged ground on which to test and practice mercantilist-inspired ideologies. Commercial and demographic statistics about the colonies would both underscore the success of the imperial enterprise and serve as a measure of its wealth. Such statistics would slowly come to be important components of the ideological toolbox of symbols of power. Population counts, the extension of the boundaries of sovereign authority that they represented, and levels of colonial commerce would all be used as justifications for the human and economic costs of the colonial adventure.

At a global level, the relative simplicity of these numbered profiles veiled local-level ambiguities and complexities stemming from the statistical operations of an administration toiling to impose the practices of the modern state. In the wake of military conquests and administration, civil authorities were left to construct modernity despite the lack of personnel, credit, and framing structures. The pyramidal organization of these structures of colonial management, first elaborated at the end of the nineteenth century, were responsible for enhancing programs and financing them by means of the head (or poll) tax. From this time on, population enumeration became an enormous administrative concern, most notably in order to assert authority over colonial populations; create taxation lists, forced labor rolls,[2] and conscription lists; organize health services; recruit workers; and allocate agricultural quotas.

Based on our earlier research,[3] this essay identifies and analyzes preliminary steps in the creation of a colonial demography of French West Africa (AOF). Although preoccupied, like Great Britain, with justifying its African conquests at the end of the nineteenth century, France mimicked metropolitan practices in the colonies and made unrealistic demands, for reasons and in ways that remain to be satisfactorily explained. It is not by chance that we have chosen the period prior to 1947 for our study, a period that demographers of the time would have qualified as prescientific. From the conquest to the first attempts at postwar "development," the colonial administration constantly had to expand its reach while at the same time identifying and exploiting colonial resources. The latter was termed a process of *mise en valeur*, or "deriving value." The administration issued directives, such as *faire du noir*, or "doing with blacks," repeatedly enunciated by governors general of French West Africa and lieutenant governors of its constituent colonies. It also devoted substantial effort to launching the census as a means of exploiting both resources and populations.[4]

Beginning with the military conquest, the act of counting, whatever its technical modalities, was perceived as one of the tools for transferring sovereignty from traditional chieftaincies to French soldiers. Asking about the number of inhabitants in a conquered village took on multiple dimensions, both symbolic and real, since it measured the success and rhythm of the penetration of civilization into the last outposts of "savagery." More concretely, recording numbers allowed colonial authorities and colonial powers to splash their colors across colonial maps. Even if traditional local authorities did not immediately understand the enumeration, just as they did not understand the treaties presented for their signatures, estimates of the number of their subjects, whether falsified or true, went hand in hand with reports on pacification.

With the transfer from military to civil authority, an important transformation occurred: for the authorities of French West Africa, the census became a central part of the relationship between an administrator and his subjects. It was no longer simply a question of reporting how many people had been conquered; it was now a matter of scientifically underscoring the rights and responsibilities of French colonial subjects. Our analysis shows that the quantitative and qualitative weaknesses of the colonial administration, coupled with the slow pace of improvement, created a gap between the central administration's high expectations and the limited capabilities on the ground. Instead of developing a statistical demography, the multilayered government in French West Africa could at best produce inventories of its population, similar to the inventories of resources reported in the earliest administrative guides sent out by the Colonial Office and the Ministry of Colonies.

This essay does not concentrate on the scientific merit of colonial population data, which preoccupied French demographers from the interwar period through the 1950s. Rather, it focuses on the origins of and the concrete methodologies and procedures associated with the production of demographic statistics for French West Africa.

Prehistory of Colonial Statistics: The Numerical Census

Historians will never know with certainty how the chiefs of villages or heads of kingdoms understood questions asked by French conquerors about how many people they ruled. Misunderstandings undoubtedly tainted the first exchanges between conquerors and conquered. It is most likely that the answers to such questions grew out of the value systems of local societies. The demographic, economic, and anthropological literatures on Africa all underscore the importance given to sociodemographic reproduction. In an environment of low demographic density,[5] stemming from both historical and health conditions,[6] the need for descendants at the social level and control of one's dependants at the sociopolitical level dominated all aspects of social relations. Power was associated with both the number of subjects in the society at large and the number of subordinates within individual lineages.

At first glance, the numerical census of the first half of the colonial era appears to represent a primitive stage in the deployment of the colonial administration; characteristically the count was most often but not exclusively undertaken by military authorities.[7] The rudimentary statistical approximations signaled a nascent bureaucracy whose capacities and need for information were limited. These approximations were subject not only to underestimation but also, and we must exercise certain caution here, to overestimation, which can be understood only in reference to indigenous models of power, particularly those common to lineage-based agricultural societies. Analysis must also contend with another misrepresentation: the imposition of the nominal census, which recorded inhabitants by name, did not take place within the time limits prescribed by decrees and directives. The elusiveness of the methodologies put in place persisted longer in some administrative districts and colonies than others.[8]

To illustrate backward practices, it is telling to review the comments of new administrators, who often painted a damning picture of their predecessors to promote themselves in the eyes of their superiors. For example, Lieutenant Governor Edouard Hesling, newly arrived in Upper Volta in 1919, objected to the practices he encountered: "Presently, if we request an item of information about the colony's demography, local authorities must refer either to the taxation lists, whose numbers have been inflated by a certain proportion, and then added to the nontaxable segment of the population; the Delafosse statistics; or [those from] the *Annuaires de l'Afrique Occidentale Française* [the *French West Africa Statistics Yearbooks*]."[9] In a single paragraph, Hesling touched upon several questionable administrative practices—censuses extracted from taxation lists, the continued use of numerical as opposed to nominative censuses, and circular reasoning. He would pursue his exploration of methods in his 1923 annual report: "Notably, in Upper Volta, censuses dated back approximately six, ten or twelve years, to which were added supplementary estimates obtained through questions asked of simple village chiefs or notables and recorded without the least critical analysis. Or the number of inhabitants of a particular group was calculated by multiplying the number of huts by a certain number of inhabitants per hut, and so on."[10] The governor general of French West Africa himself elaborated on these observations when, in 1922, he issued a directive denouncing the continued practice of conducting numerical censuses, or simple headcounts, despite repeated directives to record people by name. In an eloquent overview, he identified the most frequent technical biases of the numerical census:

> Sometimes the census agent limited [his activities] to counting the number of huts in a village, which he then multiplied by a given coefficient, presumably representing the average number in a family. In other instances, he gathered only the names of the household heads for each hut, and only individuals who made up this domestic group were the object of a purely numeric census. Sometimes, they registered the names of each person in the entire population. The procedures employed during the census, and the means employed were not clearly set out. A few district officers were satisfied with declarations reported by the county or village chiefs, while others preferred to use indigenous interpreters and guards because their evaluations seemed more sincere than the declarations of interested parties. Finally, the responsibility for carrying out the census was sometimes left to the European census agents present on site.[11]

This vagueness in methods persisted and was commented on in many other directives. Attempting to bring uniformity to the process required considerable effort. And tracking and analyzing how it developed presents a particular challenge to historians.

Very quickly, however, informants and village or clan chiefs came to understand that the act of enumerating was not without consequences; in many ways, it was an attempt to transfer sovereignty from the former authorities to the new rulers.[12] The head tax, levied first in kind and then in currency, and the levy of workers to meet the recruitment goals underscored the weighty implications of estimates produced first by the military and then by census agents. In response, people throughout French West Africa resorted to dissimulation, flight, inertia, and many other forms of resistance. The administration reacted by adopting a more reliable approach—the nominal census, which recorded people by name. This transformation demanded more administrators, the formulation of new directives, and more reliable methodologies.

Founding Act: The Ministerial Directive of 1909

The elaboration of methodologies for collecting demographic data in the French Empire was the work of multiple economic and scientific interest groups. The

Office Colonial (Colonial Office) had been created by decree on 14 March 1899. Like the Imperial Institute, its British counterpart, it played the role of propaganda agent for economic interests of the state and the private sector.[13] The Colonial Office's first task was to "to centralize and make available to the public a wide range of information about the agriculture, commerce and industry of the French colonies." Beyond promoting discourse on the imperial necessity of colonialism, the Colonial Office also sounded the alarm about the "depopulation of Africa," thereby underscoring the need to adopt indicators and measures for assessing the population that only a census could provide. With the technical support of the Conseil Supérieur de la Statistique, or the High Council on Statistics, the Colonial Office also defended the collection of uniform and comparable colonial data in order to, among other things, publish yearbooks.[14] The Conseil Supérieur de la Statistique was born of the efforts of mathematicians, demographers, and statisticians who in the nineteenth century developed new techniques for formulating data and imposed common goals to promote international comparability. Established by decree on 19 February 1885, this council became a consultative body to which the Ministry of Trade turned for expertise on statistical matters.

Before examining the impact of data-collection modalities in the field, it is essential to firmly grasp the situation at the center—the Colonial Office. The introduction of an office of imperial propaganda into the apparatus of the state, the restriction of technicians to a strictly consultative role, and the retreat of the ministry nominally responsible for such matters had considerable implications for the ways that population statistics were produced and analyzed in the French Empire. A ministerial directive circulated in 1909 was the ultimate result and symbol of this trend.

In 1904, five years after its creation, the Colonial Office apparently had succeeded in framing the first draft of what soon become a broad agreement "to count" the empire. Indeed, in a directive issued on 27 July of that year, Minister Gaston Doumergue told Martial Merlin, governor general of French West Africa, about his desire for demographic data: "Considering that there is interest in publishing the population data *annually*, [emphasis added] I send you herewith twelve samples of tables devised by the Statistics Service of the Colonial Office, following review by the *Conseil Supérieur de Statistique*."[15] Doumergue's declaration confirmed the intention to formalize what was until then a random collection of data and to organize the operations around an annual nominal censuses. From this point on, the colonial "model" distanced itself from the metropolitan practice of taking a census every five years.[16]

The reaction of French West Africa's administration was immediate and demonstrated the skepticism of men in the field, as this excerpt from the governor general indicates:

> However, I cannot let you remain unaware of the fact that it is
> impossible for the administration of our colonies in Africa to complete

some tables, notably those related to the indigenous population. In vast regions of the interior, only recently come under our influence and still greatly unknown, and where we have just started setting up a relatively simple administrative organization, there does not exist a vital registration system, or any [other] sources of information that would permit the collection of the data required for these tables on the populations of these new territories. How for the provinces of the hinterland, recently subject to our authority, may [we] record among the population men and women, boys and girls, the number of children younger than 15 years old, and [the numbers] of deaths, marriages and divorces?[17]

This discrepancy between the requirements of metropolitan interests and capacities in the field was never raised. Instead, any such discussion was replaced by exchanges about strategies to meet the unrealistic expectations.[18]

The 1904 directive was succeeded by another in 1909.[19] This 204-page document charged *all* French colonies with the responsibility for producing an annual series of data tables on a variety of topics, including population. The requirements went far beyond what was demanded of regional authorities in France itself, who could rely on the support of a massive bureaucracy. Table 3.1 lists the topics that were to be treated in the required demographic tables.[20] Because so many documents have disappeared, it is difficult to uncover the dynamics that gave rise to this directive. Diachronic analysis thus must yield to synchronic examination. Despite these drawbacks, however, such analysis permits us to detect the following concerns about statistics in French West Africa:

- The imposition of colonial administrative divisions as the principal geographic units of reference effectively redefined earlier space for African populations. Beyond the toponymic changes inevitable in the convergence of two linguistic worlds, this creation of new spatial references modeled after radically different criteria of social cartography gave rise to new divisions. This new geoadministrative colonial space led to new definitions of the "Other."[21]

- The directives of 1904 and 1909, both issued by the Colonial Office with the endorsement of the Conseil Supérieur de la Statistique and with administrative support from the ministry, marked fundamental steps toward the privileging of individuals in census declarations. The numerical census had perpetuated the precolonial practice of collective declarations made by the traditional authorities. The new obligation to produce tables classifying populations by variables such as gender and age subdivided these earlier groupings. The act of enumeration became, on the one hand, an indicator of hegemony and marker of sovereignty and,

Table 3.1. Population tables prescribed by the Ministerial Directive of 15 February 1909

Number	Title	Principal characteristics	Classification variables
LIII	Summary table: Composition of the population	Europeans, Indigenous, Métis	Origin, gender, children less than 15 years (by gender)
LIV	Summary table: Population of principal cities	By city: Europeans, Métis, Other races	Origin (French or foreign)
LV	Summary table: European population	Administrative division	Origin, gender, age group
LVI	Summary table: Births among the European population	By parental characteristics: French, Foreign, Indigenous, or Métis	Status of children (legitimate or illegitimate, stillbirths) and gender
LVII	Summary table: Deaths among the European population	Administrative division	Gender and age group
LV1II	Summary table: Marriages among the European population	By partner characteristics: French, Foreign, Indigenous, or Métis	Age of partners
LIX	Summary table: Divorces among the European population	By duration of marriage	Age of partners
LX	Statistics by profession: European population	Administrative division and status (chiefs or isolated; employed or workers)	Sectors and subsectors of activity; origin and gender
LXI	Summary table: Foreign European population	By nationality	Gender and children under 15 years
LXII	Summary table: French and foreign migration in the European population	By nationality	Arrivals, departures, gender, and children less than 15 years
LXIII	Summary table: The nonwhite population	Administrative division	Legal status (French subjects, foreign subjects, "race," gender, and children under 15 years)
LXIV	Summary table: Births among the nonwhite population	Administrative division	Legal status (French subjects, foreign subjects, "race," gender, and children under 15 years)
LXV	Summary table: Deaths among the nonwhite population	Administrative division	Legal status (French subjects, foreign subjects, "race," gender, and children under 15 years)

on the other, a face-to-face encounter between the individual and representatives of colonial authority.[22]

- The classification by legal status and "race" gave way to troubling definitions, as well as new perceptions of the self and others. Take, for example, the directives' definition of Europeans: "We shall consider European populations as all the populations of white race or assimilated, whether born in Europe or not." The nonwhite population (Table 63) was defined only by its opposite: "We shall consider non-European race as all the populations which are not of white race." The first classification was obviously ambiguous, whereas the second directly impinged upon ethnic groups making up the African population. Both obliged those who were counted to fit themselves into categories that were both predetermined and fluid.[23] The definition of self, as well as the notion of the Other, was forever modified.

The most severe critic of this initiative, inspired by the colonial lobby and reinforced by central departments of the Ministry of Colonies, put his finger on the fundamental problem: "In itself, the directive amounted to a document of many hundreds of pages, mandating sixty-five different kinds of tables. The model and framework for the tables were accompanied by demands for very detailed data, along with dates for completing their collection. In addition, the tables had to correspond to numbered sections of the annual reports describing the activities of individual administrative units. The only thing not prescribed in this demented document was how these tables, formulated in Paris, would be completed and by whom."[24] The "how" and "by whom" obsessed the leaders and the administrators of French West Africa until 1947.

Multiple strategies for dealing with these demands punctuate the administrative history of French West Africa from 1909 to 1946. A long list of geographic, social, and methodological obstacles can be cited to explain the predictable failure of the 1909 directive. First and most fundamental was the human factor: French West Africa lacked the administrative competence and technical skill to respond successfully to these demands. In fact, it was necessary to adopt a broad set of regulations and other coercive measures to dissuade African populations from rejecting the "confrontation" elicited by Guy Georgy. Georgy's memoirs included a vivid description of how colonial populations were rounded up and forced to submit to being counted.[25] Such procedures and rules also lent an aura of mystery to the administrative census. Beyond a dearth of competence, administrators did not have the requisite materials or human resources needed to carry out these operations. Table 3.2 highlights quite clearly the very low number of administrators per territorial division relative to the size of local populations.

This table shows that disparities between the colonies in the interior and those on the coast were substantial—even without including data for Niger and

Table 3.2. Shortage of human resources in French West Africa: The total area of the colonies and the number of administered per administrator, 1920

Colony	Area (km²)	Number of people administered per administrator
Senegal	3,000	18,000
Guinea	3,700	25,000
Sudan	5,700	32,000
Ivory Coast	5,000	25,000
Dahomey	2,500	19,000
Upper Volta	8,000	66,000
Average per colony	4,650	31,000

Source: Observations of Lieutenant-Gouvernor Hesling on Picanon's remarks, 1924–1925, rapport no. 124, Mission Picanon, carton 3057, Affaires Politiques, CAOM.

Mauritania, whose administrative resources were the most meager. In Upper Volta, for example, an administrator managed a population and territory twice as large as the average for French West Africa overall. When Upper Volta was created, not enough civil servants were allocated to it. Many departments did not have the required personnel. To counter what became a chronic lack of administrative support, governors of the colony resorted to nepotism by taking on unqualified members of the families of administrators for technical services:[26] "Whenever possible, the wives of civil servants are hired provisionally as '*dames-employees*' to compensate, in a certain measure, for the shortage of a workforce."[27] Moreover, the colony's abysmal reputation among junior administrators assigned to serve their initial terms in Upper Volta discouraged them from requesting a return assignment. The lack of resources also undermined civil servants' motivation to launch administrative initiatives—a limitation amply noted and criticized by administrative inspection delegations from the founding of the colony.

With minimal simplification, we can spell out the main tools developed to facilitate the evolution from a numerical census to a nominal count. The census notebook,[28] or *cahier de recensement,* was a key tool for more critical population estimates because it allowed verification or cross-checking by both administrative and general inspectors. The reports of these officials teem with details about the transition from numerical to nominal censuses. The governor general pulled them together in 1922, facilitating our analysis:

1. Conduct of the nominal census included rounding up the inhabitants of each village, grouping them by household and order of appearance in front of census agents under the authority of the colonial administrators. Each head of household was obliged to declare all dependents for the tax rolls, even if absent, without regard to when they had left. Because heads of household had less power than the

census agents, these procedures, called the *faire le compte* (doing the count), became an administrative tool for exploitation.[29]

2. Census timetables were mandated to encourage long-range planning. In many colonies, the lieutenant governor published directives urging the *commandants de cercle* (local administrators) to adopt a five-year cycle for enumerations in their districts.

3. The training of African census agents became feasible largely because of the spread of primary education in French West Africa.

4. Periodic reflection on the census emanating from various levels of administration not only fueled debate but also led to the emergence and adoption of the only viable solution: the creation of a census service in each colony in French West Africa and the mobilization of technicians. Draft documents discussing such a service had been proposed before 1930, but a clear and complete presentation of this solution appeared only in a letter/directive from Governor General Joseph Jules Brévié on 7 February 1933:"The census will no longer be an operation at the level of the district, but will fall under the colony. A unit of the central administration will assume permanent responsibility for it, and that unit will be assigned one or several teams of census agents . . . who, following a carefully formulated schedule, will direct, coordinate, monitor, and centralize the task."[30] In fact, this plan for a census office in each colony was never realized, largely because French West Africa fell victim to the economic crisis of the 1930s. However, this failure does not in any way undercut the importance of the governor general's vision. It was not forgotten, even if implementation was delayed until 1945.

The *mystique* (mystery) of the census tour also had its own cost. The decision to spread data collection over five years made it impossible to achieve the goal of complete coverage that is a sine qua non of the modern scientific census. The practice also led to the adoption of arbitrary techniques of extrapolation and correction. The "rule of three" exemplified such practices: county X, last enumerated in 1928, was arbitrarily assigned the same rate of growth as county Z, enumerated in 1930, to produce a new population total for county X for 1931. These kinds of limitations and problems made it highly improbable that policies suggested by Governor General Carde in 1927 for assessing the reproduction of human capital in French West Africa would be effectively deployed and evaluated.

Changes in Practice and the Discourse on Reproduction

In 1909, following the conquest of their territory and the imposition of colonial administration, African populations were subjected to military recruitment.[31]

They were also subjected to forced labor demands without compensation and to labor recruitment with little compensation for public works (railroads and other infrastructure projects) and private enterprises such as plantations. The minimal demographic data available at the time would have made it impossible to predict the demographic impact of these and similar labor policies on the age structure of colonial populations.[32]

The French cited the need to suppress slavery, a campaign that began in the late 1880s, as a major justification for the imposition of colonial rule in what became French West Africa. From the outset, the military was called on to extend the conquest and to mobilize a workforce to assist the administration in newly conquered territories and to provide labor for commercial companies. Colonial authorities thus founded *villages de liberté* (freedom villages) to bring together freed slaves. Far from being liberated and despite protest, however, these populations of servile origins, along with other villagers, were forced to provide porters from among their ranks. At the social and psychological levels, this strategy was the best way to manipulate the community-based organization of many African societies and to push people into the emerging labor market. Although the building of transportation infrastructure and railroads in particular eventually made porterage obsolete, these new installations also intensified other forms of economic exploitation.

Local labor requirements levied on African populations, referred to as the *indigénat,* and the financial autonomy mandated by the finance law of 13 April 1900 encouraged the spread of forced labor.[33] Called *prestations,* this system of forced labor was determined to be illegal by the minister of colonies.[34] Nonetheless, it was applied throughout French West Africa, following a ruling by the governor general on 25 November 1912. The need for a workforce to build infrastructure provided the legal rationale for it. Forced labor was justified as in-kind taxation, and each colonial subject had to fulfill an annual obligation of ten to twelve days of *corvée* (labor). The requirement applied to all indigenous adult males, with the exception of those who were auxiliaries of the administration. Nearly twenty years later, in his directive of 12 September 1930, Governor General Carde redefined the obligation as "a direct tax applied to all the inhabitants without distinction of status, payable in currency or in kind depending on the contributor's choice; strictly determined, carefully controlled, elaborately regulated, both in its levels and rates as well as in its various methods of collection."[35] Fiscal pressures on colonial populations grew with the addition of this new "tax" to the existing head tax, which had already provoked substantial flight toward the neighboring English and Portuguese colonies in West Africa.[36]

Local people, along with analysts at the time, tended to view the contrasts between French and British colonialism in Manichaean terms. British authorities were not as quick as the French to resort to overt violence in recruiting the laborers necessary to produce profit. Rather, they allowed the labor market to regulate the flow of migrants. This said, the British did not hesitate to send workers back to their French colonies of origin during downturns in the economy. British labor policies regarding the flow of workers from neighboring French colonies were indeed based just as much on constraint as those of the French. However, the fact that the British refrained from forced labor heightened perceived differences between them and French colonial authorities.

Our goal here is not to put forced labor on trial yet again. That verdict has already been rendered. Rather, we wish to focus on the warnings and concerns raised about these policies in debates at the time. Of primary concern were the risks of depopulation and the failure to adhere to established quotas for recruitment of workers mandated annually by administrative memoranda and directives. Censuses were important for the overall administration of each colonial territory, but they were most critical for determining what proportion of the population would be subjected to colonial labor requirements. Colonial missions dispatched to inspect internal administrative affairs or other missions sent to investigate broader issues focused on whether optimum recruitment targets were respected and the degree to which colonial regimes adhered to the legislation that governed their operations.[37] Beyond these operations, however, the most crucial reports emanated from other missions sent out to inspect health and medical conditions. For example, in his "Rapport sur le danger proche de dépopulation que font courir à l'AOF des recrutements excessifs et mal répartis" (Report on the approaching danger of depopulation that excessive and badly distributed recruitment poses for French West Africa), François Sorel, the officer in charge of such a delegation, underscored the norms set by the administration:

> [According to] data furnished by the offices of emigration . . . : it is not possible to remove more than 2 percent of the population of a territorial group without risk of damaging it. As such, in theory, all of French West Africa, a land of 12 million inhabitants, could be expected to dispatch 240,000 workers or soldiers beyond their homelands. But upon closer examination, this number is excessive for French West Africa. First, we should not include in the 12 million total, either the population of Niger, or that of Mauritania; moreover, the Fulani . . . , who are not suited to military service, are not any more likely to be better workers. Second, given the risk of flight, it is only with great care that indigenous people living adjacent to foreign colonies should be recruited for work camps. Hence, the target for recruitment should, in all fairness, be calculated only on the basis of a population of 9 million. . . . [Even then,] it would be a mistake among a population so psychologically pressured to want to recruit close to 2 percent of the total population of 9 million. Tailoring ourselves carefully to indicators furnished by the recruitment reports of the last 8 years, it seems that aiming for a number from 1 to 1¼ percent would be within reasonable limits. . . . Rather than being allocated according to capacity of each region, recruitment has proceeded with a blindness that later

events suggest is criminal. Hence, we learn that over the course of 3 years in the district of Kong-Korogho, of 17,400 workers who left, [only] 7,693 came back to their village: a mortality rate of 55 percent. I have concluded with certainty that a large number [of them] died after being overworked; a workload was imposed . . . that they could not bear. Twelve percent of the district's population disappeared.[38]

Situations such as this encouraged the adoption of a nominal census in order to rationalize the exploitation of human resources in French West Africa.[39] In the wake of promoting mise en valeur as promulgated by Minister of the Colonies Albert Sarraut in 1921, Carde promoted the slogan *"faire du noir,"*[40] or "doing with blacks."[41] In practice, this campaign adopted a social agenda aimed at strengthening the Assistance Médicale Indigène (Service for Indigenous Medical Care), enhancing the struggle against endemic diseases such as trypanosomiasis or human sleeping sickness, notably important in Upper Volta, and regulating the use of indigenous labor. Around this time, the administration tried to establish rules for recruiting workers. The limits set for each administrative district followed the same guidelines set for military recruitment. Complementing the notion of production with that of reproduction, the governor general acknowledged that ideological preoccupations as well as economic concerns were wrapped up in the *mission civilisatrice,* or "civilizing mission."[42] Concern for both production and reproduction also reflected fear about the demographic future of subject populations, specifically following a famine in 1926. It is not surprising, then, that Carde's directives encouraged reforms in the ways that census data was collected.

However, the economic crisis of 1929 upended these attempts to bring some logic to colonial policies. Assuring the reproduction of human capital required better knowledge of the demographic structures of African populations, made possible by, among other things, a shift from population arithmetic to demographic analysis. Even more important, it depended on a real desire to measure just how policies of labor mobilization impacted the labor force at the level of the village.

From the early 1920s, a few district officers and lieutenant governors denounced the perverse effects of seasonal migration. They also acknowledged that deficiencies in the system for collecting population data made it difficult to assess the effects of such mobility. In 1934, Acting Governor General Pierre Boisson emphasized these ambiguities: "Considering the current state of the censuses, it is obviously difficult to trace exactly variations in the demographic map, and we can thus show only large-scale movements. I do not think that we are currently seeing large-scale migration. The verdict is still out, but right now I believe that the issue of flight— always tracked attentively—does not present a real concern in French West Africa."[43] Beginning with an accurate observation about the shortcomings of the census, Boisson arrived at haphazard conclusions, which were more like expressions of faith than analysis. Moreover, his conclusions contradicted extracts from reports from district officers in Upper Volta, Dahomey, Sudan, Guinea, and Côte d'Ivoire.

Their ambivalent analyses led authorities to take contradictory actions. In order to support their programs safeguarding reproduction in motion, for example, they would have had to take three measures:

- Engage in a rapid, transparent, and broad shift toward reliable, nominal five-year censuses at all levels of the administration;

- Modify their policies for exploiting human and economic resources in accordance with census results; and

- Professionalize the administrative sectors dealing with statistics.

The global economic crisis undermined any move toward the implementation of these utopian initiatives. Indeed, it further weakened a system already limited by the need to be financially self-sufficient. Internal evaluations reveal the large gap between the regulations concerning censuses and workforce recruitment, on the one hand, and the realities on the ground, on the other.

Impact of Weaknesses in the Structure for Collecting Demographic Data

For a long time, the ways in which district officers actually carried out population censuses were obscured by language.[44] Deciphering the linguistic ambiguities—as well as the silences—required a close reading of documents buried in the lower levels of the colonial hierarchy. Initially, it was necessary to determine whether population estimates were based on numerical or nominal censuses; then, one had to figure out if, in some jurisdictions, these numbers were even products of an actual count or if they were extrapolations from data collected earlier. Two complementary sources make it possible to sort out these issues: new district officers who sought to provide more accurate demographic profiles of their districts than their predecessors had compiled and colonial, general, and administrative inspectors who periodically visited the colony.[45] Known as the watchdogs of the empire,[46] the colonial inspectors were best placed to play the role of "detective" because they reported directly to the minister of the colonies or the lieutenant governor of the territory.[47] Their location in the bureaucracy enabled them to witness firsthand the great gap between the sweeping formal authority of the administration and what actually happened on the ground. Furthermore, colonial inspectors were often called upon to investigate specific problems or the performance of local administrations in times of crisis—such as those provoked by droughts or revolts. These investigations often involved detailed analysis of the census books, thus producing observations with important consequences.

The nominal census rightfully played a central role, since it served as the grid for classifying colonial subjects as taxpayers, military recruits, forced laborers, and so on.[48] The head tax weighed heavily on the domestic economy of African households. The determination of whether one was taxable or not proved quite strategic because it was intimately linked to demographic growth. During the initial stages of developing the colonial civil administration, the lack of precision in the census, which served as the basis for taxation lists, frequently provoked bitter observations. In 1905, for instance, Colonial Inspector Louis Verrier wrote:

> It thus seems, according to these repeated declarations, that each
> year of new censuses should allow us to make increasingly accurate
> lists. Unfortunately, a reading of administrative reports included here
> shows that this is not the case, and that the Lieutenant-Governor of
> Upper-Senegal-Niger has confused what was supposed to be done
> and what was actually done. Furthermore, he has mistaken his own
> wishes for realities. Indeed, even though the inspection has observed
> that a census was conducted in 1904 in the district of Timbuktu
> (Report no. 88), it must be underscored that in most other districts,
> due to the lack of recent censuses, the head tax lists were not based
> on credible information.[49]

From this time on, we can trace the issues that haunted scores of colonial reports over the next forty years—those stemming from discrepancies between recommendations and others involving the reality and weight of facts. In 1931–32, when questions were raised about the dismantling of the colony of Upper Volta, and again at the end of 1932, when a famine in Niger was under discussion, Inspector Bernard Sol identified some of the frequent problems and techniques that had been problematic for a long time: incomplete censuses; numerical censuses; incompatibility between the census rolls and the taxation lists; a large number of estimates rather than direct observations; refusal to reduce population totals, regardless of events such as the famine in Niger; and the continued use of the rule of three, which prompted some officials to replace lower population figures with supposed increases in areas that were not even counted.[50]

The continued prevalence of all of these techniques underscored the discrepancies between the census rolls and taxation rolls, two lists that should have been organically and administratively linked. In 1940–41, when important administrative changes were introduced, the mission of Colonial Inspector Jean Bourgois-Gavardin reaffirmed the credo of his predecessors: "The census, as recent and exact as possible, is the essential element and the main source of our knowledge about indigenous populations."[51] He further noted the perpetuation of a classic bias, stating, "We seem to attach only fiscal interest to the census: 'taxable,' 'non-taxable,' that's it. Moreover, the structure of the forms encourages this." He concluded, "We even sometimes seem to not attach any interest at all to the censuses."

The frequently animated dialogues between lieutenant governors and district officers on the ground and the governors general and ministers at the highest levels of the colonial administration were far from sterile. As such, reading the general inspection reports, which allow comparisons between the requisitions and recommendations from high levels of power as well as perspectives from the field, illuminates the evolution of French colonial thought about population. At the beginning, it was the spell or mystery of the census—at first numeric or limited to population totals—that focused demands for information to assess the population and data to formulate policy intervention. This bond was even stronger than the tie linking the census to demands for data to be used in formulating propaganda to underscore the power of the empire.

The demographer-statisticians' awareness of the problems faced by the peoples of French West Africa appeared somewhat obliquely in the compilations of statisticians at the level of the Statistique Générale de France, the general statistical office. For example, in an article presented in 1937 at the International Conference on Population in Paris, Hubert Ulmer correctly suggested that attempts to aggregate data across the French colonial empire were futile. Along with numerous other cautionary recommendations, as well as hints at his preference for data collected by medical doctors, Ulmer issued a challenge: "Given that it is difficult to count the population precisely and produce a complete roster of births and deaths in most of the French colonies, [using] the method of inquiry through interrogation [that is, interviews] seems altogether recommendable. We will have to aim at multiplying these 'surveys,' and, at the same time, adopt a plan that is as uniform as possible everywhere. It is only in this way that comparison of the results from the various colonies can be of use."[52]

Ulmer's wish was fulfilled in 1943 with the creation of the Service Colonial des Statistiques, or the Colonial Statistical Service.[53] And so, important transformations in state agencies and administrative practices did lead to new realities after 1940. By means of Arrêté 1950 PL, a decree dated 26 June 1945, the ministry created the Direction Générale du Plan et de la Statistique, the General Directorate of Planning and Statistics.[54] This new agency signaled that the collection and analysis of statistical data was now a professional endeavor. When young demographers and statisticians developed the first sample surveys in the 1950s, inspired by their British colleagues in Northern Rhodesia, they had to overcome the inherent bias in the metropolitan bureaucracy against the creation of large statistical databases.[55] The newly renamed "overseas territories" became a testing ground for the use of sample surveys, operations that produced a wealth of information about many societies and populations. Indeed, these French researchers devised the methodologies combining ethnographic and demographic data collection that have inspired the contemporary Demographic and Health Surveys and many similar programs.

The shock provoked by this new approach was apparent in debates that are now relegated to the archives and autobiographies of former overseas administrators. In just a few years, practice shifted from three-year intervals in data collection to cycles of five or ten years. This move signaled a new priority for the reliable and up-to-date collection of data for planning purposes.[56] Moreover, it meant that formerly separate data-collection operations had to be linked together and oriented toward clearly identified and measurable goals. In the ensuing years, a fresh generation of statisticians and demographers rallied to these new efforts to understand better the population of colonial France, rebaptized "France d'Outre-Mer," or "Overseas France," after World War II. The focus of the international institutions set up in the wake of the Bretton-Woods accords of the postwar era emphasized economic planning over the collection of demographic data. Nonetheless, it must be underscored that the evolution in the way demographic data were collected in the French Empire, as described in this chapter, led to demands for more rigorous and reliable information not only in France but in the larger international community as well.

Notes

This paper is a longer, revised version of an article entitled "Comment compter les sujets de l'Empire? Les étapes d'une démographie impériale en AOF avant 1946," which appeared in a thematic issue of the historical journal *Vingtième Siècle* 95 (July–September 2007): 63–74. We would like to thank the editors of *Vingtième Siècle* for granting permission to translate and reproduce our essay in this volume. We also wish to express our appreciation to Richard Violette of the Department of Sociology and Anthropology at Concordia University in Montreal, who translated the text into English, and to Dennis D. Cordell, who edited it. Finally, we thank D. Ian Pool and an anonymous reviewer for their very useful comments.

For the texts of original French documents quoted in this chapter, see the online appendix on the SEDET Web site, http://www.sedet.univ-paris-diderot.fr and on the Ohio University Press/Swallow Press Web site at http://www.ohioswallow.com/book/The+Demographics+of+Empire.

1. See, among others, Jacques Dupâquier and Michel Dupâquier, *Histoire de la démographie: La statistique de la population des origines à 1914* (Paris: Librairie Académique Perrin, 1985); J. Dupâquier and Alain Drouard, "La connaissance des faits démographiques," in *Histoire de la population française*, ed. Jacques Dupâquier (Paris: Presses Universitaires de France, 1988), 4:13–47; J. Dupâquier and R. Le Mée, "La connaissance des faits démographiques de 1789 à 1914," in *Histoire de la population française*, ed. Jacques Dupâquier (Paris: Presses Universitaires de France, 1988), 4:15–61; Alain Desrosières, "Histoire de la statistique: Styles d'écriture et usages sociaux," in *L'ère des chiffres: Systèmes statistiques et traditions nationales/The Age of Numbers: Statistical Systems and National Traditions,* ed. Jean-Pierre Beaud and Jean-Guy Prévost (Sainte-Foy: Presses de l'Université du Québec, 2000), 37–60; Desrosières, "Histoire des formes: Statistiques et sciences sociales avant 1940," *Revue Française de Sociologie* 26, no. 2 (1985): 277–310; Desrosières, *La politique des grands nombres: Histoire de la raison statistique—Textes à l'appui* (Paris: La Découverte, 1993); Desrosières, "Les spécificités de la statistique publique en France: Une mise en perspective historique," *Courrier des Statistiques* 49 (1989): 37–54; Desrosières, Jacques Mairesse, and Michel Volle, "Les temps forts de la statistique française depuis un siècle," in *Pour une histoire de la statistique,* ed. INSEE (Paris: INSEE/Economica, 1987), 1:509–17; "Les bases législatives et réglementaires de l'appareil statistique public," in *Pour une histoire de la statistique,* 2:851–913; Harald L. Westergaard, *Contributions to the History of Statistics* (New York: Agathon Press, 1968).

2. *Prestations* were legal obligations to provide labor imposed on colonial populations in each territory. Lists of these laborers, or *prestataires,* were derived from census results.

3. Raymond R. Gervais and Issiaka Mandé, "From Crisis to National Identity: Migration in Mutation, Burkina Faso, 1930–1960," *International Journal of African Historical*

Studies 32, no. 1 (1999): 59–79; Gervais, "Contrôler, compter, comparer: La production et la gestion de l'information démographique en Haute-Volta avant 1960," *Histoire et Mesure* 13, nos. 1–2 (1998): 59–76; Gervais, "État colonial et savoir démographique en AOF, 1904–1960," *Cahiers Québécois de Démographie* 25, no. 1 (1996): 101–31. This last article was reprinted in *L'AOF: Réalités et héritages—Sociétés ouest-africaines et ordre colonial, 1895–1960,* ed. Charles Becker, Saliou Mbaye, and Ibrahim Thioub (Dakar: Direction des Archives du Sénégal, 1997), 961–80; Gervais, *Contribution à l'étude de l'évolution de la population de l'Afrique occidentale française, 1904–1960* (Paris: CEPED, 1993); Gervais, "Recensements en AOF: Genèse et signification—Des exemples de la Haute-Volta coloniale," *Annales de Démographie Historique,* 1994, 339–54; Gervais, "Statistiques, langage et pouvoir dans la société coloniale," *Annales de Démographie Historique,* 1987, 57–65, and also in *Notes et Documents Burkinabè* 16, nos. 3–4 (July–December 1985): 104–18; Gervais, "De quelques statistiques coloniales," *Annales de l'Université d'Abidjan, ser. 1, History,* 12 (1984): 7–17; Gervais, "Population et politiques agricoles coloniales dans le Mosi, Haute-Volta, 1919–1940" (PhD diss., Université de Paris 7–Denis Diderot, 1991); Mandé, "Les migrations du travail en Haute-Volta (actuel Burkina Faso), mise en perspective historique" (PhD diss., Université de Paris 7–Denis Diderot, 1997); Mandé, "Les migrations de travail des Voltaïques: Panacée pour l'économie ivoirienne, 1919–1960," in *La Haute-Volta à l'époque coloniale: Témoignages, recherches, regards,* ed. Georges Madiéga and G. Massa (Paris: Karthala, 1995), 313–39.

4. During that period, the term *census* had a very different meaning than it does today. Hence, we qualified the terminology from the colonial literature with "understood" quotation marks to underscore the point.

5. See Samir Amin, "L'Afrique sous-peuplée," *Développement et civilisations* 47–48 (1972): 59–67; Anthony G. Hopkins, *An Economic History of West Africa* (London: Longman, 1973); Dominique Tabutin, ed., *Population et sociétés en Afrique au Sud du Sahara* (Paris: L'Harmattan, 1988); John C. Caldwell and Patricia Caldwell, "The Cultural Context of High Fertility in Sub-Saharan Africa," *Population and Development Review* 13, no. 3 (1987): 409–37; John Caldwell, Patricia Caldwell, and I. O. Orubuloye, "The Family and Sexual Networking in Sub-Saharan Africa: Historical Regional Differences and Present-Day Implications," *Population Studies* 46, no. 3 (1992): 385–410; A. Charton, "Le problème démographique en Afrique noire (1900–1960)," *Comptes-rendus de l'Académie des Sciences Morales et Politiques* (1967): 123–39; Catherine Coquery-Vidrovitch, "Les populations africaines du passé," in *Population et sociétés en Afrique au Sud du Sahara,* ed. Dominique Tabutin (Paris: L'Harmattan, 1988), 51–72; Pierre Pradervand, "The Ideological Premises of Western Research in the Field of Population Policy," in *Population in African Development,* ed. Pierre Cantrelle (Liège, Belgium: Ordina, 1974), 2:115–26; Landing Savané, *Les problèmes de population en Afrique* (Paris: Présence Africaine, 1987).

6. Beyond the general debate regarding the volume of the slave trade, it is apparent to us that its indirect effects on population, age structure, and political organization persisted well beyond abolition.

7. It is easy to differentiate, at least methodologically, the numerical census from the nominal census. In the first case, the objective is to obtain a numerical estimation of a population expressed in large units, such as the village or the household. In the second case, the objective is to record the name of each member of a community in order to rigorously assess both the exhaustiveness and the reliability of the information. For the enumerated, then, the question changes from "How many are you?" to "Who are you?" See Louis Lohlé-Tart and Michel François, *État civil et recensements en Afrique francophone: Pour une collecte administrative de données administratives* (Paris: CEPED, 1999).

8. Gervais, "Statistiques, langage et pouvoir." The administrative units of the French colonial system were, in decreasing scale: the three colonial federations (Afrique occidentale française, or AOF, Afrique équatoriale française, or AEF, and Indochina), the colonies, the districts (or *circonscriptions*), and the counties (or *cercles*). The basic administrative unit was the circonscription. The cercle was a unit without real power and often without an assigned administrator.

9. See his letter to the governor general, 23 January 1920, 10G7 (107), Archives Nationales du Sénégal (hereafter cited as ANS).

10. Rapport politique annuel de la Haute-Volta, 1923, 2G 23-21, 33–34, ANS.

11. Martial Merlin, "Circulaire du Gouverneur général de l'AOF au sujet du recensement de la population indigène, 3 avril 1922," *Journal Officiel de l'Afrique Occidentale Française* 18, no. 915 (22 April 1922): 245-48.

12. "In the end, as imperfect as it might be, the first census operation must have a considerable impact. Not only is it an indicator precious to our commercial and agricultural economy, which will benefit from it as much as possible; but if we limit it to the political sphere, it establishes between our administration and subjects more intensive relations from which we can expect positive effects." See Chief Administrator [Noirot] to Lieutenant-Governor of French Guinea, 30 January 1905, 22G-19, ANS.

13. Ministère des Colonies, Office Colonial, *Rapport du directeur au Conseil d'administration et au Conseil de perfectionnement sur l'ensemble du service pendant l'exercice 1905* (Melun, France: Imprimerie Administrative, 1906). This report reproduces the 14 March 1899 decree that created the Office Colonial. See also Léon Cayla, *Des offices coloniaux: Documentation et propagande* (Paris: Marcel Rivière, 1908).

14. Ministère des Colonies, Office Colonial, *Statistiques de la population dans les colonies françaises pour l'année 1906 suivies du relevé de la superficie des colonies françaises* (Melun, France: Imprimerie Administrative, 1909).

15. Lettre du Ministre des Colonies [Gaston Doumergue] à M. le Gouverneur Général de l'AOF [Merlin], 27 July 1904, 22G-19, ANS.

16. See Gervais, "État colonial et savoir démographique." The institutional rationale for this unrealistic demand remains obscure and may never be known because most of the pertinent documents have disappeared.

17. Lettre du Gouverneur Général de l'AOF à M. le Ministre des Colonies, 12 September 1904, 22G-19, ANS.

18. See, in particular, Letter from the Lieutenant-Governor of Senegal [Camille Guy] to M., Governor-General of French West Africa [Merlin], 29 September 1904, 22G 19, ANS: "There must first be recognition that the task imposed on the colonies is much more considerable than what is done in France to the same end. In effect, in the *métropole,* the population is subjected to a census only once every five years. To respect the ministerial directives, it will be necessary to proceed, under more difficult conditions than those we encounter in France, to a yearly count." See also Francis Simonis, ed., *Le commandant en tournée: Une administration au contact des populations en Afrique Noire coloniale* (Paris: Seli Arslan, 2005). This volume includes numerous testimonials and anecdotes by administrators on this topic.

19. Ministère des Colonies, Office Colonial, *Instructions pour l'établissement des statistiques des colonies françaises (Circulaire ministérielle du 15 février 1909)* (Melun, France: Imprimerie Administrative, 1909).

20. The table is taken from Raymond R. Gervais, *Contribution à l'étude de l'évolution de la population de l'Afrique occidentale française, 1904–1960* (Paris: CEPED, 1993), 17–18.

21. Gervais and Mandé, "From Crisis to National Identity."

22. Here, we paraphrase Guy Georgy, *Le petit soldat de l'Empire* (Paris: Flammarion, 1992), 79–80. In addition, see Simonis, *Le commandant en tournée.*

23. See Jean Pierre Chauveau, "La part baule: Effectif de population et domination ethnique—Une perspective historique," *Cahiers d'Études Africaines* 27, nos. 1–2 [105–6] (1987): 123–65.

24. Albert Ficatier, *Un certain regard sur une des fonctions de l'INSEE: De la statistique coloniale à la coopération technique* (Paris: INSEE, 1981), 5. After World War II, Ficatier instigated reforms in the field of demographic and statistical data gathering in the French territories.

25. Although these measures affected African populations most directly, they also impacted the colonial administration.

26. See the memoirs of the daughter-in-law of the first governor of the colony: Liliane Hesling, *Une vie comme un jour en Afrique, 1917–1957* (Le Cannet, France: 1988), and also the scathing remarks of Bernard Sol, in Bernard Sol's inspection reports, 1932. See notes 27, 29.

27. Mission Picanon, Report no. 124: Observations of Lieutenant-Gouverneur Hesling on Picanon's Remarks, 1924–1925, 21ff and 22ff, document, carton 3057, Affaires Politiques, Centre des Archive d'Outre-Mer, Aix-en-Provence (hereafter cited as CAOM). On this point, Sol observed in 1932, "At the time of the inspection mission, personnel were too few in numbers, badly allocated and of a generally mediocre quality. I did not find a single civil servant who spoke the language of the country. For the most part, this situation is the direct result of policies of rapid turnover, whereby principal administrators are never returned to the colonies of their previous colonial appointment. It is my opinion that this policy is the main cause of the divide between the administration and its subjects, and as such should be avoided." See Letter from Inspector Bernard Sol to the Ministry of Colonies, 10 November, 1932, document, dossier 2, carton 105, Affaires Économiques, CAOM. Such a policy of rapid turnover created resentment among civil servants. See Albert Londres, *Terre d'ébène* (Paris: Albin Michel, 1932), 12–13.

28. The nominative census recorded the name and household of each person in a given village or neighborhood. Information included the given name and family name (which created enormous problems because the practice led to changes in the ways that people in many societies identified themselves), along with gender, age, and "race."

29. Census agents were also supposed to register deaths. See Report no. 18, Report of the Administrative Situation of Upper Volta, p. 22, Mission Sol, Fonds Direction du Contrôle, CAOM: "As with many other parts of the administration, the censuses have been, at least in Upper Volta, mostly dominated by the common preoccupations imposed on all local administrators—financial distress and the necessity to balance the budget. This connection may at first glance seem surprising. Nevertheless what we are suggesting is the absolute truth, in the sense that there was a period (1925–1926) when we did not hesitate to round up numbers (*faire le compte*) to produce budgetary surpluses while maintaining what seemed to be reasonable taxation rates, and later, when a less cynical administration replaced the previous one, reversion to the truth, far from being completed, came to pass in small and over-cautious steps, as always out of concern for budgetary stability."

30. "Demographic Census of the Group: Correspondance and Instructions, 1927–1937," 22G 75(132), ANS.

31. Marc Michel, "Le recrutement des tirailleurs en A.O.F. pendant la Première Guerre Mondiale: Essai de bilan statistique," *Revue Française d'Histoire d'Outre-Mer* 60, no. 221 (1973): 644–60; Myron Echenberg, "'Faire du nègre': Military Aspects of Population

Planning in French West Africa, 1920–1940," in *African Population and Capitalism: Historical Perspectives*, ed. Dennis D. Cordell and Joel W. Gregory (Boulder, CO: Westview Press, 1987), 95–108; Echenberg, *Colonial Conscripts: The Tirailleurs Sénégalais in French West Africa, 1857–1960* (Portsmouth, NH: Heinemann, 1991).

32. For the most part, the main concern of doctors was to know if morbidity in the work camps and the mistreatment suffered by the workers would in the long term alter the "race of producers and reproducers," thus leading to demographic imbalance—namely, the depopulation of certain regions such as the Mossi homelands. Doctors asked those who received the reports to reflect on ethical problems caused by the transport, arrival, housing, and working conditions of workers recruited for the various work camps and holdings. See document, Rapport de l'inspecteur des services sanitaires, 1H 26(26), ANS. See the report on Upper Volta, p. 50, quoted in Saliou Mbaye, *Sources de l'histoire démographique des pays du Sahel conservées dans les archives (1816–1960)* (Bamako: USED, 1986), 59.

33. The finance law also required that each colony cover expenses incurred by the French presence as well as costs for building infrastructure.

34. "Following the colonial occupation, fiscal regulations had to adapt to different conditions in each overseas territory, and evolved differently in different areas. In the immediate wake of occupation, when the means at our disposal for laying the foundations of colonial rule were precarious in regions recently subjected to French influence, recourse to the requisition of labor was necessary to assure a work force in regions where people refused to respond. These requisitions were practiced for a long time without rules or oversight, to the point where we worried about subjecting them to legal bases and limits. The 1912 regulation was a first step towards this end." See Circulaire du Gouverneur général de l'AOF au sujet du régime des prestations, 12 September 1930, K120(26), ANS.

35. Ibid. The original French text reads as follows. "Un impôt direct et l'étendit à tous les habitants sans distinction de statut, payable en argent ou en nature au gré du contribuable, strictement déterminé, soigneusement contrôlé, minutieusement réglementé, aussi bien dans son assiette et ses tarifs que dans les divers modes de recouvrement."

36. See literature quoted by Issiaka Mandé as well as the article by A. I. Asiwaju, "Migrations as Revolt: The Example of the Ivory Coast and the Upper Volta before 1945," *Journal of African History* 17, no. 4 (1976): 577–94; A. I. Asiwaju, "Political Aspects of Migration in West Africa: The Example of French Colonies with Particular Reference to the Ivory Coast and the Upper Volta up to the 1945," *Afrika Zamani*, nos. 6–7 (1977): 73–101; Dennis D. Cordell, Joel W. Gregory, and Victor Piché, *Hoe and Wage: A Social History of a Circular Migration System in West Africa* (Boulder, CO: Westview Press, 1996); Sidiki Coulibaly, "Colonialisme et migration en Haute-Volta (1896–1946)," in *Démographie et sous-développement dans le Tiers-Monde*, ed. Danielle Gauvreau, Joel Gregory, Marianne Kempeneers, and Victor Piché (Montreal, Canada: Centre for Developing-Area Studies, 1986), 73–110; Thomas M. Painter, "Making Migrants: The Early Development of Seasonal Migrations among Zarma Cultivators in Niger, c. 1900 to c. 1930" (PhD diss., State University of New York–Binghamton), 1984.

37. Colonial administrator Adolphe Albert Marie Taillebourg was steadfast in his concern for the well-being of Voltaic workers recruited for the two biggest railroad construction projects in French West Africa. His official reports described in sensitive and exacting detail the perils and human consequences of recruiting African workers in an atmosphere of European economic self-interest, Eurocentrism, and the most vile racism. Moreover, he had the capacity to step back and analyze the ultimate impact of such practices on the ethical and economic well-being of the colonial enterprise in general and Upper Volta in

particular. See Issiaka Mandé, "Colonial Administrator Adolphe A. M. Taillebourg: Rigid Devotee of the Law or Humanitarian?" in *The Human Tradition in Modern Africa,* ed. Dennis Cordell (Lanham, MD: Rowman and Littlefield, in press [2011]).

38. See Rapport sur le danger proche de dépopulation que font courir à l'AOF des recrutements excessifs et mal repartis, 12 octobre 1931, K60 (19), ANS. Sorel's position on demographic matters conforms with dominant thinking in the medical milieu of AOF. The analysis and ideology were largely inspired by data and studies done on the epidemiology of the European workers in the nineteenth century. Thus, their statistical analyses presented in reports supported their discourse on the absence of public health policies on work sites and agricultural domains. These medical doctors also feared that excessive recruitments would bring demographic stagnation or worse a decline of population in AOF, echoing the fear in France in the interwar period. In a note written ten years later, we learn that this norm of more than ten percent was widely accepted in French West Africa, and continued to evolve without being questioned because it was higher than in the Belgian Congo. See report, Les dispositions en main-d'œuvre de l'AOF, Dakar, 23 July 1941, K172 (26), ANS.

39. Sarraut correctly identified the primary factor for productivity: population. See Albert Sarraut, minister of colonies, directive issued 21 February 1921 [no. 6], "A/s Accountancy of the Population in 1921," "Demographic Census of the Group: Correspondence and Instructions, 1927–1937," 22G 75 (132), ANS. This directive was reprinted in *Les Annales Coloniales* 22, no. 23, dated 18 February 1921.

40. Jules Carde, *Discours prononcé par M. J. Carde, Gouverneur Général de l'AOF à l'ouverture de la session du Conseil de Gouvernement, décembre 1927* (Gorée, Senegal: Imprimerie du Gouvernement Général, 1928), 42: "You are aware that 'faire du noir' is one of the principal goals that I set for myself in French West Africa. This formula, I can assure you, has had good press, since it responds directly to an essential need."

41. Sarraut, "A/s Accountancy of the Population." We underscore the justification for this notion of association, whereby "a farflung possession will no longer be a simple trading post, a storehouse of wealth, or a path that the conquered will follow to trade spices and sell off merchandise, [made possible] by pressuring an indigenous race that can be exploited without end. The colonies are not only markets: they are living entities, human creations, interdependent parts of the French state, where scientific, economic, moral and political progress will grant access to the most lofty of destinies, as in other parts of the national territory."

42. See Carde, *Discours prononcé par M. J. Carde* (p. 43): "These arms must be multiplied, and it is to this end that our projects of aid, prevention, and health are devoted, along with contributions from a variety of different budgets."

43. Lettre du G.-G. p.i. (Boisson) à Ministère des Colonies, 31 May 1934, 1Q310 (77), ANS.

44. Gervais, "Statistiques, langage et pouvoir."

45. The negative impact of modernity also played a role in mediocre censuses, as indicated in the following insightful quotation:

> The only conclusion that we can draw for certain from these remarks is the imprecision of the numbers provided for the censuses. Aside from a lack of administrative personnel, which threatens to become chronic and which hinders all work of this type, we must, unfortunately, realize that the building of numerous roads and the use of the automobile, instead of engendering the more frequent

contact with indigenous groups, more often leads administrators to neglect too much those who live away from passable roads. In a recent report on the subject, the Inspector of Administrative Affairs suggested that we must recognize that far too often the districts' administrations leave much to be desired; the dealings of chiefs are not monitored with the necessary care; the tour of the Administrator by car is too quick; and if he actually does it with his family, which is often the case, he is worried about not tiring them out and providing a suitable camp site. He rapidly passes through [towns and villages], does not stay in less hospitable areas where supplies are less than ideal, does not venture into regions without roads, and is eager to get back to the colony's capital. District officers no longer go on horseback except for a few exceptions and no longer visit villages which are far from the roads. The chiefs, left to themselves, prevent their subjects from lodging complaints, win the loyalty of interpreters and guards, and trick their district officers.... Each [district officer] has a tendency to become only a sedentary office manager and to transform his collaborators into scribes while maintaining relationships with the indigenous masses only through the mediation of the chiefs, who obviously in the case of the smarter ones, provide him an attractive portrayal of the country's condition.

See Lettre du Lieutenant-Gouverneur de la Haute-Volta au Gouverneur-Général, 28 September 1931, K121 (26), ANS.

46. Raymond Garner, "Watchdogs of Empire: The French Colonial Inspection Service in Action: 1815–1913" (PhD diss., University of Rochester, 1970).

47. See Michel Gentot, *Les autorités administratives indépendantes* (Paris: Montchestien, 1991); J. Ménier, *Les inspections générales* (Paris: Berger-Levrault, 1988); Pierre Milloz, *Les inspections générales ministérielles dans l'administration française* (Paris: Economica, 1983); Pierre Sanner, *Un siècle d'Inspection d'Outre-Mer* (Paris: Académie des Sciences d'Outre-Mer, 1983); and http://www.sedet.jussieu.fr/sites/Afrilab/documents/Archives/Gervais/Gervais.htm.

48. The lieutenant governor confirmed this use of the census:

It is useless to carry out a nominal census of the entire population. What must be done is to determine nominally which individuals who registered on regulatory lists or taxation lists are subject to administrative or fiscal obligations. The other elements of the population should simply be included in the total numbers:

- the census rolls in light of the annual draft for military service;
- the roster of forced laborers;
- the roster of taxpayers subject to personal taxation.

The first two only target adult males.... But, it is completely different for the role of personal taxation which will demand the nominal enumeration of *almost the entire population* [emphasis in original], since, it is not only men of all ages, but also women and children of both genders beginning at the age of eight who are subject to the head tax. We can thus deduce that the operation of the nominal census and the establishment of lists of rolls each year will be a burdensome task and will take considerable time. We may even ask ourselves if the complications which accompany such a census, coupled with the reduced

> resources in personnel and illiterate indigenous chiefs, will not seriously hamper its execution, and if this is not the precise reason that up until this point, the nominal census of tax-payers has been put off from year to year and has never been done.

See Lettre du Lieutenant-Gouverneur de la Haute-Volta au Gouverneur-Général de l'AOF, 23 January 1920, 10G7 (107).

49. See Report no. 78, Administration of Districts, signed by Verrier (Rapport d'ensemble), 16 October 1905, nonpaginated, Verrier Mission in Upper-Senegal-Niger, 1904–05, carton 895 (bound version), Fonds Direction du Contrôle, CAOM.

50. Report no.2, Financial Situation, signed by B. Sol, pp. 51–52, Sol Mission in Upper Volta, 1931–32, carton 948, Fonds Direction du Contrôle, CAOM.

51. See Report no. 15, Contact between the Administration and the Indigenous Population, signed by Bourgeois-Gavardin, 28 August 1941, pp. 2–3, Bourgeois-Gavardin Mission, 1940-41, carton 970, Fonds Direction du Contrôle, CAOM.

52. Hubert Ulmer, "Quelques données démographiques sur les colonies françaises," in Congrès International de la Population, 1937 (Paris: Hermann, 1938), 6:111–27.

53. Alain Ficatier, "La coopération statistique avec les pays en voie de développement," in ed. INSEE, Pour une histoire de la statistique (Paris: INSEE/Economica, 1987), 2:839.

54. "Arrêté portant création de la Direction Générale du Plan et de la Statistique," Journal Officiel de l'Afrique Occidentale Française 41, no. 2171 (7 July 1945): 523–24.

55. Gervais, "État colonial et savoir démographique."

56. "Before undertaking such a plan, it is necessary to have a complete and precise inventory of needs, resources and means. This inventory must be kept up to date by continuous research; all this is the work of the documentation and statistical services." See Governor-General of French West Africa to the Governors, Commissionaires and the Administrateur Superior of the Group, Directive no. 25SG, 17 January 1945, signed by Y. Digo, for the touring G.-G., General Secretary of the Governor-General, 22G-42 (17), ANS.

4

Makwerekwere

Separating Immigrants and Natives in Early Colonial Natal

THOMAS V. MCCLENDON

Modern colonial states found themselves in one of two anxiety-provoking situations. In what Philip Curtin calls "true empire" colonies, small numbers of officials from the imperial center attempted to rule overwhelming numbers of indigenes, who responded with varying degrees of cooperation and resistance. In what Curtin calls "settlement empire" colonies, relatively small numbers of settlers from Europe expropriated land from indigenous peoples, either by conquest or submission or through the decimation of local populations as a result of introduced diseases.[1] In its early stages, the southern African British colony of Natal combined characteristics of both colonial models. In the late 1830s, Dutch-speaking emigrants from Britain's Cape Colony occupied the area and carved out a niche for themselves in the region by defeating the Zulu kingdom, whose heartland lay to the northeast. A few years later, Britain annexed the territory claimed by the Dutch-speakers. Britain then encouraged the immigration of Anglophone white settlers in a movement comparable to the immigration of 1820, when Cape officials encouraged Anglophone settlement along the eastern frontier of its recently acquired Cape Colony. But Natal's officials continued to rule over an indeterminate number—perceived to be rapidly growing—of Africans who had never formally submitted or been conquered and who were not especially vulnerable to European-borne diseases. From the earliest stages of white settlement and rule in Natal, then, officials and settlers alike frequently expressed their worries over

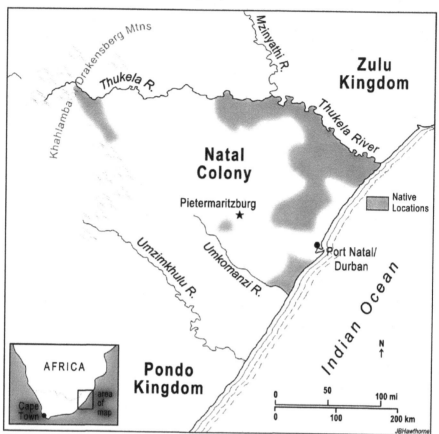

Figure 4.1. Colonial Natal

the origins, identities, customs, and location of indigenous people. These anxieties reflected fundamentally ambiguous attitudes about the presence of Africans and the expansion of African populations.

The colonies and settler republics that became today's South Africa considerably predated the imposition of European empires on most of Africa in the late nineteenth century, and they differed from all but a handful of the later colonies by encouraging permanent European settlement. The southern African colonies and settler republics were all descendants of the Cape Colony, which became part of the British Empire in 1806, during the Napoleonic Wars. The Cape Colony was in turn an outgrowth of the Dutch East India Company's seventeenth-century settlement at Cape Town, where the Mediterranean climate enabled the cultivation of grains and fruits in the European repertoire just as it precluded the introduction of standard African crops. Although the first century and a half of white settlement in the Western Cape had resulted in the political and social devastation of indigenous Khoisan-speaking herding and foraging populations, by the time the British arrived on the scene considerable numbers of white and brown settlers were penetrating inland, raiding cattle, and seeking labor from larger-scale Bantu-speaking farming and cattle-keeping societies to the east and north. On the eastern frontier, this migration of settlers led especially to a series of wars between colonial forces and Xhosa-speaking peoples.

In addition, the British arrived in southern Africa in the midst of their own debates about slavery and freedom. Although the debates centered mainly on sugar-producing islands in the Caribbean, they played out in the empire as a whole. As a result, the British takeover of the Cape Colony had a significant impact on labor polices, and the empire's ability to mobilize decisive military power allowed the colony to strengthen or expand its borders in the drive to absorb more land and labor. Both Britain's abolition of the international slave trade in 1807 and its emancipation of slaves in 1838 therefore had significant impacts in southern Africa, as settlers were forced increasingly to look to local populations for labor. At the same time, those local populations stood in the way of the settlers' desires to exert exclusive control over vast stretches of land.

Natal was no exception in regard to colonial anxieties and ambiguities about Africans within and beyond colonial borders, and this is reflected in a key problem in the historiography of early colonial Natal. White observers broadly agreed that from the late 1830s, after white settlement of the region that became Natal colony, the African population increased rapidly. They disagreed, however, about whether this population growth stemmed from communities returning to lands they had fled in the "wars of Shaka," who founded the Zulu kingdom in the generation before white occupation, or whether these people were mostly new immigrants seeking refuge from the Zulu kingdom or other nearby polities. These questions—and the underlying issues of land, labor, and not least of all taxation— consumed colonial officials trying to craft and implement policies related to land tenure for whites, the establishment and development (or not) of reserves for Africans, and methods of establishing authority and maintaining peace. These questions pertained to a colony that was open to white settlement but overwhelmingly populated by Africans who remained relatively independent economically for several decades and on whose productive capacities the colony depended for much of its revenues and food supply.[2] Officials and settlers sought to define who was within the empire and what rights and obligations that status carried. Whites viewed the Africans in their midst and nearby as culturally alien but threateningly indigenous. Their alterity could be used as a reason to exclude them from land whites wished to claim, even as their numbers could be tapped for supplies of labor and/or streams of revenue. Meanwhile, their local knowledge, alien culture, and feared ability to mount organized violence threatened the colonial enterprise with undue expense or even potential collapse.

Like most historical questions, the questions surrounding the movements of population into and out of Natal in the early nineteenth century are much more complicated than at first imagined. There are a number of subsidiary issues. For example, to what extent was the region that became the colony of Natal "devastated" or depopulated during Shaka's reign in the neighboring Zulu kingdom? Between the initial immigration of Dutch-speaking farmers (and their "colored" servants) from the Eastern Cape and just after the British annexation, evidence suggests that there were some large-scale movements of people into the region. To what extent were they composed of people previously displaced from Natal or their descendants? Was the rise in African population in the first years of white settlement and British colonization as dramatic as contemporary officials suggested? It is impossible to give definitive or precise answers to these questions. The best we can do is to consider the evidence and interrogate it in new ways. This examination will help us understand the demographic anxieties of a nascent colony on the outer fringe of the British Empire.

In early British-ruled colonial Natal, officials were consumed with questions of immigration and emigration. They sought to classify occupants of the colony not only by race and religion but also, with respect to blacks, by whether they should be counted as "aboriginal" to the territory or whether they were "refugees" from the neighboring Zulu kingdom or other areas beyond the borders. Natal became a colony in 1843 when Britain annexed the "district of Port Natal," eventually defining its borders as lying between the Thukela, Mzinyati, and Mzimkhulu rivers and the Drakensberg (uKhahlamba) Mountains.[3] Five years earlier, Dutch-speaking emigrants from the eastern seaboard of Britain's Cape Colony had entered the region and clashed with the Zulu kingdom, which claimed authority over at least part of the area. After the Dutch-speakers (also known as Boers, whose descendants call themselves Afrikaners) defeated the Zulu at the battle of Ncome (Blood) River in December 1838, Zulu king Dingane was toppled by his brother Mpande, who assumed the throne with the support of the Boer forces. In return for that support, Mpande agreed to cede most of the area that became Natal, and the Boers proclaimed a state called the Republic of Natalia.[4] The British, however, kept a close eye on the region. British traders had been settled at Port Natal (later Durban) since the mid-1820s and had long urged the British government to take a more active role in the region in order to free them from dependence on the Zulu royal house.[5] Port Natal's bay was the best harbor between Delagoa Bay (in present-day Mozambique) and the Cape Colony, so an empire based on free-trade imperialism that already had a strong colonial foothold in the subcontinent and that wished to protect the sea routes to its prime territorial possession—India—could not afford to ignore either the port or its hinterland. The British were also concerned about the activities of those they called Dutch Emigrant Farmers (the Boers), whom they still considered British subjects. Boer raids on African communities in and near Natalia, leading to enserfment of children from raided communities as "apprentices," flew in the face of the recent emancipation of slaves in the British Empire.[6] The Natalians' plan to remove a large proportion of the African inhabitants to an area beyond their southern border also excited British nervousness about the potential destabilizing influence on the Cape Colony's already war-torn eastern frontier.[7]

During Natal's first decade as a British colony, official reports repeatedly cited a rapid rise in the African population to about 100,000, attributing the increase to immigration. In 1852, Henry Cloete, the recorder, put it as follows:

> I made every possible inquiry both from the Dutch and British
> Emigrant farmers as to the numbers of what might be termed
> aboriginal tribes they had found on their arrival in the District. . . .
> In round numbers the *really aboriginal kaffirs* found in the District at
> that time appeared to have been about 5000 or 6000. . . . I made a
> broad distinction between the aboriginal kaffirs and the *interlopers* or
> Zulus and others who had come for safety into the District.[8]

Cloete's testimony shows that officials believed they were being inundated by immigrant Africans. The 1852–53 Native Affairs Commission argued, following a proposal forwarded from the colony's by Diplomatic Agent to the Native Tribes (later Secretary for Native Affairs) Theophilus Shepstone, that 30,000 or 40,000 Africans should therefore be removed from Natal.[9] They attributed the rush of immigration to their own establishment of peace in the region, which they saw as a restoration of conditions prevailing before Shaka's reign (c. 1816–28). They understood Shaka's Zulu kingdom to have launched a period of searing warfare that had caused survivors to flee to other regions. Given the renewed peaceful conditions, they believed, African communities were crossing mountains and rivers in order to settle in the colony. Some of the migrants were returning to lands from which they had been previously displaced by Zulu raiding—though the Commission report also held that "Kafirs have little attachment to any particular locality." Others were new refugees from despotic rule within the Zulu kingdom, northeast of the colony's Thukela River boundary.

Whatever their source, officials saw the migrants as a problem that impinged on their project to establish colonial order. Although immigrants were a potential source of labor, they were also among the many claimants to land. Claimants included Dutch-speaking settlers who, continuing a tradition established by cattle ranchers in the early colonial Cape, had staked out vast claims to land just before British annexation as well as mission societies and established African chiefdoms and communities. Added to this mix was an influx of about 5,000 sponsored immigrants from Britain between 1849 and 1852, mostly artisans, traders, and farmers.[10] In this situation, colonial officials wished to stem the flow of African immigrants, and they even gave serious consideration to removing a large proportion of Africans to an area beyond the colony's southern border, much as their Boer predecessors had planned.

Shepstone's removal plans, which I have discussed at length elsewhere, grew out of these competing demands for land.[11] In 1847, the colony's lieutenant governor, Martin West, appointed a "Locations Commission," headed by Shepstone, to designate portions of the colony for exclusive African occupation in order to limit African numbers on and entitlement to white-claimed land. The commission recommended a system in which each location—or reserve, as these lands were later called—would be ruled by a white superintendent in charge of African chiefs. The locations would also feature such staples of interventionist "civilizing" colonialism as missions and industrial schools, and they would nurture a Westernizing peasant class. Although the colonial government did designate locations, the rest of the plan was immediately shelved as entailing large expenditures that the fledgling colony could ill afford and that the imperial government was unwilling to subsidize. Frustrated in his attempts to implement such a plan, which he considered essential for the long-term development of the colony's African subjects, and worried that the influx of white settlers might lead to demands for dismantling the reserves, Shepstone proposed a series of plans for removing portions of the African population from the colony. In the 1854 version, he offered to lead up to half of the Africans in Natal to an area south of the colony. There, he would be the paramount ruler and would implement the civilizing plans the colony had failed to embrace. His subjects would be productive peasants and craftspeople, and they would also form a labor reserve for the neighboring colony. Although the 1852–53 Native Commission endorsed an earlier version of this plan and although the plan received a tentative go-ahead from the lieutenant governor, higher imperial authorities vetoed it as an unwarranted and potentially expensive expansion of British sovereignty.

By the mid-1850s, the colonial government's policy toward Africans developed into what nonetheless came to be known as the Shepstone system. This system entailed rule through chiefs and customary law, reserves, and direct and indirect taxation but only minimal efforts toward the "civilization" of Africans except in the relatively small and scattered reserves assigned to Christian missions. But as both white and black populations continued to grow and as land speculators came to dominate much of the land outside the reserves, officials continued to worry about the sources and histories of African communities.

The debate, so crucial for colonial actors in the 1840s and 1850s, has also been reflected in the historiography of the region since the late nineteenth century. Looking at this problem through its historiography can help us think about how to interpret problems of insider and outsider status within the empire and in Natal, and it also helps us analyze colonial ambivalence about the presence and provenance of African subjects.

In the mid-1960s, Edgar Brookes and Colin Webb dated the refugee problem to the years before British annexation, under the trekkers' Republic of Natalia: "The scattered tribes had emerged from hiding and many were crossing over from Zululand into Natal, though not on as large a scale as in the [postannexation] years 1843–5." As a result, the Volksraad, or settler governing body, passed a law limiting the number of squatters on each trekker farm to five families. In 1841, the Volksraad proposed to remove the surplus of Africans to an area south of the republic. This prospect gave the British one of the pretexts for annexation two years later, though ironically, as we have seen, Shepstone, as an official of British colonial Natal, would make a similar proposal only a few years later.[12] In 1843, after the British declared Natal to be under their jurisdiction but before they established a British administration, 50,000 refugees are said to have arrived in the colony from Zululand as a result of political disturbances in the kingdom.[13] Brookes and Webb claim that this flood of refugees added to a steady stream coming before and after it. Although the trekkers saw the immigrants as "Zulus," Brookes and Webb, picking up a theme that goes back at least to George McCall Theal in the late nineteenth century, argued that some were merely returning to areas from which the forces of Shaka's Zulu kingdom had displaced them.[14]

Theal divided the Africans of Natal into three groups: those present "before the wars of Tshaka" who had never left, those driven out by Shaka who returned after the advent of white settlers in 1838, and "refugees" not from Natal who had arrived after 1838.[15] The apparently uncontrolled immigration of Africans, combined with the colony's initial failure to confirm title to trekker land claims, led to a steady out-migration of Dutch-speakers. Brookes and Webb go on to argue that Shepstone's "locations" policy was the inevitable result of the large number of Africans in the colony, which they put at 100,000 in 1845, without citing sources for their estimate. Shepstone is said to have coaxed "from 80,000 to 100,000" of them into vaguely defined areas set aside as locations in 1847. For the next several years, much political discussion in Natal revolved around the size of the locations, which white settlers, new and old, saw as using labor they deemed rightfully theirs.[16]

Writing in 1971, just five years after Brookes and Webb, David Welsh emphasized the importance of these demographic questions, taking them up as the central issue of the short introduction to his book arguing that the system of native administration in Natal colony established the "roots of segregation" and apartheid in South Africa.[17] Welsh summarizes the apparent history of the rapid growth of African population in Natal:

> The Voortrekkers and most of the English colonists who came to Natal in the 1830s and 1840s believed that the territory contained only very few Africans who could legitimately claim to be aboriginal inhabitants. Numerous witnesses lent credence to this view. . . . In 1838, estimates of the African population of Natal varied from 5,000 to 11,000 [citing Shepstone's evidence to the 1852–53 Commission]. In October 1839 Mpande revolted against the Zulu king, Dingane, and crossed the Tukela [*sic*] into Natalia "with fully half of the Zulu population." Delegorgue estimated the number at 17,000 [citing the 1883 Native Laws Commission and John Bird]. By 1841 the African population of Natal was estimated at between 20,000 and 30,000, and by 1843, when the British Commissioner, Henry Cloete, commenced his investigation into land claims, at between 80,000 and 100,000.[18]

The implication of this summary is that there was a meteoric rise in the numbers of Africans in the colony between 1838 and 1843. However, it is not possible to glean from the evidence any firm conclusions about how many Africans lived in the area that became Natal at any particular moment in the nineteenth century. A census was not even attempted until the 1880s. Therefore, it is impossible to give precise parameters to white claims of rapid increase in that population in the early years of colonization, though officials collected what evidence they possessed in connection with a Select Committee considering "documentary tribal titles."[19] What evidence they had was self-serving and necessarily portrayed in round numbers. Though the numbers presented do not correspond precisely to actual people, they certainly indicate some movement of people. More important, they reflect colonial ambivalence about African subjects and neighbors.

As Welsh argues, the idea that most Africans in the colony were "refugees" without legitimate claims on the land was to have important ramifications for Natal's land policies. A page later, however, Welsh asserts that the refugee premise was decisively refuted by later research in oral history by Shepstone. Shepstone's evidence suggested that Natal had been "thickly inhabited" before Shakan times; warfare emanating from the Zulu kingdom had later depopulated the region. Shepstone concluded that the people flowing into Natal after the beginnings of substantial white settlement in 1838 were "aboriginal inhabitants" rather than alien refugees.[20]

This idea that Natal had been depopulated by Zulu war parties forms a central premise of what John Wright has called the "mfecane stereotype" that pervaded southern African historiography until the mid-1990s.[21] Norman Etherington's recent *Great Treks* provides a useful summary of the unraveling of the idea of "the mfecane" as a result of the work of Wright, Julian Cobbing, and other historians.[22] The mfecane debates have had two major implications. First, scholars have decentered the Zulu kingdom and an all-powerful Shaka as the motors of alleged massive violence and population displacements across early nineteenth-century southern Africa. Second, they have begun reintegrating colonial and African histories that had been segregated by apartheid conceptions of history and by an academic Africanist tradition dating from the 1960s that sought to valorize African agency and capacities for empire building. Leaving aside Etherington's conclusions about the wider region in this period,[23] his discussion of Natal shows that the idea of "devastation" resulted from the self-interested claims of white settlers, combined with a British assumption that disturbances in areas east of the Cape frontier resulted from people being driven south by Shaka. James Stuart's Zulu informants, circa 1900, further reinforced these ideas. Heirs of both supporters and opponents of Shaka agreed that he was a fearsome and unprecedented warrior king. However, the evidence now suggests that there were large states in the region before Shakan times, showing that Shaka's state was not unprecedented and that the effects of Zulu power in Natal were less severe and less direct than accounts such as those of the early settlers had indicated.[24] Timothy Keegan argues that the British annexation of Natal itself points to the fallacy of the "empty land" idea: "Fears of destabilization grew out of the evident fact that large numbers of Africans inhabited the territory that the trekkers settled in, despite the self-serving myth that it was an empty land."[25]

Many scholars have explored the notion of "empty" or "vacant" land as a foundational justification of colonialism in southern Africa. For instance, Julian Cobbing's article that initiated the mfecane debates argues, in reference to the British traders at Port Natal, that "mendacious propaganda was insistently relayed back to the Colony that Natal had been totally depopulated by the Zulu."[26] In a broader sense, Cobbing argues that the idea of a depopulating series of wars—the mfecane—in the early nineteenth century provided convenient cover for white settlement and dominion over southern Africa. Clifton Crais points to the larger white "myth of the Vacant Land" asserting that whites and "Bantu-speaking Africans" arrived in South Africa about the same time.[27] A text favored by the apartheid government in the 1970s promoted this idea quite directly. "The Afrikaner cattle-farmer advanced . . . until in 1770 at the Great Fish River he encountered the vanguard of the Black or Bantu peoples who, during the course of centuries, had been migrating slowly southwards on a broad trans-continental front."[28]

Crais lays blame for this myth at the door of Theal, "the acknowledged grandfather of South African history."[29] Theal, however, drew on earlier settler constructions that emerged in the context of frontier wars and a growing discourse of black barbarism. At the time of the 1834–35 war on the Eastern Cape frontier, Crais argues, the settler press displaced the self-knowledge of an imperialist colonial society by asserting that African opponents were "an expansive, conquering and violent people,"[30] which was, rather, an excellent description of colonial forces in southern Africa. Like Cobbing, Dan Wylie argues that the white pioneers of Natal engaged in similar displacements by asserting the idea of "depopulation" of the territory under Shaka. The empty-land claim of one such pioneer, the Port Natal trader Henry Francis Fynn,

> is contradicted in his own and other accounts. He claims that the 225 miles between Port Natal and the Mpondo (a doubling of the actual distance) contained "no inhabitants" and that only north of the port could the marauding Zulus plunder grain. This is contradicted, for example, by James King's account of the immediate vicinity of Port Natal . . . in which King notes that "Indian corn" was being grown there "in abundance."[31]

Since Natal, both as a Boer settlement and as a British possession, was a political offshoot of the Cape Colony, myths of depopulation during the so-called wars of Shaka and a wider notion of supposedly empty land in southeast Africa were common currency by the time of the British annexation of Natal in the 1840s. The myths, enhanced as Etherington argues by faulty mapmaking in the 1820s and 1830s, carried over from two centuries of white settlement in the Cape Colony.

They now circulated more rapidly through the nascent press of a self-consciously modern British colony and continued to be generated during the early decades of British rule by, for instance, the publication of Fynn's heavily reedited diary.[32]

Keletso Atkins takes up the issue of the influx of "refugees" into Natal in connection with her investigation of labor in colonial Natal. Writing during the early stages of the mfecane debate, she notes the critique of the devastation theory but nevertheless seems to accept that there was a significant displacement of population from late precolonial Natal, repeating the main essentials of the story of population movements outlined in Brookes and Webb.[33] She is more concerned, however, with what happened to people coming into Natal in the 1840s and 1850s. During the first two decades after the British annexation of Natal, she argues, "the central focus of foreign and domestic relations in the region consisted of attempts by both the English and [Zulu king] Mpande to staunch the outward surge of people and cattle from Zulu country."[34] In order to stem the flow of people, Natal's officials agreed by the mid-1840s to restore to Zululand any cattle arriving with refugees. Implementing this plan, however, proved difficult. In 1854, the colony adopted a law that was uncomfortably similar to the disguised slavery practiced by the Boers in the name of "apprenticeship," through which Boer communities had long absorbed orphaned or abducted Africans as dependent workers. The Natal policy required able male refugees entering the colony to labor for settlers for three years. The settlers hoped this policy would both reduce the volume of the refugee flow and help solve the perceived labor shortage in the colony. It would also have the convenient side effect of depressing wages. However, it turned out that the nascent colony lacked the coercive power to implement such an ordinance on a wide scale.[35] The key question for Atkins is what drove the flow of refugees into Natal. She argues that although some were seeking asylum from persecution, a "great majority" were from communities that were bent on reestablishing themselves in Natal in the wake of the partial breaking up of Zulu power in the 1830s. This is a plausible argument, but the only evidence Atkins cites in support of it is an 1864 memorandum from Shepstone referring to the influx of a large number of men with Mpande during the Zulu kingdom's "breaking of the rope" in 1839–40, and the citation makes it nearly impossible to find the referenced document.[36] She also speculates extensively on efforts by immigrants from the Zulu kingdom to reconstitute family structures in Natal, arguing that the male-centric refugee regulations posed considerable difficulties in this process.[37]

Carolyn Hamilton's book on Shaka and the "limits of historical invention" throws new light on the late precolonial and colonial histories of Natal and Zululand.[38] Hamilton argues that white observers circulated both positive and negative stories about Shaka, drawing in both cases on indigenous discourses that offered contrasting accounts of Shaka's rule as a source of order or a source of chaos. In order to demonstrate Shepstone's reliance on various images of Shaka as models for his native administration, Hamilton discusses Shepstone's research on "the historical grounds for African land claims in Natal."[39] Drawing on Wright's doctoral dissertation,[40] she contends that the two pieces produced by Shepstone in 1863–64 and published in the appendix to the Cape Native Laws Commission report relied on testimony given by about fourteen oral informants.[41] These are apparently the memoranda that Welsh mentions, and one must be the source to which Atkins's citation obliquely makes reference. Shepstone, according to Hamilton, used the Zulu discourses on order under the firm rule of Shaka, in contrast to Natalian chaos, as a justification for his own autocratic methods; in Shepstone's usage, the geographic stereotype was reversed to assert order in the colony as contrasted with chaos in the Zulu kingdom. More important for present purposes, the Shepstone memoranda justified the indigeneity of Natal's African population, though it consigned them to the less favorable land—the land that was to become locations. Shepstone put it as follows:

> When the Boers arrived in what is now Natal in 1838, all the broken
> and bushy country, as well as all the forest country, was, as a rule,
> occupied by natives . . . and all the open country not; this was the natural
> result of the political condition of the inhabitants with regard to the
> Zulus; under such circumstances it will be obvious, that it is impossible
> to name all the localities occupied by different tribes, or to decide that
> any one locality was the only spot which any one Tribe occupied.[42]

So, in Shepstone's view, most of the "tribes" living in colonial Natal had aboriginal rights to be there—but not to any particular piece of land and certainly not to the better-watered and richer-soiled agricultural land that lay along the road from Durban to the interior. More important, the scattered nature of aboriginal occupation of what became Natal precluded African claims against white, or state, ownership. In other words, his analysis, though careful and partially based on oral testimony, is a useful reflection of the ambiguity colonial authorities felt about the African populations in their midst and on their borders. He seems to be saying that these people are ours, we need them, and they have a long-standing right to be here, but they must now be present in a way that is useful to us, not disruptive of or threatening to our productive use and enjoyment of this land.

This brings me back to Welsh. Despite the fundamental ahistoricism of his argument that the Shepstone methods of native administration in Natal constituted the "roots of segregation" in the vastly different circumstances of twentieth-century South Africa,[43] Welsh is on to a critical issue. As he puts it, "The belief that the large majority of Africans in Natal were 'refugees' with no legitimate claim to land rights profoundly affected the final land settlement, and, indeed, became an important element in the colonists' 'social charter.'"[44] Mahmood Mamdani raises a similar concern in analyzing the way that ascribed indigeneity was a necessary condition of full citizenship in postcolonial Central Africa and became a concept with murderous results.[45] The irony, of course, is that in a colonial situation, it was only English- and Dutch-speaking whites—immigrants and descendants of immigrants—who were entitled to full citizenship. However, the idea that most Africans in the colony were also recent arrivals enabled settlers and officials to fantasize that they had arrived in an empty land. Shepstone was more pragmatic as well as somewhat more protective of the Africans he hoped to civilize. He therefore marshaled evidence of indigeneity, even while being careful to assert that it did not invalidate any white claims to land. His proposal to remove up to half of Natal's African population was not directed at any particular subgroup of Africans resident in Natal. The eagerness with which the settler-dominated commission of 1852–53 latched on to this proposal, however, again reflected the widespread white belief that blacks in the colony were interlopers, there primarily to serve white masters. This was unfortunately a belief that reappeared in the mid-twentieth century, under the direction of a powerful white supremacist state that possessed at least temporary power to deliver "surplus" people "back" to the areas from which they were deemed to have strayed.[46]

The evidence suggests that there may well have been a large rise in the African population of the territory in the early years of white settlement, due to a variety of causes. First, a significant number of people crossed into Natal during the Zulu kingdom's "breaking of the rope." Second, others continued to cross the river as "refugees," spurred no doubt by a variety of economic, affective, and political motives.[47] And with the threat of raiding and tribute collection erased within the colonized territory, people no doubt took up residence in more open areas, where their presence was more noticeable to white officials. In addition, much of the idea of "vacant" land in African colonial history rests on white misunderstanding—however willful—about African sovereignty and land use. Land that appeared empty from an exclusive title or commercial farming point of view often consisted of fallow fields connected to a community's long rotation through shifting cultivation or grazing land that was being used seasonally through transhumance practices.[48] Ironically, later white cattle farmers adopted the practice of seasonally moving cattle between higher and lower elevations in Natal, giving much of their land an appearance of emptiness, and large amounts of white-owned farmland remained underused for decades.[49]

Much of the perception of a black population increase probably amounted to a slow dawning on white officials of the real nature of the situation into which they had plunged—ruling a large and fragmented African population while catering to the perceived needs of a small but vocal white population. White settlers and colonial administrators felt a rising anxiety in the face of a large and apparently growing population of Africans whose political organization, land use patterns, and relationship to powerful African neighbors were largely mysterious. Would a thinly populated white colony be able to monopolize land and political power in the face of a rapidly growing black population, with many of these people apparently returning to a region from which they had recently departed? Would a thin administrative presence be able to render the colonized population "legible" to the state for purposes of implementing taxation and indirect rule?[50] As Donald Moore paraphrases Marx and Engels in reference to Zimbabwe, a spectre was haunting Natal, "the spectre of racialized dispossession."[51] That spectre triggered recurring anxiety about the presence, and number, of black inhabitants of the colony.

Drawing borders—creating new maps on top of old ones—has the effect of redefining rights of inclusion and exclusion. I was somewhat shocked several years ago when an otherwise progressive South African woman giving a presentation at the University of California–Los Angeles (UCLA) argued that many of postapartheid South Africa's ills could be attributed to a spiraling influx of illegal aliens. While we in the audience listened politely, it was all but certain that undocumented foreign nationals were trimming hedges and blowing leaves within a short distance of where we sat.

This was my first introduction to South Africa's postapartheid politics of indigeneity. That political development, though unfortunate, is hardly surprising in a country with astronomical unemployment and searing poverty that is nevertheless relatively wealthy by contrast to its neighbors. Hawkers from Mozambique, Congo, and Zimbabwe crowd Johannesburg's pavements while upscale immigrants from Nigeria and beyond compete for professional positions. At the same time, the politics of "black empowerment" enable the rapid economic rise of a select few, leading to a more equitable distribution of wealth across racial boundaries at the higher end of the scale, even as the poor and hopeless remain disproportionately black. Middle-class whites, the beneficiaries of apartheid's distributive mechanisms, continue to prosper but argue that they are no longer considered truly South African under the new dispensation. A racial politics of indigeneity has developed, with some people asserting rights based on "first people" status, others arguing for blackness as the marker of belonging, and some whites still cling to notions of objectively defined merit while conveniently ignoring the sordid histories that delivered their superior levels of education.[52]

Jean and John Comaroff called attention to South Africa's new politics of indigeneity in an article on the controversy over "alien" and "invasive" plant species in the Cape.[53] They argued that the rhetoric deployed in relation to the problem of alien species in a fragile ecosystem merges seamlessly into the rhetoric of national rights and exclusivity raised against the *makwerekwere*—the neologism for African foreigners, especially undocumented ones—in South Africa.[54] There is some poetic justice in the rise of nativity as a supreme value in a land formerly ruled through a racial hierarchy that placed white immigrants and their descendants at the pinnacle. Nevertheless, there are disturbing aspects of this trend. Mahmood Mamdani has argued persuasively that the genocidal politics of recent Central African history grows out of understanding some people as indigenous and hence first-class citizens and others as latecomers and hence second-class pseudocitizens.[55] Similar issues have arisen in various parts of the continent, often with tragic results.[56]

Mamdani's compelling argument, combined with the Comaroffs' discussion of the rhetoric of nationhood in South Africa, helps point to the importance of this aspect of early colonial history in Natal. A finding of indigeneity or its absence was the key to the colony's attitude toward its subjects, though no degree of indigeneity would trump the superior racial claims of whites. The officials of this young colonial state were faced with an apparently growing and clearly alien subject population. They were surrounded by independent African states with the capacity to resist imperial aggression and, it was feared, to threaten colonial security. The colony at this stage lacked the means to render its subject population legible through such measures as census taking and regulation of marriage practices, practices it was only to initiate in 1869.[57] Its officials found themselves befuddled by the recent and disorderly historical movements of their new subjects. As a result, the colony sought to define them—or at least a preponderance of them—as outsiders with limited rights to the land or to the protection of the government. Shepstone, whose protective urges were driven by the fear of revolt and balanced by his urge to legitimate exploitation, used African testimony to conclude that even those African communities that had considerable ties to the land could not claim any particular parcel of land. As a result, Africans could not interfere with the broad civilizing project of early Victorian colonialism, which focused on taming and transforming the land to make it commercially productive, even if Africans' own transformation was not yet its direct object.

Notes

1. Philip Curtin, *The Rise and Fall of the Plantation Complex: Essays in Atlantic History*, 2nd ed. (Cambridge: Cambridge University Press, 1998), 14–15.

2. John Lambert, *Betrayed Trust: Africans and the State in Colonial Natal* (Scottsville, South Africa: University of Natal Press, 1995).

3. John Bird, *The Annals of Natal, 1495–1845* (1888; repr., Cape Town: C. Struik, 1965), 2:165–68, 299–300, 465–66. These boundaries corresponded roughly to the area the Zulu kingdom had ceded to the Boer settlers in 1839.

4. Ibid., 1:536–40.

5. Dan Wylie, *Savage Delight: White Myths of Shaka* (Pietermaritzburg, South Africa: University of Natal Press, 2000), 91–94; Charles Rawden Maclean, *The Natal Papers of "John Ross": Loss of the Brig "Mary" at Natal with Early Recollections of That Settlement and among the Caffres*, ed. Stephen Gray (Durban, South Africa: Killie Campbell Africana Library, 1992), 153.

6. See, e.g., Bird, *Annals of Natal*, 1:624–25, 635–39; Keletso Atkins, *The Moon Is Dead! Give Us Our Money! The Cultural Origins of an African Work Ethic in Natal, South Africa, 1843–1900* (Portsmouth, NH: Heinemann, 1993), 16.

7. Bird, *Annals of Natal*, 644–45. It is notable that the resolution in support of this plan claimed that most "Kaffirs" then in Natal (in 1842) were from elsewhere and "had no right or claim to any part of the country, they having only come amongst us after the emigrants had come hither, with a view of being protected by us."

8. Testimony of Henry Cloete, Recorder, to Native Affairs Commission, 3 November 1852 (emphasis added); see also testimony of Rev. Louis Grout in the same file, SNA 2/1/2, Pietermaritzburg Archives Repository (hereafter cited as PAR).

9. Natal Native Affairs Commission, 1852–53, 41, PAR; Thomas McClendon, "The Man Who Would Be *Inkosi*: Civilising Missions in Shepstone's Early Career," *Journal of Southern African Studies* 30, no. 2 (2004): 251–70.

10. Charles Ballard, "Traders, Trekkers and Colonists," in *Natal and Zululand from Earliest Times to 1910: A New History,* ed. Andrew Duminy and Bill Guest (Pietermaritzburg, South Africa: University of Natal Press, 1989), 126.

11. McClendon, "Man Who Would Be *Inkosi.*"

12. Edgar Brookes and Colin de B. Webb, *A History of Natal* (Pietermaritzburg, South Africa: University of Natal Press, 1965), 37–38, 45–46; McClendon, "Man Who Would Be *Inkosi.*"

13. Brookes and Webb, *History of Natal,* 47–50.

14. Ibid., 50.

15. George McCall Theal, *History of South Africa,* vol. 3, 3rd ed. (London: Allen and Unwin, 1916), 229.

16. Brookes and Webb, *History of Natal,* 52, 59, 65, 69–70. Much of this reiterates evidence and conclusions given in Edgar Brookes and N. Hurvitz, *The Native Reserves of Natal* (Cape Town: Oxford University Press, 1957), 1–4.

17. David Welsh, *The Roots of Segregation: Native Policy in Natal, 1845–1910* (Cape Town: Oxford University Press, 1971), 2–5.

18. Ibid., 2, citing Bird, *Annals of Natal,* 2:311.

19. Welsh, *Roots of Segregation,* 2.

20. Ibid., 3–4.

21. John Wright, "Political Mythology and the Making of Natal's Mfecane," *Canadian Journal of African Studies* 23, no. 2 (1989): 272–91.

22. Norman Etherington, *The Great Treks: The Transformation of Southern Africa, 1815–1854* (New York: Pearson Longman, 2001), 329–49. For a useful collection of interventions into the Mfecane debates, see Carolyn Hamilton, ed., *The Mfecane Aftermath: Reconstructive Debates in Southern African History* (Pietermaritzburg, South Africa: University of Natal Press, 1995).

23. In another piece, Etherington has suggested that the idea of empty land in the southern African interior resulted from poor mapping practices in the early nineteenth century. Norman Etherington, "A False Emptiness: How Historians May Have Been Misled by Early Nineteenth Century Maps of Southern Africa," *Imago Mundi* 56, no. 1 (2004): 67–86. My thanks to Karl Ittmann for bringing this piece to my attention.

24. On large states, see Etherington, *Great Treks,* 31–35. For Zulu power in Natal, see Wright, "Political Mythology."

25. Timothy Keegan, *Colonial South Africa and the Origins of the Racial Order* (Cape Town: David Philip, 1996), 343n15.

26. Julian Cobbing, "The Mfecane as Alibi: Thoughts on Dithakong and Mbolompo," *Journal of African History* 29, no. 3 (1988): 487–519. In fact, the source Cobbing cites, at 509–10n111, suggests that not only what became Natal but also in fact the entire territory from Pondoland (south of Natal) to Delagoa Bay had been "conquered and laid waste" by the Zulu king Shaka. George Thompson, *Travels and Adventures in Southern Africa,* vol. 2, ed. Vernon S. Forbes (1827; repr., Cape Town: Van Riebeeck Society, 1968), 249.

27. Clifton Crais, "The Vacant Land: The Mythology of British Expansion in the Eastern Cape, South Africa," *Journal of Social History* 25, no. 2 (1991): 256. Archaeological evidence shows that farming communities were well distributed in South Africa, including the area that became Natal, from the first millennium CE. Peter Mitchell and Gavin Whitelaw, "The Archaeology of Southernmost Africa from c. 2000 BP to the Early 1800s: A Review of Recent Research," *Journal of African History* 46, no. 2 (2005): 209–41. Nevertheless, I have heard the old myth repeated by a well-educated and politically liberal white South African as recently as 2006.

28. W. J. de Kock, *History of South Africa* (Pretoria: Government Printer for the Department of Information, 1971), 11. My thanks to Dennis Cordell for providing this quote.

29. Crais, "The Vacant Land," 266–67.

30. Ibid., 266.

31. Dan Wylie, "'Proprietor of Natal:' Henry Francis Fynn and the Mythography of Shaka," *History in Africa* 22 (1995): 414; cf. Bird, *Annals of Natal,* 1:73–76 (paper written by Fynn between 1834 and 1838, in which Fynn calls Natal "totally depopulated"), and Bird, *Annals of Natal,* 1:103. Shepstone, by contrast, argues in an 1875 paper that although "wave after wave of desolation" had "swept over the land," the region was not depopulated. Rather, "many thousands" remained but were reduced to a "hopeless and wretched" condition. Bird, *Annals of Natal,* 1:158–59.

32. Wylie, "'Proprietor of Natal'"; Etherington, "False Emptiness."

33. Atkins, *The Moon Is Dead!* 9–13. The critique of the devastation theory is made at 147n3.

34. Ibid., 13.

35. Ibid., 17–22.

36. Ibid., 22.

37. Ibid., 18–54.

38. Carolyn Hamilton, *Terrific Majesty: The Powers of Shaka Zulu and the Limits of Historical Invention* (Cambridge, MA: Harvard University Press, 1998).

39. Ibid., 90.

40. John B. Wright, "The Dynamics of Power and Conflict in the Thukela-Mzimkhulu Region in the Late 18th and Early 19th Centuries: A Critical Reconstruction" (PhD diss., University of the Witwatersrand, 1989).

41. Cape of Good Hope, *Report and Proceedings of the Government Commission on Native Laws and Customs, 1883,* pts. 1 and 2 (Shannon: Irish University Press, 1970), 415–26.

42. Theophilus Shepstone, "Historic Sketch of the Tribes Anciently Inhabiting the Colony of Natal, as at Present Bounded, and Zululand," 1864, Report of Select Committee (7 November 1862) on Granting Natives Documentary Tribal Titles to Land, in Colenso Papers A204, v. 144, c. 1280/9, PAR.

43. I am grateful to John Wright for alerting me to the ahistoricism in Welsh's argument.

44. Welsh, *Roots of Segregation,* 2–3.

45. Mahmood Mamdani, *When Victims Become Killers: Colonialism, Nativism and the Genocide in Rwanda* (Princeton, NJ: Princeton University Press, 2002).

46. Surplus People Project, *Forced Removals in South Africa: The Surplus People Project Report,* vols. 1–5 (Cape Town: Surplus People Project, 1983).

47. Although contemporary officials tended to stress political motivations, Atkins, in *The Moon Is Dead!,* emphasizes the role of affective motivations such as marriage and the reconstitution of families.

48. See, e.g., Donald S. Moore, *Suffering for Territory: Race, Place and Power in Zimbabwe* (Durham, NC: Duke University Press, 2005), 166–68; Robin Palmer and Neil Parsons, eds., *The Roots of Rural Poverty in Central and Southern Africa* (Berkeley: University of California Press, 1977), 6–8.

49. Thomas V. McClendon, *Genders and Generations Apart: Labor Tenants and Customary Law in Segregation-Era South Africa, 1920s to 1940s* (Portsmouth, NH: Heinemann, 2002), 24; Moore, *Suffering for Territory,* 131; Palmer and Parsons, *Roots of Rural Poverty,* 7–9.

50. For legibility, see James Scott, *Seeing Like a State: How Certain Schemes to Improve the Human Condition Have Failed* (New Haven, CT: Yale University Press, 1999).

51. Moore, *Suffering for Territory,* ix.

52. See the discussion of immigration and a new South African identity in Lauren B. Landau, "Transplants and Transients: Idioms of Belonging and Dislocation in Inner-City Johannesburg," *African Studies Review* 49, no. 2 (September 2006): 125–45.

53. Jean Comaroff and John L. Comaroff, "Naturing the Nation: Aliens, Apocalypse and the Postcolonial State," *Journal of Southern African Studies* 27, no. 3 (2001): 627–51. Other pieces discussing xenophobia and nationalism in southern Africa include: Gerhard Mare, "Race, Nation, Democracy: Questioning Patriotism in the New South Africa," *Social Research* 72, no. 3 (2005): 501–30; Francis B. Nyamnjoh, "Local Attitudes towards Citizenship and Foreigners in Botswana: An Appraisal of Recent Press Stories," *Journal of Southern African Studies* 28, no. 4 (2002): 755–75; and Jonathan Crush and David A. McDonald, eds., "Special Issue: Transnationalism, African Immigration and New Migrant Spaces in South Africa," *Canadian Journal of African Studies* 34, no. 1 (2000). A recent news item suggests that in Nigeria, people often suffer discrimination on the basis of being "foreign" to a given region within the country. Alex Last, "Nigeria Discrimination Condemned," *BBC News,* 25 April 2006, available at http://news.bbc.co.uk/2/hi/africa/4943700.stm, accessed 25 April 2006.

54. The term is said to be based on what foreigners' speech patterns sound like to South African ears. Gerhard Mare, "Race, Nation, Democracy," 507 and 507n1. See also Phaswane Mpe, *Welcome to Our Hillbrow* (Pietermaritzburg, South Africa: University of Natal Press, 2001).

55. Mamdani, *When Victims Become Killers.*

56. Peter Geschiere and Stephen Jackson, "Autochthony and the Crisis of Citizenship: Democratization, Decentralization, and the Politics of Belonging," *African Studies Review* 49, no. 2 (September 2006): 1–14.

57. In 1869, the colony imposed regulations on marriage designed to raise new revenue while simultaneously limiting polygyny and protecting against forced marriage. Thomas McClendon, "Coercion and Conversation: African Voices in the Making of Customary Law in Natal," in *The Culture of Power in Southern Africa: Essays on State Formation and the Political Imagination,* ed. Clifton Crais (Portsmouth, NH: Heinemann, 2003), 49–63.

5

Counting and Recounting

Dislocation, Colonial Demography, and Historical Memory in Northern Gabon

JOHN M. CINNAMON

In heavily forested, sparsely populated northern Gabon under French colonial rule, the 1920s constituted a demographic low water mark, characterized by extensive dislocation, famine, and the depopulation of the large Minkébé forest along the Western Ivindo basin. Formal colonization spared this region until after the turn of the twentieth century, but the 1910s saw a disastrous concessionary company system, cession of a broad band of northern Gabon and Congo to German Cameroon, extensive population mobility, and the unprecedented violence of World War I as French and African troops fought to reconquer the previously ceded territory before pressing into Cameroon. After the war, France, itself hard-pressed and broke, pushed its Gabonese colonial subjects to the wall. Increased labor recruitment and taxation led to widespread subsistence crises in the mid-1920s and to important displacements and relocations of populations.

How did colonial officials and later social scientists understand these demographic processes? How is this period remembered today in Gabonese oral histories of colonialism? Unsurprisingly, differing accounts emphasize distinct priorities. Whereas French officials were obviously preoccupied by imposing colonial order, Africans sought to maintain a measure of maneuverability in an increasingly constricted field. Administrators, in spite of the difficulties of quantifying highly mobile and often reluctant populations, endeavored to tell at least part of the story by numbers. Accounts from the 1920s are filled with impressions of population decline, high mortality, and impending demographic disaster.[1] Gabonese male elders to-day are more concerned with recounting key events, processes, and movements and with reasserting a historical connection to abandoned landscapes and to kin dispersed on opposite sides of the forest. When seen in the context of labor re-cruitment, displacement, and the depopulation of Minkébé forest, oral accounts contribute toward a qualitative demographic history. In spite of their differing priorities, there is a remarkable concurrence between colonial reports, later studies by social scientists, and oral histories recorded since 1990.

To suggest this dynamic relationship between counting and recounting, I begin with two examples from 1923: the murder of a colonial chief and colonial reports on the demographic consequences of colonial policy. After a brief outline of the history of Minkébé region between first contact in 1888 and the closing of Minkébé post in 1927, I turn to a more detailed discussion of oral and written accounts of the murder. This discussion leads to an assessment of colonial demographic knowledge production between 1910 and 1930, the development of colonial population studies by French colonial official and geographer Georges Bruel, and a brief discussion of the mid-twentieth-century anthropology and geography of Georges Balandier and Gilles Sautter. The goal is to sketch the contours of an equatorial African demo-graphics of empire that includes colonial and social science understandings along with an understanding of the remembered experiences of Africans.

Two Accounts

In August 1923 in the Gabonese rain forest to the north of Makokou, the colonial chief (*chef de terre*) Ango Nkume was killed while touring villages to collect taxes. His main assailants were two brothers, Mefwé and Akule, who were also agnatic kinsmen of the slain chief. The brothers had, it seems, resented Ango's arrogance and abuses of power—complaints frequently leveled at colonial chiefs. Afterward, they fled north into the sparsely populated Minkébé forest, where they eluded co-lonial justice at the margins of Makokou Subdivision. Five months later, they finally surrendered and were incarcerated. Upon their release, instead of staying in Ma-kokou Subdivision where they would have been marked men, they crossed the for-est to settle near the northern border post of Minvoul, where many inhabitants of Minkébé forest had been resettled after the closure of Minkébé post in 1927. In the 1990s, elders in both Minvoul and Makokou still vividly recounted this murder.

Also in 1923, colonial reports lamented the demographic impact of the bur-geoning coastal timber industry, which added to colonial coffers but also led to insatiable demands for workers from interior labor reserves. Populations in the northern Woleu-N'Tem Circonscription (District) had been weakened by the 1918 influenza pandemic, sleeping sickness, smallpox, and famine in 1922–23, but labor recruitment nonetheless proceeded apace.[2] Administrators complained of "reprehensible" (*condemnable*) recruitment practices and expressed deep concern over "the rarefaction of labor" that resulted from "the exodus of natives (*indigènes*) toward the coast." A high number of able-bodied men were being removed from interior regions, including the Woleu-N'Tem and the Ivindo, where population was "already insufficient"; the development (*mise en valeur*) of interior regions was thus "eviscerated."[3]

These two accounts both pertain to northern Gabon in 1923 but otherwise convey distinct, culturally shaped representations of a colonial landscape in transition. The demographic subtext is obvious in the second account drawn from colonial archives. Here, we see an almost classic materialist perspective on the relation between production and reproduction. The demands of colonial production required labor migration that robbed interior labor preserves of workers, thereby undermining subsistence production, tax revenue collection, and reproduction of interior populations.[4] In the post–World War I era, many colonial administrators in French Equatorial Africa (AEF) concurred that population, especially in Gabon, was declining, but they weighed indigenous and colonial causes differently.[5] Later social scientists have highlighted the demographic, socioeconomic, and cultural crises that shook the foundations of Gabonese village-based societies during the colonial period.[6] One goal of this chapter is to explore the demographic understandings of colonial officials whose job it was, albeit with insufficient personnel and resources, to administer vast regions while producing usable knowledge about the people they sought to control, tax, and count. How, in turn, did these administrative concerns give rise to colonial demography and, after World War II, professional social science?

The account of Ango Nkume's murder appears a less likely place to look for African imaginings of what European demographers find compelling. Indeed, if demographics remains confined to census counts, birthrates, age-sex pyramids, and mortality (aside from Ango Nkume's), this murder tells us little. If, however, we wish to gain insight into how some Gabonese experienced and subsequently remember and narrate the shifting distribution of villages and colonial power across the landscape, and especially what demographers call depopulation, migration, and displacement, then Ango Nkume's murder, examined in more detail in the pages ahead, serves as a pertinent starting point. When set against the written record, oral histories of this murder shed light on how Africans perceived the prerogatives, impact, and limits of the colonial state; the demographic legacy of German occupation and World War I; labor recruitment; tensions between taxation and reciprocal exchange; subsistence collapse and famine in the 1920s; village displacement; and the lived violence of colonization.

One way to view the murder of Ango Nkume is as what anthropologist Sally Falk Moore calls a "diagnostic event." According to Moore, such unstaged events, along with local commentaries of them, reveal "ongoing contests and conflicts . . . and the efforts to prevent, suppress, or repress them."[7] When it comes to colonial demographics, the term *diagnostic* is apt given the preoccupation with mortality, depopulation, and displacement as social and moral pathologies. Also pertinent here is Moore's observation that "events involving a number of persons are the *crossroads* where many different interests and visions of things intersect."[8] The murder of

Ango Nkume took place at a spatial crossroads—at the intersection of paths that led to Makokou, Minkébé, and Cameroon. Moreover, the crossroads where Ango Nkume died was a site where competing colonial and African interests clashed. It was a space on the cusp of depopulation as people were moved northward and southward from the expanding emptiness of Minkébé forest, an emptiness produced by colonial policy and lamented by colonial officials and northern Gabonese. It is also possible to think of crossroads more metaphorically. If the colonial officers and later social scientists examined in this essay were concerned with classifying and counting populations and measuring unfolding processes of birth, marriage, death, and migration, the equatorial Africans who lived these processes have sought to remember and "recount" displacement and relocation. Accounts of the murder are thus also situated at the crossroads of two forms of culturally situated knowledge: demographics of empire and historical memory.

The murder of Ango Nkume both intersects with and departs from colonial accounts of demographic knowledge production. Until the early 1920s, under-staffed colonial officials were so preoccupied with imposing a colonial system on often recalcitrant Africans, struggling against undercapitalized and uncooperative concessionary companies and the incursions of German trade agents, and mo-bilizing for the World War I effort that they had neither time nor resources for systematic census taking or population study. After the war, the dual require-ments of tax collection and labor recruitment for coastal logging camps shaped census taking, as did the perception that families in the Gabonese interior were in disarray. During the 1920s, labor recruitment, famine, and village displacement (or *regroupement*), both voluntary and compulsory, contributed to a sense of rapid population decline, which officials attributed to cultural factors and to colonialism itself. An initial shift from the everyday pragmatics of colonial data collection and reporting toward a more systematic social science is indicated in the work of colo-nial administrator, bibliographer, and geographer Georges Bruel (1871–1944), who himself noted the challenges of colonial census taking and the apparent popula-tion decline in the first decades of the twentieth century. In the post–World War II period, French social scientists, in particular the anthropologist Georges Balandier (b. 1920)[9] and the geographer Gilles Sautter (1920–98),[10] worked in Gabon and Moyen Congo to assess the demographic, social, and cultural "crises" produced by the colonial situation. Both Balandier and Sautter made extensive use of earlier colonial reports, which they sought to read systematically. At the same time, they were constrained by a colonial apparatus then still in place.

Outline of Minkébé History

Although populated by Fang- and Chiwa-speaking villagers at the beginning of the twentieth century, Minkébé forest had been almost completely depopulated by the 1930s, becoming a "no-man's-land" that six decades later would attract the attention of international conservationists.[11] In 1888, Paul Crampel was the first Frenchman to travel through the Western Ivindo basin and to pass through the future Minkébé forest. The inhabitants of the region were enmeshed in the local, regional, and long-distance dynamics of their own volatile social landscape. They would scarcely have understood the fateful implications of the 1884–85 Berlin Conference, which signaled impending European colonization. Crampel encountered a region in motion, characterized by high population mobility, long-distance trade, and the interplay between alliance building, exchange, and violence. His geographic descriptions provide tantalizing information on trade routes, agriculture, regional politics, the ubiquity of imported guns, and the use of forest resources in northern Gabon as it was increasingly drawn into overland and global trade networks.[12]

In ensuing years, a number of other French explorers passed through the region.[13] When Capitaine A. Cottes traveled in northern French Congo from 1905 to 1908, he found and expelled numerous German and British traders from territory claimed by France.[14] The French finally began to establish a colonial administration in the northern Woleu-N'Tem Circonscription in 1907 and in the Ivindo in 1908. Reading through archival reports from the years prior to World War I, one is struck by the disorder and chaos of the colonial administration as it attempted to impose centralized state structures and tax collection on a region of independent villages linked by clan ties, marriage, commerce, ritual practices, and conflict. The region was well supplied with trade rifles and gunpowder through the overland trade and newly established concessionary companies. Mobile groups could attack other villages, trading posts, or caravans that marched single-file along forest paths.[15] During the first years of colonialism, most attention went to quelling resistance, especially in the Djouah River valley east of the Ivindo. Exactions by concessionary company agents also provoked incidents west of the Ivindo. As already noted, insufficient manpower and resources meant that little effort was devoted to undertaking censuses or demographic surveys.

A key stated goal of the colonial government was economic development (mise en valeur). Unprepared for the expense that such development would require, the French chose in the 1890s to emulate Leopold II's highly profitable but brutal Congo Free State. Private European investors and firms were granted commercial monopoly rights over vast concessions. In return, they were to raise revenues, pay rent to the colonial state, carry out certain administrative functions, build roads and bridges, and invest in other infrastructural improvements. By most accounts, the concessionary regime in French Equatorial Africa was an economic and political disaster.[16] The Société du Haut-Ogooué (SHO) was the largest, best-organized, and most successful concessionary company in Gabon, but it made most of its profits by providing goods and services to the French colonial administration itself. Prior to World War I, the main company in the Minkébé region was the Ngoko-Sangha (NGS) Company. The NGS was undercapitalized, with few trading posts and few agents as well as insufficient, poor quality, overpriced merchandise. Colonial officials continually bemoaned the NGS's deplorable business practices, which contributed to commercial stagnation in northern Gabon and Congo.[17]

Minkébé post was founded on the Nounah River, a right-bank tributary of the Ivindo, in 1910. In November 1911, to resolve a conflict in Morocco, France ceded a large swath of northern Congo, including Minkébé, to Germany.[18] When World War I broke out in 1914, the French army mobilized to recapture northern Gabon and southern Cameroon. By the end of 1915, the French had largely routed the Germans, who burned villages and terrorized populations as they fled. Demographically, the German occupation proved turbulent. According to French sources and oral traditions, many people fled southward to escape from German impositions and violence, including Ango Nkume's eventual assassins, Mefwé and Akule.

During and after the war, France, itself devastated and impoverished, pushed its colonies harder and harder. Excessive labor migration, combined with taxation and colonial food and roadwork requisitions, culminated in a collapse of the subsistence economy and widespread famine from 1922 to 1925 in the regions of Oyem, Mitzic, and Makokou, to the west and south of Minkébé forest.[19] Minkébé itself was spared but afterward faced growing isolation as populations on its periphery were moved to the principal roads to repopulate the hardest-hit villages. Writing on Minkébé region, Ndong Akono notes that in 1925, the administration required concessionary companies to meet annual quotas or face fines. This led to abuses and "demographic regression": "poverty, insecurity, depopulation, and disintegration of the village unit, basis of the entire economy."[20] The Minkébé area was "closed" in 1927, in part due to its growing isolation and difficult access over frequently flooded river valleys. Most of its remaining inhabitants were relocated to Minvoul, just south of the Cameroon border. It is against this backdrop of colonial trauma, war, labor recruitment, famine, and dislocation that I situate colonial understandings of demographics and the murder of Ango Nkume.

The Murder of Ango Nkume

The murder of canton chief Ango Nkume figured prominently in 1923 Ivindo Circonscription administrative reports. Surprisingly perhaps, these reports largely concur with oral histories of the event recorded seven decades later in both Minvoul and Makokou—on opposite sides of Minkébé forest. As a diagnostic event, this murder and stories about it provide suggestive insights into African and European imaginings of the colonial encounter as well as unfolding demographic processes. In the 1990s, elders' stories pointed to the increasing demands and uneven authority of the colonial state, tensions between taxation and gift exchange, ongoing mobility and displacement, and the separation and remembered unity of clans across the emerging emptiness of Minkébé forest. Colonial accounts of the murder also convey demographic concerns: knowledge production, tax collection, regroupement, labor recruitment, monitoring, and control of populations. The versions presented here—one by the son of the principal assailants from Minvoul, another by an elder from Makokou, and a third assembled from colonial reports—differ in emphasis and details but not essentials.

Ango's murder occurred in 1923, two years before devastating famine hit the Makokou region. Akule Mefwé, the son of the assailants,[21] spoke briefly about the 1925 famine. His elders seem to have suffered from a food shortage but did not face the ravages people faced farther to the south and to the west. He also hinted that his fathers had defended their village against the hungry people who sought to intrude there. The famine prompted the French government to displace the villages in the vicinity of Nkarenzox in order to replenish the population along the main Ovan-Makokou caravan road between them. This, in turn, created a depopulated zone to the south of Minkébé post. Upon their release from incarceration, Ango's assailants followed former Minkébé residents across the forest to Minvoul. Tracking their movements serves as a sort of demographic reckoning of the changes brought by colonialism.

In a 1990 interview near the northern town of Minvoul, elder Akule Mefwé said that his clan (*ayong*), the Esanzwi (also Esinzwi, Esindux), was "one person" but had dispersed, ending up in Minvoul, Makokou, and Ndjolé on the middle Ogooué, as well as in present-day Cameroon and Equatorial Guinea. Akule Mefwé himself had been born in Cameroon, had moved to Minkébé subdivision, and had then gone to Makokou before finally settling in Minvoul. His own biography thus illustrates the high residential mobility of the early colonial period. His "fathers" (*bətarə*) had lived in Gabon but moved to German territory, where the Germans "honored" them.[22] When the war reached Cameroon in late 1914, Akule's fathers fled southward to join their brothers in Makokou subdivision. There, they settled in the village of Nkarenzox at the crossroads of several paths that led downriver and to Minkébé, Makokou, and Cameroon. These paths thus linked the villages of the region to one another, to colonial posts, and to downriver logging camps toward the coast where young men sought work. In the 1920s, the people of the region moved, either voluntarily or through coercion, to the main footpaths and caravan routes "to hold the road." From an administrative point of view, this relocation would facilitate road maintenance, surveillance, tax collection, census taking, and labor recruitment.[23] It was there that Mefwé and Akule had a dispute with their brother, the chief. As wealthy men (*minkunkume*), Mefwé and Akule held and protected "a lot of people"; as warriors, they also fiercely defended them. When the whites sent Ango Nkume to collect taxes, Mefwé and Akule sent word that they would not pay them but only give the chief a "skinny dog." Ango Nkume responded that for their insolence, he would arrest them and march them naked through all the villages. They said, "We'll see that when we see it!"

When Ango Nkume came to collect the taxes, he passed by the crossroads and continued downriver without stopping in the village of Akule's fathers. His fathers were surprised but concluded that they had no dispute with him. They sent their two oldest sons, the narrator's older brothers, to deliver a gift of chickens, sheep, and plantains to the village where Ango was collecting taxes. When Ango saw the sons, he had them seized and beaten until welts rose on their bodies. Furious, the brothers went to wait for Ango Nkume on the path downriver, outside the village where the chief was. Alerted by women, Ango went with his men to where his brothers were waiting. Mefwé said, "So you're stubborn [*ukukur*] like that? If you have a problem with me, why don't you come to see me? I sent food to you, and instead, you want to kill my children? What is the dispute?"

Ango said, "You're still speaking? Are we not going to arrest you just now?" Ango's men came, and a fight broke out. Ango fell dead. Mefwé was also hit on the head by a gun barrel. His brother Akule came to his defense. Akule forced the others to flee and carried Mefwé back to the village.

The "white man" from Makokou investigated the affair. After taking refuge in the forest for several months, Akule and Mefwé turned themselves in. The brothers spent time in prison, but the white man said that Ango Nkume had acted like "an animal of the forest" (*tsit e y'afan*). Ango, like many colonial chiefs, abused his authority and thereby acted like a "wild animal." His denial of clanship and refusal of his brothers' gift was a clear violation of social norms.[24] Mefwé and Akule refused to allow Ango Nkume to use the exigencies of colonial tax collection as a way of subordinating his reciprocal obligations to them. The beating of Mefwé and Akule's sons thus underscores the tensions between a gift economy and a colonial system in which state agents could both extract resources and exercise power through violence. Instead of reciprocating by way of a return gift, Ango responded with "negative reciprocity" by beating the gift givers' sons. As warriors (*mimvu*), Mefwé and Akule were obliged to respond. These events also point to the unevenness of state control, especially far from posts at the margins of administrative districts, and to volatile residence patterns during the early colonial period.

Upon their release from prison, Mefwé and Akule saw that "the region [*si*] was bad" and decided to return to the side [*éfa*] from which they had come— toward Minkébé. Ango Nkume had lived at Nzing-Meyong, close to Makokou. Nkarenzox was two nights from Makokou for most people—one night for young men. "In route, they slept in the villages of their in-laws." Nkarenzox was three nights' walk from Minkébé. Leaving Nkarenzox toward Minkébé, they did not go through villages but "penetrated into the forest." When they left Nkarenzox to go to Minvoul, the people of Minkébé had already moved to Minvoul.[25]

Bifele Alphonse, an Ibifal elder from near Makokou, lived 500 kilometers by road from Minvoul, but he told a substantively similar version of these events. Shared memories of the murder point to a common past in spite of the colonial dispersal of populations. Bifele noted, for example, that the conflict had taken place "at the crossroads where Mefwé and Akule lived." He emphasized that the murder was an internal Esindux [Esanzwi] affair, which suggests that by the 1920s, colonial state politics had penetrated clan politics. He did not mention the assailants' incarceration but said that in the aftermath of the murder, they had fled to Minvoul: "That's where you can find them. They came from here. Besides, the same people who are in Minvoul were people from here." Bifele thus reiterated the important theme of spatial separation but ongoing genealogical connection.

The murder of Ango Nkume, like the emptying of Minkébé forest, was remembered not only as a story of colonial displacement but also in terms of kinship.

Like Akule Mefwé, Bifele referred to the imposition of taxation, abuse of colonial power, violation of the gift economy, the importance of crossroads in a shifting colonial landscape, and flight across the forest. The uncanny similarities in their accounts make sense in light of the shared history and kinship of Fang-speakers living today in Makokou and Minvoul. Stories of the murder express shared memories anchored in the now depopulated northern Gabonese landscape. As Christopher Tilley puts it, "Narrative is a means of understanding the world in relation to agency. Narratives link locales, landscapes, events, and experiences together."[26]

Colonial administrative accounts of the murder obviously express different priorities (for example, punishing recalcitrants, maintaining order, or tax collection), but they also concur in many essentials. In January 1923, some eight months before his murder, Ango Nkume had been sent out to oversee improvements to the footpath, construction of villages, and development of food production, "following instructions of the administrator." In order "to bring the local people to recognize the advantages and benefits of our occupation, . . . frequent tours, acceptance by the population of an authoritarian and active chief, exercise of justice, [and] a reasoned tax collection" were needed.[27]

On arrival in the Ivindo region in August 1923, the new *chef de circonscription,* Capitaine Krieger, left to find Ango Nkume's assassins. Krieger soon recognized that the authority of the colonial administration and "tribal and canton chiefs" was spread very unevenly across the sparsely populated territory and needed "to be reaffirmed continually." Unable to find Mefwé and his accomplices, he sought out Mefwé's father-in-law in the village of Alo Mélégué, located just a few kilometers south of the boundary of Minkébé Subdivision.[28] There, Krieger's troops fought with villagers who were armed with spears, rifles, and bows. Two villagers were killed, including Mefwé's father-in-law, whom Krieger considered the "leader of resistance." In addition, Krieger's troops captured four men and confiscated a number of trade rifles and bows. He complained of the abundance of illegal gunpowder in the village.

Krieger noted that all women and children had fled Alo Mélégué eight days before his arrival. Furthermore, all consumable cassava had been uprooted and carried away. Mefwé, who apparently sought refuge in the village of Yem, passed through the village the day before Krieger's arrival and told men to post a guard. Krieger, unsure as to whether Yem was in Makokou or Minkébé Subdivision, decided against sending a column there; he did not know if he would find an empty village or armed resistance. He notified the chief of Minkébé Subdivision, where branches of the "Essiduz" (Esindux) lived. "But as Mefwé [was] undesirable there, long wanted for having stolen women," he would have risked capture by his enemies. Finally, Krieger asked why Mefwé would have killed Ango Nkume:

> Mefwé, a great sorcerer in his tribe, very brave for a Pahouin, had
> difficulty accepting to obey a chief named by the whites. Also, this

tribe, isolated at the northern edge of the *circonscription* five days from Makokou, does not often see the circumscription chief. For a long time, the area has not been visited. In the entire area, 30 km around, there is a bad path, impracticable in *tipoye* [sedan chairs], which links the "Essinduz" villages. They've only occasionally seen *tirailleurs* [West African riflemen] . . . have not paid one *sou* [a small coin] of the taxes they have been assessed for the current year, an indication, in my opinion, that they are not in hand.[29]

Here, Krieger acknowledged that colonial control remained weak, especially in relatively inaccessible zones such as the headwaters of rivers and at the edge of subdivisions. He also admitted that, even in the postwar period, big men and "sorcerers" had not fully submitted to colonial rule. It is difficult to know how Krieger would have understood the term *sorcerer*. Among Fang-speakers, access to medicines and invisible powers would necessarily have been a component to emerging as a warrior (*mvu*) or wealthy man.

Subsequent Ivindo Circonscription reports provide additional information about the affair. In September 1923, Mefwé remained "in the bush with four armed men." In October, the circonscription chief entered into negotiations with the brothers, "still hidden in a forest camp near the Minkébé border." Apparently, Mefwé had received serious head wounds in an altercation between his "band" and the "Pahouins from Angouma."[30] Finally, in February 1924, Mefwé and Akule "responded to a summons" and were under arrest before the Indigenous Tribunal.[31] Mefwé claimed that he had not wanted to kill Ango Nkume, "from whom all the natives . . . had endured, it seems, major extractions and provided numerous services."[32]

All three recountings of Ango Nkume's murder and its aftermath reveal the links between the colonial situation, clan politics, event history, memory, and demographic processes. The murder took place at an important crossroads that linked the soon-to-be-abandoned Minkébé, Makokou, and downriver—toward timber camps, commerce, and the seat of colonial government in Libreville. The murder also underlined the potentially violent tensions between colonial labor and resource extraction—in this case, in the form of taxes—and the differing roles clan brothers could play in the emerging colonial order. After the murder, the assailants successfully eluded capture by moving back and forth across uncertain boundaries between Minkébé and Makokou subdivisions. The murder coincided with severe food shortages to the west in Oyem and Mitzic, whose populations had been heavily hit by labor recruitment, food requisitions, and roadwork at the expense of crop production. It also preceded the "great hunger" of 1925 in Makokou region, which in turn resulted in the definitive displacement of villages such as Nkarenzox to the southwest to repopulate the main Makokou-Ovan and secondary Makokou-Angouma roads hard hit by famine, which created a growing "emptiness" around Minkébé post.

Oral Histories of Displacement

Elders from Minvoul as well as younger people with historical ties to Minkébé retain powerful memories of clan and marriage ties to Fang-speakers in Ogooué-Ivindo Province. They also recall colonial displacement and dislocation, which they attribute to a number of factors, including German colonial violence, World War I, French colonial policy, and the great famine of 1925. After the 1997 creation of the Minkébé Wildlife Reserve, renamed Minkébé National Park in 2002, these themes took on renewed moral and political salience.

Many of the elders I interviewed in 1990 had been born in Minkébé in the 1910s and 1920s before being relocated to Minvoul. Nze Mengwe André, Esamesel of Evela, said that the Germans had built Minkébé. After the French ceded the northern Gabon territories in 1911, they urged the inhabitants of Minkébé to move southward into French territory, saying "'Leave this side. The Germans are going to come. They're liable to kill you.'" Some people took the French advice; others stayed. After World War I, some people left for Makokou, and others moved to Djoum in Cameroon or Souanké in Moyen-Congo. Those who remained in Minkébé eventually moved to Minvoul.[33]

In 1990, elders recalled both German merchandise, for which their fathers had traded rubber, and German violence, which had provoked flight toward Mvadhi and Makokou. According to Nze Mboule Emmanuel, an Mvua elder, his fathers fled the Germans, saying, "'We're following our brothers who stayed in Makokou.' We died too much here—the Germans killed us too much. That was how they separated—some went to Makokou and some remained, fleeing into the forest. It was the Germans that separated us." He explained how the Germans had brought a lot of merchandise, but during the war with the French, they had also brought a lot of death. "When the Germans knew that the French were going to take the land, it was then that they finished people—finished people."[34]

When asked about the famine that had raged elsewhere in northern Gabon in the 1920s, former Minkébé residents said that they had heard about it but that they themselves had not seen it. Afterward, the French had "broken" (ebuli) Minkébé and removed its people to Minvoul. To make way for the displaced Minkébé populations, "the white man removed" the inhabitants from the northern path to install them on the Oyem road south of present-day Minvoul.[35]

When I was finally able to return to Minvoul in summer 2005, most of the elders I had interviewed in 1990 had died, but Minkébé remained an anchor of historical memory, especially in light of the new national and transnational interest in Minkébé National Park, which Minvoul residents claimed as their patrimony. Oye Dzabe André, an Esikôk born around 1920, said that his fathers had arrived relatively late from Cameroon. He noted that his people had suffered greatly under the Germans. "They would insert a spear through the anus . . . , killing people and leaving them standing" so that others coming upon them thought at first that they were still alive.[36] Commerce also contributed to mobility and village relocation during the early colonial period. Other elders referred in passing to the NGS (Ngoko-Sangha) and the CFSO (Compagnie Forestière Sangha-Oubangui or "Seflisso") concessionary companies that had exchanged clothes, salt, machetes, or coins for rubber. The complaints about exorbitant prices and insufficient, inferior merchandise so prevalent in colonial records seem to have dropped out of the oral tradition. In 2005, few elders recalled that the Germans had been superior merchants or even traders at all.[37]

Other elders linked population movement to the famines of the mid-1920s and to colonial policy in the late 1920s that had led to the closing of Minkébé post. Meyong Mendzigha Pierre, from Mebem on the road to Evela, said that during the famine of the mid-1920s, the Esabon from Minkébé had gone to find their brothers who were dying of hunger near the former post of Angouma on the Mvoung River. He also noted the destruction of Minkébé in 1927 and the displacement of its populations between 1927 and 1933. Some went to Makokou and some to Congo, but most had gone to Minvoul. Biteghe-Bi-Otsima René, a retired nurse, said that his fathers had not wanted to leave Minkébé in the first place. "There was wealth there. The forest was fertile. There was hunting, large game, . . . wild fruits to gather."[38]

Following the creation of Minkébé Reserve, a group of Libreville residents originally from Minvoul had organized to represent Minvoul to the World Wildlife Fund and the Gabonese government. In August 2002, I met with Ango Ndoutoume François, a customs agent from Minvoul who founded the nongovernmental organization (NGO) Avole Israël. Ango told a story of rupture and displacement as a way of claiming access to Minkébé's resources:

> All who live in Minvoul are deported [déportés]. This deportation is
> at the origin of our problem today. All people in the department are
> behind. We were displaced and this displacement created conflicts. . . .
> Populations who were already there were also deported from Minvoul
> to make way for the displaced Minkébé populations. . . . When we
> came from Minkébé, our force was in our [ancestor] relics. We fought
> mystical battles and there was loss of human life. We no longer have
> our origins. They were at Minkébé.[39]

Ango explained how the French colonial administration had irresponsibly decided to displace Minkébé. Because Minkébé was swampy and difficult to get to, the governor had made the decision to close it. But there was another, hidden reason. "At that time we didn't know what existed at Minkébé. We were displaced wrongly. Why? So we couldn't benefit from the riches that were at Minkébé." Now, he concluded, this forest, rich in biodiversity, in flora and fauna, interested the entire world. Thus, in an age of global conservation and increased timber extraction, narratives of displacement provide a way to reconnect to a spiritually (and economically) vital homeland.

Colonial Perceptions of Displacement and Depopulation

If African knowledge about the displacement and depopulation of the post–World War I years remains embedded in oral histories, colonial knowledge emerges in administrative reports and in the simultaneous rise of colonial social science. From the very beginnings of colonial occupation in northern Gabon during the first decade of the twentieth century, colonial officers assessed the impact of policy, commerce, and interventions on colonized populations. Some administrators drew on their experiences in writing colonial reports to synthesize and systematize knowledge production. Later academic social scientists also built on the foundations and concerns of colonial report writing. To illustrate this transition from report writing to colonial and then academic social science, I shift focus here and in sections that follow to the demographic concerns of colonial officials, the published writings of administrator-bibliographer-geographer Georges Bruel, and finally the post–World War II social scientists Georges Balandier and Gilles Sautter. Although Bruel did not serve in northern Gabon, he did work in central Gabon as well as Congo, Ubangi-Shari, and Chad from 1896 to 1911. His writings illustrate the challenges faced by colonial demographers as well as the growing concern about depopulation in the years following World War I. Anthropologist and sociologist Georges Balandier and geographer Gilles Sautter arrived in colonial Brazzaville in the late 1940s. Both Balandier and Sautter wrote extensively about depopulation in colonial northern Gabon, and, as will be suggested, the questions and concerns raised in colonial reports substantially influenced them. Late colonial social science, though critical of the impact of the colonial situation, nonetheless remained rooted in the demographics of empire.

As noted earlier, insufficient staffing of newly created colonial posts, complaints about the nefarious practices of concessionary companies, "incursions" by agents from German companies, the cession of the northern regions to Germany in 1911, and World War I characterized the early years of the French colonial presence in northern Gabon. Substantial population mobility resulted as Africans sought to adjust to, evade, or resist the German and French presence. The chief officers of the Ivindo and Woleu-N'Tem circonscriptions frequently argued for more systematic implantation, contact with African populations, and data collection. In 1910, for example, Capitaine Debieuvre, military commandant of the Ivindo Circonscription, which then included Minkébé forest, detailed the difficulties, incompetence, and violence of the early colonial encounter. Luxuriant forests, numerous swamps, and narrow footpaths made penetration and circulation arduous. Moreover, inexperience and incomplete knowledge of the Ivindo basin had led to grievous political errors, "including exactions, arbitrary repression, [and] arrests in spite of assurances of immunity," as well as the summary execution of eleven Sangha-Sangha (Bɛkwil) chiefs who had been summoned to Viel post on the Djouah River. Debieuvre, sounding what would become a familiar refrain in colonial reports, accused the NGS concessionary company of having "struck a lamentably disastrous blow to our policy in the regions near German concessions. Fines inflicted on the villages by the factory agents, arbitrary arrests, threats of administrative intervention, blows, pillaging of houses and villages, when it is not genuine armed repression; all things well done to increase our unpopularity."[40]

By 1918, the impact of World War I made itself felt in a number of ways, including higher prices, scarcer imported goods, and food shortages in 1917–18:

> The principal causes of this regression are the recruitment of *tirailleurs*
> which has thrown a certain perturbation into the lives of the local
> people, an unusual drought, harmful to food cultivation to the point
> of provoking food shortages everywhere, whose consequence has been
> a fall of production already so weak, the Spanish flu panicking the
> populations of the interior and leaving numerous victims everywhere,
> the rarefaction and the rising prices of trade articles, the restriction on
> both imports and exports, the considerable rise in freight charges and,
> above all, the almost absolute lack of maritime military transport.[41]

At the end of the war, administrators assessed the damage both to the colonial effort and to the peoples they sought to govern.[42] Labor recruitment took much time and effort on the part of an already insufficient colonial administration, deprived interior circonscriptions of their "best workers and best taxpayers," "profoundly disorganized indigenous life," and would have "a repercussion that will make itself felt after 1918."[43]

In the years after World War I, the colonial administration expressed deepening alarm over declining population numbers. In 1921, the population of the colony was clearly in regression, due, in part, to lower birthrates, poor nutrition, and high mortality in both adults and children. A variety of causes were cited—natural, social, economic, and those resulting from the colonial regime itself. Portering, alcoholism, syphilis, sleeping sickness, other endemic illnesses, and flu added to the misery.[44] In the military circonscriptions, the administration was struck by "the apathetic character of the populations . . . that in the past [had] lived in the state of primitive liberty" but had "disintegrated and continually diminished at our contact."[45] A July 1924 report on the situation in Gabon demonstrates the underlying contradictions in colonial paternalism. The report decried the devastating human impact of exploitative colonialism and called both for protecting interior regions as "reserves of men *and* foodstuffs" and for displacing cultivators to feed coastal timber camps. "The disaggregating of tribes" needed remedy, including "the reconstitution of human capital," "the formation of the family," and the "protection of the child." This effort would also require the creation of large agglomerations under effective chiefs and the rebuilding of family and marriage ties "destroyed by the indirect consequences of our contact."[46]

Colonial reports on Minkébé from 1922 to 1925 provide conflicting portraits of how colonial officials viewed the region prior to shutting down the post. On the one hand, Minkébé was presented as the most stable and prosperous subdivision in the Woleu-N'Tem. On the other, it was described as a backwater in a swampy region that was subject to flooding in the rainy season, too far from Oyem, too isolated, and too inaccessible, in spite of its amenable populations, generally energetic and cooperative chiefs, and abundant food production. Although Minkébé was never hit directly by the severe food shortages of the 1920s, low fertility, high infant mortality, migration, and labor recruitment depleted its populations.[47]

In the decade following World War I, colonial officers also struggled to balance the growing needs of the forest industry—the economic motor of the colony— and what they perceived as the social, alimentary, economic, and reproductive viability of depopulated interior regions. By 1930, after two decades of commercial stagnation and colonization, Minkébé region stood empty. The colonial records explored here narrate the cumulative demographic impact of the disastrous concessionary regime, as well as German and French colonization. These themes also emerge in the scientific publications of colonial administrator, geographer, and bibliographer Georges Bruel, whose career exemplifies the transition from colonial report writing to colonial social science.

Georges Bruel, "the scientific inventor of A.E.F."

Bruel began his career as a colonial administrator in Ubangi-Shari and Chad, but according to his biographer, Marcel Soret,[48] he always found time to combine administrative and scientific work. Between 1896 and 1911, he undertook cartographic, topographic, geographic, meteorologic, ethnological, historical, and demographic research. While on periodic leave in France, he prepared publications and organized conferences on the colonies. From 1909 to 1911, Bruel founded and directed the Geographical Service of French Equatorial Africa. Later, he served as a bibliographer, and from 1918 to 1935, he published several geographic works that synthesized colonial knowledge on French Equatorial Africa.

In 1911, Bruel published *Notes géographiques sur le bassin de l'Ogooué,* based on topographic, geographic, and ethnographic surveys of the middle Ogooué and Ngounié River basins during a four-month period in 1907–8. His goal was "to give an image of the country as exact as possible."[49] Rehearsing a claim he would make throughout his career, Bruel underlined the difficulties in collecting exact census data and linked colonial knowledge production to resource extraction: "A general individual census will only be possible in the very distant future and will only be useful for tax collection when a vital registration system is organized." To remedy the immediate situation, he proposed a model for estimating population and population density based on a colonial tribal paradigm that sought "to classify these tribes, to define the zones they currently inhabit, to evaluate finally their importance as well as their kilometric density."[50] Bruel listed thirty-eight "tribes," including Fang (Mfang), Chiwa (Moshébo), and Babongo (Pygmies).[51] He acknowledged the difficulties in "[classifying] these tribes in a rational fashion," not because of the permeability and flexibility of cultural-linguistic boundaries but "because their morphological, physiological, linguistic, and sociological characters have hardly been sketched." Nonetheless, to obtain a first approximation of population, he proposed counting the number of villages per tribe, then using sample data from each tribe to estimate the average number of inhabitants per house and the average number of houses per village. This approach would allow the estimation of total population in each tribe. Population density could then be calculated by locating the villages on a map within a grid that defined the area and dividing the number of people by the area they occupied.

In his first major geographic synthesis on French Equatorial Africa, completed in 1914 but not published until 1918 due to the outbreak of World War I, Bruel included chapters on anthropology, disease, and demography. In a chapter on "Anthropologie," he sought "to avoid all confusion and ambiguity" by adopting a classification system put forth by colonial anthropologist Maurice Delafosse.[52] This schema classified populations based on origin, common anthropological and ethnographic characteristics, and language. The categorizations included "race" (white and black), family, group, people ("an ethnic grouping characterized by common origins and history and generally speaking a common idiom"), tribe, and subtribe.[53] Bruel went on to outline anthropometric measurements compiled from selected surveys, including mean height, cephalic and nasal indexes, facial angle, and prognathism.

In the "Demographie" chapter, Bruel noted that no systematic census had yet been undertaken and that "published general figures" were based on small sample surveys or "estimates without serious basis." Even for regions that had submitted to colonial authority, exact census figures were unavailable because few detailed maps existed (small villages were frequently "only known second hand") and because during visits by colonial officials "many people [were] absent from the village or in hiding." Bruel also lamented the fact that systematic enumeration had taken a back seat to counting taxpayers (*contribuables*): adult men and women were counted, but old people and children were not.[54] Again, he proposed a tribally based method of estimating populations by calculating the average number of inhabitants in a sample of villages. "One must naturally inquire after the visitors, those who are absent, those who are engaged as workers or porters for a short period, etc."[55]

Bruel considered the population of Gabon "the most difficult to estimate," for Gabon had been the last of the equatorial African colonies to be "occupied somewhat systematically." He initially estimated the population of Gabon to be 1.3 million, before subtracting 230,000 to 250,000 people who had been lost to Germany after the cession of a portion of northern Gabon. In this 1918 publication, Bruel voiced little concern about population decline.[56] At that point, he merely recommended a food crop policy that would prevent famine and foster rapid population growth; this, in turn, would create "a more abundant work force" and additional taxpayers and consumers.[57]

In a shorter, updated 1930 edition, Bruel again pointed to the inadequacy of local population counts. Local administrators, obliged to move quickly across large areas and "lacking necessary personnel," could provide only very approximate demographic estimates that had not been subjected to "a reasoned critique." Bruel also substantially lowered his earlier estimates of Gabon's population, from over a million in 1914 to just 468,000.[58] Why had population not grown during the colonial period? He cited "the disorganization we have voluntarily created in the constitution of indigenous society, alcoholism, polygamy, which resulted in 'sexual overtaxing' [surménage sexuel] of married men and a high proportion of unmarried men, infant mortality and, above all, epidemics—malaria, smallpox, sleeping sickness, and the Spanish Flu of 1918—that had spread through the increased mobility and mingling of populations." Bruel reiterated many of these arguments in his 1935 study. In the demography chapter, he noted that Gabon had the lowest population density in AEF (1.79 per square kilometer).[59] He also observed that although "no serious inquiry [had yet] been undertaken by the administration, . . . missionaries, merchants, and subaltern functionaries [were] unanimous in declaring that at least in Gabon, depopulation [was] rapid."[60] In addition, Bruel suggested that "long distance displacements" of both these men and families provoked a "huge loss . . . from the social and demographic point of view."

The cash-strapped colonial administration had done "very little . . . to vanquish the evil of depopulation."[61] Bruel proposed "realistic" policies, adapted to particular milieus designed to stabilize families and promote natality and to insist that labor migrants return home at the expiration of their contracts. He opposed the wisdom of having families or even entire villages migrate to logging camps, which resulted in delinquency, vagabondage, the "rupture of households," and "complete disorganization."[62] Thus, although Bruel did not concentrate specifically on northern Gabon, his broader treatment of AEF and his efforts at an initial demographic synthesis came to express the growing concerns with depopulation that preoccupied colonial officials on the ground. Like his better-known counterpart in West Africa, Maurice Delafosse—both a "colonial inquirer" and a "manager of colonization" who operated "between the colonial world and the university world"[63]—Bruel also prefigured the colonial social science that emerged after World War II.

Late Colonial Social Science: Balandier and Sautter

Not until after World War II did professional social scientists begin to investigate the demographic impact of empire in Gabon. Although freed from the tasks of carrying out colonial policy on the ground, they, like their colonial predecessors, sought to assess the economic, social, and demographic impact of colonialism. Both social scientists profiled here, Georges Balandier and Gilles Sautter, devoted considerable attention to depopulation, displacement, and demographic decline, particularly in northern Gabon. From 1946 to 1952, Balandier worked for the Institut Français d'Afrique Noire in Senegal, Mauritania, Guinea (Conakry), and

Congo-Brazzaville. He arrived in Brazzaville in 1948 to open a department of social sciences at the Institute d'Études Centrafricaines. There, he began to study social and cultural change among Kongo-speakers; the following year, he expanded his research to Fang-speakers in Gabon. In *Ambiguous Africa,* he detailed his impressions of devastation, poverty, corrosion, and fragmentation caused by the dual impact of "a destructive climate" and colonialism. In Lambaréné, on the Ogooué River, for example, he wrote, "One quickly senses that here, civilizations have been corroded and peoples debilitated in less than a century by contact with our economic, administrative, and religious imperatives."[64] He also included a demographic dimension, noting "the dispersion of human groups, their fragmentation across a country which is too vast and engulfs them," and "inadequately populated" regions that left him "haunted by the theme of isolation."[65]

Balandier also made extensive use of colonial reports. As he saw it, the colonial administration acknowledged its responsibility for the "intractable crisis" faced by Gabonese and Congolese villagers. The administration "wanted to understand and permitted me access to sources of information until then reserved for its exclusive use. I completed a systematic perusal of the archives, then dispersed in diverse places."[66] Indeed, Balandier drew heavily on colonial sources in his important 1955 study, *Sociologie actuelle de l'Afrique noire.* He laid out the contours of "the colonial situation" in Gabon and Congo, which he described as "a complex, total social phenomenon that linked colonizers and colonized in an ongoing dynamic of conflict, adaptation, and crisis." Colonial crisis, as he saw it, put into question "the quasi-totality of society, its institutions, social groups, and symbols."[67]

Although colonial crisis was institutional, social, and symbolic, it was also a product of demographic and economic disruption. In Gabon, the exigencies of the colonial economy led to "the demographic impoverishment and denaturation of villages," leaving them "below the minimum level they could tolerate, and leading to dispersion and growing mobility."[68] Beginning in the 1920s in northern Gabon, increased labor recruitment adversely impacted "the (already mediocre) demographic situation in recruiting zones."[69]

Balandier noted that "very early, local administrators [had] recognized the social and demographic consequences" of labor recruitment, "which gravely affected the peoples of Gabon without satisfying the demands of entrepreneurs." Although labor recruitment did not start in the Woleu-N'Tem and the Ivindo region in earnest until 1921, already a 1915 study had expressed surprise at the weakening and diminishing Fang populations that had been "so prolific in the past."[70] According to Balandier, worries about the impact of labor recruitments had long dominated colonial concerns, which, in turn, led to the recognition of "the poor demographic situation and the state of exhaustion of the Gabonese peoples . . . that pushed certain authors of reports to foresee their 'disappearance.'"[71]

Balandier cited a 1938 political report that linked changes in "the demographic and economic base" to "the principal disruptions of Fang society," with "catastrophic consequences," including "long and cruel famines," "dispersions," and "disparate regroupements." The demographic situation seems to have stabilized in Woleu-N'Tem after 1930, particularly through the creation of a peasantry that produced cocoa and coffee, but colonial concerns over "the demographic problem" and the population structure continued into the 1940s. Balandier cited a 1946 report by the Commission de la Population that raised, "once again, questions relative to the demographic drop, 'family disorganization,' and the consequences of work camps, recruitment, and malnutrition."[72] Preoccupations with demographic crisis thus persisted through the colonial era and formed an important refrain in Balandier's own analysis of the colonial situation in northern Gabon.[73]

Balandier's concern with colonial demography was shared by his colleague, geographer Gilles Sautter. Sautter's massive 1966 study, *From the Atlantic to the Congo River: A Geography of Underpopulation*, was based on research undertaken between 1948 and 1953 in Gabon and Moyen-Congo, over the same years when Balandier was in the field. Like Balandier, Sautter also paid close attention to the demographic impact of colonialism, including "the destruction of populations, emigration *en masse*, botched agricultural attempts, economic failures—which have left no trace in the countryside besides emptiness and absence."[74]

In a long chapter on Gabon's northern Woleu-N'Tem region, Sautter provided a comprehensive overview of precolonial and colonial geography. He wrote at length on concerns closely connected to colonial demographics: migration, population density, household and village organization, bridewealth circulation, the impact of concessionary companies, the colonial economy, famine, labor recruitment, agricultural and subsistence production, factors of depopulation and administrative responses, village regroupement, and cocoa.

For reasons of space, I focus here on Sautter's brief discussion of the evacuation of Minkébé. In a pre–World War I sketch map, he counted no fewer than 163 villages east of the longitude of Minvoul. He consequently estimated the population between Minvoul and Minkébé to be at least 10,000 inhabitants, not counting villages east of Minkébé. At one time, Minkébé had anchored the population corridor between the Woleu-N'Tem and the Ivindo, constituting "a sort of *plaque tournante*" (turntable, hub) between the colonial posts of Oyem and Minvoul to the west, Akwafim and Djoum in Cameroon to the north, Souanké in Congo to the east, and Mvahdi and Makokou on the Ivindo to the south. "Today," he wrote, "the region is deserted." An examination of colonial reports from the late 1920s and 1930s revealed that numerous villages in Minkébé subdivision had been "transferred" to the west, the southwest, and around Minvoul, "executed by administrative means." By 1929, according to colonial reports, people remaining in these "unhealthy regions" tended spontaneously to move to Minvoul or Oyem. In 1933–34, individuals and villages sought to take refuge in "the bush" not far from their former villages, but eventually, an expedition rounded up the "last holdouts," leading to "almost total abandonment."[75]

Sautter noted that administrative reports portrayed relocation as advantageous for Minkébé inhabitants, who were lost in a remote region, "delivered unto themselves" too far from "zones of exploitation" or "roads of evacuation," and who needed "to improve their material conditions." He concluded, however, that the decision to close Minkébé and displace its populations stemmed more from administrative convenience. Faced "with a group of villages too far off to be administered and looked after effectively, but insufficiently populated to justify the heavy expenses in such a poor territory,"[76] the administration chose to close Minkébé Subdivision and relocate its inhabitants. Here, Sautter's explanation partially echoes present-day understandings of Minvoul residents, who see their displacement from Minkébé as a matter of administrative convenience but who also suspect more insidious efforts to exclude them from Minkébé's fabulous hidden wealth.

Remembering Colonial Demography

This essay has focused on two themes in the production of emptiness in Minkébé forest following World War I. The first has to do with alternative demographic narratives told by colonial administrators and present-day Gabonese elders about displacement, relocation, and a murder in the 1920s. The second has to do with how colonial and later academic social science arose from concerns similar to those written about by men on the spot. In closing, I wish to return to the relation between demographics of empire and African storytelling traditions as alternate, overlapping, and complementary versions of the past. In a 1990 study of colonial demographics in Central Africa, historian Bruce Fetter argued, "If the human experience is to be measured rather than simply described, demography is its most basic indicator. No discipline treats phenomena more essential to our lives than birth, death, and migration." Fetter underlined the importance of trying to analyze even "the defective data" produced by colonial administrators.[77] In a chapter on French Equatorial Africa, the late Rita Headrick reassessed colonial census figures for Chad, Central African Republic, Moyen-Congo, and Gabon; her goal was to rectify the count and to explain discrepancies. Here, I have focused more on colonial displacements, how colonial officials and later social scientists understood these relocations, and how in turn these processes are remembered by Africans.

In contrast to Fetter, the editors of a recent volume on African oral history make the following claim: "But if African oral history—as opposed to oral tradition research—meant adding an 'African voice' or another perspective to archival histories, it was also, by the late 1980s and early 1990s, a way to access a more true, more accurate, and more authentic colonial experience than that which could be teased out of the writings of white male administrators and their official reports."[78]

My purpose here has not been to argue that oral histories of the murder of Ango Nkume necessarily provide a truer, more authentic recounting of the concerns of colonial demographers. Such histories do, however, present a complementary way to tell the story. The particular story recounted here, chosen in part because of its narrative density, provides a window on past unity and conflict, separation, and displacement. It conveys a sense of culturally located human agency—a conflict between clan brothers over gift giving and taxation, new forms of authority, and colonial state power. The biographies of Ango's assailants and their son's memories intersect with regional processes of migration, resettlement, and flight that were integral to the early colonial situation.

When placed in the larger context—of social alliance, exchange, and conflict; the coming of French and German explorers, traders, and colonizers; the cataclysm of World War I; and the abandonment of the region a decade after the war—the murder of Ango Nkume sheds light on both the demographic history of a colonial landscape and how that history is remembered and represented. In the 1980s and 1990s, Minkébé still figured prominently in the historical imagination of elders in Minvoul and Makokou, and it served as a crucial marker in the construction of social memory and identity. The murder of Ango Nkume was a small but significant episode in a historical anthropology that emerges at the intersection of memory, demography, colonial agency, and a social landscape in flux. In the minds of elders and town dwellers whose kin were removed from Minkébé forest in the 1920s, such stories take on new salience in the age of global claims to Gabon's forest wealth. Yet even as the Gabonese tend to ascribe causation and intention to the colonial agents who removed them from their patrimony, colonial documents and social science cite the exigencies of colonialism itself. In the end, however, one is struck by the surprising convergence between oral histories and colonial accounts of Ango Nkume's murder, especially when set against unfolding processes of movement and depopulation during the 1920s. In this sense, the murder of Ango Nkume stands at the crossroads of diagnostic event history and demographics of empire.

Notes

I would like to thank colleagues Susan Paulson, Doug Rogers, Cameron Hay-Rollins, Kay Phillips, Eric Minzenberg, and Geoffrey Owens and the editors of this volume for their close readings and generous suggestions on this essay.

1. Karl Ittmann notes that prior to the 1930s, British colonial officials also remained concerned about underpopulation, "especially in Africa." Ittmann, "Demography as Policy Science in the British Empire, 1918–1969," *Journal of Policy History* 15, no. 4 (2003): 430.

2. Note sur la situation politique du Gabon (8 September 1923), series 4(1) D 24, reel 51 M1 47 (1), Archives Nationales Section Outre-Mer, Aix-en-Provence, France (hereafter cited as ANSOM). I consulted these documents on microfilm at the Gabonese National Archives in Libreville.

3. Colonie du Gabon, Rapport du 4eTrimèstre 1923, series 4(1) D 24, reel 51 M1 47 (1), ANSOM.

4. Dennis D. Cordell and Joel W. Gregory have underlined similar contests between colonial labor recruitment and subsistence production in the more densely populated region of colonial Upper Volta during the interwar period; see Cordell and Gregory, "Labour Reservoirs and Population: French Colonial Strategies in Koudougou, Upper Volta, 1914 to 1939," *Journal of African History* 23, no. 2 (1982): 205–24.

5. Rita Headrick, *Colonialism, Health and Illness in French Equatorial Africa, 1885–1935* (Atlanta, GA: African Studies Association Press, 1994), 104.

6. See, for example, Georges Balandier, *Ambiguous Africa: Cultures in Collision,* translated from the French by Helen Weaver (New York: Meridian, 1966); Balandier, *Sociologie actuelle de l'Afrique noire: Dynamique sociale en Afrique Centrale,* 4th ed. (1955; repr., Paris: Presses Universitaires de France, 1982); and Gilles Sautter, *De l'Atlantique au fleuve Congo: Une géographie de sous-peuplement,* 2 vols. (Paris: Mouton, 1966). Both Balandier and Sautter are discussed in this essay.

7. Sally Falk Moore, "Distinguished Lecture: Explaining the Present—Theoretical Dilemmas in Processual Ethnography," *American Ethnologist* 14, no. 4 (1987): 730.

8. Sally Falk Moore, "The Ethnography on the Present and the Analysis of Process," in *Assessing Cultural Anthropology,* ed. Robert Borofsky (New York: McGraw-Hill, 1994), 365, emphasis added.

9. Georges Balandier's foundational writings on "the colonial situation" (1951, 1982 [1955]; English translations 1966, 1970) have recently been rediscovered by practitioners and critics of the burgeoning field of colonial studies. See Balandier, "La situation coloniale: Approche théorique," *Cahiers Internationaux de Sociologie* 11 (1951): 44–79, and Balandier, *Sociologie actuelle.* Recent reconsiderations of Balandier's early colonial work include *Cahiers Internationaux de Sociologie* 110, thematic issue, "Georges Balandier, lecture et relecture" (2001), and Frederick Cooper, *Colonialism in Question: Theory, Knowledge, History* (Berkeley: University of California Press, 2005).

10. Gilles Sautter studied geography and history at the Sorbonne before being assigned to the offices of ORSTOM (Office de la Recherche Scientifique et Technique d'Outre-Mer) in Brazzaville from 1948 to 1953. He began to publish on geography, population, and economic production in Gabon and Congo in the early 1950s and published his *doctorat d'état* (advanced state doctorate) thesis, a massive two-volume account on the "geography of underpopulation" in equatorial Africa. See the following works by Sautter: "Le cacao dans l'économie rurale du Woleu-N'Tem," *Bulletin de l'Institut d'Études Centrafricaines* 1 (1950): 7–24; "Les paysans noirs du Gabon septentrional: Essai sur le peuplement et l'habitat du Woleu-N'Tem," *Cahiers d'Outre-Mer* 14 (1951): 119–59; "Le régime des terres et ses modifications récents aux environs de Brazzaville et au Woleu-N'Tem," *Bulletin de l'Institut d'Études Centrafricaines* 7–8 (1954): 201–9; *De l'Atlantique au fleuve Congo: Parcours d'un géographe—Des paysages aux ethnies, de la brousse à la ville, de l'Afrique au monde,* 2 vols., coedited with Chantal Blanc-Pamard (Paris: Éditions Arguments, 1993).

11. In 1997, after the World Wildlife Fund had campaigned for several years, the Gabonese government created Minkébé Integral Game Reserve. In 2002, this reserve became Minkébé National Park.

12. L. Mizon, "Voyage de Paul Crampel au nord du Congo Français," *Bulletin de la Société de Géographie de Paris,* sér. 7, 11 (1890): 534–52; Harry Alis, "Voyage d'exploration de M. Paul Crampel dans le nord du Congo Français," *Tour du Monde* 60, 2nd sem. (1890): 321–36; Alis, *A la conquête du Tchad* (Paris: Hachette, 1891); John M. Cinnamon, "Landscapes of Mobility, Violence, and Exchange in Nineteenth-Century Gabon," paper presented at the Annual Meeting, African Studies Association, Boston, 30 October–2 November 2003; Cinnamon, "Mobility, Genealogical Memory, and Constructions of Social Space in 19th-Century Northern Gabon," in *The Spatial Factor in African History: The Relationship of the Social, Material, and Perceptual,* ed. Allen M. Howard and Richard M. Shain (Leiden, the Netherlands: Brill, 2005), 177–219.

13. Sautter cites missions by Alfred Fourneau (1898–99), Henri Lesieur-Font-Trilles (1899–1901), Cambrier (1905), Dujour (1907–8), A. Cottes (1905–8), and Périquet (1910–11); see Sautter, *De l'Atlantique au fleuve Congo*, 845n.

14. A. Cottes (Le Capitaine), *La Mission Cottes au Sud-Cameroun (1905–1908)* (Paris: Ernest Leroux, 1911).

15. Guillaume Ndong-Akono-Mbiaga, "Contribution à l'histoire de Minkébé et de Minvoul des origines à 1960" (Mémoire de Maîtrise, Université Omar Bongo, Libreville, 1984), 78.

16. See Catherine Coquery-Vidrovitch, *Le Congo au temps des grandes compagnies concessionaries: 1898–1930* (Paris: Mouton, 1972).

17. For example, a February 1911 report lamented the fact that "the N.G.S. company, deprived of all merchandise for more than 2 years, has not exploited the country and has had to abandon its factories one after the other. Under the cover of its privilege as a concessionary, it has caused the gravest prejudice to the national interest and to that of the colony in rendering impossible the exploitation of natural resources of the soil"; Colonie du Gabon, Résumés des rapports mensuels pour le mois de Février 1911, series 4 (1) D6, reel 51 M1 23, ANSOM. An April 1911 report from the huge Ivindo Circonscription noted, "The N.G.S. has no factory . . . on the right bank of the Ivindo. This hinders our influence and lets Germans drain all of the natural riches of the country"; Colonie du Gabon, Résumés des rapports mensuels pour le mois d'Avril 1911, series 4 (1) D6, reel 51 M1 23, ANSOM. Over a decade later, a September 1922 Woleu-N'Tem monthly report noted that the NGS, "charged by contract with the *mise en valeur* of the country," had one trader at Minkébé, who "mope[d] in the middle of out-of-date goods [*vieilleries*] marked at fantastic prices"; Rapport Mensuel Woleu N'Tem, September 1922, series 4 (1) D 23, reel 51 M1 46, ANSOM. As villagers moved closer to trading posts with superior merchandise or, after World War I, to work in the downriver logging camps, these commercial failures would, of course, have had a demographic impact.

18. In the postwar Versailles Treaty, the territories ceded in 1911 reverted to France.

19. Labor recruitment was for porterage and, especially in the 1920s, for work in the downriver timber camps. Northern Gabonese, however, did not face compulsory (and often deadly) recruitment to work on the massive Congo-Océan railroad project in Moyen Congo (1921–34). Large numbers of workers were recruited from Ubangi-Shari and Chad, but Headrick and Coquery-Vidrovitch follow Sautter in noting that Gabonese workers, already insufficient, were spared to work in the timber industry, a key source of colonial revenue; Headrick, *Colonialism, Health and Illness,* 278; Coquery-Vidrovitch, *Le Congo,* 194; Sautter, *De l'Atlantique au fleuve Congo,* 273. Jean Suret-Canale, however, notes that Gabonese, among others, were marched over long distances to "these homicidal construction sites!": Suret-Canale, *French Colonialism in Tropical Africa, 1900–1945,* trans. Till Gottheiner (New York: Pica Press, 1971), 202–3.

20. Ndong-Akono, "Contribution à l'histoire de Minkébé," 72.

21. Akule Mefwé follows Fang kinship terminology and refers to himself as the "son" (*mon*) of both his father and his father's brother. By this logic, he also refers to both men as "father" (*esa* or *tarə*).

22. As used here, the Fang term *batarə* (my fathers) refers to senior clan agnates and is used interchangeably with the term *bəmvama* (my grandfathers, ancestors). Of course, "my fathers" also refers to the narrator's father and his father's brother, who are central actors in his narrative.

23. Writing more broadly on French Equatorial Africa, Cordell notes that *regroupement* was initiated by the administration in the 1910s; Dennis D. Cordell, "Extracting

People from Precapitalist Production: French Equatorial Africa from the 1890s to 1930s," in *African Population and Capitalism: Historical Perspectives*, ed. Dennis D. Cordell and Joel W. Gregory (Boulder, CO:Westview Press, 1987), 144. Regroupement, labor migration, and voluntary relocation all contributed to the increasing isolation of Minkébé region in the 1920s.

24. The expression "animal of the forest" is the narrator's term. Fang-speakers use it to criticize behavior that violates prevailing social norms. By refusing reciprocal social relations with his clan brothers, Ango Nkume dehumanized himself.

25. There is some confusion here in Akule Mefwé's narrative. Earlier, he said that his fathers returned to the side of Minkébé, whereas here, he noted that Minkébé had already been closed. I do not know how long they remained in prison or whether they were released before or after the closing of Minkébé post. Nonetheless, the ambiguity of the narrative on this point captures the demographic fluidity of this moment of transition.

26. Christopher Tilley, *A Phenomenology of Landscapes: Places, Paths and Monuments* (Oxford: Berg, 1994), 32.

27. Circ. de l'Ivindo, Rapport mensuel, Jan. 1923, series 4 (1) D 26, reel 51 M1 49 (1), ANSOM.

28. Rapport sur la Sit. Pol. Col. du Gabon," 3e trim. 1925, series 4 (1) D 24, reel 51 M1 47, ANSOM.

29. Rapport du Capt. Krieger, Cmdt de la Circ. de l'Ivindo, to Lieut. Gouv. Gabon, 22 Août 1923, series 4 (1) D 24, reel 51 M1 47, ANSOM.

30. Col. du Gabon, Circ. de l'Ivindo, Rapport Mensuel, Sept. 1923, Rapport Mensuel, Oct. 1923, series 4 (1) D 26, reel 51 M1 49 (1), ANSOM. A 1924 report notes that the Angouma region and its "turbulent" natives had to be "firmly held" to avoid rebellion or hostility; Rapport Mensuel Ivindo, Feb. 1924, series 4 (1) D 29, reel 51 M1 52 (2), ANSOM. Angouma post had been created on the Upper Mvoung River in 1912 following the evacuation of "New Cameroon." Populations in this region had been slow to recognize colonial rule, pay taxes, or perform labor requisitions. The post was evacuated during World War I, reoccupied in 1917, and definitively closed in 1922. I have undertaken research among populations who had lived on the Makokou-Angouma road until they were finally moved to the main Ovan-Makokou road in 1953. For inhabitants of this region, Angouma, although only occupied for ten years, remains an important spatial and historical marker.

31. Col. du Gabon, Rapport Pol, 1er trim 1924, series 4 (1) D 28, reel 51 M1 51, ANSOM.

32. Rapport Mensuel Ivindo, Fév. 1924, series 4 (1) D 29, reel 51 M1 52 (2), ANSOM. Colonial reports do not specify how long the brothers were incarcerated.

33. Nze Mengwe André (Esamesel, Evela), interview by the author, 27 August 1990.

34. Nze Mboule Emmanuel (Mvua, Ikok), interview by the author, 25 August 1990. Cordell and Gregory underline similar processes of competition for labor and population loss in West Africa, in "Labour Reservoirs and Population," 207, 215, 221. They focus on Koudougou District in Upper Volta. There, French timber operations from Côte d'Ivoire competed with better-run British businesses in the Gold Coast. As in northern Gabon, French policies exacerbated a 1931 famine in Koudougou District. Reports from Koudougou also expressed a growing concern with depopulation, even in this much more densely populated region.

35. Essong Emane (Esantsiman, Bilou), interview by the author, 20 August 1990.

36. Oye Dzabe André (Esikôk, Mebem village), interview by the author, 6 August 2005; Bekale Mbiaghe (Yebé, Djoum village), interview by the author, 4 August

2005; Nkoume Nze Jean (Essissep, Ellarmintang village), interview by the author, 7 August 2005.

37. I recorded information on superior German trade goods in 1990; see John M. Cinnamon, "The Long March of the Fang: Anthropology and History in Equatorial Africa" (PhD diss., Yale University, 1998).

38. Meyond Mendzigha Pierre (Esabon, Mebem), interview by the author, 6 August 2005; Biteghe-Bi-Otsime René (Essissep, Ellarmintang), interview by the author, 3 August 2005.

39. Ango Ndoutoume François (b. 1965), president of NGO Avole-Israël (Libreville), interview by the author, 5 August 2002.

40. Rapport du Capt. Debieuvre, Commandant la 1ère Compagnie du Bataillon Indigène du Gabon, Administrateur de la Circ. de l'Ivindo à M'Vadhi, sur la Sit. Pol. dans le bassin de l'Ivindo et sur les mesures à prendre en vue de la pacification et de l'occupation du secteur, M'Vadhi le 1er avril 1910, series 4 (1) D5, reel 51 M1 21, ANSOM.

41. AEF, Colonie du Gabon, Rapport sur la Situation de la Colonie du Gabon pendant l'année 1918, series 4 (1) D 16, reel 51 M1 41, ANSOM.

42. For a discussion of overall mortality in Africa during the influenza pandemic, see K. David Patterson and Gerald Pyle, "The Geography and Mortality of the 1918 Influenza Pandemic," *Bulletin of the History of Medicine* 65, no. 1 (1991): 4–21.

43. Colonie du Gabon, Affaires Politiques, Rapport Politique du 3e Trimestre 1918 (LBV, 5 Oct., 1918), and Rapport Politique du 4e Trimestre 1918, series 4 (1) D 16, reel 51 M1 41 (suite), ANSOM.

44. Rapport annuel 1921 de la Colonie du Gabon (sent 17 April 1922), series 4 (1) D, reel 51 M1 42 (1), ANSOM.

45. Col. du Gabon, Rapport Politique du 2e Trimestre 1921, series 4 (1) D, reel 51 M1 42 (1), ANSOM.

46. Rapport sur les causes de la situation actuelle de la Colonie du Gabon et sur les remèdes à y apporter, July 1924 (Rapport de Mr. l'administrateur en chef G. Thomann), series 4 (1) D 28, reel 51 M1 51, ANSOM.

47. Headrick notes that in French Equatorial Africa, "Gabon presents the clearest evidence of rising infertility during the colonial years"; Headrick, *Colonialism, Health and Illness,* 125. She points to the widespread incidence of gonorrhea, among other factors.

48. Marcel Soret, "Georges Bruel (1871–1945): Notes de Biographie," manuscript in Académie des Sciences d'Outre-Mer, Paris. Consulted online at Institut de recherche pour le développement. Horizon/Pleins textes, base de données, http://horizon.documentation .ird.fr/exl-doc/pleins_textes_5/b_fdi_16-17/22538.pdf).

49. Georges Bruel, *Notes géographiques sur le bassin de l'Ogooué* (Paris: A. Challamel, 1911), 5.

50. Ibid., 51. The tribal paradigm categorized and reinforced particular ethnic identities that could then be counted, classified, and characterized; see Benoît de L'Estoile, *Empires, Nations, and Natives: Anthropology and State-Making* (Durham, NC: Duke University Press, 2005), 15–16.

51. Bruel also proposed prompt, "detailed study of each one of these tribes . . . to collect precise data on their migrations [and] history while there is still time"; see Bruel, *Notes géographiques,* 55.

52. Like Bruel, Delafosse (1870–1926) began his career in the colonial service, where he served in West Africa (Côte d'Ivoire, Liberia, Senegal, Niger) between 1894 and 1919. Later, he taught oriental languages at the École Coloniale. Delafosse published widely on West African geography, linguistics, anthropology, ethnography, and history; Emmanuelle

Sibeud, *Une science impériale pour l'Afrique? La construction des savoirs africanistes en France, 1878–1930* (Paris: EHESS, 2002), 10–11.

53. Georges Bruel, *L'Afrique Équatoriale Française: Le pays—les habitants—la colonisation—les pouvoirs publics* (Paris: Émile Larose, 1918), 153–54.

54. Bruel also wondered whether young mothers, aged eleven to thirteen, should be classified as adults.

55. Bruel, *L'Afrique Équatoriale Française,* 343–45.

56. He cited Dr. Cureau on the "physiological misery" due to insufficient nutrition and compounded "by the profound perturbations that we brought to indigenous life and mentality from the fact of our occupation"; Bruel, *L'Afrique Équatoriale Française,* 334; Adolphe Cureau, *Les sociétés primitives de l'Afrique équatoriale* (Paris: Armand Colin, 1912).

57. Headrick cites a Bruel article published in 1927 on the population of Cameroon to illustrate the "creative naïveté" of colonial demographers: "The lack of rigor in collecting the statistics was matched by a creative naïveté in interpreting them. Georges Bruel (1927, 340–41), one of the first to realize the importance of demographic studies, tried to rectify the census figures on French Equatorial Africa by using a population model derived from that of Paris in 1921"; Headrick, *Colonialism, Health and Illness,* 95–96. Similar problems existed in much of colonial Africa. See, for example, Robert R. Kuczynski, *Colonial Population* (Oxford: Oxford University Press, 1937), and Kuczynski, *The Cameroons and Togoland: A Demographic Study* (London: Oxford University Press, 1939).

58. Georges Bruel, *L'Afrique Equatoriale Française (A.E.F.)* (Paris: Larose, 1930), 157.

59. Georges Bruel, *La France équatoriale africaine: Le pays, les habitants, la colonisation, les pouvoirs publics* (Paris: Larose, 1935), 336.

60. Ibid., 357.

61. Ibid., 339.

62. Ibid., 341.

63. Sibeud, *Une science impériale pour l'Afrique?* 10–11.

64. Balandier, *Ambiguous Africa,* 146.

65. Ibid., 149, 152–53.

66. Georges Balandier, *Histoire d'autres* (Paris: Stock, 1977), 230.

67. Balandier, *Sociologie actuelle,* 27. He had originally published a lengthy article laying out "the colonial situation" in 1951; Balandier, "La situation coloniale." As Frederick Cooper has noted, Balandier's penetrating analysis of the colonial situation was quickly overshadowed by events in the 1950s as social scientists, including Balandier himself, turned from colonialism to modernization; Cooper, *Colonialism in Question,* 33–34. At the same time, the field of demographic studies burgeoned during the 1950s. For Anglophone Africa, see, for example, L. T. Badenhurst, "Population Distribution and Growth in African," *Population Studies* 5, no. 1 (1951): 23–34; A. T. Grove, "Soil Erosion and Population Problems in South-East Nigeria," *Geographical Journal* 117, no. 3 (1951): 291–304; J. F. M. Middleton and D. J. Greenland, "Land and Population in West Nile District, Uganda," *Geographical Journal* 120, no. 4 (1954): 446–55; Glenn Trewartha and Wilber Zelinsky, "Population Patterns in Tropical Africa," *Annals of the Association of American Geographers* 44, no. 2 (1954): 135–62; Richard W. Stephens, *Population Pressures in Africa South of the Sahara* (Washington, DC: Population Research Project, George Washington University, 1958); Frank Lorimer, *Demographic Information on Tropical Africa* (Boston: Boston University Press, 1961); K. M. Barbour and R. M. Prothero, eds., *Essays on African Population* (London: Routledge and Paul, 1961).

68. Balandier, *Sociologie actuelle,* 60.

69. Ibid., 167.

70. Ibid., 168–69.

71. Ibid., 187.

72. Ibid., 197.

73. Balandier mentions Minkébé in passing. Citing Woleu-N'Tem quarterly reports from 1933 and 1934, he notes that several years after the closure of Minkébé post, the administration still had to "recuperate" villages hidden in Minkébé forest: "'The people of Minkébé hang on to their region even though they know that difficulties in access mean that it will not often be visited by representatives of the administration'"; ibid., 171–72.

74. Sautter, *De l'Atlantique au fleuve Congo,* 9. Sautter's massive study on the human geography of underpopulation in Gabon and Congo is too vast to do justice to it here. After systematically laying out his methodology and discussing the challenges of relying on colonial documents, Sautter turned to six lengthy case studies, four in Congo-Brazzaville and two in Gabon (on the southern Lakes and the northern Woleu-N'Tem). In his treatment of the northern region, Sautter traces migration history and asserts a higher than average population density and economic potential in the late precolonial period. He, too, emphasizes the demographic perturbations of the early colonial period. Beginning in the 1930s, population began to stabilize in response to the new cocoa economy, which peaked in the 1950s; Sautter, *De l'Atlantique au fleuve Congo.* In 1989, French geographer Roland Pourtier also published a two-volume study on Gabon. Like his predecessors, he relies heavily on published and archival sources from the colonial period. Pourtier refers to a "peripheral and fragmented" population and, once again, underlines the impact of colonialism: "One thing seems assured: the demographic decline of the first decades of colonization"; Pourtier, *Le Gabon,* vol. 1, *Éspace-historicité-société,* and vol. 2, *État et développement* (Paris: Harmattan, 1989).

75. Sautter, *De l'Atlantique au fleuve Congo,* 876–77.

76. Ibid., 877.

77. Bruce Fetter, ed., *Demography from Scanty Evidence: Central Africa in the Colonial Era* (Boulder, CO: Lynn Rienner, 1990), 1–2.

78. David William Cohen, Stephan F. Miescher, and Luise White, "Introduction: Voices, Words, and African History," in *African Words, African Voices: Critical Practices in Oral History,* ed. Luise White, Stephan F. Miescher, and David William Cohen (Bloomington: Indiana University Press, 2002), 15.

6

The Discourse of Overpopulation in Western Kenya and the Creation of the Pioneer Corps

MESHACK OWINO

When World War II broke out, colonial authorities in Kenya already had developed a plan to mobilize African labor for the military, and beyond that, they also had a military labor unit in place, just waiting to be given the green light to enter the war. That military unit was the Pioneer Corps. Due in large part to a pervasive colonial discourse that tended to regard Kenya, especially western Kenya, as a colony teeming with an inexhaustible supply of labor, the Pioneer Corps was created to channel African labor for military service in the war. But as the war began and African labor recruits started serving in the military, colonial assumptions about a teeming African population came under considerable strain. Labor shortages became common, and agricultural production declined in areas most affected by overzealous military recruitment. Colonial authorities realized that African labor in Kenya was not limitless after all. Complaints from conscientious colonial officials and African resistance forced them to review some of their assumptions. The limits of the Pioneer Corps led to a reassessment of some of the long-standing colonial views about African population and labor in colonial Kenya. It also demonstrated the need for colonial authorities to develop sound policies based on a concrete and realistic understanding of population dynamics in Kenya African societies.[1]

Establishing the Pioneer Corps

Colonial authorities started toying with ideas on how best to channel Kenya's labor force into colonial development as soon as Kenya became a protectorate. Their objective when they took their posts in Kenya was to transform it into an independent entity capable of maintaining itself and paying for its own administration. They believed that an understanding of Kenya's demographic characteristics would help them better plan for development and make the colony financially independent of the British government. Their major difficulty during those early years was that they did not have a very clear knowledge of the size of the population. Handicapped in this way, colonial authorities often resorted to rough estimates of Kenya's population for planning purposes. Sir Gerald Portal was one of the first colonial administrators in East Africa to try to estimate the population of Kenya.[2] In 1897, for instance, he put the population at 450,000.[3] During the same year, A. H. Hardinge, the first commissioner and consul general for East Africa Protectorate, made a working guess of Kenya's population as 2.5 million. This estimate was revised in 1902 to 4 million.[4] The reason behind this dramatic rise in Kenya's population was the redemarcation of the Kenya-Uganda boundary. The western boundary, which up to 1902 stood at Naivasha, was moved farther west to modern Busia, thus adding heavily populated sections of eastern Uganda to the Kenya Colony.

As Kenya gradually evolved into a full-fledged colony, colonial authorities continued to develop better census methods as they visualized ways in which the colony's allegedly abundant population could be mobilized.[5] In a bid to make the colony pay for itself, colonial authorities spent hours assiduously calculating the size, age, and distribution patterns of Kenya's population. They commissioned studies on the colony's demographic profile. Some of these studies, particularly those by administrators and anthropologists, concentrated on delineating the size of Kenya's ethnic communities, together with their "habits" and traits.[6] Others focused on projects, works, and activities within the various ethnic communities, essentially identifying how each could contribute to the colony's development.

By the 1930s, colonial authorities had become adept at census exercises. A 1931 estimate put Kenya's population size at 4.1 million, only 100,000 more than the population in 1902. This apparent stagnation in the population is puzzling. It may well be that the earlier estimates were not accurate, given that most of them were based on guesswork by colonial officials. However, scholars such as R. M. A. van Zwanenberg have argued that during the early twentieth century, East Africa's population actually did decline. They have noted that this period was characterized by major challenges for East African people. The entire region was afflicted by wars. It was also plagued by diseases such as smallpox, dysentery, chicken pox, measles, poliomyelitis, plague, influenza, and whooping cough. Some of these diseases were old; others were just making "their appearance . . . by at least 1890."[7] Van Zwanenberg concludes that many people died.

This was a period of tumult, confusion, and uncertainty. World War I alone claimed more than 144,000 people in the region. Van Zwanenberg argues that, due to these challenges, "there seems to have been a downwards trend in the population from the 1890's until the middle of the 1920's."[8] Beginning in the 1920s, however, the region's population, including that of Kenya, started recovering. Due in no small part to colonial medical programs to combat diseases, Kenya's population started rising. By 1931, it had climbed to 4.1 million. In 1939, it stood at 4.8 million.[9]

Census methods continued to improve. By 1948, censuses were being conducted like "a military exercise."[10] And by this time, the population of Kenya was reportedly 5.7 million.[11] Nyanza Province's share of Kenya's population throughout this period was believed to be substantial. The combined population of the Nyanza Province by 1940, including, at that time, the Nandi and the Kipsigis and some parts of the present-day western Kenya, was 1.25 million, or around one-quarter of the overall population by the beginning of the war.

When the war broke out, it was therefore not surprising to find that colonial authorities had anticipated—and laid down nearly complete plans for—the appropriation of the colony's labor for military service. Fears that war would break out in Europe were already rampant in Kenya by early 1939. As Europe moved toward war, colonial authorities in Kenya started preparing. In a critical move, the chair of the Manpower Committee of the Kenya Colony circulated a communiqué soliciting suggestions on the formation of a "Labour Corps." The communiqué tellingly suggested that Nyanza Province should provisionally contribute 3,000 men.[12] If Kenya was perceived in colonial discourses as a large labor reserve, Nyanza Province in particular and western Kenya as a whole were the focus of that perception.[13] Colonial administrators based in Nyanza further enhanced and solidified this view. S. H. Fazan, the provincial commissioner, often noted that Nyanza teemed with labor, concluding that the establishment of a military labor corps would not be a major problem for the province. Fazan described himself quite proudly as "a Provincial Commissioner of a Province with a million and a quarter natives which in the war of 1914–18 in East Africa bore the brunt of the military and civil labor requirements."[14] Fazan's enthusiasm and energy then not only transformed Nyanza Province into a labor reserve but also made it into the main base for intensive labor recruitment.[15] Although the letter from the Manpower Committee sought ways of recruiting African labor, it did not provide the actual mechanism by which this could be done. It left implementation to colonial officials on the ground.

The details of drawing manpower into the war fell to Fazan.[16] The "personal request," Fazan was to recall later in the war, was for him "to write a memorandum" on military labor service. He began by collecting suggestions from his district commissioners and recommending the formation of a military labor unit. While writing his recommendations, Fazan admitted that "the subject of Manpower . . . is constantly in [my] mind."[17] Even by the normal standard of colonial obsession with labor in Kenya, Fazan was unusual. In reports issued while serving as the provincial commissioner of Nyanza, he claimed that he could not avoid commenting about the military because the views of civil administrators were also crucial to the conduct of the war. He claimed that there had already been occasions "when the civil Administration has foreseen the needs of the military before they were declared, and consequently has been able to meet them, with more expedition and less disturbance than would otherwise have been the case."[18] The fact that the provinces were required to conduct large-scale recruitment "at short notice," Fazan observed on another occasion, "demand[ed], in my submission, that we should overhaul our recruiting organization and have it ready in advance, at least on paper and also, to some extent in the field."[19]

Fazan often argued that, through vigorous enforcement of existing laws, labor could easily be channeled into military service. He became quite influential within military circles, and the military saw him as an ally. The governor of the colony praised him for "zeal and enthusiasm." Indeed, it is no wonder that Fazan later relinquished his post in Nyanza to become a liaison officer with the military. After collecting views and opinions of colonial officials, he recommended the establishment of a military labor unit. That unit came to be called, euphemistically, the Pioneer Corps.

The Challenges of Creating the Pioneer Corps

There were several major difficulties in getting the unit off the ground. Although many scholars characterize Kenyan recruits as having generally been willing to serve in the Pioneers, the evidence suggests otherwise—indicating that recruits were very reluctant because it reminded them of the ill-fated "Carrier Corps of the First World War and everything connected with it."[20] Geoffrey Hodges has estimated that upwards of 100,000 African men died during military service in the Carrier Corps—or *Kariokor* (as it was known locally)—in East Africa during World War I. That was nearly 10 percent of the total number of men serving in British military forces in East Africa, and no compensation was given to soldiers or their families for injuries or death that occurred during the war. Service in the Carrier Corps was almost synonymous with misery and death. Thus, because of the horrible experience of *askaris* (soldiers, in Swahili) in World War I and in other colonial military expeditions, military labor units were feared and loathed. In the words of Fazan, men had "not forgotten that in the last war there were many unrecorded casualties and many gratuities owing to the dependants of deceased carriers were not paid."[21] The men knew "that the Carrier Corps was alternatively known as the Labor Corps and its head as the Director of Military Labor. Any mention of a Labor Corps [was] undoubtedly . . . associated in their minds with the carrying of loads and all the hardships of the last war, and they will not engage in it voluntarily." Askaris disliked military service, especially units associated with labor. The word *labor*, as in the "East African Labor Unit" or in the "Labor Corps," then, induced images of suffering, fear, and death.

These problems were additionally complicated because the men who served in the units were often not issued rifles. "The great complaint among the men, who are otherwise keen and proud of themselves," Fazan revealed, "is that their women will mock them if they are not armed."[22] Without rifles, the Pioneers felt ordinary, as ordinary as the despised *jo Apida* (employees of Public Works Department). As mere *jo leba* (laborers) in the army, potential recruits felt that they would not be as respected as "real" soldiers serving in, say, the Kings African Rifles.[23] Fazan came to realize that the word *labor* would impede the creation of a successful military labor unit, so he proposed that the word be removed from the name of the organization. Upon receiving the communiqué from the chair of the Manpower Committee proposing to establish a "labor corps," Fazan recalled that he and his committee immediately "headed him off the term 'Labor Corps' and chose 'Pioneer Corps' as likely to be more popular."[24]

The term *Pioneer* was well chosen. According to the *Oxford English Dictionary, Pioneers* was first used in the eighteenth century to refer to "an advance party of soldiers" whose task in eighteenth-century Western armies was "clearing and making roads." Although it accurately revealed the kinds of tasks that the proposed unit would perform, the term was deliberately opaque. It was chosen to lure askaris into the army by making them believe that they were part of a bigger plan; implicit in the term was a suggestion that the unit would be a forerunner to a successor formed during wartime.[25] By adopting the term *Pioneers* and dropping more accurate, albeit frightening, labels such as *labor,* the administration was dishonest. The term was willfully misleading and took advantage of askaris without seriously addressing their fears. And though the name change enabled the government to lure unsuspecting men into providing labor, it did not, in reality, represent a qualitative change in the nature of African military service. Like its eighteenth-century precursor, the unit had a simple mission: providing labor—clearing and building roads, among other things. Askaris would not be happy when they discovered the true mission of the Pioneer Corps because the colonial administration had failed to reveal the nature of service or address the reasons why aksaris hated labor-intensive units.

Fazan's proposal targeted certain ethnic communities. He believed that the best communities for enlistment into the Pioneer Corps were the "Kavirondo,[26] the Kamba and Meru, and some of the coast tribes [*sic*]."[27] His recommendations reflected the pervasive view in British colonial circles that some communities were "warlike" or "martial" and therefore well suited for service in combat units, whereas others were only good for labor units.[28] Assessing the suitability of various African communities for military service, Fazan noted that in terms of quality "for a Pioneer Corps . . . the Kavirondo are certainly among the best of the tribes [*sic*]."[29] And among the Kavirondo, Fazan proposed that the Luo should be targeted first because "the Luo, no doubt, would yield with a fairly good grace to conscription; the Bantu would come in not readily and there would probably be some degree of disaffection in some of the more political locations."[30] Fazan argued that the communities needed to be convinced to join the Pioneer Corps, for otherwise, "they will not engage in it voluntarily."[31] He argued that if "it was made clear" to these communities that "the Pioneer Corps will not carry loads as part of their regular duties and that they will in fact be auxiliary troops who would receive some training and at least some proportion of whom would be armed, they would come forward *for that readily enough*" (emphasis added).[32] A pledge was also made to the men, assuring them that joining the Pioneers would "not spoil their chances of getting into the KAR [the King's African Rifles]."[33] Most of these promises were never kept; when it came to joining the KAR, the Pioneers were given first preference—but usually, only the men from "martial communities" graduated from the Pioneers into the KAR. Without doubt, deception was being used to recruit unsuspecting askaris into the Pioneer Corps.

Having analyzed and prepared his recommendation on the establishment of the Pioneers, Fazan submitted it to the chair of the Manpower Committee in March 1939. In this report, Fazan also suggested the formation of an auxiliary corps. The Manpower Committee accepted the idea of establishing a Pioneer Corps but took no action on the larger proposal to establish an auxiliary corps "until after war broke out . . . but the principle to form a nucleus of 'Pioneer Corps' was approved."[34] At a subsequent meeting, held on 14 and 15 April 1939, a resolution was adopted calling for a rudimentary nucleus of the Pioneer Corps. According to Fazan: "It was agreed that the Provincial Commissioner of Nyanza, after consultation with the Provincial Commissioner, Central, and the Director of Public Works, should furnish a draft scheme for the formation of a such [*sic*] nucleus to be expanded to 1,000 strong if money was obtained for strategic roads."[35]

This meeting, moreover, came up with recommendations on specific steps to form a future Pioneer Corps. The first batch of the Pioneers was supposed to consist of a peacetime nucleus of 1,000 men, which in wartime would be expanded to a force consisting of thousands of men. Other provinces, such as Central Province, were also required to establish "peace time nuclei in similar proportion to the quota required from them in wartime."[36] A list of names of potential recruits was to be drawn up, but authorities realized in time that "if we make a provisional list of names and warn the persons listed we shall simply start a pack of rumors and nervousness all over the reserve. Whatever we may say everybody will think he is down for the carrier corps and many of the persons listed would immediately seek the shelter of other work as far away from the reserve as possible."[37] Officials knew that some men might quit the Pioneers after finding out they were being misled, and so the government devised ways of recruiting and holding the men without making them aware that they would be serving with the military labor corps during the war.

To keep the men busy as war neared without alerting them as to their true mission, the government secured a grant for the construction of roads in Nyanza. While recruiting the men under the guise of constructing roads, care was to be taken to ensure that the number of recruits was "sufficient to form a nucleus . . . and [that the men were] employed on a six months' contract or longer and that all superior staff [foremen, gangers, *nyaparas* (supervisors), and so forth] employed on the work [would] be carefully selected with a view to their eventually becoming warrant officers and NCO's."[38] Another recommendation was that the "gangs should at first be treated as ordinary road gangs in all outward respects although more care would be given to the supervision and weeding out of undesirables, but as the time approached when precautionary measures need no longer be concealed they would begin to receive some degree of drill and special training, various skilled ranks such as carpenters could be added and a proper Pioneer Corps [would] begin to take shape."[39] Given the need to keep the men ignorant of their future work, the Pioneer Corps was to be "developed as part of the Public Works Department [*Apida*] and with officers, foremen, and gangers largely drawn [from] it but . . . as development is advanced it should become independent of the Public Works Department and form a military auxiliary unit [such] as a Pioneer Corps (R.E.) [Royal Engineers]."[40] Other officials were to do the same thing in their provinces, and train the recruits "for a period which might extend to two months after which they should be moved as required for roads or other works of military importance."[41]

The budget submitted in Fazan's memorandum of 25 April 1939—for a corps of 2,000 men working for two months in Nyanza (and other provinces), including pay and rations, equipment, construction materials, and consumable stores—came in at £10,963; it was later discovered that the estimate had omitted tentage.[42] Once the Pioneers left Nyanza and were employed by the military, the monthly cost of the company—the recurrent expenditure—was estimated at £1,889. At a maximum strength of 10,000 men, a colony-wide Pioneer Corps would cost £53,800 to establish, plus recurrent expenditures. The financial secretary accepted these recommendations and budget figures and called for the expenditure of £2,000, pending "a grant from the imperial government."[43] The grant was subsequently increased from £2,000 to £2,350, to cover the working cost of maintaining the corps for two months. The initial grant available to Nyanza was estimated to be enough for the maintenance of a peacetime nucleus of "1 Assistant engineer, 2 European foremen, 1 Time keeper and clerk, 2 Asiatic Gangers, 3 Masons, 1 Carpenter, 1 Blacksmith, 2 African Sergeants, 10 Corporals, and 300 men."[44]

Recruitment for the first unit began in late May 1939. In June, some 180 men presented themselves for service in the Pioneer Corps, but when they learned of the provisional terms of service, many quit and returned home. Out of the 180 men who initially joined the Pioneers, 110 went home and 70 remained.[45] The low pay and long duration of service provoked the departure of most of the first recruits.[46] But the government soldiered on looking for men. By the first week of June 1939, training began and the number of recruits in the Pioneers increased to 80.

There were other complaints. Some askaris suffered from an outbreak of typhoid fever, which afflicted the camp due to "bad water supply" and the rocky nature of the ground. These conditions had led to the building of shallow trench latrines, which allowed fly breeding. When 300 recruits who were going to join the Pioneers were rejected on medical grounds and turned over to the Public Works Department at a wage of Kshs. 16/- and Kshs. 4/- for *posho* (maize meal), on better terms than the Pioneers were offered, "the incident rankled."[47] Some recruits, such as Okumu Aulo and Oyaga Ogola, fled the Pioneer Corps camp, and an order was issued: "*Mshike hawa watu wenye kutoroka katika* Pioneer Corps, *mlete hapa kwa mara moja*" (Arrest these people who fled the Pioneer Corps, and bring them here at once).[48] Other recruits complained about the lack of rifles. During recruitment drives, the men had been promised rifles, but they never received them. When they heard that they would not be issued rifles, many refused to enlist, and others, upon enlisting, demanded firearms. Some men even went on "strike" over the lack of rifles, and "a few malcontents were discharged."[49]

After its formation, the Pioneer Corps camped about three and a half miles beyond Ahero on the projected new route between Kisumu and Muhoroni. The officer in charge of the camp was R. Southby, reportedly an ex-officer of the Yeomanry with extensive campaigning experience.[50] Things at the camp generally seemed to be running as planned by the government. A telegram from camp officials to Nairobi reported, for example: "60 recruits expected tomorrow and full strength will be reached very shortly. Recruiting now working smoothly. . . . Men responding excellently to drill and discipline and showing pride in corps."[51] During their time with the Pioneers at the Ahero camp, the recruits constructed 18.5 miles of one road and shaped and hard-surfaced 3 miles of another. By the time they finished constructing the Ahero-Muhoroni road, the Pioneers had shortened "the distance of the Kisumu-Muhoroni section of the main road to Nairobi from 54 miles to 37 miles, besides cutting out many awkward bends and drifts."[52]

But it was soon discovered that Pioneers were spending too much time on extraneous activities such as road building, which took them away from their primary duty of training for military service in the corps. The training level of the unit at Ahero camp was found wanting. When an untrained detachment was sent to Nairobi for urgent duty in the first few days of the war, it was "not very satisfactory and returned crestfallen for further training."[53] In terms of technical skills, the corps was classified as unskilled, but there was a "fair sprinkling of technicians in its ranks and (some) can look forward to becoming semi-skilled."[54] In the latter half of October 1939, 125 Pioneers were chosen for deployment into the Royal Engineers (RE). This was a loss to the Pioneers, but those who left were "replaced by new recruits . . . [who] are equally good material."[55] As the recruits gradually adjusted to their mission in the Pioneers, they were issued safari shirts, belts and buckles, shorts, macduff shirts, caps, belt webbing coils with buckles, water bottles (*charguls*), haversacks, blankets, "messing utensils," kit bags, and sandals, locally manufactured at Nakuru Tannery. To retain their service, members of the EAMLS (East African Military Labor Service) were promised that whenever KAR recruiters visited the province on recruitment exercise, the KAR would give the Pioneers first preference, taking "likely men from the Pioneer Corps before proceeding to recruit elsewhere in the districts."[56] Thus, besides serving as the nucleus for a future unit, the Pioneer Corps also served as a source of recruits for other military units.

The Pioneer Corps put the colony on a war footing, in addition to getting some roads constructed. It placed men at the ready for war instead of waiting to recruit them hurriedly in case of an emergency. By the time war broke out, these men were expected to "have some degree of training in advance together with their N.C.O.'s and Warrant Officers."[57] Recruitment into the corps was facilitated by older members of the Pioneers, who visited rural homes looking for recruits. When the war broke out, for instance, a party of sixty Pioneers was sent out to various parts of Nyanza to recruit men for the army. The number of recruits steadily increased at the camp, reaching 350 by 31 July 1939, where it remained until further orders were issued.

As the military situation in Europe deteriorated, an order was sent on 24 August 1939 to reorganize and streamline the Pioneers. European officers selected for military service whom the Manpower Committee had already alerted arrived at the camp for duty. Some of these officers were later released for urgent civil work, but others went on to lead newly formed battalions of the Pioneers. The First Battalion was led by Major C. C. Dawson Currie and the Second Battalion by Major E. H. Tapson. The acting and founding officer of the Ahero Depot, Major R. Southby, retired before the end of September 1939. His place was taken up by Captain W. Truro Norris, who became the new officer in charge of the depot.

The order for reorganizing and restructuring the Pioneers also saw the expansion of the corps because it called for the recruitment of more men in preparation for the war. Most of these recruits were already in service and were "by this time becom[ing] used to the Corps and the conditions of service."[58] Two days after the call for men, on 26 August 1939, Major Tapson of the Second Battalion went out on a recruitment drive. Many Kenyans heeded the call for recruits and "join[ed] in large numbers." According to S. H. Fazan, "Volunteers had already begun to arrive in numbers."[59] By the time recruitment was suspended on 6 September 1939, the number in the Pioneer Corps stood at 1,900, and Fazan remarked that "the response of the natives [had] been truly amazing."[60] Most of these recruits came from Nyanza Province. This was in line with the first memorandum of the chair of the Manpower Committee, which had stated that Nyanza should "provide as many as 3,000 men" to the unit.[61] And so, by November 1939, the two battalions created by the orders of the War Office consisted almost "exclusively" of recruits from Nyanza Province.[62] Colonel Michael Blundell's First East African Pioneer Battalion, for example, was "98% Nyanza" and predominantly made up of the Luo.[63] "[The first] Rifles Engineers Company formed in Kenya and the two Pioneer Battalions wholly, in respect of their African ranks, were from Nyanza natives."[64] Blundell, whose battalion served in the Northern Frontier District and in Abyssinia, later observed in his memoir that it was composed of "men . . . [who] had all been recruited in Nyanza Province by the Provincial Commissioner."[65] Lieutenant Colonel W. H. A. Bishop wrote a letter to Fazan and thanked him "for all the trouble you have expended on these units from the outset."[66] When Italian aircraft bombed the Pioneers at Abu Haggag in 1942, Captain H. E. Humphrey-Moore, the commanding officer of 1808 Company, also underscored the origins of his troops: "Bar 40, the rest [280] of the company come from Nyanza Province."[67]

The evolution of the Pioneer Corps reached an important stage when it was officially designated by the military as a combat unit and its askaris as combatants toward the end of 1939. On 11 November 1939, the newly classified combatants of the Pioneers left Nyanza for what Fazan described as "a more active field." Their departure, he would later confess, made him "feel lonely without them."[68] Two days later, a company of the Second Battalion left. Finally, on 29 November, the remainder of the two battalions departed and were now "somewhere in Kenya, taking with them the good wishes of the provinces."[69]

Among the Luo of Nyanza, the Pioneer Corps was known simply as Panyako, a corruption of the name Pioneer Corps. It was envisaged as a better replacement for the earlier, unpopular military unit, the Carrier Corps, or Kariokor.[70] But all that buildup proved to be deceptive. The promises made to recruits when the corp was created—even its very name—simply skirted around people's reluctance to serve in labor units, without dealing with their grievances. To be sure, the unit enabled the government to take advantage of the supposedly abundant labor of Nyanza in particular and Kenya in general during World War II. But the government lied. The *East African Standard* and the *Nakuru Weekly News,* for instance, noted in their editorial analyses that "the Pioneers were misled as to their terms of service."[71]

The Limits of Colonial Assumptions about African Labor for the Pioneer Corps

The emergence of the Pioneers grew out of colonial assumptions about the inexhaustibility of the labor supply in western Kenya, yet it also demonstrated the limits of those assumptions. As the colonial administration established the Pioneer Corps and recruited men from western Kenya for the war effort, it contributed to severe labor shortages that affected food production. Africans and even some colonial officials complained about the ruthless conscription of men into the Pioneers and other colonial military units without regard to the impact on local societies. By the end of 1940, the provincial commissioner of Nyanza estimated that 82,820 Nyanza inhabitants worked for the military, government, and private European concerns. He observed in 1940 that "the provision of men for the army has been the most marked of our war contributions."[72] The number of men from Nyanza in the army and civil work climbed to 93,212 by the end of 1941; at that point, the number of Nyanza men in the army alone stood at "more than twenty thousand."[73] By January 1942, one document showed that there were 19,620 men from Nyanza in the army and 98,700 in various other labor services in the colony. Thus, more than 118,320 men from Nyanza worked for the military and the government. The contribution of the province to the military and particularly to the Pioneer Corps was very large.

To a substantial extent, this was due to the long-standing colonial views with regard to Nyanza Province and to the campaigns of Fazan himself, who often explained how labor in Nyanza and the colony as a whole could be mobilized and conveyed into military and civil duty.[74] Indeed, during the early days of the Pioneers, he boasted that "Nyanza Province is quite capable of raising and training 5 Pioneer Battalions and also of recruiting drafts for five Auxiliary Transport Battalions."[75] To justify the channeling of western Kenya's labor into the military, Fazan claimed during the early years of the war that Nyanza's population was actually higher than commonly thought—"almost exactly 40% that of Kenya."[76] When it was estimated in mid-1941 that, in spite of the alleged abundant labor in Nyanza, only .5 percent of the province's population was away on military and civil duty, Fazan proposed that the labor supply from Nyanza Province be increased to 1.5 percent because "it would have no adverse effects on the supply of labor for essential industry."[77] By 1942, the number of Nyanza recruits in the army had climbed to "nearly 30,000 men . . . and further [to] approximately 110,000 in civil employment outside of the reserve."[78] Thus, only 262,000 adult males remained in the reserves, and of them, even the colonial officials admitted, 60,274 were "totally ineffective by reason of ill-health and disablement, and the remainder are capable of agriculture."[79] By the end of 1942, the existing intensive policy of recruitment of men from Nyanza Province was therefore creating uneasiness among some colonial officials.[80]

These officials produced reports suggesting that recruits from Nyanza made up the majority of those men serving with the army. Thus, a district officer in Central Kavirondo District observed that most of the recruits in the army were from Nyanza.[81] The district commissioner of Kisumu-Londiani believed that the number of Nyanza recruits "employed by the military is in excess of [the Nyanza provincial commissioner's] estimates," and he went to the extent of suggesting that an "expert statistician" should be hired to help calculate the number of Nyanza recruits in the army.[82] Many of these men were recruited through conscription—a policy that began in 1942.[83] Conscription was quite unpopular, but it was one of the ways by which the administration tried to make up for labor shortages in military labor units such as the East African Military Service Corps and the Pioneer Corps. By 1943, excessive recruitment began to have an effect on the province. Local administrators, among them D. Storr-Fox, the district commissioner of South Kavirondo, complained about the large outflow of recruits from Nyanza into the army and various civilian projects, which he believed affected food production. The district commissioners of Central and North Kavirondo even petitioned the government for a pause in conscription in February 1943, requesting that "in the interests of increased production . . . [the government should] arrange a respite of one month during February so that there may be concerted effort on cultivation."[84] This, they argued, would augment the "number of men who would be thus home during that month to help plant up."[85]

A village elder from Alego, Siaya District, complained about overrecruitment and the exploitation of labor by the government in his home area. Expressing his objections with diplomatic metaphor, he said, "If an elephant is killed, everyone sets to the flesh with their knives, and the supply of meat seems inexhaustible.

Nevertheless, there comes a time when the bones though not yet laid bare at last begin to appear."[86]

Frustrated by the extent of government exploitation of labor in Nyanza, Storrs-Fox, the district commissioner of South Kavirondo, asked the authorities to relieve him of his duties in the civil service or transfer him elsewhere. Accusing the government of establishing a system that was taking advantage of the "poor and weak people for the benefit of those who consider themselves to be 'Herrenvolk' or 'master race,'"[87] he asked his superiors to "be so kind as to consider relieving me of my present appointment as District Commissioner, South Kavirondo"; he added that should the government "decide not to dispense with my services altogether, I would be willing and glad to continue to serve in any district or colony and in any capacity where I might be required."[88]

The problems, brought about by excessive recruitment of labor from Nyanza, were exacerbated by drought, leading to a fall in food production in the early 1940s.[89] Colonial reports for the period 1941 to 1943 show a considerable decline in the yields of food crops from Nyanza Province because of the lack of labor and rain (see table 6.1). Only rice and potatoes recorded significant increases.

When the government realized that agricultural production was dropping in Nyanza, it tried to ameliorate the problem by changing the recruitment policies that had created the Pioneers. For example, although the colonial military had earlier used a policy of ethnic-based recruitment, with each military unit recruiting from particular communities, this policy had changed by 1942. A policy of "tribal mixing" brought men from different ethnic communities together in the same military units—"martial" and "nonmartial" peoples working together.[90] Colonel A. J. Knott argued that the new policy came into being because the military had realized that "a particular tribal failing is less likely to manifest itself in a mixed

Table 6.1. Nyanza Province crop production, 1941–43 (in 200-pound bags)

	1941	1942	1943
Maize	553,797	553,771	333,847
Mtama	–	65,000	82,226
Wimbi	28,656	27,126	9,507
Groundnuts	29,600	29,600	14,026
Potatoes	387	–	7,221
Simsim	21,166	18,972	2,154
Rice	–	4,870	18,545
Beans	12,090	11,122	143
Choroko	849	840	233
Wheat	–	–	1,558

Source: Nyanza Province Annual Report, 1943, PC/NZA/1/138, KNA.

unit."[91] In reality, this new policy appears to have been occasioned at least in part by the emerging awareness within the colonial administration of the negative impact of overrecruitment in areas previously designated as "teeming" with inexhaustible supplies of labor. It gradually dawned on the administration that overrecruitment for military units such as the Pioneer Corps in western Kenya and other areas took labor away from food production and led to food shortages. By "mixing" men in military units irrespective of their ethnicity, the colonial authorities hoped to give these exhausted areas a chance to recover, as they targeted other regions to make up for any shortfall in recruitment.

Thus, the creation of the Pioneer Corps shows how demography influenced colonial policy in Kenya. It further demonstrates the limits of those policies. Western Kenya, in particular, was viewed as the source of an inexhaustible supply of labor. This perception led to the formation of the Pioneer Corps during World War II. But as men were enlisted by the government into the Pioneers and other military units, their departure led to labor shortages in agriculture. Famine became common. There were protests even among the colonial officials themselves over the excessive exploitation of African labor in western Kenya. The government was forced to address these problems by changing some of its policies and by reexamining some of its demographic assumptions. These assumptions about demography in western Kenya were tested to the limit by the creation of the Pioneers and other military units. In the end, the government was left with no alternative but to readjust its assumptions to meet the realities of wartime colonial Kenya.

Notes

1. As important as it is, the history of the Pioneer Corps and its connection to Kenya's demographic and colonial labor policies has not been fully told, with the exception of memoirs such as that of Michael Blundell, a commander of a battalion of the First Pioneer Company. See Blundell, *A Love Affair with the Sun: A Memoir of Seventy Years in Kenya* (Nairobi: Kenway Publications, 1994). Blundell's memoir is limited in scope in the sense that it is based solely on his own experiences as a European military officer whose level of interaction with the ordinary soldiers was circumscribed by military regulations and seriously limited by the racial hierarchy in colonial Kenya. Geoffrey Hodge's work, *The Carrier Corps: Military Labor in the East African Campaigns, 1914–1918* (New York: Greenwood, 1986), comes the closest to comprehending African military units and labor policies, but it deals with World War I. For British colonial Africa and labor exploitation for military service in general, see David Killingray, "Labour Exploitation for Military Campaigns in British Colonial Africa, 1870–1945," *Journal of Contemporary History* 24, no. 3 (July 1989): 483–501.

2. Sir Gerald Herbet Portal was an administrator in East Africa between 1892 and 1893.

3. R. M. A. van Zwanenberg, with Anne King, *An Economic History of Kenya and Uganda* (Atlantic Highlands, NJ: Humanities Press, 1975), 7.

4. Ibid. In this revised estimate, Uganda's population was given as 3.5 million.

5. Kenya was known as the East Africa Protectorate between 1895 and 1920. As the protectorate expanded and its administrative structures developed, it was declared a Crown Colony and renamed Kenya in 1920.

6. Many of these publications are well summarized in B. A. Ogot, "History, Anthropology and Social Change: The Kenya Case," in *The Challenges of History and Leadership in Africa: The Essays in Honor of Betthwell Allan Ogot*, ed. Toyin Falola and Atieno Odhiambo (Trenton, NJ: African World Press, 2002): 511–23. See also Charles W. Hobley, "British East Africa: Kikuyu Customs and Beliefs—Thahu and Its Connection to Circumcision Rites," *Journal of the Anthropological Institute of Great Britain and Ireland* 40 (July–December 1910): 428–52; Charles W. Hobely, *Bantu Beliefs and Magic* (London: Frank Cass, 1967); G. St. J. Orde Browne, *The Vanishing Tribes of Kenya* (London: Seeley, Service, 1925); G. W. B. Huntingford, "Miscellaneous Records Relating to the Nandi and Kony Tribes," *Journal of the Royal Anthropological Institute of Great Britain and Ireland* 57 (July–December 1927): 417–61; and J. A. Massam, *The Cliff Dwellers of Kenya* (London: Frank Cass, 1968).

7. Van Zwanenberg, *Economic History of Kenya and Uganda, 9.*

8. Ibid., 10.

9. Ibid., 12. Van Zwanenberg and King project Kenya's population backward to conclude that the population was 3.7 million in 1921, 4.1 million in 1931, and 4.8 million in 1939.

10. Ibid., 14. .

11. The census of 1948 pegged Kenya's population at 5.7 million. See van Zwanenberg, *Economic History of Kenya and Uganda,* 12, and F. F. Ojany and R. B. Ogendo, *Kenya: A Study in Physical and Human Geography* (Nairobi: Longman Kenya, 1973), 110.

12. S. H. Fazan, Nyanza Provincial Commissioner, to the Chairman of Man Power Committee, letter, 21 March 1939, The Pioneers, 1939–42, PC/NZA/2/3/21, Kenya National Archives, Nairobi, hereafter cited as KNA.

13. See, for example, Ojany and Ogendo, *Kenya;* Anthony Clayton and Donald C. Savage, *Government and Labor in Kenya, 1895–1963* (London: Frank Cass, 1974); and van Zwanenberg, *Economic History of Kenya and Uganda.*

14. S. H. Fazan, "The Pioneers: A Memorandum," 14 September 1939, The Pioneers, 1939–42, PC/NZA/2/3/21, KNA; Fazan, "A Memorandum on Military Recruitment, 5 May 1941," Recruitment of Africans for the Military, PC/NZA/2/3/67, KNA. For more on Fazan's career, see David Anderson, *Histories of the Hanged: The Dirty War in Kenya and the End of Empire* (New York: W. W. Norton, 2005), 143–45.

15. For more of this discourse, see Ojany and Ogendo, *Kenya;* Clayton and Savage, *Government and Labor in Kenya;* and van Zwanenberg, *Economic History of Kenya and Uganda.*

16. Even before he arrived in Nyanza Province, Fazan was prodigiously computing the demographic patterns of Central Province, where he served as a district officer during the 1930s; see van Zwanenberg, *Economic History of Kenya and Uganda,* 10.

17. Fazan, "Memorandum on Military Recruitment," 31 May 1941, Recruitment of Africans for the Military, PC/NZA/2/3/67, KNA.

18. Ibid.

19. Ibid.

20. Geoffrey Hodges, *Kariokor: Carrier Corps* (Nairobi: Nairobi University Press, 1999).

21. Fazan, "The Pioneers: A Memorandum on Certain Points Outstanding, 25 September 1939," The Pioneers, 1939–42, PC/NZA/2/3/21, KNA.

22. Ibid.

23. Oketch Oyugi Aton, who served with the King's African Rifles from 1941 to 1964, interview by the author, 19 December 2000. He said during the interview that African men hated the labor units. This view was shared by many other interviewees.

24. Fazan, letter, 6 July 1939, The Pioneers, 1939–42, PC/NZA/2/3/21, KNA.

25. The word *pioneer* literally means "forerunner" or "precursor," suggestive of the fact that the unit would be the nucleus of a bigger unit, which the administration intended to form during wartime. The name "Pioneer" was meant to help reduce the stigma associated with military labor units, which frustrated government efforts at enlisting men because it embarrassed and agitated those slated to serve or already serving in them. Removing the label "Labor" and replacing it with "Pioneer" also allowed the government to claim that the unit was different from earlier military labor units.

26. The origins and meaning of the term *Kavirondo* is complex. It appears to have been coined by Arab-Swahili traders who, during the nineteenth century, used it to refer to communities in western Kenya such as the Luo and Abaluhya but mainly the Luo.

27. Fazan, "East African Pioneer Corps: Memorandum on the Cost of Training a Nucleus in Peace Time," The Pioneers, 1939–42, PC/NZA/2/3/21, KNA.

28. For more detailed analysis of this issue, see Timothy Parsons, *The African Rank-and-File: Social Implications of Colonial Military Service in the King's African Rifles, 1902–1964* (Portsmouth, NH: Heinemann, 1999), esp. chap. 3.

29. Fazan, Nyanza Provincial Commissioner, memorandum entitled "Labor Corps," The Pioneers, 1939–42, PC/NZA/2/3/21, KNA.

30. Ibid. These kinds of colonial stereotypes about African ethnic groups should not have been very surprising. In the colonial period, many stereotypes circulated about African peoples. A large number of these stereotypes, as already indicated in this essay, were supposedly based on colonial and anthropological studies of African communities in Kenya.

31. Ibid.

32. Ibid.

33. Fazan, "The Pioneers: A Memorandum."

34. Ibid.

35. Ibid.

36. Fazan, "East African Pioneer Corps."

37. Fazan, memorandum entitled "Labor Corps."

38. Ibid.

39. Ibid.

40. Ibid.

41. Fazan, "East African Pioneer Corps."

42. See Public Works Department Office to Chief Native Commissioner, letter, 5 May 1939, The Pioneers, 1939–42, PC/NZA/2/3/21, KNA.

43. Fazan, "East African Pioneer Corps."

44. Ibid.

45. Nyanza Provincial Commissioner, "The Pioneer Corps: Historical Record—Preliminary Recruitment and Training," in "History of War Report," 6 March 1940, History of War, 1939–48, PC/NZA/2/3/61, KNA.

46. For more of this, see Fazan, "East African Pioneer Corps."

47. Fazan to the General Staff Officer, letter, 7 November 1939, The Pioneers, 1939–42, PC/NZA/2/3/21, KNA.

48. District Commissioner, Central Kavirondo, to Chief Elija Bonyo, Sakwa, letter, 15 November 1939, Military Recruitment, DC/KSM/1/22/18, KNA.

49. Fazan to Chief Secretary, confidential letter, 22 January 1939[?], The Pioneers, 1939–42, PC/NZA/2/3/21, KNA.

50. Ibid.

51. Divisional Engineer, telegram, 12 June 1939, The Pioneers, 1939–42, PC/NZA/2/3/21, KNA.

52. Fazan, letter, 6 July 1939.

53. Nyanza Provincial Commissioner, "The Pioneer Corps."

54. Ibid.

55. Ibid.

56. Ibid.

57. Fazan, memorandum entitled "Labor Corps."

58. Nyanza Provincial Commissioner, "The Pioneer Corps."

59. Report on History of the War, 9 March 1940, History of War, 1939–48, PC/NZA/2/3/61, KNA.

60. Fazan, "The Pioneers: A Memorandum."

61. Fazan to the Chairman of Man Power Committee.

62. Fazan, letter, "The Pioneer Corps: Band Fund," 3 November 1939, Military Recruitment, DC/KSM/1/22/18, KNA.

63. Fazan, Nyanza Provincial Commissioner, to Chief Secretary, letter, 29 December 1942, Recruitment of Africans for the Military, PC/NZA/2/3/67, KNA; see also Blundell, *Love Affair with the Sun.*

64. Nyanza Provincial Commissioner to his District Commissioners, letter, 27 December 1940, History of War, 1939–48, PC/NZA/2/3/61, KNA.

65. Blundell, *Love Affair with the Sun,* 49.

66. Lt. Col. Bishop to Fazan, letter, 12 December 1939, The Pioneers, 1939–42, PC/NZA/2/3/21, KNA.

67. Capt. H. E. Humphrey-Moore, Officer-Commanding, 1808 Company, to Nyanza Provincial Commissioner, letter, 7 March 1942, The Pioneers, 1939–42, PC/NZA/2/3/21, KNA.

68. Fazan to Lt. Col. Bishop, letter, 1 December 1939, The Pioneers, 1939–42, PC/NZA/2/3/21, KNA.

69. Nyanza Provincial Commissioner, "Pioneer Corps."

70. For detailed analysis of the East African Campaign of 1914–18, some aspects of colonial policies, and how they led to labor shortages, see Hodges, *Kariokor;* Charles Miller, *Battle for the Bundu* (New York: Macmillan, 1974); Parson, *African Rank-and-File;* Melvin E. Page, ed., *Africa and the First World War* (New York: Macmillan, 1987); Gregory Maddox, "*Njaa:* Food Shortages and Famines in Tanzania between the Wars," *International Journal of African Historical Studies* 19, no. 1 (1986): 17–34; John Overton, "The Origins of the Kikuyu Land Problem: Land Alienation and Land Use in Kiambu, Kenya, 1895–1920," *African Studies Review* 31, no. 2 (September 1988): 109–26; B. J. Berman and J. M. Lonsdale, "Crises of Accumulation, Coercion and the Colonial State: The Development of the Labor Control System in Kenya, 1919–1929," *Canadian Journal of African Studies* 14, no. 1 (1980): 55–81.

71. Fazan, quoting the two papers and complaining about their editorial in a confidential rejoinder to the chief secretary, letter, 22 January 1940, The Pioneers, 1939–42, PC/NZA/2/3/21, KNA.

72. Nyanza Province Annual Report, 1940, PC/NZA/1/1/35, KNA.

73. Nyanza Province Annual Report, 1941, PC/NZA/1/1/36, KNA.

74. Archival documents show that Fazan commented on virtually every subject of military nature in the colony during the war.

75. Fazan, "The Pioneers: A Memorandum."

76. Fazan, "Supplementary Notes to Memorandum on the Subject of Military Recruitment," 11 May 1941, Recruitment of Africans for the Military, PC/NZA/2/3/67, KNA.

77. Fazan, "Memorandum on Military Recruitment," 31 May 1941.

78. Nyanza Province Annual Report, 1942, PC/NZA/1/1/37, KNA.

79. Nyanza Provincial Commissioner, Nyanza Province Annual Report, 1942, PC/NZA/1/1/37, KNA.

80. The population of adult males in Nyanza Province, according to colonial reports, kept fluctuating. Per the Nyanza Annual Report for 1942, the population of adult males in the province stood at 398,338. However, the "Statistical Notes on Nyanza Native Manpower," another document authored by colonial administrators, puts the number of males eighteen and above at 394,917 in 1941–42.

81. District Officer, Central Kavirondo, to the District Commissioner, Central Kavirondo, letter, 22 August 1942, Institutions and Associations, 1942–45, PC/NZA/3/1/358, KNA.

82. J. D. McKean, District Commissioner, Kisumu-Londiani to Nyanza Provincial Commissioner, confidential letter, 25 February 1942, Confidential Circulars, 1940, DC/KSM/1/36/47, KNA.

83. Parsons, *African Rank-and-File,* 82.

84. Acting Nyanza Provincial Commissioner to the Chief Secretary, letter, 9 January 1943, Labor Recruitment, 1943, DC/KSM/1/17/19, KNA.

85. Ibid.

86. Nyanza Province Annual Report, 1942.

87. D. Storrs-Fox, District Commissioner, South Kavirondo, to Nyanza Provincial Commissioner, confidential letter, 20 October 1941, Confidential Circulars, 1940, DC/KSM/1/36/47, KNA.

88. Ibid.

89. See Robert Maxon, "'Fantastic Prices' in the Midst of 'An Acute Food Shortage': Market, Environment, and the Colonial State in the 1943 Vihiga (Western Kenya) Famine," *African Economic History* 28 (2000): 27–52, for a discussion of this issue elsewhere in the colony.

90. Chief Secretary to Provincial Commissioners, letter, 2 November 1942, Recruitment of Africans for the Military, PC/NZA/2/3/67, KNA.

91. Ibid.

7

Disease and Reproductive Health in Ujiji, Tanganyika

Colonial and Missionary Discourses Regarding Islam and a "Dying Population"

SHERYL A. MCCURDY

During 1948, a Roman Catholic nun working in a dispensary in Ujiji, Tanganyika, published an international call for alarm in her missionary's journal over the declining population of the largely Muslim town. Sr. Christophe Marie reported that during the interwar period, the population of Ujiji had declined from 17,000 to 8,000 residents. She claimed the main causes of the population decrease were syphilis and Islam.[1] In Ujiji, European observers alleged that venereal diseases, immorality, and Islam threatened the health of residents.

Contemporary European demographers construe population decline largely as a phenomenon related to women's fertility, but myriad factors operating in specific contexts are linked to and help explain population decline. This chapter examines how experiences and practices that emerged in response to the ivory and slave trade of Central and East Africa continued to affect a community's fertility during the German and British colonial periods. Migration,[2] social relations of production, food production, distribution and consumption,[3] gendered and generational religious practices, and status differences all contributed to the state of a community's health. Political and economic factors contributed to a couple's, family's, or mother's access to food and a healthy diet, as well as maternal health and child survival.[4] The ways in which women and men restructured their communities, when that was possible, in response to slavers' initial attacks and the continuing movement of the slave trade caravans through their midst had implications for the experience of sexually transmitted infections in the community.[5]

Although fundamental changes in people's relationships began to take place again as the ivory and slave trade era drew to an end and German colonialism began, the reproductive experiences of Swahili and Manyema women of urban Kigoma/Ujiji did not drastically change. Epidemics declined during the German colonial period, but diseases affecting women's reproductive health did not. Furthermore, the specter of the ivory and slave trade lingered, and emancipation was not declared until 1922, which undoubtedly made it even more difficult to perceive the transitions in how women and men negotiated their relationships and the types of reproductive outcomes they sought. From the perspective of health and disease, the difference between the ivory and slave trade era and the colonial period is barely noticeable. Even though medical solutions became more available as the German, Belgian, and then British colonial administrations settled in, few drugs were realistically available to the vast majority of Africans before the end of World War II.[6]

The ivory and slave traders who decimated communities west of Lake Tanganyika during the 1860s and 1870s also altered the structure of settlements along the caravan routes. As men, women, and children—some emaciated, some diseased, and some healthy—moved along the caravan routes, they came into contact with new peoples, ideas, and practices and adopted some elements of these notions, rituals, and ways of being.[7] Not surprisingly, confrontation and disease exchange commonly occurred in towns along the caravan route. Islam and ethnic associations provided inspiration and community for both the disenfranchised and the privileged as they moved east along the caravan routes and into new urban communities. As the Swahili interacted with locals in urban centers in the interior, Europeans warily noted the growing presence of mosques and Swahili costume and culture.

During the 1880s, antislavery efforts in Central and East Africa intensified, and the capacity of the Zanzibar ivory and slave traders to underwrite their expeditions dwindled.[8] By the 1890s, many of the major players in the ivory and slave trade had lost their fortunes; as their economic influence waned, so did their power and authority. The epidemics of the 1890s further reduced the ivory and slave trade network's ability to move goods and services as they had in the past. The shift from the ivory and slave trade to the mercantile economy of the German colonial period included a delayed manumission declared in 1905. As the Maji Maji war of about the same time revealed, the transition to formal German rule was established by the imposition of military authority.[9] But actual shifts in identity, status, and mobility would be contested for a long time.[10] Abolition would not be declared until 1922 by the British when they established the protectorate.[11]

Ujiji, situated on Lake Tanganyika on the far western border of German East Africa, had been the entrepôt of the central route of the ivory and slave trade connecting Indian Ocean maritime trade to Central Africa. The German colonial administrators' strategy to weaken Muslim influence had led them to establish their administrative center at Kigoma, five kilometers north of Ujiji town. They moved the port from Ujiji to Kigoma, where the new rail line from Dar es Salaam would terminate in 1914.[12] These and other actions effectively undercut Ujiji's economic domination of the region, along with the power and control of Arab and African traders in Ujiji. The railway more efficiently connected the western part of German East Africa (with its circular networks in the Great Lakes region) with the Swahili coast and with points in between.

Many European administrators, missionaries, and medical providers felt Islam, as practiced in East Africa, obstructed their economic and political plans to co-opt the local population for their own agenda: building a strong, fit, Christian workforce. Islam was easily layered onto local African practices because adherents could continue to practice polygamy, honor ancestors through local religious rites, and participate in dance competitions and other rituals and celebrations with impunity. European officials also felt Africans' adherence to Islam and local ritual life lowered the capacity of workers to fully engage a northern European work ethic.

Many colonial administrators viewed Africans as subjects who needed to be indoctrinated with more acceptable values and practices that would lead to improved health and better survival rates.[13] They alleged that venereal diseases were spread via illicit sexual encounters that took place during dance competitions and ritual association activities. Some colonial officials and missionaries characterized the rituals and emerging leisure activities that the officials detailed in their surveys as constituting spaces and occasions where immoral behavior was sanctioned, tolerated, or promoted.[14] Europeans officials also blamed polygamy for the spread of venereal diseases and, in so doing, implied extramarital sex was common. Muslims' practice of polygamy provided many Europeans with a reason to deplore the spread of Islam. The goals and concerns of the White Sisters, the French-based Roman Catholic order called in to assist in the military garrisons in Ujiji during the era of Belgian occupation, from 1916 to 1920, fit well with European colonial interests. The White Sisters too wanted to reduce Muslim influence. Their directive charged them to win converts primarily through the provision of medical services to African communities.

The reality of the poor health suffered by women and their children propelled different narratives about population decline. Depending on the decade, some Europeans blamed the famines and the rinderpest epizootic of the 1880s and 1890s; others condemned slavery and its impact on individuals, families, and communities; and still others cited the harsh imposition of German rule and the Maji Maji war of 1905–6. Of course, the cumulative effect of all these events, responses, and processes claimed many lives, forcing survivors into new life trajectories. The structural changes that emerged from these crises and the changing opportunities that women and men of different generations and statuses negotiated in response to them facilitated the emergence of unattached or precariously affiliated women and young men. Their situations and practices, stemming from the experience of instability, poverty, and insecurity, added another dimension to women's fertility, men's and women's subfecundity, and infant survival.

Germans recognized that economic factors influenced childbearing strategies, but they planned to increase fertility and child survival to build a large workforce through educational initiatives and health programs, closer inspections of the population to discourage abortion, and the promotion of Christian values. They had no intention of changing economic policies.[15]

For their part, Africans—depending on their status, ethnicity, gender, generation, religious affiliations and practices, aspirations, skills, education, health, and associational life—found opportunities and obstacles in the social, political, and economic transitions to a German colonial state, then a Belgian-occupied region, and finally a British protectorate. For example, though some German colonial administrators professed concern about Muslim influence in the local community, they tapped Swahili-speakers for key positions in their administration. Swahili men became clerks in German offices. German colonial administrators also actively recruited Manyema, formerly from the Congo and also Muslim Swahili-speakers, for positions in their *askari* (military/police) force. These young Muslim men gained paid labor positions in the colonial administration, ensuring they not only had access to goods and services but also had the purchasing power needed to acquire or use them. In addition, as government employees, they had access to European medical services that others did not.[16]

Differences in reproductive health between individuals who were involved in paid labor in colonial service and those who were not were blurred by distinctions between urban and rural living. It is likely the benefits of rural living in times of plenty greatly outweighed the risks of life in urban settings, where migration, separation from family and other social groups, loss of social and material support, and movement into new social networks probably increased urban dwellers' exposure to a range of diseases and lowered the quality and quantity of food they consumed. Others living in urban areas—children, women, and men without wage labor and only limited income-generating activities—were even less likely to be eating as well as their rural counterparts.

Relationships, duties, obligations, and practices that women, men, and children of different statuses and affiliations negotiated revealed the changing dynamics of society. Their health, particularly their reproductive health, was indicative of the relative success or failure of their own action (or inaction) within the constraints of colonial rule. The health of the African population and its decline or growth also recorded the impact of the ivory and slave trade era and subsequent programs and policies of successive colonial regimes.

The Ujiji Environs

The town of Ujiji emerged during the first half of the nineteenth century from a collection of hamlets dotting the shore of Lake Tanganyika in today's Tanzania.

Zanzibari traders who arrived in the 1830 and 1840s built their long lodge houses between the main port and the market area.[17] By the 1860s, Zanzibari ivory and slave traders had moved from their Ujiji base into the northeastern Congo area of Manyema, where, along with clients called the *waungwana,* they established political authority over communities and territory in the area.[18]

The disruption and destruction of rural societies west of Lake Tanganyika by Zanzibari slave traders led Manyema immigrants to flow into Ujiji, seeking peace and protection.[19] Some Manyema were slaves taken to the market, others were waungwana, and still others were refugees searching for work. The movements of large numbers of malnourished, physically exhausted people into Ujiji and the unsanitary conditions of daily life exposed many slave and free people to diseases to which they had no prior exposure or immunity and contributed to the rise of disease and death in Ujiji and the surrounding Ha villages.[20] During the late 1870s and early 1880s, many more Manyema immigrants arrived in Ujiji. London Missionary Society (LMS) representative Walter Hutley, who lived in the community between 1879 and 1881, claimed that some traders in Ujiji individually owned between two hundred and a thousand slaves.[21] During 1879, Hutley's senior LMS colleague, Edward Coode Hore, wrote that the slave population was the largest and most visible group in Ujiji.[22]

Mobility and Epidemics

Exposure to new diseases came later to inland East and Central Africa than to other parts of the continent. The relative isolation of the peoples of Central Africa before 1840 meant that their encounter with the ivory and slave traders was one of their first exchanges with outsiders, and subsequently, it would prove to be among the most damaging in terms of morbidity and mortality. As Gerald Hartwig and K. David Patterson have noted, "Recurrent and often devastating epidemics [in East and Central Africa] characterized the nineteenth and early twentieth centuries and, in many areas, caused substantial depopulation."[23]

The movement of the ivory and slave trade caravans west into Ujiji and Central Africa during the first part of the nineteenth century, then, exposed people in those areas to a new set of disease conditions. The men and women in the caravans, who inadvertently carried disease with them, also encountered new illnesses as they moved into these new ecological environments. All too often, neither the travelers nor those they encountered possessed the immunological protection they needed to safeguard themselves from the other group's diseases. As new populations encountered one another when the caravan stopped in town for a few days along its route, people came in contact with new illnesses, and smallpox and cholera epidemics erupted.

Ujiji, an important caravan station between the east and west, was a newly emerging urban center with its own disease environment. Crowded conditions and lack of sanitation services promoted respiratory and enteric diseases. With the continual movement of caravans and the increasing numbers of people from all around Lake

Tanganyika, the northeast Congo, and the Swahili coast coming to visit or live in Ujiji, the likelihood that epidemics would wipe out a large portion of the population increased significantly during the latter half of the nineteenth century.

The long-distance trade network and the movement of epidemics that accompanied it did more than simply bring illness and death to the people they touched; together, they initiated social, cultural, economic, political, and religious changes.[24] The ability to acquire and build individual holdings transformed what were once community-centered relationships. The ivory and slave trade and the ravages of famines and epidemics facilitated people's ability to acquire servile labor. The tensions that changing community and interpersonal relationships and slavery entailed, in combination with the extraordinary death and disease tolls and the unsettling deaths of young people and children that epidemics caused, found outlets in assault, theft, murder, witchcraft accusations, and activities involving spirit possession.[25] Manyema and Swahili women's reproductive health complaints reveal some of the responses that social disruption and slavery elicited in communities along the ivory and slave trade routes.

During the latter half of the nineteenth century, the ivory and slave trade, by then a fixture of everyday life in Ujiji, contributed to infertility, subfecundity, and infant mortality by constantly introducing newly impoverished, nonimmune, and diseased people to the community's disease pool. The Manyema waungwana (some of whom were privileged slaves) and the slave population of Ujiji succumbed regularly in large numbers to disease and death. LMS representative Hutley noted as much: "The mortality among them [the waungwana] is very great. Out of every three hundred, two hundred are said to die either here or on their way to Unyanyembe [Tabora]. Syed bin Habib brought 300 slaves here and of these 250 died."[26]

In late 1886, an unidentified Arab told the European explorer Hermann von Wissmann that mortality rates among working slaves were extremely high and that "a working slave—in distinction from the female slaves, who are put into the harem—at Ujiji is said not to stand the climate above a year."[27] Slave women in the harems wove rugs, sang and danced publicly, braided each other's hair, accompanied the caravans, organized cooking preparation, and had slave attendants of their own.[28] Their more leisurely and supervisory activities stood in stark contrast to those of individuals engaged in hard labor on the plantations. During the early 1890s, Lieutenant Sigl, a member of the antislavery expedition intent on ending Arab dominance in the region and promoting European interests, noted that 80 percent of the slave population died annually in Ujiji during the late 1880s and early 1890s.[29] Many of the victims were Manyema waungwana and slaves.[30] European comments about the extremely high number of deaths among these two groups testify to the dire straits they endured at that time.

In 1870, an ivory and slave trade caravan brought cholera to Ujiji from the coast. The epidemic was so severe that another group of porters had to be sent from the coast to transport the ivory.[31] And while the caravans traveling west carried cholera to Ujiji, the waungwana and slaves traveling east carried smallpox and relapsing tick fever to Ujiji.

During August 1876, when a smallpox epidemic struck Ujiji, Henry Stanley estimated that in a population of three thousand, some fifty to seventy-five people died each day from the disease.[32] In the Zanzibari traders' compounds where slaves lived in close proximity with their masters, both free people and slaves were counted among the dead. In 1879, David Livingstone noted that "smallpox comes every three to four years and kills many of the people."[33] During the lulls between epidemics, boats arriving at and departing from Ujiji usually carried people suffering from smallpox.[34]

The mobility of the population ensured that smallpox persisted at an endemic level, and under the right conditions (for example, when nonimmune persons mixed with contagious people), another epidemic would erupt. The arrival of large numbers of diseased individuals in caravans that included over a thousand people probably triggered the epidemics in Ujiji.[35] During the dry season of 1880, LMS missionary representative Hore wrote:

> Smallpox has been raging here for the last two months, sometime since Ujiji was crowded with hundreds of Wamanyuema emigrants and slaves—I think the smallpox came here with these people for they had it at Mtowa [west, the Congo] first and with the departure of a large caravan towards Unyanyembe [east, Tabora] the disease seemed to decline here and is now considerable lessened though not gone. There have been many deaths and I think without exception amongst the very poorest and most "miserable."[36]

A rinderpest panzootic in 1891–93 affected the whole of Africa, and the subsequent movement of people in response to the resulting famine set the stage for a smallpox epidemic in 1893 that raged on Lake Tanganyika's shores and in the Manyema area of the Congo.[37] Ujiji's inhabitants lived in a fertile area situated just north of the Luiche delta and rarely experienced serious droughts, locust invasions, or food shortages. However, during the 1891–93 rinderpest panzootic, the residents of Ujiji, like the rest of Africa, lost livestock and experienced a famine so severe that some of the poorest in the community died of starvation.[38] Fisherfolk and traders from Ujiji sold slaves and palm oil around the perimeter of Lake Tanganyika in exchange for small amounts of maize and millet, which saved the lives of many area residents.[39]

Demography, Slavery, and Gender

Various travelers and missionaries speculated on Ujiji's population size: in 1876, Stanley estimated it was 3,000; in 1883, a White Father speculated that it was 5,000; and during the 1890s, François Coulbois reported that it was between 7,000 and 8,000.[40] None of these observers conducted systematic surveys to get their estimates: thus, their impressions were just that, but they do give us an idea of the growth and size of Ujiji between 1870 and 1900.[41] The loss of slaves began before slave caravans even appeared in Ujiji, for half of the slaves routinely escaped. Of those remaining in the caravan, deaths due to starvation, ill treatment, disease, and poison arrows were common.[42] Because so many slaves arrived in Ujiji already at death's door, we would not expect many to survive very long.

Clearly, Ujiji required a continual flow of newcomers to sustain its population, people who would need, first, to be healthy and, then, to be willing and able to reproduce. The slave population was unlikely to manage this feat. As the ivory and slave trade dwindled during the late 1880s, the steady movement of slaves through Ujiji slowed, and they and many of the remaining residents of the community were in poor health. As people struggled to build new lives, they also needed to improve their diets and health.

During the latter half of the nineteenth century, slave traders violently attacked many Central African communities. Dennis Cordell illustrates how different responses to the restructuring of the Manza and Nzakara communities following their incorporation into the slave trade economy largely determined the extent of sexually transmitted infections in these groups.[43] Such infections were not extensive among the Manza, who incorporated slaves into society; unfortunately, however, they were rampant in Nzakara, where the destruction of the hierarchy led to a great number of unattached working-class women.

Many European observers in precolonial and colonial Africa blamed venereal diseases for African women's low fertility. Yet sexually transmitted infections explain some, but not all, of Manyema and Swahili women's childlessness and reduced fertility. Following their experiences of slavery and disconnection from family and clan, some women may have avoided long-term relationships in which they would have been expected to have children. African women were agents themselves, and they sometimes used different strategies—for example, abortion or infanticide—to space their children or remain childless. During different points in their reproductive careers, women might prevent pregnancies; later, they might attempt to conceive. Some unfortunate women who desired a child and who might have been fecund at an early point in their reproductive career found that they had become infertile; other women had always been infertile.

The increasing mobility of the Manyema and Swahili peoples passing through Ujiji on their way to or from the Swahili coast or the Congo helped to spread Manyema and Swahili ideas, rituals, practices, and diseases. Their associations, some of which sanctioned specific practices related to sexuality, marriage, and fertility, remain active along the former central ivory and slave trade corridor of East Africa.[44] For instance, this continual movement of the Manyema and Swahili, from west to east and back again, promoted female puberty initiation and spirit possession associations, which were informed by life experiences that included enslavement, famine, starvation, and epidemics. The chaos of social, cultural, and political disruption caused by the ivory and slave trade also promoted temporary liaisons in lieu of marriage, divorce, and remarriage and prompted Manyema and Swahili women to develop female networks of friendship and support; these were layered over or used instead of kin networks and soon extended across regions and later across state borders.

The disruption of families by the ivory and slave trade and the disruption of communities forced many women and men in Ujiji to form new patterns of social relationships that affected women's reproductive histories. Women's reproductive experiences reflected their exposure to disease and the strategies they used to survive difficult circumstances. Not every woman elected to have a child. A variety of diseases affected fertility, and people employed various strategies to explain and legitimate women's reproductive health, low fertility, childlessness, and infant health in light of their particular life experiences and strategies.

Reproducing Relationships: Disease, Abortion, and Personal Crises

According to the reports of mid- and late nineteenth-century travelers, smallpox claimed the greatest number of lives both among people traveling the caravan route and among those living in the towns they passed through.[45] Other conditions and illnesses in Ujiji that were related to fecundity during the latter half of the nineteenth century were: malaria, cholera, influenza, typhoid fever, prolapsus (prolapsed uterus), dysentery, tuberculosis, gonorrhea, syphilis, yaws,[46] and relapsing tick fever.[47]

A number of different diseases and their resulting conditions, such as anemia, caused subfecundity, reduced a couple's capacity to conceive, or made it impossible for a woman to bear a live child who survived. Smallpox affected women's fertility by inducing miscarriages, stillbirths, and neonatal mortality.[48] Malaria caused increased rates of miscarriages, stillbirths, and low-birth-weight babies, which compromised the infants' chances of survival.[49] Anemia secondary to malaria, dysentery, malnutrition, and intestinal parasitism also produced miscarriages and stillbirths.[50] In addition, in women, high fevers caused by influenza, typhoid fever, cholera, relapsing tick fever, and malaria resulted in miscarriages, stillbirths, premature births, and congenital anomalies.[51] Genital tuberculosis caused primary sterility in women.[52] And relapsing tick fever, which was endemic in the Ujiji area, is associated with "extremely high perinatal mortality."[53]

Yaws, a skin contact disease that was endemic in East Africa, played an important protective role against syphilis because the spirochetes produced from yaws protected people from acquiring syphilis. Women who contracted syphilis often experienced miscarriages, stillbirths, or neonatal deaths until the disease had progressed into a latent period; children born during this later stage of the disease generally survived.[54] Gonorrhea caused infertility by damaging the fallopian tubes through infection and scarring.[55] High fevers in men caused by influenza, typhoid fever, cholera, relapsing tick fever, and malaria reduced male sperm counts, and smallpox affected male fertility by causing male conceptive failure, as did genital tuberculosis. A range of factors contributed to declines in women's and men's reproductive health as well as infant survival. Most of them were not related to sexually transmitted infections.

The anecdotal evidence about slave mortality suggests that the slave population in Ujiji, as almost everywhere else except the United States after the 1720s, failed to reproduce itself.[56] The high numbers of slave deaths did not significantly alter the Zanzibari economy in Ujiji partly because a reliable, cheap, and abundant source of slaves existed across Lake Tanganyika in the eastern Congo. Certainly, the conditions of slavery excluded any semblance of family life for the majority of slave women who were not concubines. It is unlikely that having a child as a strategy to gain status as an adult, to gain economic support from a man, or to strengthen clan ties was part of most slave women's repertoires.[57]

African Women's Experiences

The survivors' narratives of former slaves as presented and analyzed by Marcia Wright provide some detail about adult slave women's reproductive experiences in East Central Africa.[58] For example, Narwimba, who was born around the middle of the nineteenth century, bore six children with her first husband, only one of whom survived. Because all of the infant's brothers and sisters had died, they gave the child the name Death. After Narwimba's husband died around 1880, his sister's son "was instructed to assume responsibility" for her and her child.[59] With her second husband, Narwimba again bore six children; two survived. In another case, Chisi had three children by her first husband, and one died. She had a daughter with her second husband, a child who died at age four.[60] Meli, who was a generation younger, bore her children during the German colonial period. She joined the mission station as a child, acquired a Western education, and lived in relatively privileged circumstances, residing in European-style houses with her husband, who worked for German officers and missionaries. But despite her relative wealth and privilege, only three of the five children she bore survived.

Like the parents who named their child Death, other parents called their newborn Traitor following the loss of multiple children. From a female perspective, German missionary E. Kootz noted that African mothers believed "[the child will] not stay with us. Just as the others left, so will you leave. Who can prevent it?"[61] This tragedy of children's failure to thrive and parents' fear of the pain of losing yet another child is common in societies experiencing chaos, structural violence, and the misery that accompanies both.[62]

The succession of infant deaths that couples experienced does suggest that syphilis may have played a role in their losses, but it is simplistic to attribute the cause to syphilis alone without taking into consideration the health of the mothers and infants and other diseases circulating in the environment. Smallpox and cholera epidemics, like HIV/AIDS today, claimed many people, provoking ruptures in the social fabric and straining relationships to the breaking point.[63] Some people lost kin support networks, and others felt let down by their families. A song about smallpox, popular among women and collected during the 1890s on the Swahili coast, proclaimed,

183

I am leaving you, I am leaving,
Never shall I return.
I went down with the pox,
Both the maize and the sorghum.
You thought that I would die,
And you would eat my flesh.
But now I have recovered
By the power of the Lord.[64]

Of the different types of smallpox, the varieties that people called maize and sorghum were less often fatal than the one referred to as sesame. Sesame is an oil seed rather than a grain like maize and sorghum, which puts it in a separate category. Maize is not drought resistant, whereas sorghum, sometimes interplanted with sesame, *is* to a fair degree. The attributes of the crops, the different classes of seed, or the size of the seeds may have conveyed beliefs about the severity of these types of smallpox. Associating a fatal disease with a seed or crop type during a famine and singing that "you would eat my flesh" hints at the links the local population made between disease and hunger during the smallpox epidemics of the latter half of the nineteenth century. The song also demonstrates how famine and disease brought devastation and tore apart people's lives.

Women immersed in this "social chaos" responded either with the threat, the fantasy, or the reality of embarking on their own.[65] During the latter half of the nineteenth century, many women lost husbands to epidemics, porterage, and slavery. Others left their partners, and many never bothered to contract a public long-term relationship of any sort. If Margaret Strobel's sample of the lives of slaves in a Mombasa family is representative of a larger social phenomenon (and I suspect that it is), then many former slave women were childless.[66] During the late nineteenth century, missionaries noted the contrast between fishing villages and trading centers along the upper Congo River in the eastern Congo: "There were a hundred children to be seen in a fishing village for every child to be seen in a trading village of the same size."[67] Zanzibari-established trading centers of the eastern Congo, developed in the mid-nineteenth century, came under attack in the early 1890s by agents of King Leopold II, who forced entire communities into rubber production. Resistance grew into rebellion.[68] Many people regularly congregated in these towns for commercial activities, and female slaves engaged in the commercial preparation of food.[69] Others passed through trading centers as part of caravans, in forced-labor groups, as soldiers, and as refugees fleeing from famine or the destruction of their communities. These circumstances provided the perfect opportunity for epidemics to flourish and threaten the survival of all in their wake.

Independent observers were struck by the low numbers of children in some trading towns. Their observations need to be carefully examined. A range of explanations exists for the small number of children, and the similarities and differences between locations must be explored and analyzed. In addition to few children, there were more women than men in the market towns, and these women prepared food for sale.[70] The women in these trading towns may have experienced subfecundity or infertility as a result of famine and subsequent epidemic or endemic diseases or because of chronic malnutrition, in ways that the women in fishing villages did not. A steady supply of fish from the lakes and rivers may have protected the health of people in the fishing villages by providing them with a protein-rich diet. In addition, although some of the people from these fishing settlements went off to do business in the market towns, few outsiders visited them. Hence, access to protein and relative isolation from the mixing of different populations that regularly took place in market towns could well have protected fisherfolk from epidemics and high rates of infant mortality.

Another reading of the sources considers women as actors who selected different strategies in response to their situations. Slave women understood that their situations were tenuous and the time they might remain as domestic servants could be short. One song popular among women field slaves tells the tale of many: "The slave girl has sharp teeth and bites. I want her no more, send her to the country, and let her dig."[71] LMS representative Hutley noted that slave women in Ujiji contracted sexual liaisons with men and performed domestic services in exchange for food and clothing. No doubt, some women did use this strategy, but it does not necessarily follow that they desired to conceive, bear, or raise children. It is possible, then, that childlessness and low fertility became an adapted life strategy that passed from one slave generation to the next, creating an antinatality outlook among women whose support networks had been decimated by epidemics and the ivory and slave trade.[72]

German Programs and Population Surveys

In 1896, the Germans launched measures to improve African health by establishing a hospital attached to the military station in Ujiji.[73] Sleeping sickness eradication campaigns initiated from the Ujiji hospital marked the first efforts of the German colonial administration to use European medical techniques to improve Ujiji residents' health. During 1908, Staff Surgeon Feldman treated Africans in Ujiji clinically diagnosed with sleeping sickness with Atoxyl, but he avoided instituting public health measures that would address the tick infestation in the African neighborhood of the Germans' administrative center in Kigoma.[74]

As early as 1913, German colonial administrators reported that local people's life strategies and childbearing practices had already altered in response to the changing political economy: "On the coast and in many areas . . . the feeding of children is relatively expensive, so that social objections outweigh the desire for progeny. A more important cause [of low birth statistics] is the fear of the difficulties of the last months before the birth and the birth itself." A German colonial administrative report published in 1914, echoing the many earlier mission and travel reports, claimed that the population in central Ujiji District had declined due to miscarriages, abortions, and high infant and child mortality rates.[75] In the document, the German sanitary officer in the middle district of Ujiji reported on the astonishing failure of a new generation of Africans to appear: "The small villages of on average ten men and twenty to twenty-five women seldom harbor more than two to three children. . . . The main fault according to the district doctor is polygamy."[76] The unhappy state of women under polygamy, the doctor explained, led women to select other sexual partners, which in turn led to widespread venereal disease. It is possible that concurrent sexual partnerships and sexually transmitted infections were associated with low fertility in the villages visited by this official. However, it is also possible that they were related to another phenomenon, the famine that followed the 1892 rinderpest epizootic, which was accompanied by high levels of infant and child mortality.[77] The 1914 report on maternal and child health held that high infant mortality throughout the entire Tanganyika protectorate resulted primarily from intestinal sickness and malaria.

The effects of smallpox, chronic malnutrition, dysentery, relapsing tick fever, and malaria all contributed to low fertility or childlessness in slaves and free women and men. Furthermore, German officials reported that Manyema women in Ujiji both induced abortions and experienced miscarriages secondary to syphilis. They also noted the difficulties in determining the exact cause of death:

> Without doubt, however, it is more frequent that the native abortions
> are artificially caused, although the execution and other actions
> pertaining to the abortion are kept a secret if possible. For the most
> part, it is unquestionable that the *askari* and Swahili [Manyema]
> women are most included here. The number of children cited as
> stillborn which fall under the rubric of miscarried or premature births
> is indeterminable. When asked by Europeans, the women do not
> distinguish between abortion, premature birth, or stillbirth. Further,
> the cause of death of stillborn infants who come to full term, whether
> it is a case of foul play, or whether they die immediately during or
> after birth, is indeterminable.[78]

This colonial source also reveals just how much some colonial and most missionary representatives were preoccupied by African sexuality. Since these were Muslim women, European officials found it easy to translate women's actions into a concern about the negative effects of Islam on a population.

The Swahili coast, Bukoba, Tabora District, and Uganda were other areas identified as having a "sharp decrease in the population."[79] At the time, the German colonial medical officer suspected that among "Swahili" women (as the Germans alternately referred to Manyema, Swahili, and urban Haya women), the miscarriages they experienced were due to syphilis, for "as much as fifty percent of the residents have become infected." But he also suspected that the Swahili women and askari, in particular, induced abortions. German officials' awareness of the independence and power of urban Swahili women grew when the askari in the garrison at Bukoba demanded "to be circumcised *en bloc*" because the "arabized prostitutes" refused to have sex with them.[80] Many Manyema and Swahili operated as unattached women, and some were independent agents in the urban communities of East Central Africa. Other women in East and Central Africa who bore few children were the Sudanese soldiers' partners and older women known as the "camp followers" of the local African soldiers affiliated with the German imperial forces.[81] A commandant in Iringa region noted he would like to repatriate these "promiscuous" women back to the coast.

Cultural and religious practices influenced social relationships and fertility and the choices that the Germans made as they began to establish their regime. Although the colonial administrators worried about the low fertility of certain sectors of the African population, especially among those residing in Ujiji and Bukoba and on the Swahili coast, their early medical efforts focused on large disease eradication campaigns meant to improve overall health. What they might have accomplished in Tanganyika remains unknown because the Germans lost their colonies in the aftermath of World War I.

Taking over Tanganyika Territory: Assessing Priorities and Locating Concerns

When the Belgians took over Kigoma during World War I, Congolese troops living in the African section of the town contracted relapsing tick fever in large numbers. André Boigelot, the medical inspector general of labor for the Congo, responded by invoking martial law. He evacuated the tick-infested houses and ordered them burned to the ground. Mwanga town was rebuilt on the hill a little to the south for the African residents of Kigoma.[82] The Belgians administered this western region of Tanganyika until the British took over in 1921.

In 1916, the Belgians recruited the missionary community known as the White Sisters to help provide medical care in Ujiji/Kigoma. The White Sisters set up their home near Kigoma town, the German administrative center, and soon began to extend their activities beyond the Belgian military into the Swahili community of Ujiji. Their ministrations and home visits continued with the arrival of the British administration. By 1920, they had a clinic and were seeing, on average, forty-five patients a day.[83]

The sanitation and hygiene programs initiated by the Medical Department of the British colonial administration in Tanganyika during the 1920s served a twofold purpose. First, the British concept of indirect rule justified a strategy designed to provide the greatest possible health interventions with the least possible investment. Second, the British administrators contributed to colonial economic goals by promising to promote a healthy labor force. J. B. Davey, appointed the first postwar medical director in 1920, wrote that "more than 32 percent of the total estimated revenue is expected from house, hut and poll taxes. The development of the country . . . depends upon the labor of the native."[84]

During the 1920s, British colonial officers determined that the survival of African children was key to establishing a healthy labor force, and African women were targeted to accomplish this goal. They hoped that mothers would solve the crisis of particular groups of Africans who were dying out and give birth to the healthy laborers of the future.[85] Concerns over morality in terms of alcohol abuse and sexuality, the influence of Islam, and the reputed role of venereal disease continued to loom large in European colonial debates and plans of action. Such concerns were reinforced by European racist and sexist attitudes fostered in the nineteenth century by emerging scientific notions of race, gender, and sexuality and the accompanying growth of the eugenics movement.[86] During the late nineteenth century in Europe, prostitutes were likened to Saartje Baartman, the young woman from Cape Colony who was labeled the Hottentot Venus.[87] Scientific tracts of the period claimed that the "immoral hypersexuality" of the European prostitute reflected a biological connection to Africans. By the beginning of the twentieth century in many middle- and upper-class European minds, both African women and European prostitutes represented a dangerous sexuality. Consequently, many British colonial officers believed that if they could control African women's sexuality, the levels of venereal disease would drop and increased fertility would follow.

British officials generally attributed most of the effects of high infant mortality and subfecundity to venereal diseases. As early as 1922, however, some recognized other causes:

> Other factors must have a great influence on infant mortality
> throughout the Territory. The partial immunity against malaria, tick
> fever, and other indigenous diseases acquired by native communities
> is possibly obtained at the cost of considerable numbers of lives. In
> most districts there are periods during each year when food is scarce
> and the unsuitable diet which is all that is available, combined with
> helminthic infections, results in severe intestinal disorders.[88]

Partly due to financial and staffing constraints and partly due to differences in philosophical approaches to eradicating disease (for instance, curative versus preventative medicine), this early assessment of the range of environmental, socioeconomic, and disease conditions contributing to low fertility failed to capture the imagination of administrators. Also, a comprehensive approach would have been more expensive. Instead, quick-fix campaigns to eradicate specific infectious diseases became the focus of initial colonial efforts to improve African health.

British colonial officials and medical missionaries operated on very tight budgets, which led many officials to conclude that in order to get the most economic benefit for the least amount of money, they should focus on providing curative services to Africans. They hoped not only to improve the health of the nation but also to instill in Africans a strong impression of the power of European medicines, ideas, and practices. Emerging European medical ideas and practices promised Europeans safety from local diseases, a healthy population, and a recruiting tool to engage people's minds in new ways of being and doing that were more Christian than Muslim. Injections of bismuth tartrate to treat yaws, for instance, had spectacular success, often making sores disappear after one injection.[89] European medicinal practices offered some Africans relief from symptoms, as well as entertainment and new economic opportunities.

The colonial and missionary medical discourse acknowledged the range of diseases that affected reproductive health and infant survival but chose to blame Islam, immorality, and venereal diseases for population decline. Implicit in this discourse was the notion that if the African population could be Christianized and stripped of many of its nefarious practices, Africans might become more civilized, less diseased, and more capable of reproducing.

Drawing on 233 clinical cases, Dr. J. McClark, the Kigoma medical officer in 1922, argued that venereal diseases were common in urban Kigoma. We have no evidence to support his claim or any other colonial officials' statements about the prevalence of venereal disease. Instead, we have colonial documents that detail the anxieties of administrative officials and missionaries about venereal diseases and the policies and programs they implemented. In 1922, health care workers at the Kigoma hospital treated 24 African cases of gonorrhea (16 African government employees and 8 nongovernmental employees), 68 cases of syphilis, and 141 cases of yaws. One-third of the yaws patients were African officials.[90] Men, most of them in the government service, formed the core of the patients seeking treatment. British colonial administrators noted that most Africans were not voluntarily seeking biomedical treatment for venereal disease. It is possible that those men who sought treatment felt compelled to do so for fear of losing their jobs. It is more likely that due to their close contact with the British colonial administration, they were among the first witnesses of the dramatic results of the initial yaws injections and that these observations spurred them to seek treatment.

Venereal disease and yaws may have preoccupied the White Sisters' imaginations as early as the 1920s, but a smallpox epidemic erupting in 1922 kept them busy. As attendance grew in their Ujiji clinic during the early 1920s, they found themselves treating patients for a range of complaints, including malaria, which was endemic in the area.

A smallpox epidemic that began in September 1922 claimed many victims, among them the European physician, Blackwood.[91] At their dispensary, the White Sisters saw their patient numbers increase from 40 to 50 a day in 1920 to between 60 and 70 in 1922. In addition to smallpox patients, they saw many individuals suffering from yaws and malaria.[92] Following their tour of the area during 1922, the White Sisters noted that there were very few children in Ujiji:

> Ceci est très rare. Les noirs ont très peu enfants. Tour une ville de 20.000 âmes, couvre l'est Udjiji, une seule petite école kiswahili suffit pourtant les noirs tiennent beaucoup à y envoyer leurs fils.[93]

> This is very rare. The Blacks have very few children. For the entire town of the 20,000 residents of Ujiji, only one small Swahili school more than suffices for all the Blacks to send their children to.

The White Sisters had been in the Ujiji area for several years when they made this comment. Moreover, they were not strangers to the area or to other communities in Central Africa. Their observation confirmed the earlier surveys of the German colonial administration. Although syphilis was a problem that persisted until the late 1950s when treatment became more widely available, it did not constitute 90 percent of their caseload. Out of approximately 20,000 patients they treated, on average, during the 1940s, only about 10 percent, or 1,900 people, suffered from syphilis.[94]

The culture of divorce, remarriage, and alternate relationships that was a response to epidemics, slavery, and porterage contributed to Manyema and Swahili women's experience of lowered fertility. Different types of crises limited the number of years a woman might actually be with a partner and attempting to have a child. The experience of moving around in response to a crisis and the subsequent loss of partners due to social, political, economic, and environmental circumstances also increased the likelihood that a person would have more than one sexual partner in his or her lifetime and thus increased the likelihood of contracting a sexually transmitted infection. Together, the culture of divorce, remarriage, and alternate relationships, combined with the effects of sexually transmitted infection, smallpox, malaria, tuberculosis, cholera, influenza, typhoid fever, and anemia, created an environment where couples were less likely to conceive. And even among those who did conceive, the rates of miscarriage, stillbirth, and infant and child mortality were extremely high.

With the mobility of Ujiji/Kigoma's residents ensured by rail service and a dense network of relationships along the former ivory and slave trade route, the movement of the urban community and the continuous transmission of diseases was guaranteed. Unattached women who lived in those Swahili towns had reproductive experiences that spoke to the community's history with slavery, migration, epidemics, and sexually transmitted infections. Although many women and couples wanted children and were either infertile or lost them to miscarriages, stillbirths, or early death, others opted, willingly or not, to forgo bearing and raising a child.

The parallels between the concern over the sexual behavior of Africans and its implications for the spread of venereal diseases during the colonial period has a direct correlate in the contemporary focus on changing individual behaviors to prevent HIV/AIDS. Policymakers and funders have paid little attention to the social, political, and economic aspects influencing people's lives during the epidemic.

When Meli, the woman who had arrived at the White Sisters' mission as a child, was recruited in 1936 to return to Tanganyika to assist with an orphanage, the very notion of orphanages was considered an anachronism, a European innovation introduced to deal with human suffering in the wake of the massacres and day-to-day miseries that accompanied the ivory and slave trade era.[95] Little did anyone suspect that African societies would so soon face tragedy again on such a massive scale that orphanages would once more be part of the landscape.

Notes

The research for this chapter was supported by an International Doctoral Research Fellowship, funded by the Joint Committee on African Studies of the Social Science Research Council and the American Council of Learned Societies, with moneys provided by the Rockefeller Foundation. Additional funding for the write-up was provided by the Behavioral Science Education Cancer Prevention and Control, National Cancer Institute/NIH Grant #2R25CA57712–06. The Population Research Institute at the Pennsylvania State University and the University of Texas–Houston School of Public Health provided financial assistance and office support. I thank the Tanzanian Commission for Science and Technology for permission to carry out the research, as well as Professor Kapepwa Tambila and the History Department at the University of Dar es Salaam for research affiliation. I thank Iris Berger, Dennis Cordell, Karl Ittmann, Gregory H. Maddox, Phyllis Martin, Jamie Monson, Brooke Schoepf, Pamela Scully, Carole Vance, Kerry Ward, and Marcia Wright for their comments on earlier versions of this paper.

1. Sr. Christophe Marie, "Cet S.O.S. d'Ujiji est celui de toute l'Afrique," "Soeurs Blanche," *Grand Lacs,* nos. 4, 5, 6, n.s. 106–8 (February 1948): 123–24.

2. Abdallahi Mahadi, "Migration, Sedentarisation, and Urbanisation Process in the Central Sudan before 1800 AD" (paper presented at the 2e Congrès International de Démographie Historique, Société de Démographie Historique, Paris, 4–6 June 1987), cited in Dennis D. Cordell and Joel Gregory, "Earlier African Historical Demographies," *Canadian Journal of African Studies* 23, no. 1 (1989): 2–27.

3. Claude Meillasoux, *The Anthropology of Slavery: The Womb of Iron and Gold* (London: Athlone Press, 1991).

4. Cordell and Gregory, "Earlier African Historical Demographies," 13.

5. Dennis D. Cordell, "Où sont tous les enfants? La faible fécondité en Centrafrique, 1890–1960," in *Population, reproduction, sociétés: Perspectives et enjeux de démographie sociale,* ed. Dennis D. Cordell, Danielle Gauvreau, Raymond Gervais, and Céline Le Bourdais (Montreal, Canada: Les Presses de l'Université de Montréal, 1993), 257–82.

6. Sheryl McCurdy, "Transforming Associations: Fertility, Therapy, and the Manyema Diaspora in Urban Kigoma, Tanzania, c. 1850–1993" (PhD diss., Columbia University, 2000).

7. Arjun Appadurai, *Modernity at Large: Cultural Dimensions of Globalization* (Minneapolis: University of Minnesota Press, 1996).

8. Abdul Sheriff, *Slaves, Spices & Ivory in Zanzibar: Integration of an East African Commercial Empire into the World Economy, 1770–1873* (Athens: Ohio University Press, 1987).

9. Jamie Monson, "Relocating Maji Maji: The Politics of Alliance and Authority in the Southern Highlands of Tanganyika," *Journal of African History* 39, no. 1 (1998): 95–121.

10. Laura Fair, *Pastimes and Politics: Culture, Community, and Identity in Post-abolition Urban Zanzibar, 1890–1945* (Athens: Ohio University Press, 2001); Thaddeus Sunseri, "Famine and Wild Pigs: Gender Struggles and the Outbreak of the Maji Maji War in Uzaramo (Tanzania)," *Journal of African History* 38, no. 2 (1997): 235–59.

11. Jan George Deutsch, *Emancipation without Abolition: German East Africa, c. 1884–1914* (Oxford: James Currey Press, 2006).

12. By 1894, large boats could no longer negotiate the Ujiji harbor. During 1878, the Lukugu River outlet in the Congo had opened, and it drained for the next six years, dropping the water level in Lake Tanganyika from 783 meters to 773 meters and causing the Ujiji beach to extend another 100 meters. See Beverly Brown, "Ujiji: The History of a Lakeside Town, c. 1800–1914" (PhD diss., Boston University, 1973), 2.

13. Dmitri van den Bersselaar, "Establishing the Facts: P. A. Talbot and the 1921 Census of Nigeria," *History in Africa* 31 (January 2004): 69–102.

14. London Missionary Society representative Walter Hutley reported that the men's and women's dance he observed seemed a rather sedate affair, without any associated immoral behavior. See Hutley, *The Central Africa Diaries of Walter Hutley, 1877 to 1881,* ed. James B. Wolf (Boston: Boston University Press, 1976), 254.

15. Anonymous, "Famillien-Nachwuchsstatistik über die Eingeborenen von Deutsch-Ostafrika," *Deutsches Kolonialblatt* (1914), 440–41. I thank Thaddeus Sunseri for translating this report.

16. Dr. J. McClark, "Kigoma and Ujiji: Extracts from a Report," *Annual Medical Report, Tanganyika Territory, 1922* (Dar es Salaam: Government Printers, 1923) 126.

17. Edward Coode Hore, *Missionary to Tanganyika, 1877–1888: The Writings of Edward Coode Hore, Master Mariner* (London: Frank Cass, 1971), 8; Richard Burton, *The Lake Regions of Central Africa* (St. Clair Shores: Scholarly Press, 1971), 53.

18. David Northrup, *Beyond the Bend in the River: African Labor in Eastern Zaire, 1865–1940,* Ohio Center for International Studies, Monographs in International Studies, Africa Series no. 52 (Athens: Ohio University Press, 1988), 23–33; Deogratias Kamanzi Bimanyu, "The Waungwana of Eastern Zaire, 1880–1900" (PhD diss., University of London, 1976), 68–97. By the 1870s, the term *waungwana,* though it literally meant "free men" or "free women," had become synonymous with *gentlefolk.* See Jonathan Glassman, *Feasts and Riots: Revelry, Rebellion, and Popular Consciousness on the Swahili Coast* (Portsmouth, NH: Heinemann, 1995), 61–64. Also see Walter Hutley's report from Urambo, "Mohammedanism in Central Africa" [14 November 1881], Council for World Mission Archives (formerly London Missionary Society), Incoming Letters, Central Africa Archives, CAMP microfiche, box no. 4, folder no. 2, jacket D, page 7 (hereafter cited as CWMA/IL/CAA). Jérôme Becker refers to the *Ouguana* as the "gentlemen" of the coast; see Becker, *La vie en Afrique* (Paris: J. Lebègue, 1887), 2. Glassman found that in the earlier caravans from the coast, *vibarua* slaves were often used as caravan porters, and they called themselves *waungwana.*

19. The word *Manyema* first appeared in print in 1872 in Henry M. Stanley, *How I Found Livingstone* (repr., New York: Arno Press, 1970), 426, 463. Stanley used the term to refer to both the people and the place.

20. Marc H. Dawson, "Socioeconomic Change and Disease: Smallpox in Colonial Kenya, 1880–1920," in *The Social Basis of Health and Healing in Africa,* ed. Steven Feierman and John M. Janzen (Berkeley: University of California Press, 1992), 90–103. Dawson's essay illustrated that it is the social reaction to famine or population movement that triggers epidemics, not malnutrition. For details on social reactions to famine, see Gregory Maddox, "Mtunya: Famine in Central Tanzania, 1917–1920," *Journal of African History* 31, no. 2 (1990): 181–97; Maddox, "Gender and Famine in Central Tanzania, 1916–1961," *African Studies Review* 39, no. 1 (1996): 83–101; Maddox, "Njaa: Food Shortages and Famines in Tanzania between the Wars," *International Journal of African Historical Studies* 19, no. 1 (1986): 17–34; see also Megan Vaughan, *The Story of an African Famine: Gender and Famine in Twentieth-Century Malawi* (New York: Cambridge University Press, 1987).

21. Hutley, "Mohammedanism in Central Africa."

22. Hore to Mullens, Ujiji, 16 April 1879, Box 2, Folder 1, Jacket B, CWMA/IL/CAA.

23. K. David Patterson and Gerald W. Hartwig, "The Disease Factor: An Introductory Overview," in *Disease in African History: An Introductory Survey and Case Studies,* ed. Gerald W. Hartwig and K. David Patterson (Durham, NC: Duke University Press, 1978), 3–24.

24. Gerald W. Hartwig suggested that in Kerebe, in northwestern Tanzania, disease and long-distance trade introduced changes in "lineage relationships, increasing accusations of sorcery, and a desire for a servile population." See Hartwig, "Social Consequences of Epidemic Diseases: The Nineteenth Century in Eastern Africa," in *Disease in African History: An Introductory Survey and Case Studies,* ed. Gerald W. Hartwig and K. David Patterson (Durham, NC: Duke University Press, 1978), 25–45.

25. Hutley, *Central Africa Diaries,* 107, 117, 152, 196, 206, 227.

26. Ibid., 105.

27. Hermann von Wissmann, *My Second Journey through Equatorial Africa, from the Congo to the Zambesi, in the Years 1886 and 1887* (Westmead, UK: Gregg International Publishers, 1971), 246.

28. Jane Moir, *A Lady's Letters from Central Africa: A Journey from Mandala, Shire Highlands to Ujiji, Lake Tanganyika and Back in 1890* (Blantyre, Malawi: Central Africana, 1991), 31–32. Stephen Rockel, "Caravan Porters of the Nyika: Labour, Culture and Society in Nineteenth-Century Tanzania" (PhD diss., University of Toronto, 1997), 238–47. For more about Manyema women's activities, see Sheryl McCurdy, "Fashioning Sexuality: Desire, Manyema Ethnicity, and the Creation of the Kanga, c. 1880–1900," *International Journal of African Historical Studies* 39, no. 3 (2006): 441–69.

29. Lieutenant Sigl, "Ujiji," *Le Mouvement Géographique,* February 4, 1894, 14.

30. Hore to Mullens, Ujiji, 16 April 1879, CWMA/IL/CAA/2/1/B, as cited in Brown, "Ujiji," 104.

31. James Christie, *Cholera Epidemics in East Africa: An Account of the Several Diffusions of the Disease in That Country from 1829 till 1872* (London: Macmillan, 1876), 236, 246, 258. Christie suggested that the 1858–59 epidemic made its way to Uganda at least, where J. H. Speke discussed it with Buganda ruler Mutesa. Three earlier cholera epidemics had struck the Swahili coast, in 1821, 1835–36, and 1858–59. There is limited evidence on the extent to which these epidemics affected Central Africa. However, each had its origins in cholera outbreaks on the Arabian Peninsula, and the outbreaks of the 1835–36, 1858–59, and 1869–79 epidemics coincided specifically with the pilgrimages to Mecca in 1835, 1858, and 1865. See Christie, *Cholera Epidemics,* 98–99, 104–8, 150. For other references to the epidemics, see also David Livingstone, *The Last Journals of David Livingstone* (Hartford, CT: T. W. Bliss, 1875), 331.

32. Henry M. Stanley, *Through the Dark Continent* (New York: Harper, 1878), 2, 62–63.

33. Livingstone, *Last Journals,* 305.

34. Hutley noted smallpox cases in January, May, and October 1880. See Hutley, *Central African Diaries,* 152, 173, 214.

35. Hutley to Whitehouse, Ujiji, 23 February 1880, CWMA/IL/CAA/Fiche 36. Marc Dawson described how the movement and crowding together of large, disparate groups of people into new places triggered smallpox epidemics in Kenya; see Dawson, "Smallpox in Kenya, 1880–1920," *Social Science and Medicine* 13B, no. 4 (1979): 245–50.

36. Hore to Whitehouse, Ujiji, 20 July 1880, CWMA/IL/CAA/Fiche 41–42.

37. The influx of nonimmune peoples from the countryside into the fishing communities of Lake Tanganyika and the towns of the northeastern region of the Congo following the rinderpest epizootic and famine created the environment for smallpox to spread quickly. Many died from starvation, smallpox, or both. Sidney Langford Hinde, *The Fall of the Congo Arabs* (London: Methuen, 1897), 177; Beverly Brown and Walter T. Brown, "East African Trade Towns: A Shared Growth," in *A Century of Change in Eastern Africa,* ed. W. Arens (The Hague, the Netherlands: Mouton, 1976), 183–200.

38. Hinde, *Fall of the Congo Arabs,* 177; Brown and Brown, "East African Trade Towns," 183–200; Lionel Decle, *Three Years in Savage Africa* (London: Methuen, 1898), 311. The central plateau and coast of East Africa were also severely affected by the rinderpest panzootic, with reports of 90 percent of the livestock lost. James L. Giblin suggested that the rinderpest panzootic might have been, in part, responsible "more broadly for the collapse of patronage and depopulation during the 1890s famines"; see Giblin, *The Politics of Environmental Control in Northern Tanzania, 1840–1940* (Philadelphia: University of Pennsylvania Press, 1992), 129.

39. White Fathers' 1892 Kibanga Diary, cited in Brown and Brown, "East African Trade Towns," 190.

40. Brown, "Ujiji," 87–88.

41. I have not found sources that describe how they arrived at their population estimates.

42. Hutley, *Central African Diaries,* 293; Hutley to Whitehouse, Ujiji, 23 February 1880, CWMA/IL/CAA/Fiche 36; Lovett Cameron, *Across Africa* (London: George Philip and Son, 1885), 177; Livingstone, *Last Journals,* 255. Travelers' and slaves' narratives noted the ill treatment; for an extreme example, see Ned Alpers, "Story of Swema: Female Vulnerability in Nineteenth Century East Africa," in *Women and Slavery in Africa,* ed. Claire Robertson and Martin Klein (Madison: University of Wisconsin Press, 1983), 185–219.

43. Cordell, "Où sont tous les enfants?" 257–82.

44. See Sheryl McCurdy, "Learning the Dance, Initiating Relationships," in *In Pursuit of History,* ed. Jan Vansina and Carolyn Keyes Adenaike (Portsmouth, NH: Heinemann, 1996), 41–56.

45. Stanley, *How I Found Livingstone,* 543. Lovett Cameron and Thomas Heazle Parke both noted the extent to which the disease was prevalent along the ivory and slave route. See Cameron, *Across Africa,* 77. Parke, the medical officer for the Emin Pasha Expedition, observed that a large proportion of the Zanzibaris [*waungwana*] with whom he traveled had suffered from smallpox. See Parke, *My Personal Experiences in Equatorial Africa: As Medical Officer of the Emin Pasha Relief Expedition* (New York: Scribner's, 1891), 24.

46. Burton, *Lake Regions,* 318, 320, 321; Stanley, *How I Found Livingstone,* 533.

47. Charles M. Good, "Tick-Borne Relapsing Fever in East Africa," in *Disease in African History: An Introductory Survey and Case Studies,* ed. Gerald W. Hartwig and K. David Patterson (Durham, NC: Duke University Press, 1978), 46–87, 83n5, which cites Edward Hindle, "The Relapsing Fever of Tropical Africa: A Review," *Parasitology* 4, no. 3 (1911): 184.

48. Joseph A. McFalls and Marguerite Harvey McFalls, *Disease and Fertility* (Orlando, FL: Academic Press/Harcourt Brace Jovanovich, 1984), 60, 533.

49. Ibid., 108, 120, 122.

50. Ibid., 55.

51. Ibid., 61; V. H. Jongen, Jos van Roosmalen, Johannes Tiems, Jacqueline Van Holten, and Jose C. F. M. Wetsteyn, "Tick-Borne Relapsing Fever and Pregnancy Outcome in Rural Tanzania," *Acta Obstetricia et Gynecologica Scandinavica* 76, no. 9 (1997): 834–38.

52. McFalls and McFalls, *Disease and Fertility,* 98.

53. Jongen et al., "Tick-Borne Relapsing Fever." Out of 1,000 pregnancies, 436 resulted in perinatal death and another 39 in miscarriages.

54. Renee Pennington and Henry Harpending, *The Structure of an African Pastoralist Community: Demography, History and Ecology of the Ngamiland Herero* (Oxford: Oxford University Press, 1993), 128–29.

55. Ibid., 127, citing Mark A. Belsey, "The Epidemiology of Infertility: A Review with Particular Reference to Sub-Saharan Africa," *Bulletin of the World Health Organization* 54, no. 3 (1976): 319–41; D. C. W. Mabey, G. Ogbaselassie, J. N. Robertson, J. E. Heckels, and M. E. Ward, "Tubal Infertility in the Gambia: Chlamydial and Gonococcal Serology in Women with Tubal Occlusion Compared with Pregnant Controls," *Bulletin of the World Health Organization* 63, no. 6 (1985): 1107–13; W. Cates, T. M. M. Farley, and P. J. Rowe, "Infections, Pregnancies and Infertility: Perspectives on Prevention," *Fertility and Sterility* 47, no. 6 (1987): 964–68.

56. For an exception to the rule, a slave population that did replace itself through reproduction, see Hilary Beckles, *Black Rebellion in Barbados: The Struggle against Slavery, 1627–1838* (Bridgetown, Barbados: Antilles Publications, 1984). Fertility rates in Barbados averaged around 3.0 per slave woman.

57. Meillasoux, *Anthropology of Slavery.*

58. Marcia Wright, *Strategies of Slaves and Women: Life Stories from East/Central Africa* (New York: Barber Press, 1993), 47–52.

59. Ibid., 27.

60. Ibid., 88.

61. Ibid., 191.

62. See Nancy Scheper-Hughes, *Death without Weeping: The Violence of Everyday Life in Brazil* (Berkeley: University of California Press, 1993), which deals with similar reactions to tragedies of this kind in late twentieth-century Brazil. For a contemporary African novel that discusses spirit children, who come but never really mean to live among us, see Ben Okri, *The Famished Road* (New York: Anchor Books, 1991).

63. Asa Briggs suggested the massive death tolls resulting from the nineteenth-century cholera epidemics around the world tested political authority and leadership as the disease moved along mercantile routes, spread quickly in response to mass religious celebrations, and intensified class divisions. See Briggs, "Cholera and Society in the Nineteenth Century," *Past and Present* 19, no. 1 (1961): 76–96.

64. J. W. T. Allen, ed. and trans., *The Customs of the Swahili People: The Desturi za Waswahili of Mtoro bin Mwinyi Bakari and Other Swahili Persons* (Berkeley: University of California Press, 1981), 134.

65. The term *social chaos* is an adaptation of Jean Allman's use of *gender chaos.* See Allman, "Rounding Up Spinsters: Gender Chaos and Unmarried Women in Colonial Asante," *Journal of African History* 37, no. 2 (1996): 195–214.

66. Margaret Strobel, "Slavery and Reproductive Labor in Mombasa," in *Women and Slavery in Africa,* ed. Claire Robertson and Martin A. Klein (Madison: University of Wisconsin Press, 1983), 111–29. Seven of the eighteen slave women attached to one household never married and never had children. Another four married but had no children. Five slave women who were not concubines had seven children among them. Finally, two concubines had a total of five children between them.

67. Robert Harms, "Sustaining the System: The Middle Zaire," in *Women and Slavery in Africa,* ed. Claire Robertson and Martin A. Klein (Madison: University of Wisconsin Press, 1983), 95–110. In the early 1950s, when reliable demographic data were finally becoming available, it was possible to trace a belt of low fertility that extended from the Swahili Coast inland to the former ivory and slave trade communities at least as far as Stanleyville, Congo, in what used to be called the Manyema area. The Swahili community in Stanleyville, Congo, referred to as *Arabisés* during the colonial period, had a very low age-adjusted fertility rate of 1.46, or approximately 1.5 children for each woman. See

Valdo Pons, *Stanleyville: An African Urban Community under Belgian Administration* (London: Oxford University Press, 1969), 86. Manyema living in Dar es Salaam during the 1950s also had low fertility. See J. A. K. Leslie, *A Survey of Dar es Salaam* (Oxford: Oxford University Press, 1963), 247. Swahili women along the coast also had low fertility. See R. E. S. Tanner, "The Relationships between the Sexes in a Coastal Islam Society: Pangani District, Tanganyika," *African Studies* 21, no. 2 (1962): 70–82.

68. Jean Stenghers and Jan Vansina, "King Leopold's Congo," in *The Cambridge History of Africa,* vol. 6, *From 1870–1905,* ed. J. D. Fage and Roland Oliver (Cambridge: Cambridge University Press, 1985), 313–58.

69. Meillasoux argued that women in a slave economy depended on their productive rather than reproductive capacities. The greater numbers of women compared to men also limited exposure to the possibility of becoming pregnant. See Meillasoux, *Anthropology of Slavery,* 311.

70. Ibid., 311.

71. Allen, *Customs of the Swahili People,* 125.

72. Swahili and Manyema women continued to have lower fertility than other Tanzanian women throughout the colonial and postcolonial periods. Richard Burton noted the Swahili women on Zanzibar had small families. See Burton, *Zanzibar: City, Island, and Coast* (London: Tinsley Brothers, 1872), 436.

73. Amon J. Nsekela and Aloysius M. Nhonoli, *Health Services and Society in Mainland Tanzania: A Historical Overview 'tumetoka mbali'* (London: Academic Press, 1976), 14; John Iliffe, *Tanganyika under German Rule, 1905–1912* (Cambridge: Cambridge University Press, 1969), 15.

74. David F. Clyde, *History of the Medical Services of Tanganyika* (Dar es Salaam: Government Press, 1962), 6, 31.

75. Ibid., 440. All quotations in this paragraph are from this document and page, unless otherwise stated.

76. Ibid., 441. The middle district of German-administrated Ujiji may refer to Mpanda District, which later, under the British administration, fell under Kigoma Region. District Officer C. M. Coke, Kigoma, reported in 1943 that this southern region was dramatically underpopulated, due, he believed, to the early age of marriage of young girls. Coke lectured the people of the district that their early marital practices forced young girls into sexual intercourse before their bodies were mature, with the inevitable result that the young women would be childless in their old age. See C. M. Coke, Kigoma District Officer's Report, Western Province, Dar es Salaam, Tanzania National Archives.

77. The Culwicks suggested that women's low fertility in southwestern Tanzania during the 1930s and 1940s was one of the lasting effects of the Maji Maji War in 1905–6. See Arthur T. Culwick and G. M. Culwick, "A Study of Population in Ulanga, Tanganyika Territory," *Sociological Review* 30, no. 4 (1938): 50–84.

78. Anonymous, "Famillien-Nachwuchsstatistik," 441. In the 1930s, British Western Provincial Commissioner F. J. Bagshawe also complained about childless Manyema women and their partners, the Manyema soldiers, and sought information about what herbs they used as abortifacients. The *liwali* (Muslim judge) informed him that women used herbal contraceptives to prevent pregnancy. See F. J. Bagshawe's Diaries, vol. 15, pp. 92–93, Rhodes House Library, Oxford.

79. In Tabora District, the provincial commissioner wrote that the low birthrate was "due to the absence of many thousands of men who went to the coast to work" and the temporary liaisons women and men contracted instead of marriage. See F. J. Bagshawe,

"Western Province," *Annual Report of the Provincial Commissioners, Tanganyika Territory* (Dar es Salaam: Government Printers, 1934), 44–45. For a discussion of population decline in Bukoba and Uganda, see Birgitta Larsson, *Conversion to a Greater Freedom: Women, Church, and Social Change in Northwestern Tanzania under Colonial Rule* (Uppsala, Sweden: Acta Universitatis Upsaliensis, 1991), 162; Megan Vaughan, "*Curing Their Ills: Colonial Power and African Illness* (Stanford, CA: Stanford University Press, 1991), 132–38.

80. O. F. Raum, "German East Africa: Changes in African Life under German Administration, 1892–1914," in *The History of East Africa,* ed. Vincent Harlow and E. M. Chilver (Oxford: Clarendon, 1965), 163–207.

81. Wright, *Strategies of Slaves and Women,* 204–5, citing M. von Prince, *Eine deutsche Frau im Innern Deutsch-Ostafrikas* (Berlin: Liebmann, 1903), 61, 79.

82. Wright, *Strategies of Slaves and Women,* 204–5.

83. *Rapports Annuels,* 1920–21, White Sisters Archive, Rome.

84. J. B. Davey, *Annual Medical Report, 1922, Tanganyika Territory* (Dar es Salaam: Government Printer, 1923), 26.

85. Birgitta Larsson used this term in her discussion of Haya sexuality. See Larsson, *Conversion to a Greater Freedom,* 162.

86. For a detailed and eloquent discussion on this topic, see Vaughan, *Curing Their Ills,* 129–54.

87. The Hottentot Venus was the name used to refer to Saartje Baartman, a twenty-five-year-old woman from what is now South Africa who was exhibited in European cities between 1810 and 1815 so that Europeans could see her large buttocks and fantasize about her genitalia. See Qureshi Sadiah, "Display Sara Baartman, the Hottentot Venus," *History of Science* 42, no. 2 (2004): 233–57. After Baartman's death at age twenty-five, the physician George Curvier performed her autopsy and preserved her sexual organs, ostensibly for the posterity of science but more realistically as part of a larger European project that grew out of Europeans' fascination with cataloging, defining, and reifying their own ideas about a hyper-African sexuality. See Sander Gilman, *Difference and Pathology: Stereotypes of Sexuality, Race and Madness* (Ithaca, NY: Cornell University Press, 1985), 76–108; Londa Schiebinger, *Nature's Body: Gender and the Making of Modern Science* (Boston: Beacon Press, 1993), 143–83.

88. Senior Commissioner of Tabora District, "Vital Statistics and Infant Mortality," *Annual Medical Report, Tanganyika Territory, 1922* (Dar es Salaam: Government Printers, 1923), 100–101.

89. Marc Dawson, "The Anti-yaws Campaign and Colonial Medical Policy in Kenya," *International Journal of African Historical Studies* 20 (1987): 417–37.

90. J. McClark, "Kigoma and Ujiji: Extracts from a Report," *Annual Medical Report, Tanganyika Territory, 1922* (Dar es Salaam: Government Printers, 1923), 126.

91. *Rapports Annuels,* 1922, White Sisters Archive, Rome.

92. Ibid., 1a, 2a.

93. Ibid., 4a.

94. Ujiji dispensary records, 1945–49, White Sisters Archive, Rome.

95. Wright, *Strategies of Slaves,* 120.

8

Disease and Environment in Africa

Imputed Dynamics and Unresolved Issues

GREGORY H. MADDOX

One of the great ironies of debates about African populations turns on the pivot of disease. Although much current public and scholarly debate centers on the recent rapid expansion of African populations, scholars in a number of fields have begun to argue that African populations remained relatively low until the recent past because of the pressure of a variety of diseases. This essay reviews some of the literature on the relationship between demographic variables, disease, and environment refracted against evidence drawn primarily from eastern Africa. It argues that monocausal explanations for population growth or decline need to be replaced by more nuanced explanations that include disease environments as well as changes in the physical environment and social and political conditions. Historians must combine their own ability to discuss economic, political, and social context with a careful analysis of the biological and scientific evidence generated by scientific models to ensure the assumptions used in the creation of the models do not overly distort the resulting conclusions.

It is striking that scholars can still speak of this region of the world, the one longest occupied by humanity and its ancestors, as a frontier. The idea that African societies are in some way "new" to these landscapes flows from certain assumptions about how people lived in these landscapes and particularly how many people lived there. In short, if, as John Iliffe most famously has argued, eastern Africa—and almost all of Africa—was lightly populated before the twentieth century, we must ask why.[1] The simplest answers given usually cite some combination of disease and environment. The archaeologist Brian Fagan succinctly glosses this neo-Malthusian view:

> Yet Africans have often triumphed over environmental adversity. They created great kingdoms—Ghana, Mali, Zimbabwe—traded indirectly with the far corners of the earth, and fashioned great art and flamboyant cultures. But many have always lived on the edge. Regions like the southern fringes of the Sahara are so arid and unpredictable that it took remarkable ingenuity and environmental knowledge to survive there. Famine and disease stalked farmer and herder alike even when population densities were low. In the twentieth century, when colonial governments upset the delicate balance of climate and humanity on a continent that had never supported vast numbers of people or huge urban civilizations, these social disasters have come more frequently. Europe suffered through repeated subsistence crises during the Little Ice Age. Africa is enduring far more serious food shortage in the late twentieth century, caused by a combination of drought, population growth, and human activity.[2]

K. David Patterson and Gerald W. Hartwig, in their overview of disease in African history, have argued along similar lines: "African disease environments, frequently augmented by tropical climatic conditions, have always exacted a significant toll on human life and energy."[3]

Indeed, the twin specters of disease and environmental disaster lurk throughout the literature on African history. Philip Curtin's early work that helped spark the growth of the field of African history in the United States started with the argument that western Africa's deadly disease environment helped explain the Atlantic slave trade and the difficulty Europeans encountered in the conquest of Africa as compared to the Americas.[4] Works by William H. McNeill, Alfred W. Crosby, and Sheldon Watts repeated and elaborated these arguments.[5] All these works asserted that the combination of Old World infectious diseases such as smallpox and vector-borne diseases such as malaria, yellow fever, and trypanosome-caused human and animal diseases led to low African population densities.

As a result, population—demographic change—has long concerned writers about Africa. First colonial administrators and then scholars of modern Africa have engaged in a long-standing debate over the state of African populations before the later nineteenth century and then under colonial rule. Colonial officials and then academics disagreed about both the basic demographic variables and the starting points. Until the middle of the twentieth century, colonial observers tended to worry about shrinking populations.[6] They generally, in turn, assumed that population had always been low. After World War II, concerns turned to the rapid growth in population.[7] Colonial observers attributed the growth to improved health care and sanitation and cited it as a danger to the sustainability of African environments.[8] John Iliffe, however, has asserted that health care made relatively little impact on demographic variables until well after World War II and that much of the earliest phases of population growth in Africa in the twentieth century came because "feast and famine waned together" as colonial infrastructure development helped reduce the incidence of crisis mortality.[9]

Later scholars have tended to agree that in many parts of Africa, populations underwent a demographic crisis in the late nineteenth and early twentieth centuries; however, several have argued that before that time, populations had stabilized in eastern and southern Africa.[10] The crux of the debate centers on whether African populations achieved a degree of control of both their physical and disease environments. Writers such as Helge Kjekshus, Juhani Koponen, and James L. Giblin have forcefully argued the former against the views cited in the opening of this chapter.[11] They have suggested that in particular places, African societies attained a measure of control over the environment and developed social institutions that ensured a degree of stability in populations. Giblin's work in particular has argued that although no society could totally control the effects of climatic variability and exposure to disease, in northeastern Tanzania before the intensification of the caravan trade in the second half of the nineteenth century, African communities developed practices that allowed the maintenance of cattle herds in areas that would harbor the tsetse fly during the twentieth century, preventing their occupation.[12]

Most arguments emphasizing population stability come from particular case studies; as Juhani Koponen has pointed out, communities in Africa could reach "equilibriums" in local contexts.[13] In some cases, scholars begin with an observed or presumed stability and then construct explanations that skip ahead of scientific verification. In addition to cyclical climatic variations, political and economic events could alter or disrupt such situations. Patterson and Hartwig, for example, suggest that the apparently greater degree of contact between western Africa and the outside world, especially since 1500, has meant that such equilibriums in that part of the continent were more disrupted than those in eastern and southern Africa.[14]

Models and Evidence

Given the long history of these concerns, what questions concerning the relationship between disease, environment, and population in Africa still need answers? First, it is important to understand both environment and demographic factors as being specific, not generalized to the continent as a whole. At a broad level, for instance, West Africa's demographic history seems strikingly different from that of eastern or southern Africa. The Sudanic regions of West Africa have an ancient history of regular contact with the Mediterranean world through the medium of caravans across the Sahara. The coastal regions, from the Senegambia through the Guinea Coast and the Bight of Biafra to what is now Angola, became directly incorporated in the world economy starting in the fifteenth century. Over the next four hundred years, at least 11 million individuals left the region as slaves in the Atlantic slave trade. Scholars have debated the demographic effect of this trade on Africa, with some suggesting that long-term population losses remained low.[15] Others have argued that the demographic drain on affected African communities reduced population in the region over the long range.[16] Several factors come into play in these calculations. Some scholars see the impact of New World food crops and the fact that Africans exported more men than women and retained the women in situations where they often bore children as mitigating the population losses due to the slave trade and the greater circulation of infectious disease.[17] The external slave trade ended in the mid-nineteenth century, but commodity trade increased. Perhaps due to this more intense contact with the outside world, populations in West Africa seem not to have suffered declines as severe as those of eastern and central Africa in the late nineteenth and early twentieth centuries.[18]

This conclusion remains speculative. Evidence for reconstructing such changes is difficult to find, and scholars too readily rely on assumptions and models that often obscure important localized as well as chronological variations. In the case of the effects of the Atlantic slave trade, multiple factors interacted in chronologically specific ways. Many epidemiological models, however, search for regular patterns and equilibrium states. Historians cannot dodge this methodological problem, but they can use and have used evidence generated out of such models by situating that evidence in the context of changing conditions.

In different environments in the past, African societies exhibited several types of demographic regimes. To understand these differences, we must consider the variation in the ways that African societies lived in their environments. Geologic factors, climatic change, and conscious and unconscious human agency shaped African landscapes. And neither geologic factors nor the climate is constant. In this context, geologic change includes not just dramatic events such as earthquakes or volcanic eruptions but also erosion and sedimentation. Climate varies in extremely long cycles of glaciation and warming; in medium-term cycles, such as the current global warming that has occurred since the 1850s; and over much shorter, decade-to-decade and year-to-year cycles. Humans have sought to make landscapes both more productive in terms of food and safer for humans vis-à-vis, in William McNeill's words, macro– and microparasites.[19] All of these changes alter the possibilities for the development and transmission of different types of diseases.

One of the key elements of disease environments in Africa has been the existence of malaria. Parasites of the *Plasmodium* family cause malaria. Four species can infect humans (others infect other mammals), with *Plasmodium vivax* and *Plasmodium falciparum* causing the most common cases of malaria in humans. Malaria parasites coevolved with mammals and with mosquitoes of the *Anopheles* family that feed on mammalian blood. The parasite spends part of its life cycle in both the mosquito and its mammal victim and feeds on the red blood cells of its host. The malaria parasites that infect humans all appear to have originated in Africa and spread with hominids out of the continent. Malaria can cause sickness and widespread death. Individuals can achieve short-term resistance to the disease if constantly exposed to it, but resistance to the most deadly variant caused by *P. falciparum* comes at the price of high childhood mortality. *P. vivax* can survive dormant in a host's liver and then reemerge, causing a "relapsing" fever.[20]

James Webb recently produced a synthesis that combines findings in microbiology with the historical disciplines regarding the impact of the evolution of malaria parasites on the growth of human populations in Africa. He notes that *P. vivax* developed about 2 million years ago and quickly became "a scourge of the hominids." The existence of the disease reduced human population growth in the moistest environments in Africa. When modern human populations began to spread outside of Africa at some point between 100,000 and 50,000 years ago, they moved into environments that did not have *P. vivax*.[21]

The rapid growth of human populations outside Africa after about 50,000 years ago occurred in part because of the lack of the disease in other parts of the Old World, although *vivax* established itself in much of the temperate, tropical, and semitropical Old World. In Africa, Webb argues, the development of a genetic defense against the parasite, known as "Duffy negativity," prevented the *vivax* parasite from invading hemoglobin and allowed the dramatic expansion of African population. The trait, almost universal in western and Central Africa today, developed and became fixed in the human population after some humans departed for other parts of the world. As a result, *vivax* malaria has disappeared from Africa (it remains common in Asia and Latin America), whereas the more deadly *falciparum* malaria has become the major strand of the disease on the continent. Webb argues that *falciparum* gradually spread with humans as they developed the skills and tools necessary to exploit the resources of the moister areas of Africa, even as the extent of such environments varied over the last 50,000 years due to climate change. In particular, he points to riverside settlements across the continent that provided both access to greater food resources and exposure to malaria. Webb's argument suggests that African societies, just as those outside Africa, pursued technological innovations that in turn brought greater risks; eventually, those humans who survived did so because they possessed a genetic mutation that allowed them to exploit those resources.[22]

A second example of the way that disease environments deeply patterned the development of human societies in Africa comes from eastern Africa in the period after the domestication of cattle in the northeastern part of the continent. Archaeologists have discovered evidence for the domestication of cattle in western Egypt as early as 11,000 years ago.[23] Although the evidence is still sketchy, some archaeologists believe they can reconstruct a rough history of the spread of cattle keeping south of the Sahara prior to 5,000 years ago.[24] However, humans do not seem to have been able to take livestock south of the arid savannas until about 4,000 years ago. Diane Gifford-Gonzales has argued that the presence of tsetse flies carrying trypanosomiasis prevented humans from entering the moister savannas and woodlands. Tsetse and trypanosomiasis are ancient and seem to have evolved with the large game animals of Africa. It took a thousand years for humans to develop the ability to control the exposure of cattle to disease, which allowed such animals to move south. Humans altered the environment by clearing land for agriculture and by burning, which reduced that habitat for tsetse and the game on which it feeds.[25]

These deeper historical relationships between human populations and disease point to the need to look beyond single-cause, onetime changes in biological relationships to explain demographic regimes. In both of the cases outlined earlier, dynamic relationships between humans, microbes, other animals, and domesticates helped create variable relationships. Since these biological relationships can change over long time periods, historians must relate them to changes in human societies.

In short, historians must combine their own ability to discuss economic, political, and social context with an awareness of biological and scientific discourses. Historians, of course, have excelled at this effort. Numerous case studies have examined both particular diseases and diseases in particular environments.[26] The difficulty has lain in generating the kind of conclusions that will engage not just historians but also researchers in demography, public health, and epidemiology. Too often, historical studies involve a search for errors, and that comes across as undermining the basis for knowing anything about disease and environment. In identifying the origins of much scientific knowledge about health or environment in "colonial science," historians sometimes come close to rejecting any legitimacy for scientific knowledge at all.[27] It is imperative for historians to frame their arguments in terms that impact other debates. The remainder of this paper seeks to outline some elements of a productive approach to the study of disease in African history.

Historicizing the Interaction between Disease and Environment

Following Patterson and Hartwig, we can consider a couple of central transitions in African population history. Before the development of agriculture, foraging populations seem to have lacked the numbers to sustain endemic diseases, although they were susceptible to diseases that were carried by vectors and/or had hosts in animal populations, such as malaria and trypanosomiasis. Hence, little evidence exists for diseases such as smallpox in the deep past, but diseases such as malaria and human sleeping sickness and nagana in livestock caused by trypanosomiasis seem to possess great antiquity.

Part of the argument for the low population densities of Africa relates to these two types of diseases. Malaria inhibits population growth in areas of high rainfall, and trypanosomiasis prevents the raising of animals in rain forest regions and makes much of eastern and southern Africa very difficult to open to agriculture.[28] Foraging communities would have avoided the environments that produced human sleeping sickness, and human communities developed biological defenses for malaria. They needed these defenses due to the range of the various species of *Anopheles* mosquitoes that carry the disease-causing microbes. In the wettest regions of Africa, exposure was constant; in most of the rest, it tended to be seasonal.[29]

The development of agriculture gradually created more-settled populations and led to a greater propensity for the spread of viral and bacterial diseases. Settled populations allowed some diseases to become endemic. Webb suggests the development of settled agricultural populations brought humans into more regular contact with *falciparum* malaria sometime after 10,000 years ago.[30]

The movement of agricultural communities into the African rain forests created the conditions for the emergence of the sickle-cell trait in human populations. Richard Carter and Kamini N. Mendis state: "The intense transmission that induced early immunity simply concentrated the mortality due to *P. falciparum* malaria into the youngest age groups. *P. falciparum* had become a killer of human beings which, historically and still today, has few rivals."[31] As a result, human populations evolved several defenses against this relatively new killer. The sickle-cell trait became the most effective of these mutations in one sense. The trait causes red blood cells to elongate. Children inheriting the trait from just one parent have one-tenth the chance of dying from malaria compared to children without the trait; however, those inheriting the trait from both parents suffer from sickle-cell anemia and die young, probably before reaching reproductive age in premodern societies. This trait gives heterozygotes a critical survival advantage during early childhood and allows them to almost uniformly acquire immunity to the worst effects of malarial infection. In areas of holoendemic malaria, up to 30 percent of individuals carry the sickle-cell trait from one parent, and up to 10 percent of babies born are doomed to an early death from sickle-cell anemia—"the cost of endemic *P. falciparum* malaria to a human population."[32] Human populations in four regions of Africa developed different versions of the trait, and populations in the Mediterranean, India, and Middle East also carry it. Anthony C. Allison, one of the researchers instrumental in discovering the relationship between the sickle-cell trait and malaria, argues that in East Africa, frequencies of the trait follow very closely the prevalence of malaria.[33]

Several important diseases either moved back and forth between domestic animals and humans or made the evolutionary jump from the former to the latter. Likewise, settled populations could both control some diseases more easily and also create the environment for the concentration of other disease vectors. Clearing land for agriculture in areas where tsetse could survive reduced the danger to humans (although not necessarily as much for domestic animals, which still required grazing lands) even as it created more opportunities for the *Anopheles gambiae* mosquitoes that carried malaria. Webb suggests that the development of limited immunity in populations exposed to malaria combined with higher-yielding agricultural practices to create an "immunological gradient" that facilitated the expansion of communities speaking Bantu languages.[34] Several scholars have made the case that African societies developed the means to control exposure to tsetse for both humans and animals in different contexts. James Giblin has argued that in East Africa, cattle-keeping communities practiced limited exposure to tsetse as a way of building up immunity to trypanosomiasis among their herds. The resulting landscape consisted of broad areas kept relatively clear of bush by fire and agriculture, divided by belts of bush hosting both tsetse and the game reservoirs of infection.[35] It is worth noting that such methods of control and exposure work mostly in savanna-type environments where human clearing is not overwhelmed by rainfall.

Even then, such control remained precarious. Changes in population density caused by political disruption or forced by climatic variation such as drought could result in the loss of the ability to maintain such control locally. Roderick McIntosh has argued that in the Inner Niger Delta, successive wetter and drier periods resulted in what he describes as "pulses" of population. Both agricultural-ists and stockkeepers moved farther north in wetter periods and "collapsed" back south to the Niger in drier periods. He suggests this process underlies the eth-nic diversity and perhaps even the caste system among the Mande-, Taureg-, and Fulbe-speaking peoples in the region.[36] James Webb has also shown how climate helped shape the contours of population in the western Sahel.[37] In regard to what is now central Tanzania, I have proposed that cyclical changes in climate or even conjectural events such as severe famines could have led to the repeated ebb and flow of population. In that region, people would move into the grazing lands of the central plateau and eastern Rift Valley during wetter years. The ability to keep cattle drew people into the region from the wetter but often tsetse-compromised south and east. I think this "pulsing" of population explains the strong clan con-nections across ethnic boundaries in the region. A study of clan origin claims among the Gogo people shows that a majority of them claim origins among the Hehe to the south or Kaguru or Sagara to the east.[38]

The regular disruptions helped create long-term webs of connections across environmental frontiers. These links took a variety of forms. In central Tanzania, stock owners "loaned" stock to other stock holders in different areas in order to ensure the survival of some of their herds. These loans were often reciprocal, with individuals exchanging stock. This relationship gave each member a source of support in case a drought or epidemic struck the herd in their direct possession.[39] For the Pare Mountains of northeastern Tanzania, I. N. Kimambo has documented how an intricate network of social and trade relationships among the Pare people served to give them access to food in times of emergency and specialized products such as salt and metal in more normal times.[40] In many highland regions in East Africa, communities held land up and down slopes to take advantage of different ecosystems at different altitudes. The higher, better-watered elevations served as refuges in case of drought on the lowlands. Among the Chagga peoples of Kili-manjaro, social and political ties ran up and down the mountain so strongly that they organized states along those lines.[41] Similar patterns exist among the Arusha and Meru of Mount Meru,[42] in the Uluguru Mountains,[43] in the Usambaras,[44] and in the Kenya Highlands.[45] In the Mbulu highlands of north-central Tanzania, the Iraqw people used support from the colonial government and then the inde-pendent government to recolonize the plains surrounding their highland refuge over the course of the twentieth century.[46]

Demographic and land use patterns also reflected the biological defenses to disease developed in human populations.[47] The earliest studies to fully explain the relationship between sickle-cell trait, malaria infection, and childhood mortality took place in East Africa. In the 1950s, Anthony Allison first documented that people in regions with an endemic, year-round transmission of malaria—in this case, the area around Lake Victoria Nyanza and along the East African coast—had frequencies of the sickle-cell trait that approached 30 percent. The frequencies then declined in a gradient that followed the intensity of malaria transmission to almost 0 percent in the cool highlands of Kenya and Tanzania, which never saw the transmission of malaria.[48]

This discovery helped lead to an understanding of the way malaria works in holoendemic environments, where exposure to the disease occurs throughout the year. Such areas see a high degree of the sickle-cell trait, and as a result, populations develop immunity to malaria through repeated exposure. This process leads to very high childhood mortality rates and often high fertility rates. In dry lowlands, which have an extended dry season, malarial exposure is correspondingly seasonal. Historically, childhood mortality from malaria in these areas generally was lower, but because immunity was not as widespread, adult mortality was higher.[49] In addition, maternal mortality in modern populations in such areas is higher, as it undoubtedly was in the past. The literature has not explored this in the historical context.

In East Africa, the coastal area, the lowland regions around the Great Lakes, and the river valleys all have this type of environment, and one such area, the Kilombero Valley of southern Tanzania, has become a center of global malaria research because of the intensity of transmission there.[50] In semiarid areas, in which exposure to malaria was short and in some years nonexistent, a wet year that allowed an extended breeding season for mosquitoes permitted more exposure and the spread of malaria from wetter areas.[51] It often resulted in epidemic-like episodes. The effect of human action on the landscapes complicates the simple environmental schema of malaria exposure. Clearing land for agriculture increases the niches for the survival of *Anopheles gambiae* and hence expands the areas prone to longer periods of exposure to malaria over the course of the year.[52] In most moist uplands, heat rather than moisture governs exposure to malaria.[53] Warmer and wetter years could and can lead to malaria epidemics in higher altitudes than normal, as happened in 2005–6 in Hai District on Mount Kilimanjaro in Tanzania and in the central Kenyan Highlands.[54] In all cases, where a rough equilibrium developed, it has remained fragile.

Mobility among African populations exposed people to new diseases environments. Long-distance contact through trade and migration brought new diseases from different environments and circulated infectious diseases. There is great debate about the degree of this circulation. Some scholars point to long-standing trade networks in the Sahel and along the East African coast as having created circulation. Other scholars argue that there was very little circulation before the year 1500. Sheldon Watts suggests:

Environments of this sort were often associated with a lived-world in which community members were geographically stable. This situation comes close to those found in West African regions still unblitzed by the commercial trade in slaves. Here in time of peace, the generality of the population seldom traveled far from the cluster of villages or the large urban settlements in which they had been born. Within this *pays* and those immediately adjacent, they found their spouses, did their farming and marketing, buried their dead and did whatever else normal people do. Biologically, this relatively restricted region served as a unified disease environment.[55]

Scholars contend that the degree of movement (and the number of people involved) was relatively small and that contact tended to occur in stages. Allison's evidence from the gradient in the sickle-cell trait in East Africa supports this conclusion, since such a gradient would not have existed if people had constantly moved between disease zones.[56]

Yet diseases moved among African populations. Roderick McIntosh has suggested that people abandoned Jenne-Jeno and eventually built Jenne in the Inner Niger Delta because of a population collapse due to the spread of plague across the Sahara in the fourteenth century.[57] Certainly, by the time of extensive contact with Europeans after 1500, epidemics of smallpox, cholera, and plague had become common in port towns and along trade routes. The Yoruba peoples, for example, worshiped a specific god of smallpox.[58] By the nineteenth century, when written records became more copious, smallpox and cholera epidemics struck regularly along trade routes in Africa.[59]

In eastern Africa, the nineteenth century saw a dramatic upsurge in violence and population movement. As a result, both famine and disease seem to have become more common in the region. Helge Kjekshus has most famously argued that the more rapid circulation of disease played a major role in population decline in what eventually became mainland Tanzania,[60] and Juhani Koponen has supported this assertion with more detailed evidence from early travelers and missionaries.[61] The crisis that Mike Davis has labeled a "Victorian Holocaust" saw the population of eastern Africa probably fall and continue to fall until 1920.[62] Marc Dawson contends that population growth only began in Kenya after 1930.[63]

The modern era has seen the continued development of new landscapes and increasing amounts of movement between them. Urban and industrial landscapes have brought the most dramatic changes, as documented by works such as that of Randall M. Packard.[64] He argues that the particular conditions of industrial labor in southern Africa led to widespread suffering from tuberculosis. In general, communicable diseases of all sorts spread more rapidly. The influenza epidemic of 1918–19 provides a striking case. Medical authorities reported the first cases in West Africa in August 1918. Cases quickly sprang up in southern Africa and then in East Africa. Death rates reached up to 5 percent of the total population in the affected areas—a staggering total in a short period.[65] In Accra, which normally saw only a few deaths per day, Patterson reports that deaths peaked at fifty-nine per day in early October 1918 and declined after the middle of the month.[66] In what has become central Tanzania, the Gogo people remembered the time as *Kapatula,* meaning "shorts," after both the short pants that the British wore and the short time before death came. The British had occupied the area in 1916, having taken over from the Germans, and they continued to requisition food for their troops. The epidemic followed a famine.[67]

"Globalization" in the aftermath of colonial conquest and the development of mechanized transport further increased the velocity of circulation. In the twentieth century, urbanization brought the rapid spread of some diseases, such as tuberculosis and venereal diseases. Meredeth Turshen has suggested that for Tanganyika, after the British took control of the colony there was a general deterioration in health.[68] Marc Dawson and Osaak Olumwullah have made similar arguments for Kenya.[69] The severity of malarial transmissions also increased in some cases. Public health measures under colonial rule were erratic and often ineffectual. The British in East Africa and the Belgians in the Congo engaged in massive efforts to resettle human populations and reshape landscapes to control both human and livestock exposure. However, such grand efforts to manage the tsetse fly probably had less to do with the reduction of the disease problem after the middle of the twentieth century than with the spread of cultivation.[70] Efforts to control malaria failed in most cases (in a few urban areas, sanitation succeeded in reducing it), even though interventionists in public health generally dominated the debate.[71] The effects of colonial conquest and the accordant mortality crisis affected demographic trends in different parts of Africa well into the colonial era. A. T. and G. M. Culwick documented the reduced population growth in southern Tanganyika into the 1940s as a result of the mortality of both conquest and especially the suppression of the Maji Maji Revolt by the Germans in 1905.[72]

Although the debate over the impact of colonial conquest is critical, the central fact of East African and African population history in the twentieth century remains the dramatic growth that began at some point after World War I. The great debate concerns the relative role of fertility and mortality in causing the rapid expansion of African populations. The variety of evidence, especially when considering the importance of disease environment in the equation, gives a confusing picture. The "received wisdom" of Western social science holds that population growth resulted from declining mortality in the era after World War I coupled with historically high fertility rates. John Iliffe argues that crisis mortality—mortality from famines, epidemics, and wars—declined while fertility remained relatively constant.[73] A generation of historical scholarship has challenged this simplistic vision. Scholars such as Cordell and Gregory, Turshen, Koponen, and Dawson have argued that death rates did not fall but birthrates rose.[74] Such arguments do not apply universally. The "malaria thesis" argues that in holoendemic populations, high birthrates and high childhood death rates existed in order to stabilize population. For instance, Shane Doyle cites both oral and written sources to suggest that the Banyoro of Uganda had practiced high fertility in the face of a hostile disease environment.[75] But in other cases, especially where societies escaped the pressure of malaria, populations may have reached other types of equilibrium.[76] In the densely population highlands in the Great Lakes and the Eastern Arc Mountain regions of eastern Africa, for instance, population seems to have reached a relatively low-fertility/low-mortality equilibrium. The area that included Kagera and Kigoma in western Tanzania and Buganda in Uganda became one of the focal points of British concern in regard to falling African populations.[77] There, fertility rates remained low into the colonial era. Juhani Koponen has suggested that African families raised fertility by decreasing polygamy, reducing the length of time during which mothers breast-fed babies, and reducing the marriage age for women especially.[78] The variety of demographic regimes explains the divergences of the evidence, of course. The demand for labor in the colonial economies of Africa, more than any fall in mortality, still explains sustained population growth better than any other factor.

There are questions about the pattern of mortality decline since the 1940s as well. Mortality fell erratically across the continent and the region of East Africa. A variety of factors combined to create this fall. Crisis mortality during food shortages declined in many areas after World War I and World War II almost everywhere. A number of health interventions had incremental effects in reducing mortality and morbidity. During the 1950s, the introduction of penicillin, even if it did not reach all areas of the continent, reduced mortality for a number of diseases. The widespread use of chloroquine to treat malaria began to reduce mortality at the same time. The movement to urban areas and, to some extent, improved sanitation in those areas also played a role; urbanization in Africa in the twentieth century generally reduced mortality by providing more regular access to food and to whatever health care was broadly available.

But the decline in mortality only explains part of the population growth in eastern Africa. Many Africans and African communities remain decidedly pronatalist, with surveys reported to show that Africans favor more children than any other comparable group.[79] African women continue to have more children than women of any other region in the world. The UN Human Development Report estimates that total fertility per woman in sub-Saharan Africa declined from an average of 6.8 in 1970–75 to 5.5 in 2000–2005. Although Oceania and the Arab states had rates comparable to Africa's in 1970–75, no other region in the world had a rate of over 3.7 per woman by 2000–2005. Both the generalized discussion of attitudes and the gross regional figures hid diversity (again). Fertility rates have fallen in southern and eastern Africa. South Africa's fertility rate has already dropped to 2.8 per woman, and southern Africa may see a stabilized population in the next few decades. Parts of East Africa have seen fertility rates decline since the 1970s also, but countries around the Great Lakes—especially Burundi and Uganda—still have fertility rates of over 6.5 per woman.[80]

Population in the Time of HIV

Although concern about rapid growth remains central to African demography, the emergence of HIV/AIDS has dramatically altered the landscape. In this context, the rapid spread of HIV/AIDS from the 1970s on can be understood as operating in much the same way as earlier epidemics, though with consequences that are more long term and more acute. John Iliffe makes two important points about the effects of HIV on Africans and African populations. He notes that the disease's unique combination of characteristics—"mildly infectious, slow acting, incurable, fatal"[81]—meant that HIV spread slowly from its origin in the western equatorial region, probably making the jump between the chimpanzee and the mangabey monkey to humans sometime between 1915 and 1950. It spread earliest in what is now the Democratic Republic of the Congo, and Kinshasa became the first center of diffusion, with cases retrospectively identified back to the 1970s. From that epicenter, it spread rapidly through East Africa in the 1980s and into southern Africa in the 1990s. The virulence of the epidemic in Africa came about because Africa suffered first.[82]

As is not unusual, general perceptions of the effects of HIV on African demographics have varied tremendously. Visions of "depopulation" have sprung from the heads of some in the media. Demographers have had to create complex dynamic models to estimate the effect because "one can expect the age pattern of AIDS-related deaths to change over time as the epidemic alters the age-structural dynamics of the population," and "a number of other downstream effects of the epidemic are now becoming manifest: the lower fertility of HIV-infected women, the increased mortality risks of 'AIDS orphans,' and the synergistic relationship between HIV and tuberculosis, to name a few."[83] The Joint United Nations Programme on HIV/AIDS (UNAIDS) estimates that due to HIV, the African population will be 13 percent lower in 2050 than would otherwise be expected.[84] This figure, like all continental demographic abstractions, hides important regional differences. The epidemic peaked first in central and eastern Africa, causing life expectancy to fall in a number of countries during the 1980s and 1990s. Its spread into southern Africa in the 1990s and caused even greater concern. In southern Africa, infection rates have approached 20 percent. In eastern Africa, infection rates peaked at over 12 percent in the 1980s but fell to about 7 percent in the first decade of the twenty-first century.[85] HIV infection, however, seems to have peaked in western Africa at about 5 percent, for reasons that are not fully understood yet.[86] The number of HIV and AIDS cases, however, will continue to rise, even if new infections finally begin to decline everywhere in the continent.

The net effect of HIV/AIDS on the total population varies dramatically, and changing conditions have made early professional estimates obsolete. Better treatment, even if not the widespread provision of antiretroviral drugs, means longer life spans for victims. In southern Africa, reduced life expectancy due to HIV has intersected with failing fertility rates and hastened the point when total population will stabilize. In eastern and central Africa, some countries, even with a high HIV load, continue to see rapid population growth. Uganda expects its population to triple in the fifty years between the beginning of the century and 2050. Tanzania and Kenya, by contrast, have seen gradual declines in population growth, driven both by increased mortality due to HIV (which may, in turn, be beginning to decline) and declining fertility, which seems set to continue for the foreseeable future.[87]

Africa's populations remain the least well understood in the world. The diversity of African demography, environmental, and disease landscapes has meant the search for generalizations and models has constantly come up short. This brief survey is really more a caution than a specific agenda for research. Historians must do what they do best—explain the complex interaction of multiple factors that produce the observed outcomes of the past. In particular, environmental historians can bring a nuanced reading to the history of disease and population in Africa.

Yet even in this endeavor, we must remember that one of our tasks is eventually relevance. The historian's narrative encompassing the multiplicity of causes and the reality of constant feedback may give a more elegant overall picture than a demographer's model of the same historical juncture, but it obviously lacks the solidity of the numbers. The narrative succeeds by encompassing the whole range of the demographer's margin of error in its words. Yet rather than deride the demographer's search for certainty, historians must provide relevant guides to complexity, exactly what demographers look for in the literature of other disciplines.

Notes

1. John Iliffe, *Africans: The History of a Continent* (Cambridge: Cambridge University Press, 1995), 1–2.

2. Brian Fagan, *Floods, Famines and Emperors: El Niño and the Fate of Civilizations* (New York: Basic Books, 1999), 204.

3. K. David Patterson and Gerald W. Hartwig, "The Disease Factor: An Introductory Overview," in *Disease in African History: An Introductory Survey and Case Studies,* ed. Gerald W. Hartwig and K. David Patterson (Durham, NC: Duke University Press, 1979), 3–4.

4. Philip D. Curtin, "Epidemiology and the Slave Trade," *Political Science Quarterly* 83, no. 2 (1968): 190–216; Curtin, *Migration and Mortality in Africa and the Atlantic World, 1700–1900* (Burlington, VT: Ashgate/Valorium, 2001); Curtin, *Disease and Empire: The Health of European Troops in the Conquest of Africa* (Cambridge: Cambridge University Press, 1998); and Curtin, "The End of the 'White Man's Grave?' Nineteenth-Century Mortality in West Africa," *Journal of Interdisciplinary History* 21, no. 1 (1990): 63–88.

5. Sheldon Watts, *Epidemics and History: Disease, Power and Imperialism* (New Haven, CT: Yale University Press, 1997); William H. McNeill, *People and Plagues* (Garden City, NY: Anchor/Doubleday, 1976); and Alfred W. Crosby, *Ecological Imperialism: The Biological Expansion of Europe, 900–1900* (Cambridge: Cambridge University Press, 1986).

6. Karl Ittmann, "Population, Race and Power in the British Empire, 1890–1970" (paper presented at a workshop entitled "The Demographics of Empire," Texas Southern University, 8 and 9 November 2002); Monica M. van Beusekom, "From Under-population to Overpopulation: French Perceptions of Population, Environment, and

Agricultural Development in French Soudan (Mali), 1900–1960," *Environmental History* 4, no. 2 (1999): 198–219.

7. R. R. Kuczynski, *Demographic Survey of the British Colonial Empire,* vol. 2, *South Africa High Commission Territories, East Africa, Mauritius, Seychelles* (Oxford: Oxford University Press, 1949); A. T. Culwick, "The Population Trend," *Tanganyika Notes and Records* 11 (1941): 13–17; and A. T. Culwick and G. M. Culwick, "A Study of Population in Ulanga, Tanganyika Territory," *Sociological Review* 30, no. 1 (1938): 365–79.

8. Christopher A. Conte, *Highland Sanctuary: Environmental History in Tanzania's Usambara Mountains* (Athens: Ohio University Press, 2004).

9. John Iliffe, *The African Poor: A History* (Cambridge: Cambridge University Press, 1987), 155–63, quote on p. 159.

10. See the essays in Dennis D. Cordell and Joel W. Gregory, eds., *African Population and Capitalism: Historical Perspectives,* 2nd ed. (Madison: University of Wisconsin Press, 1994); Mike Davis, *Late Victorian Holocausts: El Niño Famines and the Making of the Third World* (New York: Verso, 2001).

11. James L. Giblin, *The Politics of Environmental Control in Northeastern Tanzania, 1840–1940* (Philadelphia: University of Pennsylvania Press, 1993); Juhani Koponen, *People and Production in Late Precolonial Tanzania: History and Structures* (Uppsala, Sweden: Scandinavian Institute of African Studies, 1988); and Helge Kjekshus, *Ecology Control and Economic Development in East African History: The Case of Tanganyika, 1850–1950* (London: Heinemann, 1977).

12. James L. Giblin, "Trypanosomiasis Control in African History: An Evaded Issue?" *Journal of African History* 31, no. 1 (1990): 59–80; Giblin, "East Coast Fever in Sociohistorical Context: A Case Study from Tanzania," *International Journal of African Historical Studies* 23, no. 3 (1990): 401–21; and Giblin, *Politics of Environmental Control.*

13. Koponen, *People and Production.* Historians of Europe and of Latin America have made similar arguments about the specificity of demographic regimes. See E. A. Wrigley and R. S. Schofield, *The Population History of England, 1541–1871: A Reconstruction* (Cambridge, MA: Harvard University Press, 1981); Robert H. Jackson and Edward Castillo, *Indians, Franciscans, and Spanish Colonization: The Impact of the Mission System on California Indians* (Albuquerque: University of New Mexico Press, 1995), 41–59.

14. Patterson and Hartwig, "Disease Factor," 6.

15. Joseph C. Miller, *Way of Death: Merchant Capitalism and the Angolan Slave Trade* (Madison: University of Wisconsin Press, 1989); David Eltis, "Europeans and the Rise and Fall of African Slavery in the Americas: An Interpretation," *American Historical Review* 98, no. 5 (1993): 1399–1423; and Eltis, *The Rise of African Slavery in the Americas* (Cambridge: Cambridge University Press, 2000).

16. Patrick Manning, *Slavery and African Life: Occidental, Oriental and African Slave Trades* (Cambridge: Cambridge University Press, 1990), 84.

17. Roland Oliver, *The African Experience* (London: Weidenfeld and Nicolson, 1991) 128–29.

18. Manning, *Slavery and African Life,* 80–85.

19. William H. McNeill, *Plagues and Peoples* (Garden City, NY: Anchor/Doubleday, 1976).

20. David J. Bardley, "Malaria," in *Disease and Mortality in Sub-Saharan Africa,* ed. Richard G. Feachem (Oxford: Oxford University Press, 1991), 193; Richard Carter and Kamini N. Mendis, "Evolutionary and Historical Aspects of the Burden of Malaria," *Clinical Microbiology Reviews* 15, no. 4 (2002): 564–94.

21. James L. A. Webb, Jr., "Malaria and the Peopling of Early Tropical Africa," *Journal of World History* 16, no. 3 (2005): 272–74. Webb draws heavily on Carter and Mendis, but he disputes several of their conclusions based on evidence indicating that agriculture, and hence settled and more dense populations, had developed in Africa earlier than was assumed in the research on which Mendis and Carter based their analysis.

22. Ibid., 275–80.

23. R. F. Marshall and E. Hildebrand, "Cattle before Crops: The Beginnings of Food Production in Africa," *Journal of World Prehistory* 16, no. 2 (2002): 99–143; Fred Wendorf and Romuald Schild, "Nabta Playa and Its Role in Northeastern African Prehistory," *Journal of Anthropological Archaeology* 17, no. 2 (1998): 97–123.

24. Augustin F. C. Holl, "Western Africa: The Prehistoric Sequence," in *Encyclopedia of Precolonial Africa: Archaeology, History, Languages, Cultures, and Environments,* ed. Joseph O. Vogel (Walnut Creek, CA: Alta Mira Press, 1997), 305–12.

25. Diane Gifford-Gonzalez, "Early Pastoralists in East Africa: Ecological and Social Dimensions," *Journal of Anthropological Archaeology* 17, no. 2 (1998): 166–200; Gifford-Gonzalez, "Animal Disease Challenges to the Emergence of Pastoralism in Sub-Saharan Africa," *African Archaeological Review* 17, no. 3 (2000): 95–139.

26. See, for example, Osaak A. Olumwullah, *Dis-ease in the Colonial State: Medicine, Society, and Social Change among the AbaNyole of Western Kenya* (Westport, CT: Greenwood, 2002); Marc H. Dawson, "Smallpox in Kenya, 1880–1920," *Social Science and Medicine* 13B (1979): 245; Meredeth Turshen, *The Political Economy of Disease in Tanzania* (New Brunswick, NJ: Rutgers University Press, 1984); and Megan Vaughan, *Curing Their Ills: Colonial Power and African Illness* (Stanford, CA: Stanford University Press, 1991).

27. Watts, *Epidemics and History,* presents a prime case at a broad level. Although the hectoring tone may be deserved at the level of historical analysis, researchers and policymakers probably write off the work as another case of science bashing. See James Fairhead and Melissa Leach, *Misreading the African Landscape: Society and Ecology in a Forest-Savanna Mosaic* (Cambridge: Cambridge University Press, 1996), 46–52, for a discussion of these issues in a context of environmental science.

28. Renee L. Pennington, "Disease as a Factor in African History," in *Encyclopedia of Precolonial Africa: Archaeology, History, Languages, Cultures, and Environments,* ed. J. O. Vogel (Walnut Creek, CA: Alta Mira Press, 1997), 45–48.

29. Webb, "Malaria," 276; Bardley, "Malaria," 193.

30. Webb, "Malaria," 278; Carter and Mendis, "Evolutionary and Historical Aspects," 575–76.

31. Carter and Mendis, "Evolutionary and Historical Aspects," 579.

32. Ibid., 570–71; Webb, "Malaria," 280–82.

33. Anthony C. Allison, "Two Lessons from the Interface of Genetics and Medicine," *Genetics* 166, no. 4 (2004): 1591–99. See also Walter A. Schroeder, Edwin S. Munger, and Darleen R. Powars, "Sickle Cell Anemia, Genetic Variations and the Slave Trade to the United States," *Journal of African History* 31, no. 2 (1990): 163–80.

34. Webb, "Malaria," 288–89.

35. Giblin, "Trypanosomiasis Control in African History"; Kirk Arden Hoppe, *Lords of the Fly: Sleeping Sickness Control in British East Africa, 1900–1960* (Westport, CT: Praeger, 2003); and John Ford, *The Role of the Trypanosomiases in African Ecology: A Study of the Tsetse Fly Problem* (Oxford: Clarendon, 1971).

36. Roderick J. McIntosh, "The Pulse Model: Genesis and Accommodation of Specialization in the Middle Niger," *Journal of African History* 34, no. 2 (1993): 181–220; McIntosh, *The Peoples of the Middle Niger: The Island of Gold* (Oxford: Blackwell, 1998).

37. James L. A. Webb Jr., *Desert Frontier: Ecological and Economic Change along the Western Sahel, 1600–1850* (Madison: University of Wisconsin Press, 1995).

38. Gregory H. Maddox, "Networks and Frontiers in Colonial Tanzania," *Environmental History* 3, no. 4 (1998): 436–59; Peter Rigby, *Cattle and Kinship among the Gogo: A Semi-pastoral Society of Central Tanzania* (Ithaca, NY: Cornell University Press, 1967); and Mathais E. Mnyampala, *The Gogo: History, Customs, and Traditions,* ed. and trans. Gregory H. Maddox (Armonk, NY: M. E. Sharpe, 1995).

39. Gregory H. Maddox, "'Leave, Wagogo! You Have No Food!': Famine and Survival in Ugogo, Central Tanzania, 1916–1961" (PhD diss., Northwestern University, 1988), chap. 2; L. E. Y. Mbogoni, "Food Production and Ecological Crisis in Dodoma—1920–1960: Colonial Efforts at Developing the Productive Forces in Peasant Agriculture" (master's thesis, University of Dar es Salaam, 1981).

40. I. N. Kimambo, "Environmental Control and Hunger in the Mountains and Plains of Northeastern Tanzania," in *Custodians of the Land: Ecology and Culture in the History of Tanzania,* ed. Gregory Maddox, James Giblin, and I. N. Kimambo (London: James Currey, 1996), 71–95.

41. Sally Falk Moore and Paul Pruitt, *The Chagga and Meru of Tanzania* (London: International African Institute, 1977).

42. Thomas Spear, *Mountain Farmers: Moral Economies of Land and Agricultural Development in Arusha and Meru* (Berkeley: University of California Press, 1997).

43. Pamela A. Maack, "'The Waluguru Are Not Sleeping': Poverty, Culture, and Social Differentiation in Morogoro, Tanzania" (PhD diss., Northwestern University, 1992).

44. Christopher A. Conte, *Highland Sanctuary: Environmental History in Tanzania's Usambara Mountains* (Athens: Ohio University Press, 2004).

45. Bill Bravman, *Making Ethnic Ways: Communities and Their Transformations in Taita, Kenya, 1800–1950* (Portsmouth, NH: Heinemann, 1998).

46. Y. Q. Lawi, "Where Physical and Ideological Landscapes Meet: Landscape Use and Ecological Knowledge in Iraqw, Northern Tanzania, 1920s–1950s," *International Journal of African Historical Studies* 32, nos. 2–3 (1999): 281–310; Katherine Ann Snyder, "'Like Water and Honey': Moral Ideology and the Construction of Community among the Iraqw of Northern Tanzania" (PhD diss., Yale University, 1993).

47. Maryinez Lyons, "Diseases of Sub-Saharan Africa since 1860," in *The Cambridge World History of Human Disease,* ed. Kenneth F. Kiple (Cambridge: Cambridge University Press, 1993), 298–305.

48. Allison, "Two Lessons," 1591–99.

49. Carter and Mendis, "Evolutionary and Historical Aspects," 568.

50. Nassor Kikumbih, Kara Hanson, Anne Mills, Hadji Mponda, and Joanna Armstrong Schellenberg, "The Economics of Social Marketing: The Case of Mosquito Nets in Tanzania," *Social Science and Medicine* 60, no. 2 (2005): 369–81; T. Smith, G. Killeen, C. Lengeler, and M. Tanner, "Relationships between the Outcome of *Plasmodium falciparum* Infection and the Intensity of Transmission in Africa," *American Journal of Tropical Medicine and Hygiene* 71, supplement 2 (2004): 80–84.

51. See David F. Clyde, *History of the Medical Services of Tanganyika* (Dar es Salaam: Government Press, 1962), 24, for a description of a malaria epidemic in 1901–2 in German East Africa.

52. James C. McCann, *Green Land, Brown Land, Black Land: An Environmental History of Africa, 1800–1990* (Portsmouth, NH: Heinemann, 1999), 113.

53. Bardley, "Malaria," 193–98.

54. Charles Llewellyn and Dr. William Krekamoo, USAID Tanzania, personal communication; M. K. Arness, R. D. Bradshaw, K. Biomndo, and G. D. Shanks, "Epidemiology of Highland Malaria in Western Kenya," *East African Medical Journal* 80, no. 5 (2003): 253–59.

55. Watts, *Epidemics and History,* 225.

56. Allison, "Two Lessons," 1592–93.

57. McIntosh, *Peoples of the Middle Niger,* 148.

58. J. D.Y. Peel, "Syncretism and Religious Change," *Comparative Studies in Society and History* 10, no. 2 (1968): 123.

59. Gerald W. Hartwig, "Economic Consequences of Long-Distance Trade in East Africa: The Disease Factor," *African Studies Review* 18, no. 2 (1975): 63–73.

60. Helge Kjekshus, *Ecology Control and Economic Development in East African History: The Case of Tanganyika, 1850–1950* (London: Heinemann, 1977).

61. Juhani Koponen, "War, Famine, and Pestilence in Late Precolonial Tanzania: A Case for Heightened Mortality," *International Journal of African Historical Studies* 21, no. 4 (1988): 637–76; Koponen, *People and Production.*

62. Davis, *Late Victorian Holocausts.* See also the case studies in Douglas H. Johnson and David M. Anderson, eds., *The Ecology of Survival: Case Studies from Northeast African History* (Boulder, CO: Westview Press, 1988).

63. Marc H. Dawson, "Health, Nutrition, and Population in Central Kenya, 1890–1945," in *African Population and Capitalism: Historical Perspectives,* ed. Dennis Cordell and Joel Gregory (Boulder, CO: Westview Press, 1987), 210–12.

64. Randall M. Packard, *White Plague, Black Labor: Tuberculosis and the Political Economy of Health and Disease in South Africa* (Berkeley: University of California Press, 1989).

65. Sandra M. Tomkins, "Colonial Administration in British Africa during the Influenza Epidemic of 1918–19," *Canadian Journal of African Studies* 28, no. 1 (1994): 69–72.

66. K. David Patterson, "The Influenza Epidemic of 1918–19 in the Gold Coast," *Journal of African History* 24, no. 4 (1983): 488.

67. Gregory H. Maddox, "*Mtunya:* Famine in Central Tanzania, 1917–1920," *Journal of African History* 31, no. 2 (1990): 181–98.

68. Meredeth Turshen, "Population Growth and the Deterioration of Health: Mainland Tanzania, 1920–1960," in Cordell and Gregory, *African Population and Capitalism,* 187–200.

69. Olumwullah, *Dis-ease in the Colonial State;* Dawson, "Health, Nutrition, and Population," 210.

70. Hoppe, *Lords of the Fly;* Maryinez Lyons, *A Social History of Sleeping Sickness in Northern Zaire, 1900–1940* (Cambridge: Cambridge University Press, 1992).

71. David F. Clyde, *Malaria in Tanzania* (London: Oxford, 1967).

72. Culwick and Culwick, "Study of Population in Ulanga"; A. T. Culwick, "Population Trend," 13–17.

73. Iliffe, *African Poor,* 162–63; also see, for example, Veena Soni Raleigh, "Trends in World Population: How Will the Millennium Compare with the Past?" *Human Reproduction Update* 5, no. 5 (1999): 501–2.

74. Juhani Koponen, "Population Growth in Historical Perspective: The Key Role of Changing Fertility," in *Tanzania: Crisis and Struggle for Survival,* ed. Jannik Boesen, Kjell J.

Havnevid, Juhani Koponen, and Rie Odgaard (Uppsala, Sweden: Scandinavian Institute for African Studies, 1986), 33–42; Dennis D. Cordell, Joel W. Gregory, and Victor Piché, "African Historical Demography: The Search for a Theoretical Framework," in Cordell and Gregory, *African Population and Capitalism*, 14–34; Marc H. Dawson, "Health, Nutrition, and Population," 201–17; Turshen, "Population Growth," 187–200; and Dennis D. Cordell and Joel W. Gregory, "Earlier African Historical Demographies," *Canadian Journal of African Studies* 23, no. 1 (1989): 5–27.

75. Shane Doyle, *Crisis and Decline in Bunyoro: Population and Environment in Western Uganda, 1860–1955* (Athens: Ohio University Press, 2006), 34–38.

76. Ibid., 218–20.

77. Culwick, "Population Trend," 13–17.

78. Koponen, "Population Growth," 40; see also, for example, Maack, "'Waluguru Are Not Sleeping,'" chap. 2.

79. John Cleland and Steven Sinding, "What Would Malthus Say about AIDS in Africa?" *Lancet* 366 (2005): 1899.

80. United Nations Development Programme, *Human Development Report 2005, International Cooperation at a Crossroads: Aid, Trade and Security in an Unequal World* (New York: UNDP, 2005), 235.

81. John Iliffe, *The African AIDS Epidemic: A History* (Athens: Ohio University Press, 2006), 158; see also Susan Hunter, *Black Death: AIDS in Africa* (New York: Palgrave Macmillan, 2003).

82. Iliffe, *African AIDS Epidemic,* 3–18.

83. Patrick Heuveline, "HIV and Population Dynamics: A General Model and Maximum-Likelihood Standards for East Africa," *Demography* 40, no. 2 (2003): 222.

84. Cited in Raleigh, "Trends," 504.

85. Cleland and Sinding, "What Would Malthus Say?" 1899–1901.

86. Ibid., 1901.

87. Ibid., 1902–3.

9

Reproducing Labor

Colonial Government Regulation of African Women's Reproductive Lives

MEREDETH TURSHEN

Women's reproductive capacity and women's sexuality have always been objects of policy, whether governmental, religious, societal, or private. The breadth of policies—from macroeconomic to microeconomic, social to political—that affect population growth is striking. Government policies, the subject of this chapter, range widely: wars and military recruitment; emigration and immigration policies; tax systems; benefits such as family allowances or, more broadly, social insurance schemes; public health and maternity services (whether free or available on payment of a fee); contraceptive and abortion laws; public housing and taxes or exemptions on private housing; laws that assign adult women the status of minors and that regulate family affairs such as minimum age at marriage; penalties for adultery; policies that cause hunger and starvation and policies of famine relief; policies that cause disease to spread and public health measures to prevent or arrest contagion; education policies, whether free or not and whether available to girls and boys alike, and language requirements that pose barriers to education; race and sex barriers to employment; and, finally, even the death penalty.

Every colonial government in sub-Saharan Africa employed some or all of these policies in efforts to regulate population growth. Most of the policies fall into one of two categories: either their intention was to alter the demographic structure of the population (pronatalist or antinatalist policies) or their demographic impact was an unintended or inexplicit consequence (for example, laws

punishing adultery).[1] Note that women more often bore the burden of such policies than men and that the only direct regulations on men's reproductive lives
involved intercourse with minors and forced intercourse.[2] Ultimately, widespread
poverty and the lack of equal opportunity laws for social advancement had the
greatest impact on women's reproductive lives. The impoverishment was neither
incidental nor accidental: when large regions were so impoverished that wage labor became part of the life cycle, the supply of laborers flowed most predictably.[3]

In colonized Africa, sexual control was a fundamental class and racial marker
embedded in a wider set of relations of power, though the underlying relationships between gender prescriptions and racial boundaries were rarely explicit.[4]
Sexuality was tied to politics at several levels and in numerous ways: men shuttled
between male-only hostels at the workplace and family life in the village (a way to
reproduce a labor force cheaply), but such migratory patterns could also foster social disorder and political dissonance. Ostensibly, colonial powers saw stable family
life as a way to depoliticize discontents. But paradoxically, colonial regimes divided
families and segregated regions of reproduction from the sites of production, thus
creating migrant labor systems. Yet they also tried to tie them back together. European administrators repeatedly linked family ideology and political agendas
in Africa, and they argued about the costs and consequences of domesticating
African reproductive practices. Frederick Cooper and Ann Stoler ask why sexuality was so politicized under certain colonial conditions and not others.[5] Why did
family organization become so central at certain moments of economic restructuring and political crisis and remain ignored at other times?

Historically, all African societies, like all societies across the globe, had population
regimes, managing family size through a variety of social controls and practices.
These controls included infanticide; birth spacing through prolonged breast-feeding
and the imposition of taboos on sexual relations before a baby was weaned; the use
of herbal contraceptives, abortifacients, and manual techniques to interrupt pregnancy; age at marriage; and social controls on sex between unmarried couples.[6]
Many of these controls and practices changed after colonial conquest.

The foundations of colonial control of African women's lives were, first and
foremost, customary laws. Marriage and property arrangements were the basis of
sexual relations and therefore of demographic trends. Changes in these arrangements
followed the introduction of colonial control and the codification of custom into
law. Feminist research on colonial history, together with what historians have un-
covered about the impact of colonial conquest on the economy and ecology of
African societies, reveals a picture of how colonial government regulations affected women's reproductive lives.

This chapter examines colonial government population policies in sub-Saharan
Africa in the twentieth century, focusing on the interwar period. I try to avoid
interpretations that are economically reductionist or instrumentalist without ob-
scuring the reality of the pronatalist or antinatalist intention of colonial demographic
policies. A discussion of gender relations, rather than of impacts on women alone,

helps avoid determinist arguments. We know that white colonists appropriated the material bases of masculine identity among African men by regulating cattle, labor, and land; we know, too, that they also intervened in African men's rights to control "their" women and children, "directly through laws governing marriage practices and family residences, and indirectly through the provision of alternatives to patriarchal control for young men and women."[7] Far from being passive victims of these machinations, women tried to use colonial intervention to their advantage to create more opportunities for themselves and to escape male control.

The chapter begins with some background and a general discussion of the demographic impact of changing gender relations in the colonial era. It then turns to the shifting public/private divide caused by the imposition of statutory law and the creation of customary law, in particular marriage laws. The next section deals centrally with direct intervention to control population growth by the use or denial of maternity services and birth control; it is followed by another section on disease dispersion and environmental disruption. The chapter ends with brief discussions of three areas of colonial policy that had far-reaching demographic consequences: education, famine relief, and taxation.

Background

In any general discussion of the demographic impact of changing gender relations in the colonial era, issues of race and class emerge as central determinants of policy. Reproductive policies are about who has how many children. In African colonies, the fundamental policy issue was labor: the colonists' demands always exceeded the number of African workers available to them. Natalist policies were designed to increase the next generation of workers. Authorities employed a number of measures to secure the labor force they wanted. They coerced adult men to work through systems of *corvée*, legally required unpaid labor; levied taxes in cash that forced them out of the subsistence sector; and introduced migratory work structured by the combined policies of supporting mining and agricultural enclaves in some regions, creating labor reserves in others, and depriving still others of any investment at all. The need for more African workers conflicted with concerns about population growth in the settler colonies where Europeans worried about land distribution. Population densities were always relevant to land availabilities (for farming and for grazing). In settler colonies, there was also an issue of racial ratios, which resulted in policies to discourage black reproduction and encourage white reproduction.[8]

In the category of unintended consequences, Elizabeth Schmidt emphasizes the results of an earlier colonial policy adopted during the occupation of Southern Rhodesia (contemporary Zimbabwe), which led people on the margins of African society to take advantage of the erosion of indigenous authority structures.[9] Women challenged male control over their mobility, sexuality, and productive and reproductive capacities. Because European missionaries and the colonial state found customs such as forced marriage, polygyny, and child pledging, or the betrothal of young girls to older men, to be repugnant, they initially encouraged a degree of female emancipation. However, the resulting "crisis of authority in the rural areas foreshadowing the possibility of a total breakdown in law and order, forced state officials to reconsider. . . . By the 1920s, a backlash against female emancipation was well under way."[10]

A recent analysis of the contemporary phenomenon of "missing women," by age and disease, confirms that relative to developed countries and some parts of the developing world, there are far fewer women than men in India and China. Moreover, the study has added the startling new observation that as a proportion of the total female population, the number of missing women is largest in sub-Saharan Africa. The absolute numbers are comparable to those for India and China:"For the year 2000, around 1.53 million women are missing in sub-Saharan Africa for that year alone, which is not that different from the Chinese and Indian estimates of 1.73m and 1.71m respectively."[11] Most analyses of India and China have emphasized a skewed sex ratio at birth, which may indicate sex-selective abortion or female infanticide. Although this may be true of China, it does not account for data from India or sub-Saharan Africa, where sex ratios at birth are, if anything, skewed to more girls and where missing women are spread over the entire age spectrum.

> In sub-Saharan Africa, much of the female deficit is to be found at younger ages. Malaria is an important component, and so is maternal mortality: much more so than in India. But the dominant source of missing women is HIV/AIDS. We estimate that there are over 600,000 excess female deaths each year from this source alone. That said, it is still true that the percentage of missing women in sub-Saharan Africa is comparable to that in India or China even if HIV/AIDS is ignored.[12]

Are there historical roots to this demographic deviation, and are they to be found in colonial policies? For all their worry about declining population and failure to meet labor needs, colonial authorities did not seriously investigate demographic issues. In regard to French Equatorial Africa, Rita Headrick notes the administration's failure to organize studies of fertility or mortality. She also observes that demographic reasoning was "preposterous" and that establishing tax rolls was the only motive for counting heads.[13] Although the "censuses" showed a rise in population, all the qualitative evidence pointed to depopulation, at least until the 1920s. In this volume, Raymond Gervais and Issiaka Mandé make a similar argument for French West Africa.

Policy seemed to flip from pronatalist to antinatalist in the interwar years, a period that Jean Allman describes as one of gender chaos.[14] The critical decade of the 1930s opened with the Great Depression and closed with the declaration of World War II. This period highlights the extent to which colonial regimes subordinated social policy to labor policy. Frederick Cooper notes a sharp break in both British and French thinking about the relationship of wage labor to African society in the 1940s as World War II and "the weaknesses in imperial economies that it revealed underscored British and French need for their empires."[15] Although the French believed their colonies had less potential manpower than those of the British, it was the Belgians who pioneered elaborate social investments in the reproduction of the labor force and protecting the health and fertility of workers' families; Nancy Hunt claims that such measures were anomalous in colonial Africa before 1945.[16]

The British began to rethink the labor question in the late 1930s. In the 1920s, the imperial myth that led Europeans to portray themselves as bringing a slave-ridden, barbarous continent under civilized and progressive rule had given way to another—and contradictory—vision of rural Africa as tradition bound but stable, living in the organic harmony of ancient social structures. Such perceptions led to praise for and the reinforcement of indirect rule. French officials also viewed Africa through a pastoral lens, which led to support for development through peasant production within traditional communities. Both the British and the French thought of urban workers as a detribalized, floating population, more an aberration or a pathology than a normal part of colonial society.[17] Cooper believes that colonial officials eventually had to reconcile themselves to the limits of their own power to exploit African resources and labor systematically. They publicly lamented the mediocrity of imperial economic accomplishments; but subsequent calls for a new round of interventionist development in the 1920s and 1930s in both Britain and France came to little. All of this changed after World War II, which devastated the European economies and saw the rise of movements for self-determination.[18]

The perceived interrelationship of gender and work had also changed in French colonies. From a characterization of men as averse to steady and productive labor, sapped by slavery and the violence of savage life, and of women engaged in agricultural production, the prevalent images morphed to others of potentially productive African men and women who remained primitive cultivators and the bearers of backward culture. Both French and British colonial governments calculated the costs of social reproduction independently from the market wage and sought to separate industrial culture from African culture.[19] The consequences of changed perceptions of gender and work played out in new population trends.

Changing Gender Relations in the Colonial Era

Colonial authorities never simply imposed Victorian ideology, and they invented "traditions" in both metropolitan and colonial contexts. Debates in the postcolonial period shifted away from the impact of colonialism to issues of the construction of gender, male and female, by both colonizers and the colonized.[20]

Schmidt has examined critiques of "androcentric functionalism," an interpretation of colonial labor policy that held that mining and agricultural interests, driven by the need for male labor, dictated the fundamental characteristic of the migratory labor system. That system channeled only men to the mines, forcing women and children not just to fend for themselves in rural areas but also to subsidize the male workers who were paid subsistence wages as single men—even though they sent a portion of those wages back to their women.[21] Schmidt argues that in the case of Southern Rhodesia, this policy grew out of gender struggles among Africans as well as struggles between labor, capital, and the state. Of special interest is her observation that senior African chiefs and headmen colluded with colonial authorities to confine women to the rural areas:

> For it was women who solidified kinship alliances through their marriages. The bridewealth received for daughters procured wives for the sons, and daughters-in-law produced children for the patrilineage. The labor of women generated food crops and guaranteed continued access to lineage land, for any unused land was returned to the common domain. Because husbands frequently sent a portion of their wages home to their wives, the retention of wives in the rural areas gave senior men some access to those wages, cash income that would otherwise be unavailable to them. For all these reasons, older men struggled to maintain control over women—over their labor, cash, children, and other resources; over their mobility; and over their marriages.[22]

Jane Parpart has found much the same sort of collusion between British colonial authorities and rural African authorities in Northern Rhodesia (today's Zambia). Both parties recognized the connection between the control of women's sexual behavior and the authority of those who controlled society—women's freedom was a threat to chiefly authority and therefore to the system of indirect rule.[23]

Schmidt also argues that control of women's behavior was essential to the maintenance of colonial rule: "The refusal of women to marry their appointed partners, their persistence in entering into adulterous liaisons, and their flight to missions, mines, farms, and urban areas posed a serious threat to African male authority, and, consequently, to the entire system of indirect rule."[24]

According to Hunt, women most often appeared in the colonial record when moral panic surfaced, settled, and festered. Prostitution, polygyny, adultery, concubinage, and infertility were the loci of such angst throughout the historical record of Belgian African colonial regimes.[25] Megan Vaughan, who has done considerable research on the British colonies of Nyasaland (today's Malawi) and Northern Rhodesia (today's Zambia), says that "the problem of women" was colonial shorthand for issues related to changes in property rights, rights in labor, and generational relations.[26] Dramatic economic changes lay beneath these problems and placed enormous strains on relations between genders and generations, which colonial authorities chose to describe in terms of degeneration, uncontrolled sexuality, and disease.

British, French, Belgian, and Portuguese officials dictated colonial policy, no doubt in response to the interests of mining, commercial agriculture, missionaries, settlers, and their metropoles. However, they did not always succeed in either imposing or implementing the policies they wanted, in part because African women and men resisted or rejected them. The examination of official discourses in the form of commission reports, parliamentary debates, and the texts of laws brings to light the categories the state used to rule its subjects. Such categories established the boundaries of behavior. In South Africa, gender histories reveal that different policy discourses and legislation referred to African women in a variety of ways "as mothers, as wives, as blacks, as workers—steeping those constructs in racial, sexual and class ideologies."[27] In so doing, state policy and practices also constructed women as objects of rule, "reproducing or restructuring normative gender meanings and subordinate social and political identities through the same process."[28] Struggles among Africans and between Africans and colonial authorities surfaced in the use of law to institutionalize changed gender relations.

Shifting the Public/Private Divide: The Imposition of Statutory Law and the Creation of Customary Law

In British colonial Africa, indirect rule had very specific implications for mediating gender conflict, shaping gendered boundaries, and reformulating the mechanisms of gender subordination.[29] Such shifts affected fertility rates. Indirect rule facilitated the colonization of the domestic sphere through marriage, divorce, adultery, childbirth, death, and inheritance. It enabled Europeans to enter the private world of African families, "the world where children were born, the sick were healed, meals were cooked, babies were bathed, marriages were negotiated, and deaths were mourned."[30] The missions were often handmaidens of the state, inculcating values such as hard work and discipline that both parties agreed upon and even implementing state policies—especially where the state was shorthanded, as in education and medical work.

Law works as a mechanism of power, contributing to the creation of the categories of persons and rights fundamental to the workings of any society.[31] Definitions of the terms *husband* and *wife,* laws about marriage in customary and common law, the very fact of marriages being recorded and contestable in court, assumptions about domestic arrangements that inform labor regulation, and the definition and regulation of "normal" sexuality are all fundamental to the material and moral constructions of gender integral to state formation.[32] The imposition of two bodies of law—statutory and customary—as well as the ability to create customary law as a brace for colonial rule gave European regimes exceptional control over the interwoven factors of land and labor and the fruits of both.

The development of customary law focused first on the law of persons and then on the law of property.[33] Customary laws, governing marriage and inheritance, opened inroads to labor discipline, which "was achieved through a systematic assault on the access of African cultivators to the land."[34] Martin Chanock confirms that customary law "must be understood . . . as a product of the struggle for control of labour in the changing conditions of the rural economy."[35] After the end of slavery, family producers could not respond to the market through their former practice of intensifying the exploitation of their slaves. Yet squeezing household labor was a more convenient strategy than finding labor outside of the household, which made the labor of wives vital and emphasized the marital bonds that tied wives to their work. It also led ambitious commercial farmers to struggle to maintain control over the labor of their children, aggravating conflict within marriage over rights to children and the products of their labor.

However, a major consequence of the transformation of labor power into a commodity was the erosion of the basis of customary kinship. As rural households became increasingly dependent on commodity relations, they were caught up in a struggle for control of labor power between generations. Custom became a weapon in the battle against the economic independence of dependants.[36] African chiefs and headmen had a shared interest with colonial authorities in making customary law and inventing traditions. As Schmidt notes, all shared the fear of losing the labor of both sexes, as well as money and control of the agricultural economy.[37] Such concerns produced the neotraditional reaction that was solidified in customary law. But these struggles were also usually couched in other terms—morality, rights and wrongs, duty, propriety, correct marriages, and the moral health of the community.

In village life, there really was no clear-cut distinction between the realms of public and private. Customary practice was not rule bound. But Western law is, so colonial judges picked among customs and chose the ones that suited their purposes. According to Chanock, Northern Rhodesian colonial authorities favored a public model of law.[38] When it came to interpreting African testimony, they chose versions that supported their positions. Then they presented their rulings as an improvement on custom. This invention marked an unwillingness to consider the real position of women in customary legal systems. Colonial authorities invested chiefs with new judicial powers, and chiefs and headmen had an interest in exaggerating their "traditional" powers. In reality, the political economy of colonial capitalism created what were thereafter labeled as customary legal systems.

Marriage and Divorce Laws

Marriage was a central arena in which labor and land conflicts played out. Marriage laws were all-important in regulating sexuality, procreation, labor, and property rights. Because these laws created links between traditional social organization and state authority, colonial administrators hoped they would ultimately preserve the stability of the colonial regimes. But as Barbara Cooper has shown for the French colony of Niger, marriage was not a static arrangement; it underwent tremendous change in the twentieth century, shaped and reshaped by the rapidly changing political economy.[39] The French attempted to legislate matters relating to women and marriage as the basis of marriages shifted to become more remote and further from women's control.

British colonial authorities required African couples to register their marriages (including those performed under customary rites), purportedly to keep tax records current. Similarly, the registration of divorces freed husbands from paying taxes for their wives.[40] African men saw marriage as an important labor strategy, and they wanted more wives for labor, especially as cash cropping opened up new avenues for revenue.[41] In systems in which land could not be bought or leased, men also saw polygyny as a way of acquiring more land.[42] An accentuated and narrower version of custom became a new weapon in the hands of married men, one with which to control the labor power of their immediate dependents.

Schmidt maintains that the colonial state in Southern Rhodesia created customary law in an effort to coerce women into staying with their husbands.[43] The state feared the consequences of female emancipation and sought to legitimate customs that would justify continued female subordination. So-called customary laws were established when the concerns of the informants, who were mainly male chiefs and elders with vested interests in controlling women, coincided with the moral predilections and administrative purposes of colonial officials.[44] But picking and choosing led to contradictions: Europeans deemed some patriarchal customs repugnant and outlawed them even though they reinforced others.

For example, colonial child custody laws, which threatened to deprive women of their children and which were contrary to the more flexible arrangements of African custom, show how the state pressured women to remain with abusive or disaffected husbands, a policy that had perhaps unintended pronatalist consequences. Yet child marriage and forced marriage, which also had pronatalist consequences, were considered repugnant to the European sense of morality. The Southern Rhodesian Native Marriages Ordinance of 1901 outlawed child pledging and required that a woman's consent be obtained before a marriage could take place. The age of first marriage was set at twelve for girls.[45]

Two issues arose in connection with marriage and divorce laws. The first was adultery, which was cast as a problem of declining control over women that clearly warranted legal reform. Africans testified that the offender usually resolved adulterous liaisons privately by paying compensation for the affair. But colonial authorities invented "traditional penalties" for adultery—death, mutilation, or enslavement. They then criminalized adultery and made the punishment payment of fines or imprisonment. This strategy made their treatment seem far more lenient than their caricature of African tradition. Whereas custom did not hold women responsible for adultery, chiefs colluded with colonial authorities to punish female indiscipline by fining adulterous women.[46] The criminalization of adultery was a response to demands of male migrant laborers who worried that their women would be unfaithful while they were away, and the courts provided a mechanism for securing their control. It would seem that fining adultery was more about the recruitment of labor than about African sensibilities.

In Southern Rhodesia, European officials frowned on the custom of African husbands allowing wives who had left them to return and instead encouraged

African men to divorce unfaithful wives and reclaim the bridewealth. This pressure led African families to push their daughters to remain with their husbands even in situations that were life threatening.[47] Was punishing adultery a population policy? Did keeping women from committing adultery through threats of court proceedings and fines force them to remain in marriages where the exposure to pregnancy was higher?

The second issue is polygyny, a common practice in both animist and Muslim areas. Missionaries vigorously opposed polygyny, and European powers aligned with the Catholic Church condemned the practice. Some African women, perceiving monogamy and the right of the wife to her husband's property as advantageous, ran away to missions, angering their men. According to Hunt, polygyny came to signify depopulation for Belgian authorities, "the moral risk of the African 'race' being unable to reproduce itself (and the economic risk of an insufficient labour supply)."[48] The Belgians also opposed postpartum abstinence and prolonged breast-feeding because they thought these practices supported polygyny (and curbed the birthrate). The actual demographic implications of polygyny are less important here than colonial perceptions.[49]

Control of Population Growth

It was not only the law that shifted the public/private divide: direct intervention in pregnancy and childbirth did so as well. Colonial authorities presented their rationales for intervention quite transparently, asserting that depopulation through disease or high rates of infant mortality was a threat to the labor force.[50] Although they could not link diseases such as trypanosomiasis to women's behavior, they certainly could and did link epidemics of venereal disease (today referred to as sexually transmitted infections) to women.

Wars, which set in train famines, exoduses, and spikes in death and disability, are primary determinants of population patterns. Yet the dynamics of population in war zones and in the aftermath of war are poorly studied aspects of demography; even today, few assessments go beyond the enumeration of internally displaced persons and refugees. In wartime, census bureaus usually do not collect health and population data, and conflicting estimates of mortality and morbidity are part of the propaganda of warring sides. War-related mortality is sex- and age-selective and specific, with higher deaths rates in three groups—adult men and young boys who are fighting, the elderly (usually disproportionately women), and children.[51] The higher mortality among adult men produces more widows and more female-headed households in war-torn societies. Yet war creates a pronatalist environment, putting pressure on women to bear more children, which affects their reproductive choices and results in phenomena such as the baby boom after World War II. Demographers have done almost no research on this phenomenon in the aftermath of other wars, although scattered observations suggest it might be widespread.

One historical question is how changes in breast-feeding practices and postpartum abstinence contributed to the decline in birth-spacing intervals and to population growth and the deterioration of maternal and infant health in twentieth-century Africa. In the early 1920s, Belgian Congo authorities tried to alter infant feeding practices and to distribute milk to mothers and infants, initiatives linked to a discourse that viewed African birth-spacing customs as insidious.[52] The purpose of the programs was to reduce infant mortality by teaching African women about child rearing, cleanliness, and hygiene; by improving diet with weaning foods; by suppressing the practice of prolonged postpartum lactation; and by ending the ban on postpartum sexual relations. Behind the moralizing was the colonists' concern about the impact of population loss, infertility, and low birthrates on growing industrial labor requirements. In the Belgian Congo, according to Hunt, such concerns led to pronatalist policies, including family allowances; expansion of medical services; laws to repress abortion, prostitution, and polygyny; maternity gifts; and tax exemptions for monogamously married men with more than four children.[53]

The Belgians, who were responsible for an estimated 10 million deaths in the Congo in the nineteenth century, expressed concern for the health of the Congolese in the colonial era. They melded patriotism, greed, and labor demands in their new pronatalist policies.[54] Hunt quotes one of the European women leading the new health project as saying in 1926: "Without black labor, our colony would never be able to send to Europe the wealth buried in its soil. Help us by all means in our ability to protect, to care for the child while educating indigenous mothers, it is a duty. We need black labor. . . . To protect the child in the Congo is a duty, not only of altruism, but of patriotism."[55] The British were little better in the Gold Coast, according to Allman, where authorities regularly exposed the contradictions in their policies and perceptions, as well as the bankruptcy of their social welfare policies.[56]

In view of this broad range of factors, the narrow focus of population studies—and research in the applied field of population control—on fertility, almost always on women and today usually on chemical and surgical birth control, seems curious.

Birth Control and Contraception

European powers imposed their religious, racial, class, and gender prejudices on their colonies—in the legislation they adopted to govern their subjects and in their parochial attitudes toward women and childbearing. Moreover, labor force requirements drove their decisions. The British conflated sexuality and reproduction even as they pursued what were, in fact, antinatalist policies, yet they maintained bans on abortion and contraception long after the British women's movement achieved change at home in the 1930s. For the French, Belgian, and Portuguese administrations, these bans were consonant with their pronatalist policies. The Belgian law against abortion dates from 1867; it was repealed in Belgium in 1990. The French laws of 1810 (article 317) and 1939 (article 87) were the basis of laws in colonial Burkina Faso, Burundi, Cameroon, Chad, Comores, Congo (Brazzaville), Congo (Kinshasa), Côte d'Ivoire, Gabon, Guinea, Madagascar, colonial Mali, Mauritania, Niger, Rwanda, Senegal, and Togo. In 1923, the French confirmed the

1920 ban on abortion, extended it to cover attempted abortion, and increased the punishment for abortion providers; for the woman seeking an abortion, the crime was classified as a civil liability.[57] As Asian, Middle Eastern, and African countries liberated themselves from colonial rule in the decades after World War II, few new governments repealed those laws. Most still retain the ban on abortion.[58]

Writing in 1985 about Cameroon, Gwan Achu has noted that pronatalist government policy had its roots in culture and in French colonial legislation "against contraception and abortion, discriminatory taxation in favor of married persons, family allowances and other travel, leave, transfer, retirement, housing and educational benefits and concessions for persons with large families as well as an elaborate network of mother and child health care centers."[59] Although the ban on sales of contraceptives, adopted in 1920, was rescinded in France in the late 1960s, it remained in force in Cameroon until 1980. Cameroon's current abortion law, also adopted in 1980, continues the prohibition on dissemination of information about abortion, bans abortifacients, and permits abortion only for therapeutic reasons or for pregnancy due to rape.[60]

An obvious and effective way to regulate population growth is to control maternal mortality by providing maternity services. Even today, fertility control drives the safe motherhood initiatives of the World Health Organization (WHO).[61] Maternal mortality was and remains exceedingly high in sub-Saharan Africa. The failure of colonial public health services to persuade African women to use hospitals for birth and to let obstetricians assist them is evidence, to my mind, of anti-natalist policies. Colonial health services likewise failed to appreciate traditional midwives or to assist them with training and acquiring a minimum of material. Because pregnancy and childbirth entail considerable health risks and because abortion rates are nearly constant, independent of the legal status of abortion, prohibitions on abortion and contraception correlate with high maternal and infant mortality.[62] In colonial Ghana in the 1930s, the British admitted that they did not have great confidence in the science of obstetrics, that there was an insufficient number of biomedically trained midwives, that there was no hospital to cope with high-risk deliveries, and that they had few facilities to deliver babies.[63]

In colonial Kenya, pronatalist policies focused on how and when girls were circumcised, where women could give birth, and how premarital pregnancy was managed. Beginning in the 1920s, girls' sexuality, fertility, and initiation practices were the subject of heated debate and intense gender, generational, and political negotiations.[64] Native authorities, in conjunction with British colonial agents and the police, instituted the forced circumcision of girls in the name of preventing population decline.[65]

In Uganda, British concern over reproduction and population size intensified from 1907 through 1924. Colonial administrators developed institutions and ideologies to cope with an epidemic of sexually transmitted diseases, to promote the family as a unit of reproduction, and to reform motherhood. The British admitted that syphilis arrived through increased contact with Europeans and added that Christianity transformed it into an epidemic by setting women free from the bonds of polygynous marriages and abolishing dire punishments for adultery. The administration worked to instill shame and to change the sexual behavior of individuals. At the end of World War I, the administration's medical service and its missionary allies promoted motherhood through the Maternity Training School (MTS) in an effort to make more women reproduce, make them better mothers, and lower infant mortality levels. In the 1920s, the administration and the missions attempted to shape African family structures and private life by employing MTS-trained midwives in health and education initiatives.[66]

Colonial authorities were also aware of infertility as a cause of population decline. Much has been written on the African infertility belt, and many have speculated on the causes—whether they are related to the end of slavery, the sterility panic that blurred the discussion of fertility with discourses on degeneration and trauma, or the spread of sexually transmitted infections.[67] I will discuss the epidemic of venereal disease in greater detail, but here—under the rubric of birth control and contraception—it is startling to note two absences in colonial policy: the lack of gynecological facilities to diagnose and treat infertility and the failure to distribute condoms to combat this contagion.[68]

Disease, Dispersion, and Environmental Disruption

Policies that cause disease to spread and public health measures to arrest or contain contagion can affect population growth rates directly. During periods of epidemic disease and famine, slave raiding so weakened African populations that colonial conquest was facilitated. Jill R. Dias describes Portuguese conquest as following waves of malaria and sleeping sickness in northern Angola and sweeping plagues of rinderpest in the south; in addition, there was a major epidemic of smallpox, and an almost uninterrupted sequence of drought, flood, and locusts marked the 1900s and 1910s, culminating in the terrible famines of 1911 and 1916 in the south:

> These disasters weakened African rulers at a moment when Portuguese military pressures were at their most intense. In some regions, excessive losses of manpower and cattle hastened the military defeat of chiefs through their inability to mobilize resistance on the scale of previous decades. This was most evident in the south of Angola, where the deaths of around a quarter of a million people from starvation between 1911 and 1916 undoubtedly facilitated Portuguese victory over the Kwanyama in 1915. In the north, the uninterrupted epidemic of sleeping sickness between the 1890s and 1910s also aided Portuguese conquest.[69]

Maryinez Lyons examined trypanosomiasis (human sleeping sickness) in the Congo, where the Belgian conquest created an extraordinary ecological crisis that affected all aspects of life, including food production, social relations, and individual existence; it also resulted in devastating epidemic disease, increased endemic disease, severe malnutrition, and lowered resistance to disease. The colonial administration was aware that a demographic crisis brought about by epidemic sleeping sickness could seriously affect the future exploitation of the northern Congo, for which a plentiful supply of labor would be vital.[70] The control of population mobility—effected by the imposition of a cordon sanitaire, which entailed relocation and consolidation of villages as well as quarantine of sick Africans—was the principal feature of campaigns against sleeping sickness. The fallout from travel restrictions in terms of economic life, payment of taxes, and social relations was unprecedented.[71]

Carol Summers describes a similar situation in Uganda, where from 1900 to 1920 between 250,000 and 330,000 people died of trypanosomiasis in an epidemic that shocked the protectorate administration into action. The population continued to shrink, however, even after the epidemic waned, and the administration turned its attention to the low birthrate, which was attributed mainly to venereal disease, especially syphilis.[72] Authorities estimated that 70 percent of pregnancies among the Baganda ended in miscarriage, stillbirth, or infant death within the first week after birth, primarily the result of congenital syphilis. F. J. Lambkin, head of the commission Britain sent to investigate the epidemic, argued that "medical intervention against syphilis was necessary, feasible, and potentially cost-effective. Too many actively infectious cases in young, productive adults had caused substantial debility to an already depleted work force."[73]

Colonial medical authorities discussing maternal and infant welfare in the 1920s and 1930s blamed social diseases (prostitution, adultery, and their concomitants, syphilis and gonorrhea); poverty; the poor hygienic practices of native midwives; the carelessness of African mothers who fed their children inappropriately; superstition; and, in a departure from victim-blaming rationales, the lack of sufficient medical aid. Barbara Cooper notes that even today, public health authorities still level such accusations, shifting responsibility from the state to mothers.[74] In parts of the Gold Coast, infant mortality rates exceeded 70 percent, yet colonial authorities failed to tie them to economic exploitation—the effects of migrant and forced labor, cash cropping, and taxation—preferring to underscore their own supposed moral superiority by calling for better education for African mothers, whom they considered failures.[75]

Venereal disease causes pregnancy loss, neonatal mortality, and sterility. Unchecked, it acts as a control on population growth. Physicians in the past often confused syphilis with endemic yaws. Infertility is a classic symptom of gonorrhea but not of syphilis.[76] In Tanganyika, the fear was that low fertility, caused by widespread venereal disease, would lead to the depopulation, if not the extinction, of the Haya from the Bukoba region[77] In Uganda, colonial administrators allowed missionaries to take the lead in the post–World War I campaign against syphilis and paid for the missionary-administered "social purity" campaign and maternal health programs.[78] Southern Rhodesian colonial authorities were so concerned about venereal disease that they imposed medical examinations on single African women who traveled to urban and industrial areas.[79] The focus on women and venereal disease in urban centers found an echo in South African colonial policy in the interwar years.[80] Women who suffered from venereal disease were affected socially and economically more than men because husbands repudiated wives who did not bear children.[81]

From the colonial administrators' viewpoint, widespread venereal disease posed several problems with implications for population control. First, colonists blamed women who were sterile or aborted spontaneously for aggravating the perceived shortage of labor. Second, they blamed women for spreading venereal disease to men rather than seeing them as victims of diseased partners, corroborating notions that women were immoral. Third, the prevalence of these diseases confirmed colonial suspicions that women who ran away to towns were prostitutes who spread infection,[82] reinforcing ideas about the need to control women's mobility. Taken together, these considerations fostered the belief that women should be under the control of fathers or husbands, a concept that underlay the general colonial policy of designating adult women as minors for life.

What is striking about colonial efforts to control rates of population growth is the disparate levels on which policy operated—at one extreme were microlevel attempts to change breast-feeding practices, for example, and at the other extreme were macrolevel policies such as taxation. The next section examines the impact of several broader social and economic policies on demographic trends. Education exposed Africans to European ideas of modernity and the ideals of Christian family life. Famine relief reduced mortality from starvation. And taxation profoundly affected gender norms and relations.

Colonial Education Policies

Nineteenth-century missionaries training for the priesthood from Great Britain, France, and later the United States, who were supported by the Phelps-Stokes Education Fund, laid the foundations for European education in Africa.[83] European evangelical missions taught literacy and manual skills, whereas the Anglican and Catholic missions had a more academic focus. Taking most of the credit for the establishment of schools in sub-Saharan Africa in the early 1900s, mission officials began to pressure their governments for more support of their efforts in education. After World War I, the governments of Great Britain and France acknowledged that education was an important aspect of colonial policy and increased grants to mission schools. The value of African agricultural exports increased in the postwar period and African territories were becoming more profitable, justifying investments in African education. As mass education began taking root in Europe the use of schools as centers for colonial activity also encouraged educational spending.

According to Bob White, France had a very tight grip on the development of educational systems in its colonies.[84] In 1922, the French colonial administration restricted missionary activity in education. The establishment of a new school in the colonies required government permission, teachers had to be government certified and teach the government curriculum, and French had to be the exclusive language of instruction. It might be said, then, that France supported mission schools only insofar as they spread knowledge of French and cultivated loyalty to France. The education given in the state schools was entirely secular.

In addition to promulgating French, French colonial education in sub-Saharan Africa tailored enrollment to estimates of job availability for graduating students. The system had "European" and "African" tracks. The European schools were selective and aimed at educating an African elite to fill the lower ranks of the colonial civil service, whereas African schools delivered popular education. Primary schools fell into three categories: village, regional, and urban. The village schools were African, and the regional schools, much fewer in number, were transitional. Urban schools were almost entirely European, and they closely followed the structure and curriculum of schools in the *métropole*.[85]

Depending initially on missionary schools, British colonial administrations became involved in formal education in Africa later than the French. Their activities were also much less visible. At first, the British government encouraged missionary education by granting church establishments full administrative freedom and providing occasional grants-in-aid. Such a laissez-faire attitude relieved the colonial regime of responsibility for educational administration and policy formation. The French had embarked on such endeavors before 1900. Even after the British increased expenditures for education, the strong influence of missions in the British colonies eventually led to the creation of a dual system of education. Mission and state schools existed side by side. British colonial education policy did eventually establish priorities for education, emphasizing curricula and activities adapted to meet local needs and conditions. The British system also privileged the use of local languages in primary school instruction and directed greater attention to the education of girls.[86] The influence of missionaries, who often held negative, demeaning, and racist views of African women, on the type and content of education offered to girls cannot be overstated.[87] Although they justified their civilizing experiments as efforts to improve the status of women, missionaries tried to reduce African women to the position of nineteenth-century European housewives.[88] They taught women to cook (often on electric stoves, never mind that there was no electricity in the villages), mend, and wash and iron clothes, as well as how to wean their infants and decorate their homes (with no regard to poverty). Some of these women were destined to work as maids in European households.[89] Was there a pronatalist motive behind the state funding of missionary education? Was it part of the push in the early years of colonial power to control the population?

Gertrude Mianda, writing about the Belgian Congo, maintains that the colonial educational system distanced women from salaried work, even as it prepared men for it. Schools trained a minority of women for "feminine work" in nursing, elementary school teaching, and infant care, a focus that Mianda attributes to Christian education and colonial legislation that restricted wives' freedom to work outside the home.[90] Hunt remarks that if colonial administrators assumed that working wives would bear fewer children and that female schooling and formal sector employment would influence fertility rates, they would have met with disappointment and contradictions.[91] Colonial pride in the introduction of formal education was unambiguous. Credit for reducing the death rate from famine was less clear because the relief measures so often ignored the policies that created famine conditions, as detailed in the next section.

Famine Relief

The relation of famine to starvation and death, frequently stemming from crop failures due to drought, flood, and infestation, is well documented.[92] Famine acts as a check on population growth, even when it is not responsible for outright population decline. And famines were recurring phenomena throughout the colonial era. Joseph C. Miller suggests that drought caused the reversal of an underlying tendency toward population growth in west-central Africa: "The overall level of population thus probably increased little from the moment when Bantu-speaking farmers and herders first exceeded densities that could survive extended periods of failed rains. Pulses of growth repeatedly gave way to shudders of partial collapse, to be succeeded once again by a new phase of expansion."[93] And as Amartya Sen has observed of the great Bengal famine of 1942, more people died of disease epidemics attendant on famine than from starvation. Miller confirms this pattern in west-central Africa:

> Outbreaks of disease paralleled the chronology of drought in an epidemiological sequence familiar from many other regions. Africans weakened by malnutrition and exhausted by dispersal into the bush or by flight into lowlands became particularly vulnerable to endemic pathogens. Retreat from drier watersheds into moist river valleys or to the coast carried people into disease environments where they possessed few immunities. Eighteenth-century droughts commonly culminated in mounting mortality.[94]

Dias notes increased mortality rates from disease among the African population of Angola particularly following droughts:

> Malarial fevers, diseases of the digestive tract, especially those described as "dysentery" or "diarrhoea," and respiratory diseases, including bronchitis, pneumonia and tuberculosis, were the most common and widespread endemic diseases in Angola by the nineteenth century. Together they were responsible for approximately half the deaths reported annually in Luanda, excluding years of smallpox epidemics,

from the 1850s.... Malnutrition also favoured the outbreak of
epidemic diseases. The principal infectious/contagious diseases which
recurred in epidemic form in Angola from the sixteenth century
onwards were yellow fever, smallpox, measles, influenza, and possibly
bubonic plague and trypanosomiasis (sleeping sickness).[95]

Whole families emigrated during hunger crises, and Dias surmises that the
recurrence of more prolonged drought crises resulted in a permanent drift of
people toward more fertile, densely populated areas. "Such fugitives from hunger
would also have provided chiefs in Kasanje or the Ovimbundu kingdoms with a
ready supply of slaves to sell for shipment overseas."[96] What is interesting about
this for the purposes of this chapter is that we know more men were sold into
overseas slavery and more women were retained for domestic slavery. The question is whether this enslavement of women further depressed population growth,
since we know that slave women had fewer children than free married women.[97]
Dias does not investigate the gender dimensions of famine in her essay.

Each year between 1911 and 1927, major famines visited some large area of Africa.
Droughts were the chief cause, but new tax systems, crop exports, declining trans-
Saharan commerce, and labor migration exacerbated their impact.[98] Public famine
relief in the British colonies was modeled on the Indian Famine Codes of the 1880s
and consisted of policies designed to fend off starvation: a ban on the export of foods
from affected areas and food-for-work programs, which usually employed men on
road-building schemes, paying workers in grain. Even when authorities considered
importing food—usually thought too costly and impractical—they distributed relief
in the context of food-for-work programs, an approach still used today by the World
Food Program. In some places, authorities restricted the use of grain to brew beer,
required Africans to store food and seed for the following year, enforced the cultivation of drought-resistant root crops, and fixed price ceilings.[99] The emphasis was on
short-term relief and not on the development of agriculture, communications, and
infrastructure; that is, the focus was never on preventing future famines.

When famine threatened, administrators regularly blamed food shortages on
overpopulation as well as poor farming practices and improvidence, despite a general concern, especially in the early years of colonialism, that population growth was
slow and insufficient to provide the necessary labor for the development of commercial agriculture and mining. In explaining overpopulation, colonists fell back
on rationales that exonerated them from any blame; instead, they praised colonial
conquest for putting an end to deadly tribal warfare and slave raids that depopulated areas even when they were not lethal.[100] Yet colonial authorities extracted too
much food from subsistence farms for administrative requirements and for sale in
towns, and they collected taxes on a timetable that coincided with metropolitan
fiscal years, not the vagaries of local weather patterns.[101] Iliffe attributes the decline
in famine mortality after 1927 to a combination of manioc cultivation; vaccination
against smallpox; the substitution of motor vehicles for human porterage; and, more

generally, "effective government, good transport, wider markets, and some increase in average wealth."[102] At the same time, he acknowledges that endemic poverty, undernutrition, and chronic malnutrition replaced periodic famine mortality as the chief problems of subsistence. "The decline of famine mortality during the later 1920s and 1930s removed one of tropical Africa's chief constraints on population growth . . . a general demographic expansion now became apparent."[103]

I have discussed elsewhere the demographic implications of famine relief: starvation killed the young and the old, but though it spared those in their reproductive years from death, it did depress their ability to reproduce. In famine years, population growth nearly halted, but with the next harvest, adults were able to recover. In sexual relations, men could once again hold erections and produce sperm, and women could again ovulate, menstruate, become pregnant, and bear children. Famine relief both lopped off the peaks in mortality and permitted couples to reproduce. Only child health suffered as chronic malnutrition set in. Famine relief was never of sufficient quantity or quality, and the main preventive measure—the planting of manioc—was of such low nutritional value as virtually to ensure chronic malnutrition.[104]

Marcia Wright points out another incidental demographic effect of famine: colonial economic units at the southern tip of Lake Tanganyika in Northern Rhodesia employed single men in significant concentrations in an atmosphere that undermined the authority of chiefs. "This was especially true in critical times of famine, which meant hard work and short rations," she observes. Furthermore, chiefs were not easily able to maintain control of their many wives, "who tended to develop their own strategies for amelioration, seeking sexual and social relations outside the royal monopoly and rebelling and running away in groups."[105]

Yet another way in which famine affected demography involves the aid it gave to the process of European displacement of Africans and expropriation of African farms, which triggered complex processes of impoverishment and threatened to make the effects of famine more severe. Dias describes the process by which African families lost control of land to foreigners during such crises in Angola:

> Successive crop failures bankrupted hundreds of small African coffee and peanut producers, forcing them to sell or abandon their plots to local or incoming purchasers and creditors. . . . Expropriation of African farmland was further aided by mortality and flight during repeated smallpox epidemics. This process resulted in a major redistribution of property in Cazengo [Angola] in favour of European settlers and the replacement of a predominantly African, smallholding economy by large-scale plantations.[106]

The impact on women related to the commercial boom in commodities for which men required their labor, leading to the neglect of food production. Where rubber was extracted, expansion of the trade aggravated the situation because women, who normally cultivated food crops, were the ones who prepared rubber for trade. Emergency famine relief, with its contradictory effects on rates of population growth, was a response to hunger crises created largely by colonial policies; it never was intended to solve underlying problems such as the way that taxation policies contributed to food shortages and famines.

Taxation

Taxes affected African women, although colonial states officially collected taxes from African men (in most cases), on the assumption that the family was patriarchal. The hut tax, for example, set a precedent for treating African women as legal minors, although the state took for granted that women were economically productive members and that agriculture was the major source of income. In South Africa, according to Sean Redding, "later taxes combined with the development of migrant labor and the declining availability of arable land in the reserves to restructure women's roles dramatically." Some whites hoped that the hut tax would lead to the decline, if not the extinction, of polygyny and that African women would concentrate on domestic duties, leaving their men to do the monetarily productive labor; based on Victorian ideals of English womanhood, they envisaged African women committed to monogamous marriages in which they were the junior, silent partners. Taxation was the basic context for colonial administrations' interest in marriage laws, as discussed previously.[107]

The British tradition of a strong civil service and a local value-based tax stands in contrast to the French approach of centralization and area-based taxes. In Anglophone countries, the state generally administered property taxes locally, and the revenues supported local government. Most Francophone countries had a central government property tax. Francophone countries generally have detailed and codified tax systems with complex administrative structures. According to Riël C. D. Franzsen and Joan M. Youngman, in the absence of a tradition of a strong civil service, these systems are almost impossible to maintain and have contributed to the decline of ancillary revenue sources such as the property tax.[108] In Lusophone colonies, the property tax was generally a national tax.

Belgian authorities introduced the single women's tax in Usumbura in 1942; they required all urban women residents without husbands—whether divorced, widowed, or never married—to pay. Each woman had a special tax book in which authorities stapled a tax receipt for each year she paid, along with other tickets for payment of water, property, and road taxes. The penalty for not paying was imprisonment. What motivated this tax?[109] Was it a morality tax, as Hunt argues, based on the assumption that all women living alone were prostitutes? Did it also have an indirect pronatalist demographic appeal, since single women were unlikely to bear as many children as married women?

The Cape Colony first imposed the hut tax on men in 1870: "Although it did little to change women's social, cultural and economic status by itself," Redding writes, "[it] did set a precedent for treating African women as legal minors." Combined with the development of migrant labor and the declining availability of arable land in the reserves, taxes restructured women's roles dramatically. "Taxes were by no means the only or the primary cause of this restructuring, but they were an integral part of the foundation."[110] The hut tax, which could not be paid in kind, assumed that women and unmarried men were legal minors and dependents, a status that was alterable for men through marriage but not for women. Reasons for the hut tax's longevity include whites' ideas about gender relations, the proper sexual division of labor, and opposition to polygyny. A tax on each wife acted as an (ineffectual) economic disincentive to having multiple wives.

Yet, as Redding points out, the hut tax by itself did not impose a high enough price either to deter polygyny or to propel men into wage labor. It did, though, lay the "legal groundwork for social, cultural and economic changes in African women's roles, changes that would be catalyzed by additional taxation, the development of migrant labor, population growth, and the impact of legislation that severely restricted women's choices."[111] Women had neither security of tenure nor legal right to property. The state effectively taxed women without according them the status of taxpayers or adults. As husbands and sons more commonly spent longer periods of time engaged in migrant labor, women had to take greater responsibility for the actual physical payment of taxes. Those who remained in the rural areas suffered the brunt of the consequences of nonpayment even though they were not in any legal sense liable. The punishments for nonpayment of taxes could be severe; the man could be tried and stood virtually no chance of being acquitted. After the trial, the police could seize the family's livestock and other movable property; they could imprison him; or they could confiscate his usufruct title to the land, evicting his whole family in the process, and assign the land to someone else. Although the state rarely resorted to these punishments, women procured the money in several ways—by taking a lover who could be coaxed into providing the cash; by borrowing from white traders or wealthier and often male relatives; by engaging in commercial farming, selling produce, eggs, or wool; or by renting out their plots to other African farmers or allowing them to farm on the halves, a set of sharecropping arrangements that were illegal. Still others became migrant laborers themselves, leaving their extended families to occupy the land.[112] Taxation (and other economic requirements) forced women out of family life in the rural areas, often pushing them into illegal occupations in the towns.

Summing Up

This chapter describes colonial administrators' attempts to bend reproductive trends to their requirements for labor through a wide range of policies. Marriage, adultery, divorce, child custody, and inheritance laws were crucial arenas in which to reassert patriarchal control, leading to collusion between chiefs and headmen, on one side, and colonial officials, on the other. Colonial policies that controlled women's behavior, including their reproduction, were not only directly about birth control but also about using the control of women to rule societies and ultimately to control men's labor and the supply of male labor. Gender and generational relations directly organized social relations of production in precolonial African societies. Attempts by colonial administrations to reorganize productive relations meant disruption of, if not an assault on, familial and gender relations and powers; attempts to reorder gender precipitated shifts in economic power and in demographic patterns.[113]

Male representatives from African communities encountered the colonial legal system at a point of insecurity in which wage labor was eroding their control over the labor of women and young men. They represented African customary law to colonial rulers in ways that emphasized their control over women, interpretations that colonial legal procedures rendered even more rigid. African patriarchal gender values converged with the colonial administrators' and judges' own patriarchal views and their administrative interests in controlling African women and strengthening the capacity of chiefs to govern locally.[114] By monopolizing criminal law and punishment, the colonial regimes introduced distortions into customary law. Chanock wonders, "In a situation of growing class differentiation, whose resource was custom?"[115]

Chanock has described the processes by which the British shaped customary law in Africa and also the ways in which public issues, such as labor power and landownership, and private issues, such as kinship relations, were inextricably linked:

> With the development of migrant labour, both labour power and goods could be sold as commodities. Household heads obtained cash through the transformation of their dependants' labour power into commodity form, and gradually rural production for cash sale also developed. Household heads therefore encouraged dependent men and women to labour in various ways for money. The production of commodities, which enabled dependants to have access to cash independently of elders, both accentuated the fragmentation of households and produced "custom" as an ideological response to this fragmentation.[116]

The attempts of colonial administrators to influence women's reproductive lives were congruent with the moral values that Christian missionaries sought to instill in Africans and wanted to see reflected in the law. Although colonial administrators and missionaries held many religious values in common, particularly regarding the proper role of women in society, some missionary beliefs conflicted with the reproductive outcomes that the state desired. The two groups compromised because missionaries needed state subsidies and the state needed and used missionaries to implement regulations that were intended to control the population. African women and men resisted some of those policies and used others for their own purposes. Women and men also clashed with each other. And older men were at odds with younger men and women in their struggles for some semblance of independence, autonomy, and power vis-à-vis colonial authorities.

In this chapter, I have tried to tease out the demographic consequences of colonial policies and to call attention to the motivations underlying some of them, whether to promote or to restrict population growth. I have not discussed the issue of population densities, although population distribution and migration clearly influenced mortality from disease. My primary focus is on gender—that is, on the impact of colonial policies on women and relations between genders and generations. Some of the central questions of this chapter raise issues for further research. For example, what were the demographic implications of the customs that colonial states codified in customary law, and what were the demographic consequences of the prohibition of some customs and the criminalization of others under statutory law?

Notes

This essay could not have been written without the generous assistance of many historians. Not trained as a historian myself, I relied heavily on their work. I particularly want to thank Elizabeth Schmidt, Barbara Cooper, Nancy Hunt, Elisha Renne, Dennis Cordell, Asma Abdel Halim, and José Curto. I thank them for their own work as well as for their responses to my requests for references. Special thanks are due to Dennis Cordell for so kindly reading the first draft and making useful comments.

1. These are not inflexible categories: the French and Belgians seemed more conscious of the pronatalist impact of benefits and allowances than the British, and they used them to increase the birthrate (read labor force, even as they gave other justifications for their policies). The British had no less need for labor but seemed haunted by Malthusian beliefs that welfare provisions such as "poor laws" constituted a "negative" check on population, enabling large families to survive. Catholic European powers—France, Belgium, Portugal—adhered to (pronatalist) church doctrine.

2. Prosecution for rape in colonial Africa focused on black male assaults on white women; the same concern did not extend to white or black assaults on black women.

3. Frederick Cooper, "From Free Labor to Family Allowances: Labor and African Society in Colonial Discourse," *American Ethnologist* 16, no. 4 (1989): 751.

4. Ann Stoler, "Making Empire Respectable: The Politics of Race and Sexual Morality in 20th-Century Colonial Cultures," *American Ethnologist* 16, no. 4 (1989): 634–60.

5. Frederick Cooper and Ann L. Stoler, "Introduction: Tensions of Empire—Colonial Control and Visions of Rule," *American Ethnologist* 16, no. 4 (1989): 614.

6. Dennis D. Cordell, Joel W. Gregory, and Victor Piché, "African Historical Demography: The Search for a Theoretical Framework," in *African Population and Capitalism: Historical Perspectives,* ed. Dennis D. Cordell and Joel W. Gregory (Boulder, CO: Westview Press, 1987), 14–32.

7. Amy Kaler, *Running after Pills: Politics, Gender, and Contraception in Colonial Zimbabwe* (Portsmouth, NH: Heinemann, 2003), 180–81.

8. Barbara Brown, "Facing the 'Black Peril': The Politics of Population Control in South Africa," *Journal of Southern African Studies* 13, no. 2 (1987): 256–73.

9. Elizabeth Schmidt, "Negotiated Spaces and Contested Terrain: Men, Women, and the Law in Colonial Zimbabwe, 1990–1939," *Journal of Southern African Studies* 16, no. 4 (1990): 622–26.

10. Ibid., 622.

11. Siwan Anderson and Debraj Ray, "Missing Women: Age and Disease," *Review of Economic Studies*, forthcoming. Paper cited in *Journal of Economic Literature Classification*, nos. J11, J16, O53 (2009): 2.

12. Ibid.

13. Rita Headrick, *Colonialism, Health and Illness in French Equatorial Africa, 1885–1935* (Atlanta, GA: African Studies Association, 1994), 96.

14. Jean Allman, "Making Mothers: Missionaries, Medical Officers, and Women's Work in Colonial Asante, 1924–45," *History Workshop Journal* 38, no. 1 (1994): 23–47.

15. Cooper, "From Free Labor," 746.

16. Nancy Hunt, *A Colonial Lexicon: Of Birth Ritual, Medicalization, and Mobility in the Congo* (Durham, NC: Duke University Press, 1999).

17. Cooper, "From Free Labor," 751.

18. Ibid.

19. Ibid., 755–56.

20. Nancy Hunt, "Placing African Women's History and Locating Gender," *Social History* 14, no. 3 (1989): 359–79.

21. E. Schmidt, "Patriarchy, Capitalism, and the Colonial State in Zimbabwe," *Signs* 16, no. 4 (1991): 732–56. This was also true for migration related to commercial (plantation) agriculture. See Dennis D. Cordell, Joel W. Gregory, and Victor Piché, *Hoe and Wage: A Social History of a Circular Migration System in West Africa* (Boulder, CO: Harper and Row, 1996), esp. 231–86.

22. Schmidt, "Patriarchy," 735.

23. Jane Parpart, "Sexuality and Power on the Zambian Copperbelt, 1926–1964," in *Discovering the African Past: Essays in Honor of Daniel F. McCall,* ed. Norman Bennett, Boston University Papers on Africa 8 (Boston: African Studies Center, Boston University, 1987), 53–72.

24. Schmidt, "Patriarchy," 741.

25. Nancy Hunt, "Noise over Camouflaged Polygamy, Colonial Morality Taxation, and a Woman-Naming Crisis in Belgian Africa," *Journal of African History* 32, no. 3 (1991): 471–94.

26. Megan Vaughan, *Curing Their Ills: Colonial Power and African Illness* (Stanford, CA: Stanford University Press, 1991).

27. Linzi Manicom, "Ruling Relations: Rethinking State and Gender in South African History," *Journal of African History* 33, no. 3 (1992): 456.

28. Ibid.

29. Allman, "Making Mothers," 28.

30. Ibid., 29–30. One illustration of this intrusion was the annual staging of a "baby show," which required mothers to register births, regularly attend the welfare clinic, and (for extra points) have their babies vaccinated.

31. Martin Chanock, *Law, Custom and Social Order: The Colonial Experience in Malawi and Zambia* (Cambridge: Cambridge University Press, 1985).

32. Manicom, "Ruling Relations," 460.

33. Martin Chanock, "A Peculiar Sharpness: An Essay on Property in the History of Customary Law in Colonial Africa," *Journal of African History* 32, no. 1 (1985): 65–88.

34. Cooper, "From Free Labor," 749.

35. Chanock, *Law, Custom and Social Order,* 14.

36. Chanock, "Peculiar Sharpness," 67.

37. Schmidt, "Negotiated Spaces."

38. Martin Chanock, "Making Customary Law: Men, Women, and Courts in Colonial Northern Rhodesia," in *African Women and the Law—Historical Perspectives,* ed. M. J. Hay and M. Wright (Boston: Boston University Press, 1982), 60.

39. Barbara Cooper, "La rhétorique de la 'mauvaise mère,'" in *Niger 2005: Une catastrophe si naturelle,* ed. Xavier Crombé and Jean-Hervé Jézéquel (Paris: Karthala, 2007), 199–226.

40. Chanock, *Law, Custom and Social Order,* 172.

41. Judith Byfield, *The Bluest Hands: A Social and Economic History of Women Dyers in Abeokuta (Nigeria), 1890–1940* (Oxford: James Currey, 2002), 65.

42. Chanock, "Peculiar Sharpness," 73.

43. E. Schmidt, *Peasants, Traders, and Wives: Shona Women in the History of Zimbabwe* (Portsmouth, NH: Heinemann, 1992), 106.

44. Chanock, quoted in ibid., 108.

45. Ibid., 111.

46. Margaret Strobel, "African Women," *Signs* 8, no. 1 (1982): 109–31.

47. Schmidt, *Peasants, Traders, and Wives,* 116.

48. Hunt, "Noise over Camouflaged Polygamy," 475.

49. As a group, polygynous marriages tend to produce more children than monogamous marriages because women marry young and remarry quickly after death or divorce; however, individual women in polygynous marriages appear to have fewer children because of (short-term) separations and the older age of husbands. See M. Gareene and E. van de Walle, "Polygyny and Fertility among the Sereer of Senegal," *Population Studies* 43, no. 2 (1989): 267–83, and G. Pison, "La démographie de la polygamie," *Population* 41, no. 1 (1986): 93–122. Fertility is also usually lower for women who have a number of marriages because more time is spent without regular sexual intercourse between liaisons and the incidence of venereal disease may be higher. See Claire Robertson, "Post-proclamation Slavery in Accra: A Female Affair?" in *Women and Slavery in Africa,* ed Claire C. Robertson and Martin A. Klein (Madison: University of Wisconsin Press, 1983), 220–45.

50. In their rudimentary attempts to enumerate the population, colonial officials were unable to determine which factors were responsible for population decline. Dennis D. Cordell, "Où sont tous les enfants? La faible fécondité en Centrafrique, 1890–1960," *Population, reproduction, sociétés: Perspectives et enjeux de démographie sociale,* ed. Dennis D. Cordell, Danielle Gauvreau, Raymond R. Gervais, and Céline Le Bourdais (Montreal, Canada: Les Presses de l'Université de Montréal, 1993), 257–77.

51. See Meredeth Turshen, "Definition and Injuries of Violence," in *Interventions: Activists and Academics Respond to Violence,* ed. E. A. Castelli and J. R. Jakobsen (New York: Palgrave, 2004), 29–35.

52. Nancy Hunt, "Le bébé en brousse: European Women, African Birth Spacing and Colonial Intervention in Breast Feeding in the Belgian Congo," *International Journal of African Historical Studies* 21, no. 3 (1988): 401–32.

53. Ibid., 403–4.

54. According to Hunt, "Noise over Camouflaged Polygamy," 473, once the Congo became a colony, Belgians felt guilty about King Leopold's excesses and were eager "to bring in a new humanitarian era, introduce reforms and approach the civilizing task with earnestness and vigour."

55. Hunt, "Le bébé," 405.

56. Allman, "Making Mothers," 31.

57. Bartha Maria Knoppers, Isabel Brault, and Elizabeth Sloss, "Abortion Law in Francophone Countries," *American Journal of Comparative Law* 38, no. 4 (1990): 889–922.

58. Ibid. Colonial policies and the Catholic Church continue to dominate government regulation of birth control practice in sub-Saharan Africa. Since independence, the following countries have amended the law to allow abortion when the woman's life is at serious risk: Burkina Faso, Central African Republic, Chad, Gabon, Guinea, Madagascar, Mauritania, Niger, and Senegal. In many of these countries, more than one physician must attest to the necessity of an abortion—this in countries where the ratio of physicians to population was on the order of 0.19 per 10,000 population even after independence!

59. Emmanuel Gwan Achu, "Origins and Elements of the Population Policies of Cameroon Republic," *Revue Science et Technique* 3, nos. 1–2 (1985): 116–28.

60. Center for Reproductive Rights, "Les droits des femmes en matière de santé reproductive au Cameroun: Rapport alternatif," available at http://reproductiverights.org/sites/crr.civicactions.net/files/documents/SRCameroon00fr.pdf, accessed 4 April 2010.

61. For example, the lead story in *Safe Motherhood*, the newsletter of the WHO initiative, speaks of women bearing the cost of high fertility in Nigeria and how men control the use of contraceptives and decisions about family size, whereas a report on a Safe Motherhood workshop in Asia emphasizes access to family planning (vol. 25, no. 1 [1998], available at https://apps.who.int/rht/pdf_files/25_safemotherhood.en.pdf, accessed 5 April 2010). See also the report of an October 2009 UN Fund for Population Activities (UNFPA) meeting in Addis Ababa, Ethiopia, at which health ministers from around the world agreed that swift action had to be taken to reduce the number of women dying during pregnancy and childbirth. The ministers seemed to agree that family planning was the most cost-effective way of tacking the problem; see http://news.bbc.co.uk/2/hi/health/8327144.stm, accessed 5 April 2010.

62. Knoppers, Brault, and Sloss, "Abortion Law."

63. Allman, "Making Mothers," 32.

64. Lynn Thomas, *Politics of the Womb: Women, Reproduction, and the State in Kenya* (Berkeley: University of California Press, 2003).

65. For more on this and outstanding specific examples from among the Meru, see Anne-Marie Péatrik, *La vie à pas contés: Génération, âge et société dans les hautes terres du Kenya (Meru-Tigania-Igembe)* (Nanterre, France: Société d'Ethnologie, 1999), 429–506.

66. Carol Summers, "Intimate Colonialism: The Imperial Production of Reproduction in Uganda, 1907–1925," *Signs* 16, no. 4 (1991): 787–807.

67. Cordell, "Où sont tous les enfants"; Nancy Hunt, "Fertility's Fires and Empty Wombs in Recent Africanist Writing," *Africa* 75, no. 3 (2005): 421–35; Anne Retel-Laurentin, "Influence de certaines maladies sur la fécondité: Un exemple africain," *Population* 22, no. 5 (1967): 841–60.

68. Hunt, "Fertility's Fires," and Alan Jeeves, "Public Health in the Era of South Africa's Syphilis Epidemic of the 1930s and 1940s," *South African Historical Journal* 45, no. 1 (2001): 79–102.

69. Jill R. Dias, "Famine and Disease in the History of Angola, c. 1830–1930," *Journal of African History* 21, no. 3 (1981): 375. Not until the very end of the nineteenth century did Portugal develop systematic colonization policies for Africa, when officials promoted military campaigns against rebellious African rulers, encouraged white settlers to migrate to Africa, and put Africans under the control of the Portuguese state as either compliant assimilated Africans (*assimilados*) or natives (*indigenas*) subject to forced labor. Cristiana Basto, "Medical Hybridisms and Social Boundaries: Aspects of Portuguese Colonialism

in Africa and India in the Nineteenth Century," *Journal of Southern African Studies* 33, no. 4 (2007): 767–82.

70. Maryinez Lyons, *The Colonial Disease: A Social History of Sleeping Sickness in Northern Zaire, 1900–1940* (Cambridge: Cambridge University Press, 1992), 2–3.

71. Ibid., 199–233.

72. Summers, "Intimate Colonialism," 789.

73. Quoted in ibid., 791. The British public saw syphilis as a disease imported by the colonial expansion, so there was a substantial British lobby for an antisyphilis campaign. For further examples, see Shane Doyle, *Population and Environment in Western Uganda, 1860–1955: Crisis and Decline in Bunyoro* (Athens: Ohio University Press, 2006), and Jan Kuhanen, *Poverty, Health and Reproduction in Early Colonial Uganda* (Joensuu, Finland: University of Joensuu Publications in the Humanities, 2005), 630–34.

74. Cooper, "La rhétorique de la 'mauvaise mère.'"

75. Allman, "Making Mothers."

76. Mead Over and Peter Piot, "HIV Infection and Sexually Transmitted Diseases," in *Disease Control Priorities in Developing Countries,* ed. D. T. Jamison, W. H. Mosley, A. R. Measham, and J. L. Bobdilla (Oxford: Oxford University Press, 1993), 455–527.

77. Birgitta Larsson, *Conversion to Greater Freedom? Women, Church and Social Change in Northwestern Tanzania under Colonial Rule* (Stockholm: Almqvist and Wiksell International, 1991), 89.

78. Summers, "Intimate Colonialism," 794.

79. Lynette Jackson, "When in the White Man's Town: Zimbabwean Women Remember *Chibeura,*" in *Women in African Colonial Histories,* ed. Jean Allman, Susan Geiger, and Nakanyike Musisi (Bloomington: Indiana University Press, 2002), 191–215.

80. Karen Jochelson, *The Colour of Disease: Syphilis and Racism in South Africa, 1880–1950* (New York: Palgrave, 2001).

81. Larsson, *Conversion,* 88.

82. See Luise White, *Comforts of Home* (Chicago: University of Chicago Press, 1990), which is the history of women prostitutes in Nairobi during the interwar period.

83. Bob White, "Talk about School: Education and the Colonial Project in French and British Africa (1860–1960)," *Comparative Education* 32, no. 1 (1996): 9–25.

84. Ibid.

85. Ibid.

86. Ibid.

87. Allman, "Making Mothers"; Hunt, "Noise over Camouflaged Polygamy"; and Schmidt, "Patriarchy."

88. Nancy Hunt, "Domesticity and Colonialism in Belgian Africa: Usumbura's Foyer Social, 1946–1960," *Signs* 15, no. 3 (1990): 447–74; Nakanyike Musisi, "Colonial and Missionary Education: Women and Domesticity in Uganda: 1900–1945," in *African Encounters with Domesticity,* ed. Karen Tranberg Hansen (New Brunswick, NJ: Rutgers University Press, 1992), 172–94.

89. Jacklyn Cock, "Domestic Service and Education for Domesticity: The Incorporation of Xhosa Women into Colonial Society," in *Women and Gender in Southern Africa to 1945: An Overview,* ed. Cherryl Walker (Cape Town: David Philip. 1990), 76–96.

90. Gertrude Mianda, "Colonialism, Education, and Gender Relations in the Belgian Congo: The *Evolué* Case," in *Women in African Colonial Histories,* ed. Jean Allman, Susan Geieger, and Nakanyike Musisi (Bloomington: Indiana University Press, 2002), 157.

91. Hunt, "Fertility's Fires," 422–23.

92. Amartya Sen, *Poverty and Famines* (Oxford: Oxford University Press, 1980).

93. Joseph C. Miller, "The Significance of Drought, Disease and Famine in the Agriculturally Marginal Zones of West-Central Africa," *Journal of African History* 23, no. 1 (1982): 22–23.

94. Ibid.

95. Jill R. Dias, "Famine and Disease," 357–58.

96. Ibid., 356–57.

97. Claire C. Robertson and Martin A. Klein. "Women's Importance in African Slave Systems," in *Women and Slavery in Africa,* ed. Claire C. Robertson and Martin A. Klein (Madison: University of Wisconsin Press, 1983), 3–25.

98. John Iliffe, *The African Poor: A History* (Cambridge: Cambridge University Press, 1987), 157.

99. Holger Weiss, "Crop Failures, Food Shortages and Colonial Famine Relief Policies in the Northern Territories of the Gold Coast," *Ghana Studies* 6 (2003): 5–58.

100. Ibid.

101. For examples from several parts of Africa, see various chapters in Dennis D. Cordell and Joel W. Gregory, eds., *African Population and Capitalism: Historical Perspectives* (Boulder, CO: Westview Press, 1987), and Dennis D. Cordell and Joel W. Gregory, "Labour Reservoirs and Population: French Colonial Strategies in Koudougou, Upper Volta, 1914 to 1939," *Journal of African History* 23, no. 2 (1982): 205–24.

102. Iliffe, *African Poor,* 158.

103. Ibid., 160.

104. Meredeth Turshen, "Population Growth and the Deterioration of Health: Mainland Tanzania, 1920–1960," in *African Population and Capitalism: Historical Perspectives,* ed. Dennis D. Cordell and Joel W. Gregory (Boulder, CO: Westview Press, 1987), 187–200.

105. Marcia Wright, "Justice, Women and the Social Order in Abercorn, Northeastern Rhodesia, 1897–1903," in *African Women and the Law—Historical Perspectives,* ed. M. J. Hay and M. Wright (Boston: Boston University Press, 1982), 36.

106. Dias, "Famine and Disease," 367.

107. Sean Redding, "Legal Minors and Social Children: Rural African Women and Taxation in the Transkei, South Africa," *African Studies Review* 36, no. 3 (1993): 49.

108. Riël C. D. Franzsen and Joan M. Youngman, "Mapping Property Taxes in Africa," *Land Lines* (July 2009), 8–13, available at www.lincolninst.edu/pubs/di/1648_863_Article2.pdf, accessed 4 April 2010.

109. The tax was also economically important, contributing as much as 20 percent of urban revenues in Stanleyville. Hunt, "Domesticity and Colonialism."

110. Redding, "Legal Minors," 49.

111. Ibid., 57–58.

112. Ibid., 58–66.

113. Manicom, "Ruling Relations," 452.

114. Ibid., 451.

115. Chanock, "Peculiar Sharpness," 65–88.

116. Ibid., 67.

10

African Population

Projections, 1850–1960

PATRICK MANNING

This essay focuses on the implications of national era population studies for our understanding of colonial and precolonial populations. In it, I draw upon recent and authoritative estimates of African population totals for the mid-twentieth century in order to estimate African population totals, at regional and continental levels, for each decade from 1950 back to 1850. The principal finding in this study is that colonial era populations in Africa were significantly higher than previously thought. I conclude that the 1950 continental population of just over 220 million—now well documented—is consistent with a 1930 population of 175 million.[1] The latter figure is 25 percent higher than the 140 million for 1930 that John Caldwell and Thomas Schindlmayr have recently labeled, skeptically, as a consensus.[2] Although it is a commonplace among demographic historians of Africa that colonial officials tended to underestimate the size of the populations they ruled, the magnitude of the discrepancy proposed here is surprisingly large. A corollary finding is that the growth rates of colonial era populations in Africa were much lower than has been previously assumed.[3]

The second major finding is for African populations in the precolonial era—especially in the era of large-scale export slave trade from 1650 to the late nineteenth century. These precolonial populations are here projected, similarly, to have been significantly higher than previously thought: an 1850 population of about 140 million for the African continent. This new estimate is roughly 50 percent higher than previous estimates of the continental population for 1850, which have averaged about 100 million.[4] A corollary finding, parallel to that for the colonial era of the twentieth century, is that precolonial African population growth rates were substantially lower than those implicit in previous estimates.[5]

Precolonial demography is the issue that first attracted me to the estimation of African continental and regional populations: the desire to know the impact of the external slave trade on African population. The analysis of precolonial populations led inevitably to the need to link them credibly to colonial era and national era populations and hence to the present study. I participated in the lively scholarly discussion, especially in the 1980s, about the impact of slave trade on African population.[6] In the course of this discussion, I argued that the slave exports during the eighteenth and nineteenth centuries reduced the growth of African population everywhere and brought decline in many subpopulations. According to this logic, the population of Africa may have been larger in 1700 than it was in 1850. Yet to be calculated are my revised estimates of pre-1850 African populations, based on the higher estimates of 1850 populations that emerge from the present study. Nonetheless, it is clear that, for 1700, they will show African continental population totals substantially higher than the commonly cited figure of 100 million; further, they will show very low and sometimes negative growth rates for the eighteenth century.

The findings of the present study draw attention to the widespread assumptions of past observers that African populations were relatively small and that they were growing rapidly—in both colonial and precolonial eras. These pervasive assumptions were more than demographic estimates: they emerged out of ideologies that treated African societies as technically backward, politically immature, and socially elemental. Such views of African societies enabled observers to make aggregate generalizations without exploring the details of African social interaction. As a result, colonial administrators and even modern scholars have found it easy to assume that African populations "started" (perhaps a thousand years ago) from a small base and were able to grow rapidly throughout the era of slave exports, the wars and epidemics of the nineteenth century, the oppression of the colonial conquest, and the chaotic early days of colonial rule.

The high rates of African population growth since the 1940s cannot reasonably be projected back to earlier times—certainly not the absolute growth rates and not even the relative or comparative growth rates. The methodology underlying my population estimates is laid out here in considerable detail. This methodology combines several elements, yet it relies on standard demographic principles within each element. It compares population totals and demographic rates over time, with attention to rates of change. It relies on relatively recent data as benchmarks—that is, it begins with population estimates for 1950 and 1960. It uses disaggregated data, working with relatively small regions, and pays attention to population breakdown by age, sex, race, and free or slave status. It accounts for migration. It compares population growth rates across regions, assuming that birthrates and death rates rose and fell in similar patterns for various world regions. (Specifically, I have used growth rates from India, from 1871 to 1951, as proxies for African growth rates, and I offer arguments as to why these are the best available proxies.) As a result, the methodology has definitely compensated for previous errors and oversimplifications in African population estimates, including earlier errors on my own part. There are doubtless remaining errors: I hope the analysis is transparent enough to make them relatively easy to find.[7]

Although I argue that the implications of this study are substantial, its principal purpose is rather basic. It is to develop decennial population estimates for African territories from 1960 back to 1850, in association with crude growth rates by decade.[8] The year 1850, the effective end of the transatlantic slave trade, is chosen as the earliest date of the study. These estimates are developed for modern nations and the preceding colonial territories and for appropriate subcolonial territories where these are relevant to slave trade calculations. These territorial and subcolonial estimates are then aggregated into population estimates for geographic regions and slave trade regions of Africa. Territories of North Africa and South Africa are included in these estimates, though they were not sources of large numbers of slaves, because their inclusion strengthens the basis for the continental comparison of population size, composition, and growth rates.

In the order of presentation, I begin with a discussion and comparison of African population estimates in national, colonial, and precolonial eras. The second section summarizes the methodology of my estimates for colonial era populations. Details of these estimates follow, in eight analytical steps. The concluding section provides a restatement of the main conceptual and methodological issues highlighted by these estimates. Appendices, published separately online, discuss the error margins and summarize the decennial population estimates at territorial, regional, and continental levels.[9]

African Populations: National, Colonial, and Precolonial

African populations in the national era are known in considerable detail. Although most of Africa still does not benefit from regular and systematic enumerations of whole populations, knowledge of African populations has advanced greatly since 1950 through the careful comparison and linkage of an expanding number of surveys and censuses. Estimates reported here for 1950 and after are the 2006 estimates of the United Nations Population Division, although these figures rely in turn on repeated reconsideration of data collections and analyses since 1950.[10] African population estimates for the second half of the twentieth century depend fundamentally on the great advance in the quality of African population data collection and analysis of the 1950s and 1960s.[11] That brief era of optimism and ability to invest in social services brought sample censuses and occasional general enumerations, which in some cases still serve as an effective demographic baseline.[12] The summary reports of the United Nations Economic Commission for Africa (UNECA) in the 1960s provided the first systematic overview of African population.[13]

As shown in table 10.1, the total population of the African continent has now been estimated authoritatively at 800 million for the year 2000 and at roughly 220 million for the year 1950. These figures for Africa's national period confirm a remarkably rapid rate of growth of well over 2 percent per year, brought especially by declining death rates. The life expectancy at birth rose, for sub-Saharan Africa as a whole, from 36.7 years (1950–54) to 48.6 years (1990–94), though it declined thereafter, especially in response to the HIV/AIDS epidemic.[14] This knowledge has been summarized in two comprehensive articles by Dominique Tabutin and Bruno Schoumaker.[15]

For the colonial era (roughly 1890 to 1960), three types of new data are enriching our understanding of African populations. First, the documentation of postcolonial populations sets methodological standards and empirical figures to which the colonial era estimates must be linked. Second, there have been numerous studies of the colonial era, which rely on the exploration of published colonial documents and the surveys underlying them (although there has not yet been any attempt to aggregate these studies into global population estimates for the colonial era).[16] Third, the comparison of colonial African data with the expanding knowledge of contemporaneous data from other parts of the world provides a basis for making improved estimates of African demographic rates.[17] In my analysis of the colonial era, I have drawn on each of these types of evidence and compiled them into an array of estimates of decennial growth rates as they were affected by a range of social, political, economic, and demographic variables.

In light of the newly available information, the estimates of A. M. Carr-Saunders, Walter F. Willcox, and R. R. Kuczynski for the 1930s appear to have been too low—or, equivalently, they require unreasonably high growth rates to be made consistent with the established population figures for 1950. They can only have been consistent with the known 1950 population of Africa if growth rates were well over 2 percent per year during the 1930s and 1940s. Such growth rates have been documented almost nowhere in the world for that time period, though they are not uncommon for Africa in the post-DDT years of the 1950s and 1960s. This comparison demonstrates the need for new estimates of colonial era African populations. Table 10.2 displays 1929–34 estimates of African population by colonial era authorities, and it

Table 10.1. African population in the national era: United Nations estimates

	Population 1950	Population 2000	Average annual growth rate 1950–2000 (%)
Africa	220,263,472	817,673,000	2.66%
Sub-Saharan Africa	176,150,472	676,586,000	2.73%
West & Central Africa	90,027,000	336,684,000	2.67%
East & Northeast Africa	70,446,595	275,296,000	2.76%

Source: United Nations Population Division, "World Population Prospects: The 2006 Revision."

Table 10.2. African populations in the colonial era, various estimates			
Year	*African continental population*	*Source and year of estimate*	*Annual growth rate (%) to 1950 population of 220 million*
1929	140,000,000	Willcox (1931)	2.28%
1930	145,400,000	League of Nations	2.20%
1930	143,315,000	Carr-Saunders (1936)	2.28%
1934	145,074,000	Kuczynski (1937)	2.78%
1930	175,802,302	Manning (2009)	1.13%

contrasts those figures with my estimate for 1930.[18] In addition, the table calculates the growth rate separating each estimate from the 220 million for 1950 currently estimated by the United Nations. It amply corroborates the argument of Caldwell and Schindlmayr, who have deconstructed the estimates of world population created by Willcox, Carr-Saunders, and Kuczynski, tracing their origins and essential circularity.[19] Instead, as they argue, colonial African population estimates were generally too low. (As we will see, exceptions have been documented for French Equatorial Africa and the West African savanna under French rule.)[20]

My estimates, working from national era base populations and projecting back by decade at appropriate growth rates for each African colony, permit detailed comparison with estimates of colonial governments. Table 10.3 contrasts selected populations from British and colonial censuses with my estimates.[21] It shows that the official population figures for 1911 and 1931 were well below the population projections that result from applying appropriate growth rates to the 1950 populations for the two territories listed; comparisons for the French territories of Senegal and Congo (not shown) present smaller discrepancies.

For the precolonial era—the long era ending in about 1890—population studies of Africa must address a situation in which documents are fragmentary and in which there tends to be more information on the migrations of enslaved Africans than on settled populations in Africa. The primary issue in precolonial African population history is the magnitude of African vital rates, especially birth and death rates. On these vital rates and their modification by environmental and nutritional factors, J. C. Caldwell published a thoughtful analysis in 1985; more

Table 10.3. Colonial era population estimates, selected territories				
Territory	*1911 govt est*	*1911 Manning*	*1931 govt est*	*1931 Manning*
Gold Coast*	1,503,418	3,319,464	3,163,464	4,205,084
Kenya	2,648,500	4,140,140	2,966,993	4,873,983

*Note: Gold Coast in 1911 did not include Trans-Volta Togoland (with a 1911 population of some 350,000), annexed from Germany during World War I.

recently, Dennis D. Cordell has undertaken a major review of precolonial African population.[22] Meanwhile, publication of scattered data on coastal regions has added to the store of information on precolonial African rates of birth and death.[23] Otherwise, we have progressed little beyond the early guesses of European observers on African populations and their birth and death rates.

The secondary issue in precolonial African population history is the impact of slave trade in expanding mortality and out-migration. This is the work that has kept me interested in estimates of African population.[24] That is, the present effort at back-projection to 1850 is associated with another effort at back-projection, aimed at estimating the impact of the export slave trade on African populations from the seventeenth century to the mid-nineteenth century.[25] For three decades, off and on, I have been investigating the demographic impact of slave trade on Africa. I began with slave export estimates from a region of West Africa and turned next to a demographic model for the continent, showing that attention to the age and sex distribution of those enslaved led one to recognize that exports of young adults in slavery could easily cause population decline.[26] I then implemented this model in a simulation and, with the simulation and estimates of African regional populations, concluded that African populations declined because of slave exports—from 1730 to 1850 in West and Central Africa and from 1820 to 1880 in East Africa.[27] As a result, I projected slow growth or even decline in African population for the eighteenth and nineteenth centuries and therefore larger African populations in the seventeenth century than were previously thought.[28] As I argue, our understanding of African population in one era depends on our understanding of African population in other eras.

The discussion that follows advances the case for an African population of about 140 million in 1850. If such an analysis is sustained, its further implication is that African population in 1700 may have been as much as one-seventh of the world population rather than one-tenth. If seventeenth-century Africa is seen as having had a relatively dense and stable population rather than a relatively sparse and growing population, the resulting demographic picture is likely to have substantial implications for the understanding of precolonial African history, of the place of Africa in the world, and indeed of the contours of world population.

Population estimates for other parts of the world have gone ahead, mostly with better documentary bases.[29] In the occasional worldwide summaries of population growth, recent research on African populations has been given little attention. Angus Maddison's widely quoted summary of 2001 is shown in table 10.4.[30] Maddison's figures reaffirm the common assumption that African population was marginal on a world scale but was growing at a rapid rate in both precolonial and colonial eras: he assumed African growth to have averaged 0.86 percent per year from 1820 to 1950. But a closer inspection of these same summary figures suggests some obvious corrections to the assumptions it entails. The only regions with growth rates estimated at over 1 percent per year are South America and "Western Offshoots" (North America and Australasia)—regions known to have

Table 10.4. Maddison's estimates (2001) of world population				
Region	1820 population	1913 population	1950 population	Growth, 1820–1913 (%/year)	Growth, 1913–50 (%/year)
Africa	74,200,000	124,700,000	228,300,000	0.56	1.65
Asia	710,400,000	977,600,000	1,381,900,000	0.34	0.94
Latin America	21,200,000	80,500,000	165,900,000	1.44	1.97
Europe	224,100,000	496,800,000	572,400,000	0.85	0.38
Western offshoots	11,200,000	111,400,000	176,100,000	2.50	1.25
World	1,041,100,000	1,791,000,000	2,524,500,000	0.58	0.93

received massive numbers of immigrants. Europe shows a growth rate of nearly 1 percent and was undergoing significant out-migration in the nineteenth century, but this was also the era of the European demographic transition, in which death rates fell at an unprecedented rate. No reason is given as to what propitious African conditions allowed for growth rates nearly double those of Asia. On the face of it, therefore, Maddison's estimates for African population size in the nineteenth and early twentieth centuries are unreasonably low. In the present study, as will be described, I return to the estimation of colonial and precolonial African populations with better data and more precise methodology than I used before.

Strategy and Procedure of Analysis

The overall strategy of the population estimates is to set a framework for analysis and projection of populations, make an initial set of projections, then revise and update them. I identify a base population for each national or subnational territory in the years 1950 and 1960 and then project backward at high and low rates. In projecting populations back to 1850, I attempt to estimate variations in growth rates for each territory and each decade, relying on available demographic data and hypothesized changes in epidemiology, overseas slave trade, continental slave trade, and other social and political conditions.[31] The details of the territories analyzed, base populations, and decennial growth rates—and their interactions with each other—are described in what follows at two levels of detail. First, the eight bulleted points in this section describe the full analysis in telegraphic form. Then, the remaining sections of the chapter describe the same analysis in more discursive, detailed fashion. Details of the calculations and the results of the analysis—too voluminous to present within a chapter of a collective work—are freely available online and are stored permanently in a world-historical data archive.[32]

- Step 1—Define territories: Identify standard territories (colonies and subcolonies) that can fit with postindependence African nations, colonial era population statistics, and slave trade regions.

See the map in figure 10.1 and the territorial categories in appendix B1 and appendix B2.

- Step 2—Identify base-year populations for 1950 and 1960: From UN estimates as modified by other data, project base populations by nation for 1950 and 1960. Document or interpolate for subcolony regions, and project their populations for 1950 and 1960. Estimates are summarized in appendices B1 and B2.

- Step 3—Explore data and assumptions on growth rates, 1850–1950: For colonies and subcolonies as defined in Step 1, collect available demographic data and consider the range of possible annual growth rates for decennial periods, 1850–1950, based on empirical, comparative, and speculative approaches. This step includes comparison to contemporaneous growth rates in regions of India. The range of assumptions is displayed in figure 10.2; Indian data are summarized in appendix B19.

- Step 4—Set default growth rates, 1850–1950: Select continent-wide default (that is, estimated median continental) growth rates per decade, reflecting average or expected growth rates, 1850–1950. Estimate the decennial African populations associated with these growth rates. Estimates are displayed in table 10.5 and appendix B3, with implications shown in figure 10.3.

- Step 5—Explore regional variations in growth rates. Based on a review of empirical data (from Step 3), propose estimates of positive or negative adjustments to default growth rates caused by such situations as slave trade within sub-Saharan Africa, export slave trade, disorder from slave trade, post–slave trade recovery, migration of free people to or from adjoining colonies, population decline through colonial oppression, benefits of income growth, or varying local health conditions. Summaries of regional variations in growth rates are in table 10.6 and table 10.7; details are in appendices B4–B12.

- Step 6—Estimate growth rates revised for local conditions and slave exports: Working back from 1950 to 1850 for each region, modify growth rates based on varying local conditions including slave trade (Step 5). Revised growth rates are displayed in appendices B13 and B14.

- Step 7—Calculate low-, mid-, and high-population projections, 1850–1950: To the revised growth rates from Step 6, add tolerances of plus and minus 0.1 percent (or one per thousand) to each earlier decennial growth rate for each territory, so that there will be a high and low growth rate at each stage. Calculate low-, mid-, and high-population estimates for each region in each decade, and aggregate them as appropriate. Table 10.8 of this text compares the populations of the continent's various slave trade regions in 1850 and 1950; full details of projections are displayed in appendices B15–B18.

- Step 8—Review error margins: Discuss sources of error in data and methodology, techniques for verifying or rejecting the hypothesized population estimates, and alternative methods of analysis. This discussion is presented in appendix A.

Step 1—Defining Territories for Analysis

With the increasing availability of regional and subregional data, it is now realistic to conduct the data collection and analysis at low levels of territorial aggregation rather than at continental or subcontinental levels.[33] Results analyzed at the level of colonial territories and subterritories can then be aggregated to the levels of slave trade regions and continental regions and for Africa as a whole. Just as breaking down populations by their age and sex composition increases the precision and accuracy of the analysis, so does breaking down populations by relatively coherent subregions.

In the regional parameters of analysis, I have adopted the convention of relying on colonial and postcolonial boundaries, in an attempt to work with consistent territories throughout the three centuries of the analysis. In a modification of my earlier analysis, the territories are now organized into several types and levels. At the highest level, I identify a fairly standard set of six geographic regions for Africa (see appendix B1).[34] At the next level, I identify eighteen slave trade regions for parts of the continent that exported slaves, plus five demographic regions for North Africa and one for southern Africa (see figure 10.1 and appendix B2). North Africa and southern Africa are included in this analysis partly to achieve comprehensive estimates of African populations from 1850 to 1960 and partly because comparison of these data with other African data may improve the quality of estimates for all regions. The third level is that of colonial and national territories of the continent. But since colonial and national boundaries do not always fit the historical regions of slave trade, the fourth level consists of relevant subcolonial territories and populations by racial designation (see figure 10.1 and appendices B1 and B2). Thus, the northern portions of Gold Coast, Togo, Dahomey, and Nigeria are broken out from the southern portions of those territories, as the northern portions functioned as parts of the slave-trading system of the savanna rather than of the Atlantic coast. Similarly, Cabinda is broken out from Angola because its slaves were exported through Loango; Katanga is broken out from Congo because its slaves were exported through Angola. Further, for Mozambique, Lesotho, and South Africa, people labeled as Europeans and Asians, not liable to enslavement, are calculated separately from those labeled as Africans and Coloured, from

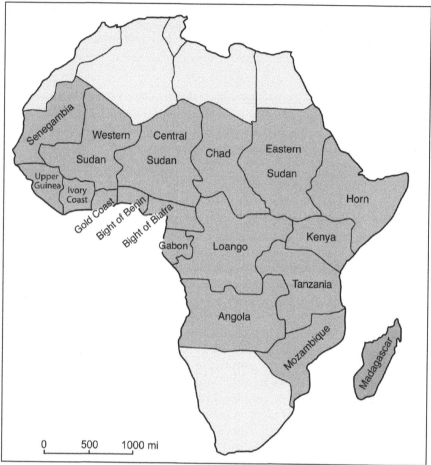

Figure 10.1. Slave-trade regions of Africa. *Map by Claudia Walters*

whom slaves were drawn.[35] In practice, this fourth and lowest level of territorial aggregation—consisting of a mix of colonial territories, subterritories, and racial groups within them—is the level at which data collection and analysis takes place. In appendices B4–B18 and the spreadsheets that underlie them, data and calculations are processed at the level of individual cells, and then they are aggregated geographically for each time period. The results are presented for colonial territories, slave trade regions, and continental regions.

A further set of considerations has been used in defining the slave trade regions and their constituent subregions. Although estimation of slave exports is not a principal or immediate objective of this study, the regions must be designed so that they are appropriate for such estimates at a later stage. Some territories exported captives uniquely into the Atlantic market, whereas others exported captives into both the Atlantic market and the trans-Saharan market. Transatlantic captives were dominantly male, but trans-Saharan captives were dominantly female. Slave exports across the Atlantic and the Sahara for each decade are therefore broken down by region of origin and also by sex, in order to project the impact of slave exports on the population of each region.[36] A second problem in the accounting of the slave trade involves regions that exported few slaves or no slaves. Such regions included southeast Cameroon, Gabon, parts of Ubangi-Shari, Southern Rhodesia, Rwanda, Burundi, Uganda, and the Orientale and Kivu regions of Congo. So far, I have included each of these regions within an adjoining slave trade region; the alternative would be to make them into separate regions. Though these regions were not active in slave exports, analyzing their population growth is important in order to yield a conclusion on whether their demographic rates were similar to or different from those of slave-exporting regions. Shona territories of Southern Rhodesia, for instance, seem to have avoided the slave trade of neighboring areas of Mozambique during the nineteenth century. Does that mean that Shona populations rose significantly in proportion to those of Mozambique in that century? Life expectancy seems to have been higher among the Shona; did their birthrates decline in compensation? I have tended to assume "natural fertility rates," which could not easily be adjusted, but this analysis of colonial era populations offers an opportunity to reconsider that issue.[37]

Step 2—Identifying Base Populations

I have chosen to identify base populations for 1950 and 1960, thus including the growth rate linking them, on the argument that this provides the most robust statement of each base population. I have based my estimates first on UN estimates of 2006.[38] (For Ghana, where the 1960 census was exceptionally strong, one may still ask whether the current UN estimates are improvements over the initial figures; for Nigeria, population estimates for 1950 and 1960 remain problematic.)[39] Both 1950 and 1960 are treated as base years, but in practice, the 1950 population estimate for each territory is used as the basis for projection of earlier populations. These figures show African continental populations of 220 million in 1950 and 278 million in 1960, linked by an annual growth rate of 2.4 percent; in that interval, regional growth rates ranged from 2.1 percent in Central Africa to 2.9 percent in southern Africa.

Step 3—Exploring Data and Assumptions on Growth Rates, 1850–1950

The main authorities with which to begin in making estimates of African demographic rates before 1950 are (1) colonial era annual reports and compilations, plus occasional large-scale reviews, notably the massive 1948 survey by R. R. Kuczynski, and (2) postcolonial scholarship reviewing the documents of the colonial era, notably the 1987 collection of essays edited by Dennis Cordell and Joel Gregory and the 1990 collection edited by Bruce Fetter.[40] There are many other commentaries on aspects of colonial African demography, on which I have drawn in varying degrees.[41] Official reports on colonial era populations are the principal sources with which the authorities have worked; the censuses and estimates for South Africa provide the longest time frame.[42]

The clear judgment of recent authorities is that colonial era population estimates systematically underestimated the size of African populations: low estimates of African population characterized censuses in South Africa as elsewhere on the continent.[43] Several related types of bias kept estimates low, and these downward biases had not been overcome even by the end of the colonial era. First, officials estimating populations did not visit or estimate for all the regions within their territory. Second, they gave prime attention to counting taxable male adults. Third, when they included female adults, they still tended to underestimate the number of children. Fourth, where populations were dispersed, many households were left out even in areas that were enumerated. Colonial officials sought to use rules of thumb—ratios of family size per house or per head of household—but these did not generally overcome the downward bias.

However, some areas under French rule were exceptions to this pattern. In West Africa, the savanna and sahelian territories that are now Mali, Burkina Faso, and Niger may have been overestimated in population, and the Central African territories that are now Central African Republic, Gabon, and Congo-Brazzaville were similarly at risk for overestimates in population. The analyses of Dennis Cordell, Joel Gregory, and Raymond Gervais are distinctive in making the case for colonial overestimation rather than underestimation of population in these territories.[44] At the same time, these studies are among the most detailed in arguing that colonial records exaggerated the rate of growth of African populations—a conclusion that is implicit in the work of all recent scholars on African population.[45]

Further, recent authorities appear to agree that colonial population estimates were often erratic and arbitrary. Annual repetitions of unchanging population figures for a region or, more commonly, annual growth at an unchanging rate provide the most common examples of arbitrary reporting. Ratios of family size per household varied sharply by year and from official to official.[46] Shifts in territorial organization compounded the inconsistencies in reporting. Tabulating and aggregating colonial estimates does not in itself provide any way of checking or correcting these distortions. As a result, the alternative adopted here—projecting back from 1950 population estimates using hypothesized growth rates—has some clear advantages as a way of estimating African populations before 1950.[47]

For the period from the 1930s to the 1960s, colonial reports on population are relatively comprehensive, including some censuses and commonly including useful qualitative descriptions of population characteristics such as migration. Prior to the 1930s, from the beginning of the twentieth century through the 1920s, colonial statistics are scattered but may include qualitative descriptions and useful comments on migration. Small colonies and urban areas, such as Gambia and Lagos, tend to have the best reports. For the nineteenth century, some statistics are available for the limited regions under colonial rule, such as Natal and parts of Senegal, but for most of the continent, one is left with guesswork. During the last

half of the nineteenth century, populations were disturbed by large-scale enslavement and migration in many areas of the continent, making them more difficult
to estimate. Nonetheless, imperial and colonial observers recorded useful estimates
of the volume of slave trade in that era.[48]

North African populations included many people with ancestry in sub-Saharan
Africa. Trans-Saharan slave trade reached a nineteenth-century plateau of some
20,000 persons per year into the 1860s and then declined; many other black people
had gone to North Africa in times before 1850. North African population figures, at
the aggregate level, give no breakdown by color, so it will require some more indirect methods to trace the links between sub-Saharan and North African populations.
Meanwhile, the aggregate estimates of population size and growth for North Africa,
along with contemporary commentaries on demographic rates, will make it possible
to assess the North African portion of the continent's population back to 1850.

These qualitative and quantitative data, in association with demographic assumptions, are now to support estimates of net population growth rates for African territories from 1960 back to 1850. To convey a sense of the outside limits of such
speculation, figure 10.2 displays estimates of population growth at low, medium, and
high rates. The figure begins (at right) with a 1960 population of 278 million and a
1950 population of 220 million and projects population back to 1850 at constant annual rates from a low of 2 per thousand (0.2 percent) to a high of 20 per thousand (2
percent). It shows that, at 0.2 percent annual growth, a 1950 population of 220 million corresponds to an 1850 population of 180 million, whereas at 2.0 percent annual
growth, the same 1950 population corresponds to an 1850 population of just over 30
million. Clearly, the reality we seek lies somewhere between these extremes.[49]

If it may be assumed that changes in population growth rates throughout the
tropics were somewhat similar, then it is relevant to consider growth rates in
the well-documented population of India as proxies for African growth rates.[50]
Appendix B19 shows decennial growth rates calculated from census returns for

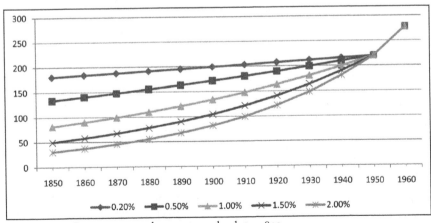

Figure 10.2. Constant growth rates, 1950 back to 1850

regions of south and central India for which the administration was consistent. The Indian case suggests that there were no growth rates as high as 2.0 percent before 1940 and that growth rates as high as 1.0 percent were rare before 1920. Of forty-one observations from 1871 to 1921, ten showed annual growth rates of over 1 percent, eight showed growth rates between 0.5 percent and 1.0 percent, nine showed growth rates between zero and 0.5 percent, and fourteen showed negative growth rates. The apparently high growth rates of the 1880s (averaging 1.2 percent) are probably an artifact of improved enumeration in 1891.[51]

India cannot, of course, be taken as a straightforward model for Africa. It was under stable British administration from the early nineteenth century. There are reasons to expect that African growth rates should have been lower than those for India, especially in the nineteenth-century circumstances of slave trade and in the tumultuous era of conquest and establishment of European administration.[52] Overall, however, the available Indian growth rates are very helpful in suggesting the range of African growth rates in contemporary periods.

Step 4—Setting Default Growth Rates

After evaluation of the data and alternative assumptions summarized in Step 3, I have chosen to project preliminary or "default" decennial growth rates for Africa as a whole, ranging from a low of 0.2 percent per year for the 1850s to a high of 1.5 percent per year for the 1940s. These are estimates of average or expected crude growth rates, not accounting for export slave trade. My overall assumption is that death rates declined at an accelerating rate from the mid-nineteenth to the mid-twentieth century, while birthrates remained relatively constant, so that net rates of population growth increased over time throughout the continent.[53] For the 1910s and 1930s, I assumed slight declines in growth rates from preceding decades because of war, economic depression, and fertility decline, in parallel with apparent declines in India. I assumed growth rates of no more than 0.2 percent in the mid-nineteenth century because of the high insecurity of that era.

Figure 10.3 shows these default growth rates and also shows the tolerance that would result from adding and subtracting a growth rate of 0.1 percent cumulatively, each decade. In appendix A, this elementary estimate of an error tolerance is shown to be consistent with a more sophisticated test of the limits of the expected error in these estimates.[54] The projection based on these

Table 10.5. Africa: default growth rates	
Decade	*Annual growth rate in percent*
1951–60	2.4
1941–50	1.5
1931–40	0.8
1921–30	1.0
1911–20	0.2
1901–10	0.3
1891–1900	0.3
1881–90	0.3
1871–80	0.3
1861–70	0.2
1851–60	0.2

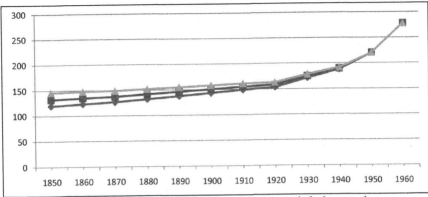

Figure 10.3. Projected continental African population at default growth rates, showing tolerances

assumptions shows low and high continental African populations of 119 and 149 million, respectively, for 1850 as compared with 220 million for 1950 and 278 million for 1960. The resulting mid-level estimates for African population—133 million in 1850 and 152 million in 1900—are significantly higher than the received estimates of Willcox, Carr-Saunders, Jean-Noël Biraben, and others.[55] The assumption of relatively low growth rates for the nineteenth century leads logically to these higher estimates of African population size in the nineteenth century and, indeed, in earlier times. (As we will see, further specification of regional growth rates yields still higher estimates of African population.) One implication is that, since these population estimates are higher than previous estimates, the negative impact of slave trade on these populations will tend to be estimated as less severe than in my previous estimates.[56]

Step 5—Exploring Data and Assumptions on Local Conditions

I turn now to the issue of regional variations in growth rates according to any specific circumstances that can be identified. Before attempting a detailed analysis of the available data, I propose a list of social circumstances for which one can project increases or decreases in population growth rates. Table 10.6 lists the eight

Table 10.6. Situational modification to growth rate

Type of modification	Maximum annual magnitude (percent)
a. Slave-trade disorder	−0.2
b. Sub-Saharan slave exchanges	+ or −0.3
c. Sub-Saharan slave exports	−0.6
d. Post-slave-trade recovery	+0.4
e. Colonial disorder	−0.4
f. Income growth	+0.2
g. Migration of free people	+ or −0.6
h. Epidemic and famine	−0.5

situations I propose, along with estimates of the magnitude of the annual effect of each situation on population growth.[57]

The first three situations or categories of modification account for the impact of slave trade. Enslavement and its demographic impact are known to have been at a high level for many African regions in the nineteenth century. Though the export slave trade across the Atlantic ended in the 1850s, exports across the Indian Ocean continued into the 1890s, and exports to the Sahara and North Africa continued to 1900. The retention of captives within sub-Saharan Africa, long a by-product of slave exports, grew as a proportion of total enslavement and continued in some regions well past 1900. The flows of captives included those from the West African savanna to Saharan oases, the enslavement of people from the periphery of the great West African states of Sokoto and Samori, and the settlement of slaves along the routes from the Upper Congo and Lake Malawi to the Swahili coast. The task of assessing these regional flows and the overall magnitude of this nineteenth-century forced migration is intractable, and few serious efforts have been made to quantify it.[58] For instance, up through the eighteenth century, the number of slaves exported from Africa may serve as an adequate index of the overall volume of African enslavement, but this approximation is no longer satisfactory for the nineteenth century.[59] The regions with the greatest slave exports after 1850 were Mozambique, Tanzania, the Horn, the Eastern Sudan, and the Central Sudan. In earlier estimates, I concluded that populations declined significantly as a result of slave exports as late as the 1880s in Mozambique and Tanzania and that growth rates were slowed significantly for the remaining slave-exporting areas in the last half of the nineteenth century.[60]

To account for the impact of enslavement, I have prepared matrixes for each African territory and each decade from the 1850s through the 1890s, and I have made rough estimates of eight variables for each cell:[61]

    i.   numbers enslaved
    ii.   number of captives retained within the territory
    iii. mortality upon enslavement
    iv.   seasoning mortality of retained captives[62]
    v.   number of captive out-migrants from the region
    vi.   number of captive immigrants to the region
    vii. seasoning mortality of immigrant captives
    viii. number of out-migrants from sub-Saharan Africa

Of these factors, *slave trade disorder* is taken to be the sum of (iii) and (iv), the enslavement-induced mortality within each region.[63] The *sub-Saharan slave exchanges* are taken to be the difference between exports and imports of captives within any region, or the level of (vi) less the sum of (v) and (vii). The *sub-Saharan slave exports* (viii)—exports across the Sahara and the oceans—have been estimated, with decennial totals shown in appendix B6.[64] These estimates begin as a mix of population sizes and rates of migration and mortality; they are converted into estimated changes in annual population growth rates for each region in each decade. The big difference here was that export slave trade and its impact halted in West and Central Africa from the 1860s but continued until 1900 in East Africa, the Horn, and the northern savanna.

The remaining five regional variations in growth rate were important especially for the twentieth century. The end of slave trade commonly coincided with the colonial conquest, at times ranging from the 1870s to after 1900: see appendices B4–B6 for the timing of colonial conquest and the end of slave trade in each territory. Once slave trade ended, the return in security is presumed to have led not only to a decline in death rate but also to an increase in birthrate. This *post-slave trade recovery* enabled growth rates to rise from default levels by an estimated 0.4 percent per year for one or two decades.

But colonial regimes, though they brought an imperial peace, also brought their own disorder. Especially for French and perhaps Belgian Central Africa, colonial regimes brought population decline, largely through fertility decline, which in turn was notably a result of disease spread in particular by African and European colonial officials. More generally, colonial recruitment of forced labor had negative effects on seasonal production cycles, thus affecting nutrition and mortality. For this type of situation, I project that *colonial disorder* brought reductions in growth rates by as much as 0.3 percent per year, for periods from a decade to as much as thirty years (see appendix B8). For other colonies, such as West African coastal colonies, *income growth,* especially through expansion of agricultural exports, brought higher fertility, adding to default rates by up to 0.2 percent per year for as long as the boom lasted. Epidemic and famine, finally, could have impacts that brought high mortality, reducing population growth rates by as much as 0.5 percent per year but usually for no more than one to three years at a time.[65]

Having established a typology of varying modifications to the prevailing rates of population growth for each time period, the next step is to apply it and categorize each African region according to the situation it faced in each period. Table 10.7 provides a qualitative summary of the modifications I have made, for each territory and each decade, to the default growth rates displayed in table 10.5. In cases where a cell is left blank, it is assumed that the default growth rate for that period is applicable to the region. Quantitative details of these modifications are shown in appendices B13 and B14, which display the categories and magnitudes of growth rate modifications that I estimated for each decade, by territory. These estimates, though preliminary and speculative, are at least explicitly identified, to encourage updating based on more thorough evaluation of the descriptive literature for each territory.

Table 10.7. Outline of modifications to growth rate			
Region	*1850s–90s*	*1900s–20s*	*1930s–50s*
North Africa	c) slave immigration g) free immigration	g) free immigration	
West African savanna	a) slaving disorder b) slave exchanges c) slave emigration	d) post-slaving recovery e) colonial disorder g) free out-migration	g) free out-migration
West African coast	b) slave exchanges d) post-slaving recovery	f) income growth g) free immigration	f) income growth g) free immigration
Central Africa	a) slaving disorder b) slave exchanges d) post-slaving recovery	e) colonial disorder h) epidemic	
Northeast Africa	a) slaving disorder b) slave exchanges c) slave emigration h) epidemic	d) post-slaving recovery e) colonial disorder h) epidemic	
East Africa	a) slaving disorder b) slave exchanges c) slave emigration h) epidemic	d) post-slaving recovery e) colonial disorder h) epidemic	f) income growth
Southern Africa	e) colonial disorder	f) income growth g) free immigration	g) free immigration

Note: See appendix B14 for details.

Step 6—*Exploring Growth Rates Revised for Local Conditions and Slave Exports*

Summarizing the estimates of Step 5 makes it possible to estimate growth rates and then populations for each territory and subterritorial region, working decade by decade from the 1940s back to the 1850s. That is, for each region within each decade, I locate and summarize the modifications to growth rate because of local conditions and slave exports (from Step 5). This process yields a revised growth rate for each decade, as well as a revised population for the beginning of each decade. Appendices B12–B14 display the data on regional growth rates calculated as a result of this process for each of the slave trade regions and for four of the ten decades under consideration.[66]

Step 7—*Calculating High- and Low-Population Projections, 1850–1960*

Results of the previous sections are computed for each territory and then are tabulated for geographic and slave trade regions. Although the detailed analysis and revision of growth rates is best conducted at the localized level of the colony or subcolony, one can also learn from review and critique of aggregate results of the estimations.[67] For instance, table 10.8 compares these estimates of

Table 10.8. Mid-level estimated populations, by slave-trade regions

	1850	% 1850 Population	1950	% 1950 Population	Difference in %
Senegambia	2,020,997	1.9%	3,529,000	2.2%	+0.3%
Upper Guinea	3,562,752	3.3%	5,892,000	3.6%	+0.3%
Ivory Coast	1,568,935	1.5%	2,505,000	1.5%	+0.0%
Gold Coast	3,043,167	2.8%	5,381,839	3.3%	+0.5%
Bight of Benin	4,114,997	3.8%	7,222,478	4.4%	+0.6%
Bight of Biafra	6,162,335	5.7%	10,852,100	6.7%	+1.0%
Forest	433,858	0.4%	639,856	0.4%	+0.0%
Loango	7,487,167	7.0%	10,555,304	6.5%	-0.5%
Angola	4,015,345	3.7%	6,377,597	3.9%	+0.2%
Mozambique	8,392,608	7.8%	10,540,905	6.5%	-1.4%
Madagascar	2,816,274	2.6%	4,234,000	2.6%	+0.0%
Tanzania	11,208,394	10.4%	14,500,789	8.9%	-1.5%
Kenya	8,260,923	7.7%	13,691,000	8.4%	+0.7%
Horn	13,522,949	12.6%	21,901,000	13.4%	+0.8%
Eastern Sudan	6,557,378	6.1%	9,190,000	5.6%	-0.5%
Chad	2,442,180	2.3%	3,086,000	1.9%	-0.4%
Central Sudan	15,940,740	14.8%	24,564,422	15.1%	+0.3%
Western Sudan	5,823,418	5.4%	8,502,161	5.2%	-0.2%
Total[1]	107,374,417	100 %	163,165,451	100 %	

Source: Appendix B18

[1] The totals refer to populations for the African regions from which captives were exported, and
  thus exclude North Africa and Southern Africa; the percentages refer to portions of those totals.

population by slave trade regions for 1950 and 1850. Figures for slave trade regions in table 10.8 are for black populations (those that were liable to enslavement), and the regions listed are limited to those in which people were enslaved. Regional percentages of continental population, shown for 1850 and 1950, indicate which regions grew and which declined during that century in relative terms. Those for which projected populations *grew* relatively included especially the Bight of Biafra and Bight of Benin but also Kenya, Gold Coast, Upper Guinea, Angola, and Senegambia. Those that *declined* relatively included especially Tanzania and Mozambique but also Loango, Eastern Sudan, and Chad. Relatively unchanged were the Horn, Ivory Coast, Madagascar, Central Sudan, and Western Sudan. For the Bights of Biafra and Benin, slave exports ended relatively early, and prosperity fed colonial era growth rates. For Tanzania and Mozambique, the prolonging of slave exports to the end of the nineteenth century slowed long-term growth.

The three Sudan regions and the Horn, though they exported slaves until the end of the nineteenth century, exported smaller proportions of their population than Tanzania and Mozambique.

A New View of African Demographic History

This essay has combined available data and updated assumptions to provide a new view of African demographic history from 1850 to 1950. This view is strikingly at variance with the picture given in previous global assessments of African population. This concluding section restates the results of the analysis, restates the methods that have led to these results, and identifies the further research needed in order to verify and pursue the results.

Results of the analysis indicate a continental African population of 140 million in 1850 that changed little to 1920, then began accelerating in its growth to a 1960 population of 280 million and a 2000 population nearing 800 million. Growth rates reached a peak in the 1960s and have since declined only slowly from that peak. The biggest numerical change in African population took place from 1950 to 2000, but the biggest change in the structure and organization of African population—the demographic regime—took place from 1900 to 1950.

The century beginning in 1850 (but especially the period after 1900) was unquestionably an era of massive demographic transformation. This analysis argues that African growth rates for the nineteenth and early twentieth centuries were lower than previously thought, with the result that African populations in the nineteenth and early twentieth centuries were considerably higher than previously thought.[68] African population thus went from a brutal steady state in the nineteenth century to an era of initiation and expansion of growth, but under colonial conditions, that by no means eliminated brutality. Africans in this period experienced dramatic changes in vital rates, accelerating rates of growth, sharp changes in migration patterns, and the beginnings of spectacular urbanization. African life expectancies—though low in comparison with those of other regions and perhaps changing with a lag—nonetheless lengthened impressively. For the early nineteenth century, life expectancies at birth are estimated to have been in the range of 20 to 25 years; life expectancies had risen to 35 years by 1950.[69] Similarly, African populations went from crude growth rates of no more than 0.2 percent to rates averaging over 2.0 percent. Of course, there was almost equally massive demographic change, far better documented, for Africa from 1950 to the present. By 1990, the life expectancy at birth was commonly over 50 years. (The subsequent HIV/AIDS epidemic, however, has reduced life expectancies in several countries back to levels of the 1960s—a devastating reversal.)

This new view of African demographic history arises not as the result of a single discovery but from the application of comprehensive methods that reach across time, space, and topics to achieve greater internal consistency and empirical fit for the interpretation. This work with scanty evidence involves the assembly of official documents and scholarly studies, but it also entails systematic modeling of demographic patterns and the comparison of data and assumptions over space and time.[70]

Most obviously, linking postcolonial to colonial African history clarified a gap in previous reasoning. For too long, scholars ignored the discrepancy between the dense populations documented since the 1960s and the much smaller populations estimated for the 1930s and before, though Caldwell and Schindlmayr sounded the alarm on the issue in 2002. The estimates proposed here, based on modifications of proxies drawn from India, yield populations that can reasonably be linked to those known for the late twentieth century. These new and higher figures for 1900–1950 are generally consistent with the understanding that official counts were systematically too low. The substantial underestimation by colonial era administrators and demographers was partly a result of their limited skills and resources. But their undercount also resulted from widely shared European views of African backwardness.

The ideological dimension to African population history has thus been significant, and it may remain so. Despite wide recognition of the high level of violence in precolonial Africa, some scholars have been willing to assume robust population growth for the eighteenth and nineteenth centuries. For the colonial era, assumptions of relatively small and rapidly growing populations were consistent with visions of African regions as frontier zones where newly arrived populations grew rapidly, and they were consistent as well with visions of colonial rule as benign and socially progressive. The more complex realities of conquest and forced labor fit better with the larger populations and slower growth rates proposed here.

The present overview of changes in African population would benefit from additional work to corroborate its outlines and, especially, to develop more detailed demographic analyses by region, time period, and topic. The overall changes in African population, dramatic though they have been, are known only in vague and inconsistent detail. When and how did the crucial transformations in fertility and mortality take place? At local levels, observers have argued that fertility rates rose in the twentieth century, though demographers tend to assume that the rise was in infant survival rather than fertility. But even if population growth came more from decreased mortality rather than increased fertility, what was the age profile of the declining mortality? How do increased African growth rates compare to those from other world regions? I hope that further efforts to identify territorially specific rates of crude population growth rates, along the lines of this exploration, may do much to indicate whether estimates of sufficient precision can be developed to yield answers on these questions. Although dispersed censuses and other enumerations exist for African populations in the nineteenth century and before, they are not set in clear context.[71] Demographic data are scattered (as with so many records on Africa) in documents created and held by a welter of individuals, agencies, and governments, in many languages and with inconsistent terms of reference. Records of European governments are more numerous from the late nineteenth century, but they are focused on tax collection rather than a systematic demographic concern. Even as censuses became more thorough in the 1960s, they were less than exhaustive, and in any case, they documented populations that had changed greatly in structure from earlier times. Research on African demographic history is not simple work, but it is valuable work, and it is to be hoped that skilled and adequately funded research teams can be supported.

Understanding the causes of Africa's pervasive demographic change, especially from 1900 to 1950, is of great importance for learning about the African past and also for historical demography in general. The possible causes of demographic change include changes in nutrition, the rise and fall of social violence, epidemics, changing immunities, the nature and effectiveness of government, public health practices, changes in the nature and availability of traditional and modern medicine, and the connections brought by commerce and communication. The commonly offered explanations for demographic transition extend only with difficulty to colonial Africa, so that further analysis of African population change may be relevant for other regions. Modern medical and public health practices, though valuable where applied, were simply not applied in sufficient degree to have brought the reductions in death rates that took place in Africa before 1940. Antimalarial campaigns beginning in the 1940s—the spraying of DDT along with the dissemination of chloroquine and antibiotics—brought rapid declines in mortality, but these changes do not explain the earlier declines in mortality. These new measures were applied unevenly across the continent, so that DDT seems to have been most effectively used in southern Africa whereas chloroquine was more important for malaria reduction in East Africa.[72] Other possible causes of demographic change include natural transformations in the epidemiological atmosphere (that is, diseases may have become less virulent), social changes resulting from the end of large-scale enslavement, improved nutrition resulting from declining oppression and expanding markets, and perhaps development of new African healing practices.

Finally, the results of this study, in arguing that nineteenth-century African population was at least 40 percent higher than the commonly cited aggregate figures, challenge the relative marginalization of Africa in studies of world history. The larger population figures imply that African societies had higher levels of productivity than is commonly attributed to them. At the same time, the stasis and even decline in African populations of the nineteenth century suggest that a combination of global conditions and domestic crises were constraining life in Africa in this era of imperialism and industrialization, when populations elsewhere in the world were growing at robust rates.

Notes

I wish to express my deep appreciation to Karl Ittmann, Dennis D. Cordell, and Ian Pool for their detailed and insightful critiques of earlier versions of this study and to Gregory Maddox for engaging me in this project and seeing me through its early stages. In addition, I am grateful to John C. Caldwell for a discussion that clearly conveyed the work of early demographers of Africa and inspired certain key analytical devices in this study. None of these individuals, however, are responsible for the specific arguments advanced here. In addition, Scott C. Nickleach verified all of the calculations and coauthored appendix A on error margins.

1. The UN 2006 estimates for continental African population are 223 million for 1950 and 281 million for 1960. UN Population Division, "World Population Prospects: The 2006 Revision," available at http://esa.un.org/unpp/.

2. John C. Caldwell and Thomas Schindlmayr, "Historical Population Estimates: Unraveling the Consensus," in *Population and Development Review* 28, no. 2 (2002): 183–204.

3. By "finding," I mean a mix of empirical, comparative, and deductive findings, rather than strictly empirical documentation. The purpose of this study is to detail the various findings and how they have been linked together.

4. Willcox estimated the 1850 population of Africa at 100 million; Carr-Saunders reduced the figure to 95 million. See Walter F. Willcox, "Increase in the Population of the Earth and of the Continents since 1650," *International Migrations*, vol. 2, *Interpretations* (New York: National Bureau of Economic Research, 1931), 76; A. M. Carr-Saunders, *World Population* (London: Frank Cass, 1964), 34–35, 42.

5. Willcox projected no population growth for Africa from 1500 to 1850; Carr-Saunders even projected population decline in that period. Both assumed rapid growth thereafter. I am certain that their growth rates for the period 1850–1930 are too high; it is even possible that their estimates of flat or negative growth rates for the period before 1850 are too high. See Willcox, "Increase in the Population," 78, and Carr-Saunders, *World Population*, 42.

6. Patrick Manning, "The Enslavement of Africans: A Demographic Model," *Canadian Journal of African Studies* 15, no. 3 (1981): 499–526; John K. Thornton, "The Demographic Effect of the Slave Trade on Western Africa, 1500–1800," in *African Historical Demography*, ed. Christopher Fyfe and David McMaster (Edinburgh: African Studies Centre, 1981), 2:691–720; Joseph Inikori, "Introduction," in *Forced Migration: The Impact of the Export Slave Trade on African Societies*, ed. Joseph Inikori (New York: Africana Publishers, 1982), 13–60; Roger Anstey, *The Atlantic Slave Trade and British Abolition* (Cambridge: Cambridge University Press, 1975); John D. Fage, "Slavery and the Slave Trade in the Context of West African History," *Journal of African History* 10, no. 3 (1969): 393–404.

7. See Step 8, in a later section of this chapter, for fuller discussions of errors.

8. In accordance with the current practice of the UN Population Division, I have defined census points as 1950, etc., and decades as 1950–59, 1940–49, etc.

9. Patrick Manning, "African Population Estimates, 1850–1960: Appendices," archived in the World-Historical Dataverse, www.dataverse.pitt.edu/archive/users.php. Included in this archive are appendix A, "Review of Error Margins," by Scott Nickleach and Patrick Manning, and appendix B, "Statistical Tables," including appendices B1 through B19 as identified in the text and notes of this chapter. The same material is also available on the Ohio University Press/Swallow Press Web site at http://www.ohioswallow.com/book/The+Demographics+of+Empire.

10. Through the work of the UN Population Division, documentation on populations since 1950 has been reworked repeatedly, so that updates as recently as 2006 have revised estimates for 1950 and all the years thereafter; see www.un.org/esa/population/unpop.htm.

11. For major collections of demographic analysis conducted during the era of decolonization, see K. M. Barbour and R. M. Prothero, eds., *Essays on African Population* (Westport, CT: Greenwood, 1961); William Brass, Ansley J. Coale, Paul Demeny, Don F.

Heisel, Frank Lorimer, Anatole Romaniuk, and Etienne Van de Walle, *The Demography of Tropical Africa* (Princeton, NJ: Princeton University Press, 1968); John C. Caldwell, *Population Growth and Family Change in Africa: The New Urban Elite in Ghana* (Canberra: Australian National University Press, 1968); and John C. Caldwell and Chukuka Okonjo, eds., *The Population of Tropical Africa* (London: Longman, 1968). See also Ansley J. Coale and Paul Demeny, with Barbara Vaughan, *Regional Model Life Tables and Stable Populations,* 2nd ed. (New York: Academic Press, 1983); and R. P. Moss and R. J. A. R. Rathbone, eds., *The Population Factor in African Studies* (London: University of London Press, 1975).

12. Chukuka Okonjo, "A Preliminary Medium Estimate of the 1962 Mid-year Population of Nigeria," in *The Population of Tropical Africa,* ed. John C. Caldwell and Chukuka Okonjo (London: Longman, 1968), 78–96; B. Gil and K. T. de Graft-Johnson, *1960 Population of Ghana,* vol. 5, *General Report* (Accra: Census Office, 1964).

13. UN Economic Commission for Africa, *Demographic Handbook for Africa* (Addis Ababa: Economic Commission for Africa, Population Division, 1968); United Nations, "World Population Prospects."

14. By 2000, life expectancies at birth declined to levels near those of 1960 in much of southern Africa.

15. Dominique Tabutin and Bruno Schoumaker, "La démographie de l'Afrique au sud du Sahara des années 1950 aux années 2000: Synthèse des changements et bilan statistique," *Population* 59, nos. 3–4 (2000): 521–621; Tabutin and Schoumaker, "La démographie du monde arabe et du Moyen-Orient des années 1950 aux années 2000: Synthèse des changements et bilan statistique," *Population* 60, nos. 5–6 (2005): 611–724. For an authoritative overview of advances in demographic studies of Africa, see Etienne van de Walle, Patrick O. Ohadike, and Mpembele D. Sala-Diakanda, eds., *The State of African Demography* (Brussels: IUSSP, 1988).

16. Dennis D. Cordell and Joel W. Gregory, eds., *African Population and Capitalism: Historical Perspectives,* 2nd ed. (Madison: University of Wisconsin Press, 1994); Bruce Fetter, ed., *Demography from Scanty Evidence: Central Africa in the Colonial Era* (Boulder, CO: Lynne Rienner, 1990). The present study develops continental estimates, but it does so deductively from aggregate populations and estimated growth rates, rather than inductively through aggregation of local studies.

17. For a convenient list of major summaries of world population data and estimates, see Angus Maddison, *The World Economy: A Millennial Perspective* (Paris: Development Centre of the Organisation for Economic Co-operation and Development, 2001).

18. Sources for table 10.2 are: Willcox, "Increase in the Population," 78; Carr-Saunders, *World Population,* 18, 34–35; R. R. Kuczynski, *Demographic Survey of the British Colonial Empire,* 3 vols. (London: Oxford University Press, 1948), 1. For other estimates of African continental population, see Maddison, *World Economy;* Jean-Noël Biraben, "Essai sur l'évolution du nombre des hommes," *Population* 34, no. 1 (1979): 13–25; C. McEvedy and R. Jones, *Atlas of World Population History* (Harmondsworth, UK: Penguin, 1978); and John D. Durand, "The Modern Expansion of World Population," *Proceedings of the American Philosophical Society* 111 (1967): 136–59.

19. Caldwell and Schindlmayr, "Historical Population Estimates."

20. See note 44.

21. Table 10.3 sources are: For Gold Coast—Kuczynski, *Demographic Survey,* 1:418–419; for Kenya—Kuczynski, *Demographic Survey,* 2:144–45; for Manning estimates—appendix B5.

22. J. C. Caldwell, "The Social Repercussions of Colonial Rule: Demographic Aspects," in *General History of Africa,* vol. 7, *Africa under Colonial Domination, 1880–1935,* ed.

A. Adu Boahen (Berkeley: University of California Press, 1985), 458–86. Caldwell's chapter was completed some years before the publication date. Dennis Cordell's forthcoming analysis of the past millennium of African population trends will update Caldwell's interpretation. See Cordell, *Rhythms of Life: Population in African History* (Cambridge: Cambridge University Press, forthcoming).

23. Antonio McDaniel's study of Liberia provides the best set of data on population in Africa before 1850, but the data center much more on immigrants to Africa rather than on locally born people; see McDaniel, *Swing Low, Sweet Chariot: The Mortality Cost of Colonizing Liberia in the Nineteenth Century* (Chicago: University of Chicago Press, 1994). For population on Angola, see José Curto and Raymond Gervais, "The Population History of Luanda during the Late Atlantic Slave Trade, 1781–1844," *African Economic History* 29 (2001): 1–59.

24. For a bibliography of major monographs and collective works on the history of the slave trade, see Patrick Manning, "Introduction," in *Slave Trades, 1500–1800: Globalization of Forced Labour*, ed. Patrick Manning (Aldershot, UK: Variorum, 1996), xv–xxiv.

25. Patrick Manning, "Local vs. Regional Impact of Slave Exports on Africa," in Cordell and Gregory, *African Population and Capitalism*, 35–49; Manning, *Slavery and African Life: Occidental, Oriental, and African Slave Trades* (Cambridge: Cambridge University Press, 1990). *Retrojection* was the charming term proposed by the late Joel Gregory for this sort of demographic speculation.

26. Patrick Manning, "The Slave Trade in Southern Dahomey, 1640–1890," in *The Uncommon Market: Essays in the Economic History of the Atlantic Slave Trade*, ed. Henry A. Gemery and Jan S. Hogendorn (New York: Academic Press, 1979), 109–141; Manning, "Enslavement of Africans."

27. Patrick Manning and William S. Griffiths, "Divining the Unprovable: Simulating the Demography of African Slavery," *Journal of Interdisciplinary History* 19, no. 2 (1988): 177–201; Manning, "The Impact of Slave Trade Exports on the Population of the Western Coast of Africa, 1700–1850," in *De la traite à l'esclavage*, ed. Serge Daget, 2 vols. (Paris: Société Française d'Histoire d'Outre-Mer, 1988), 2:111–34; Manning, "Slave Trade: The Formal Demography of a Global System," *Social Science History* 14, no. 2 (1990): 255–79; Manning, *Slavery and African Life.*

28. This project is the fourth iteration in my estimates of African populations for colonial and earlier times. Initially, I projected the impact of slave exports on the Bight of Benin, by ethnolinguistic group, from the 1930s to the 1650s. Second, I focused a broader but still simplified effort at projection on West and Central Africa. In it, I drew on colonial estimates of African populations for the 1930s and projected them back to the 1850s at constant rates of 1.0 percent per year (as a high estimate of growth) and 0.5 percent per year (as a low estimate). This approach resulted in projections that the slave trade of the Bight of Benin, for instance, drew in 1850 on a population ranging between 2.4 million and 3.5 million located in a "catchment area" including colonial Dahomey, Western Nigeria, and a portion of the Central Sudan. My third effort at projection extended this same procedure to the entire African continent, in order to estimate the effects of slave trade in all directions on African population. This fourth iteration relies on a revised and elaborated strategy of projecting populations for the years 1850 to 1950.

29. Maddison, *World Economy.*

30. Table 10.4 source is: Maddison, *World Economy*, 175, 183. Maddison's "Western Offshoots" include the United States, Canada, Australia, and New Zealand; "Europe" includes the entire territory of the former Soviet Union. I calculated the growth rates shown.

31. I retain the practice of identifying a base population for each territory at a given date and then projecting backward at high and low rates. But I have modified the procedure by identifying smaller and more specific regions within which to analyze population growth, and I have moved to identifying base populations for 1950 and 1960, rather than 1931. In projecting populations back to 1850, I now attempt to estimate variations in growth rates for each decade, through greater detail in assumptions and review of available demographic data.

32. See note 10.

33. When subterritorial data are lacking for 1950 or 1960, they may be estimated by interpolation from subterritorial data available for nearby years. This technique was used for Angola, Mozambique, and Sudan, for instance.

34. Here are the countries included in each of the six regions: North Africa—Western Sahara, Morocco, Algeria, Tunisia, Libya, and Egypt; West Africa—Mauritania, Senegal, Gambia, Guiné-Bissau, Guinea, Sierra Leone, Liberia, Mali, Burkina Faso, Côte d'Ivoire, Ghana, Togo, Benin, Niger, and Nigeria; Central Africa—Chad, Cameroon, Central African Republic, Equatorial Guinea, Gabon, Congo-Brazzaville, Congo-Kinshasa, Angola, and Zambia; Northeast Africa—Sudan, Ethiopia, Djibouti, and Somalia. East Africa—Uganda, Kenya, Burundi, Rwanda, Tanzania, Malawi, Mozambique, and Madagascar; and Southern Africa—Zimbabwe, Namibia, Botswana, South Africa, Lesotho, and Swaziland.

35. For this reason, the African continental totals shown in table 10.5 are lower by roughly 3 million than the totals in table 10.1 and table 10.4; the difference arises entirely from southern and eastern Africa.

36. Thus, captives taken in Upper Guinea were exported only across the Atlantic, captives taken in Senegambia were exported across both the Atlantic and the Sahara, and captives taken in the Western Sudan were exported in several directions—across the Sahara, to settlements within the Sahara, and across the Atlantic through Senegambia, Upper Guinea, and Gold Coast. Anticipating this procedure has reaffirmed the choice to subdivide the populations of Gold Coast, Togo, Dahomey, and Cameroon into northern and southern subgroups, as well as dividing Nigeria into its old regions of West, East, and North. (Similar adjustments are made for captives flowing in multiple directions from Chad, Sudan, Ubangi-Shara, and Mozambique.)

37. "Natural fertility rate" refers to the assumption that females were exposed without restriction to the risk of fertility. If they did not restrict their fertility, they could also not voluntarily increase their fertility. The assumption is plausible, since African women commonly married early and remarried at the death of their spouses. But there may be reasons to revise this assumption: for instance, there have been arguments that slave women had lower fertility than free women. See Martin A. Klein, *Slavery and Colonial Rule in French West Africa* (Cambridge: Cambridge University Press, 1998).

38. United Nations, "World Population Prospects." I have relied upon the 2006 estimates of territorial population for 1950 and 1960. The Tabuthin-Schoumaker survey of sub-Saharan Africa relied on the 2002 estimates, and the same authors in surveying North Africa and the Middle East relied on the 2004 estimates. I have accepted the argument that the 2006 estimates, which differ in various details from the earlier series, are to be preferred. I am thankful to Sabine Henning of the UN Population Division for generously providing a set of total African national populations for 1950 and 1960 as estimated in 2002, 2004, and 2006.

39. The official Nigerian census results for 1953 and 1962–63 are generally understood to have exaggerated the population, especially for Northern Nigeria, through an alliance

of British and Northern Nigerian figures who managed thereby to guarantee northern dominance of Nigeria at independence in 1960. The Okonjo estimate of Nigeria's 1962 population is understood to be a summary of the unrevised results from the field and hence the best available estimate. Gil and de Graft-Johnson, *1960 Population of Ghana;* Okonjo, "Preliminary Medium Estimate." Other countries for which discrepancies arose between the 1967 UNECA figures and later UN figures are Guiné-Bissau, Central African Republic, Gabon, Congo-Brazzaville, and Mozambique: in these cases, I relied on the later UN figures. Growth rates in the 1950s appear generally to have been higher in East Africa and North Africa than in West Africa. My thanks to J. C. Caldwell and Ian Pool for advice on these points.

40. Kuczynski, *Demographic Survey;* Cordell and Gregory, *African Population and Capitalism;* Fetter, *Demography from Scanty Evidence.*

41. Gilles Sautter, *De l'Atlantique au fleuve Congo: Une géographie de sous-peuplement: République du Congo, République gabonaise,* 2 vols. (Paris: Mouton, 1966); Dennis D. Cordell, *Dar al-Kuti and the Last Years of the Trans-Saharan Slave Trade* (Madison: University of Wisconsin Press, 1985).

42. Union of South Africa, *Official Year Book of the Union* (Pretoria: Government of the Union of South Africa, 1916–60). For a major recent assessment, see Tukufu Zuberi, Amson Sibanda, and Eric O. Udjo, eds., *Demography of South Africa* (Armonk, NY: M. E. Sharpe, 2005).

43. On the underestimates of colonial African censuses, see Caldwell and Schindlmayr, "Historical Population Estimates"; Tabutin and Schoumaker, "La démographie de l'Afrique au sud du Sahara," 526–29; Bruce Fetter, "Demography in the Reconstruction of African Colonial History," in *Demography from Scanty Evidence: Central Africa in the Colonial Era,* ed. Bruce Fetter (Boulder, CO: Lynne Rienner, 1990), 6–8; and Caldwell, "Social Repercussions of Colonial Rule," 482–83. In South Africa, enumerations of populations designated as European, Indian, and Coloured were fairly accurate in the early twentieth century, but African populations were underestimated there as elsewhere until midcentury.

44. On the population of French West Africa, especially colonial Upper Volta, see Dennis D. Cordell and Joel W. Gregory, "Labour Reservoirs and Population: French Colonial Strategies in Koudougou, Upper Volta, 1914 to 1939," *Journal of African History* 23, no. 2 (1982), 205–24; Raymond Gervais, "Vérités et mensonges: Les statistiques coloniales de population," *Canadian Journal of African Studies* 17, no. 1 (1983): 101–3; Dennis D. Cordell and Joel W. Gregory, "Vérités et mensonges: Les statistiques coloniales de population—A Response," *Canadian Journal of African Studies* 17, no. 1 (1983): 105–6; Raymond R. Gervais, *Contribution à l'étude de l'évolution de la population de l'Afrique occidentale française, 1904–1960* (Paris: CEPED, 1993); and Issiaka Mandé, "Labor Market Constraints and Competition in Colonial Africa: Migrant Workers from Upper Volta, 1920–1932," in Toyin Falola and Aribidesi Usman, eds., *Movements, Borders, and Identities in Africa* (Rochester, NY: University of Rochester Press, 2009), 285–304.

On French Equatorial Africa, see Dennis D. Cordell, "Où sont tous les enfants? La faible fécondité en Centrafrique," in *Population, reproduction, sociétés: Perspectives et enjeux de démographie sociale—Mélanges en l'honneur de Joel W. Gregory,* ed. Dennis D. Cordell, Danielle Gauvreau, Raymond R. Gervais, and Céline Le Bourdais (Montreal, Canada: Les Presses de l'Université de Montréal, 1993), 257–82; Gervais, *Contribution à l'étude de l'évolution.* See also Rita Headrick, ed. Daniel R. Headrick, *Colonialism, Health and Illness in French Equatorial Africa, 1885–1935* (Atlanta, African Studies Association Press, 1994);

Catherine Coquery-Vidrovitch, *Le Congo au temps des grandes compagnies concessionaires 1898–1930* (Paris: Mouton, 1972); and Sautter, *De l'Atlantique au fleuve Congo.*

45. Cordell, "Où sont tous les enfants?" In fact, the population growth rates of Gabon, Congo-Brazzaville, and Central African Republic have remained relatively low in the national period. In contrast, those in the West African sahel rose to comparatively high levels after 1950.

46. In Ruanda-Urundi under Belgian rule, from the 1920s through the 1940s, the administration made efforts to enumerate adult males, then estimated total population by multiplying the adult male total by a factor set for each year, estimating the ratio of total population to adult males. For Burundi, this factor ranged from a low of 3.602 in 1931 to a high of 4.649 in 1935—a difference of almost 30 percent within four years. See Belgium, Ministère des Colonies, *Rapport sur l'administration belge du Ruanda-Urundi* (Brussels: F.Van Gompel, 1921–39).

47. See table 10.3 and appendix B.

48. See table 10.9 for a summary of the results of those observations.

49. In the second and third iterations of my population estimates, I began with base populations taken from 1931 colonial estimates and projected them back at rates of 0.5 percent and 1.0 percent. See note 28.

50. There has been insufficient comparison of demographic rates among tropical regions. Although each region necessarily has its demographic specifics, the general parallels in ecology, disease environment, colonial domination, and scanty records require that comparative work be expanded in order to ensure that advances in the demographic study of any one region can be considered for application to other regions. Thus, the application of Indian proxies for African data is the utilization of detailed data—although from a distant and distinctive region—in place of sheer speculation on African demographic rates. In addition, as the remainder of this section shows, I proposed modifications to Indian data based on known distinctions between Indian and African demography.

51. For decennial growth rates by Indian province, from 1871 to 1961, see appendix B19. These growth rates were calculated only for Indian territories for which the boundaries remained virtually unchanged over the full century. Sources for this information are: Census of India (various titles and publishers, for decades ending 1881 to 1961); Leela Visaria and Pravin Visaria, "Population (1757–1947)," in *Cambridge Economic History of India,* vol. 2, ed. Dharma Kumar (Hyderabad, India: Orient Longman, 1984), 463–532; N. Gerald Barrier, ed., *The Census in British India* (New Delhi: Manohar, 1981); Ira Klein, "Population Growth and Mortality in British India, Pt. 1: The Climacteric of Death," *Indian Economic and Social History Review* 26, no. 4 (1989): 387–403; Klein, "Population Growth and Mortality in British India: The Demographic Revolution," *Indian Economic and Social History Review* 27, no. 1 (1990): 33–63; Klein, "Imperialism, Ecology, and Disease: Cholera in India, 1850–1950," *Indian Economic and Social History Review* 31, no. 4 (1994): 491–518; Klein, "Development and Death: Reinterpreting Malaria, Economics and Ecology in British India," *Indian Economic and Social History Review* 38, no. 2 (2001): 147–79; Sumit Guha, "Mortality Decline in Early Twentieth-Century India: A Preliminary Enquiry," *Indian Economic and Social History Review* 28, no. 4 (1991): 371–91; Tim Dyson and Arup Maharatna, "Excess Mortality during the Bengal Famine: A Re-evaluation," *Indian Economic and Social History Review* 28, no. 3 (1991): 281–97; Bidyut Mohanty, "Migration, Famines and Sex Ratio in Orissa Division between 1881 and 1921," *Indian Economic and Social History Review* 29, no. 4 (1992): 507–28. See the appendices in P. B. Desai, *Size and Sex Composition of Population in India, 1901–1961* (Bombay, India: Asia Publishing House, 1969).

52. Population practices in Africa and India differed in this period in that Indians practiced some female infanticide and selective nonnurturing and had British health services in parts of the subcontinent. Other reasons why Indian fertility rates may have been lower than African rates include Indian prohibitions against widow remarriage, in contrast to African practices of encouraging such remarriage. However, mortality rates may have been higher in Africa, compensating in part for this difference. Indian populations were undercounted—but not as seriously as in Africa. Indian data suggest a common decline in fertility rates in the early twentieth century, and African data suggest a parallel decline, at least for some regions. These comparisons should be explored in more detail.

53. The overall pattern of "demographic transition," in which populations worldwide have changed over the past two centuries from high rates of mortality and fertility to low rates of mortality and fertility (with mortality declining first), is now known to have been far more variable than was earlier thought. Nonetheless, though the exact pace of historical change in African societies is not yet known, I argue that it is appropriate to retain the general assumption of demographic transition for Africa.

54. The tolerances are cumulative: that is, the tolerance is plus or minus 0.1 percent for the 1940s, 0.2 percent for the 1930s, and 1.0 percent for the 1850s. In the statistical test of this estimate, we assumed a uniform distribution of error in growth rates of +/- 1 percent and replicated the calculation of growth rates 100,000 times, obtaining the equivalent of a Monte Carlo distribution of the continental population under our assumptions. At 95 percent confidence, we found the resulting error tolerances to be half as large as those shown in figure 10.3. See "Appendix A: Review of Error Margins," by Patrick Manning and Scott Nickleach, in the online appendix to this chapter. In a larger study of African population, from 1650 to 1950, Scott Nickleach and I are employing stochastic techniques to establish error margins for estimating rates of birth, death, and migration in Africa and for overseas migration. See Patrick Manning and Scott Nickleach, *African Population, 1650–1950: The Eras of Enslavement and Colonial Rule* (forthcoming).

55. Willcox, "Increase in the Population"; Carr-Saunders, *World Population;* Biraben, "L'évolution."

56. Manning, *Slavery and African Life,* 60–85, 179–81.

57. Categories "a" through "c" refer to the effects of slave trade within the indicated decade; category "d" refers to population growth resulting from the end to enslavement one to two decades earlier. Details of these estimates are available from the author; they are still subject to significant revision. The rubric for these estimates appears to be satisfactory in its present form.

58. Inikori, "Introduction"; Manning, "Enslavement of Africans"; Paul E. Lovejoy, "The Impact of the Slave Trade in Africa in the Eighteenth and Nineteenth Centuries," *Journal of African History* 30, no. 3 (1989): 365–94.

59. For the years before 1800, I have assumed that the number of captives retained in sub-Saharan Africa, for each region, was a constant proportion of those exported. After 1850 (and arguably earlier), the proportion of captives retained in Africa rose substantially, and there is no obvious basis for estimating their numbers. See Manning, *Slavery and African Life,* 50–53.

60. Ibid., 79–82.

61. These matrixes are available on request from the author.

62. "Seasoning mortality" refers to the mortality accompanying the captive's settlement and socialization into slave status. This phenomenon, well documented for the Caribbean, must be included in the accounting of the mortality of enslavement in Africa as well.

63. Additional factors could be added to this estimation, such as the possibility that high proportions of females in slavery might have caused their age-specific birthrates to decline, though the same factor might have increased crude birthrates.

64. Interpolation is necessary at various points—for instance, to allocate slave exports from a slave trade region among its constituent colonies and subterritories. In addition, care is required to avoid double counting, since captives exported from sub-Saharan Africa as a whole have already been exported from one of its constituent regions.

Repeated runs of the slave trade simulation led me to summarize their results in two linear equations. Where E is the export ratio (current slave exports as a fraction of African regional population), G_1 is the estimated growth rate of the African regional population from Step 4, and G_2 is the growth rate of the African regional population after accounting for slave exports. For the western coast of Africa, where slave exports were predominantly male:

$$G_2 = G_1 - 2.5\,E$$

For the slave trade across the Sahara, the Red Sea, and the Indian Ocean, where exports were predominantly female:

$$G_2 = G_1 - 3.1\,E$$

For the earlier version of this procedure, see Manning, *Slavery and African Life*, 179–81.

65. Examples included the influenza pandemic of 1918, cholera epidemics of the late nineteenth century in eastern Africa, and sleeping sickness in Central and eastern Africa in the early twentieth century.

66. Note that the variance in these growth rates reflects the difference in territorial growth rates under specific influences; the assumed margin of error for overall estimates (discussed in appendix A) is in addition to these variations.

67. See appendices B15–B17 for estimates by geographic region.

68. A further measure of the discrepancy between the estimates of the present study and previous estimates is my own 1990 estimate for the western coast of Africa, that region from Senegal to Angola that nourished the Atlantic slave trade. In *Slavery and African Life*, for the period from 1700 to 1850, I estimated populations in the range from 17 to 24 million; the present study shows a mid-level estimated population of 32 million for the same region in 1850. This revision suggests that the negative demographic impact of slave exports on Africa was smaller than I suggested in earlier work, and I am pursuing this question in further revisions of this study. See Manning, *Slavery and African Life*, 73–74; Manning and Nickleach (forthcoming).

69. John C. Caldwell, "The Social Repercussions of Colonial Rule: Demographic Aspects," in *General History of Africa*, vol. 7, *Africa under Colonial Domination, 1880–1935*, ed. A. Adu Boahen (Berkeley: University of California Press, 1985), 458–86; Tabutin and Schoumaker, "La démographie de l'Afrique," 521–621; and United Nations, "World Population Prospects." For studies of demographic history in Africa in precolonial settings, see Philip D. Curtin, *Death by Migration: Europe's Encounter with the Tropical World in the Nineteenth Century* (Cambridge: Cambridge University Press, 1989), and Louise Marie Diop-Maës, *Afrique noire: Démographie, sol et histoire* (Paris: Présence Africaine, 1996).

70. The term *scanty evidence* comes from Bruce Fetter, *Demography from Scanty Evidence*. As an example of proceeding from guesswork to specific procedures, the simulation of slave exports showed how it could be that exports of a relatively small number of persons could result in decline of the home population; see Manning, *Slavery and African Life*, 41–44, 49, 66–69.

71. For discussion of census data on Angola, see John Thornton, "The Slave Trade in Eighteenth-Century Angola: Effects of Demographic Structures," *Canadian Journal of African Studies* 14 (1981): 417–27, and José Curto and Raymond Gervais, "The Population History of Luanda during the Late Atlantic Slave Trade, 1781–1844," *African Economic History* 29 (2001): 1–59. See also McDaniel, *Swing Low, Sweet Chariot.*

72. Gregory H. Maddox, personal communication.

appendices

The appendix to chapter 3 is available online on the SEDET Web site, http:// www.sedet.univ-paris-diderot.fr. The appendices to chapter 10 are archived on-line in the World-Historical Dataverse, www.dataverse.pitt.edu/archive/users.php. Appendices to chapters 3 and 10 are also available online at the Ohio University Press/Swallow Press Web site, http://www.ohioswallow.com/book/The+ Demographics+of+Empire.

Chapter 3

Raymond Gervais and Issakia Mandé, "How to Count the Subjects of Empire? Steps toward an Imperial Demography in French West Africa before 1946," original French quotations

Chapter 10

Patrick Manning, "African Population Estimates, 1850–1960"

Appendix A. Review of Error Margins, by Scott Nickleach and Patrick Manning

Appendix B. Statistical Tables

B1: Population by territory and subregion, 1950–60

B2: Slave trade regions and subregions

B3: Default growth rates by territory and decade

B4: Revisions to default rates attributed to slave trade disorder

B5: Revisions to default rates attributed to continental slave trade

B6: Revisions to default rates associated with overseas slave trade data, 1850–1900

B7: Revisions to default rates attributed to post–slave trade recovery

B8: Revisions to default rates attributed to colonial disorder

B9: Revisions to default rates attributed to income growth

contributors

John M. Cinnamon is associate professor of anthropology and affiliate of black world studies at Miami University (Ohio). His research interests include history and memory in Equatorial Africa and the contribution of missionary ethnographers. He is currently working on a history of the Mademoiselle movement in northern Gabon from the 1950s to the present.

Dennis D. Cordell is professor of history and adjunct professor of anthropology at Southern Methodist University. He is the coeditor of *African Population and Capitalism: Historical Perspectives* and the coauthor of *Hoe and Wage: A Social History of a Circular Migration System in West Africa.* He is currently writing a history of African population.

Raymond Gervais focused his early research on African history and the demography of West Africa. His first master's thesis, in history from the University of Birmingham, dealt with the economic history of the Lake Chad region; his second, in demography from the Université de Montréal, analyzed the demographic impact of the drought in 1969–73 on Niger. Directed by Catherine Coquery-Vidrovitch, he went on to complete a PhD dissertation at the Université de Paris 7–Denis-Diderot on the economic and demographic history of Burkina Faso. Along with these topics, Gervais's publications have also explored the history of statistics in colonial French West Africa. Since 1985, he has served as a consultant on economic and social development projects throughout Africa and in other parts of the developing world.

Karl Ittmann is associate professor of history at the University of Houston. He is the author of *Work, Gender and Family in Victorian England.* He is writing a history of population policy in the British Empire.

Gregory H. Maddox is professor of history at Texas Southern University and author of *Sub-Saharan Africa: An Environmental History* and coauthor of *Practicing History in Central Tanzania: Writing, Memory, and Performance.*

Issiaka Mandé received his doctorate in African history from the Université de Paris 7–Denis-Diderot, where he is now maître de conférences in the Department of History and attached to the Laboratoire SEDET of the Centre National de Recherche Scientifique (CNRS). Mandé is the coeditor of and contributor to several collections of essays on the modern history of Africa, including *Migrations et cultures d'entreprise,* with E. Guerassimoff, C. Maitte, and M. Martini; *Être étranger et migrant en Afrique au XXème siècle,* with Catherine Coquery-Vidrovitch, Odile Goerg, and F. Rajaonah; and *Historiens africains et la mondialisation,* with B. Stefanson.

Patrick Manning is Andrew W. Mellon Professor of World History and director of the World History Center at the University of Pittsburgh. He is the author of *Navigating World History: Historians Create a Global Past* (2003), *Migration in World History* (2006), and *The African Diaspora: A History through Culture* (2009). His Web site is http://www.worldhistorynetwork.org/manning.

Thomas V. McClendon is a professor of history at Southwestern University. He is the author of *Genders and Generations Apart: Labor Tenants and Customary Law in Segregation-Era South Africa, 1920s to 1940s,* and of *White Chief, Black Lords: Shepstone and the Colonial State in Natal, South Africa, 1845–1878.*

Sheryl A. McCurdy is associate professor at the University of Texas–Houston School of Public Health. She is coeditor of *"Wicked" Women and the Reconfiguration of Gender in Africa* and publishes in history, social science, and public health journals. Her current research on the social networks of heroin users in Tanzania is funded by the National Institute on Drug Abuse.

Meshack Owino is an assistant professor of history at Cleveland State University, Cleveland, Ohio. He is currently working on a manuscript on the experience of Kenya African soldiers in World War II.

Meredeth Turshen is a professor at the Edward J. Bloustein School of Planning and Public Policy, Rutgers University. She has written four books, most recently *Women's Health Movements: A Global Force for Change.* She has also edited five volumes and is currently editing a sixth, *African Women: A Political Economy.*

index

Page references in *italics* denote illustrations.